Yankees in the Courthouse

A Florida Civil War & Reconstruction Biography

Book 3 in the

Palmetto Pioneers

Series

Cindy Roe Littlejohn

Palmetto Pioneers

P R O S E ·

Monticello, Florida

Dedication

In Memory of Dee Counts

Derylene Delp Counts (Dee) was Monticello and Jefferson County's longtime historian, generously volunteering countless hours at the Keystone Genealogical Library. She devoted herself to preserving and sharing the county's history, helping hundreds trace their Jefferson County roots through her research and guidance.

Dee's historical writings—including several articles and books, such as her pictorial and narrative history of Jefferson County, Florida—earned her wide recognition. She had a rare gift: the ability to take dry, dusty records and transform them into engaging and informative stories that brought our shared heritage to life.

She freely shared her knowledge through civic organizations and conferences, and her expertise helped to ensure the historical accuracy of the first two books in this *Palmetto Pioneers* series.

Dee blessed this community with her passion, talent, and generous spirit. She will be deeply missed by all of us she leaves behind.

In Memory of James Sledge

Dr. James Seymour Sledge provided me with the best information on our Walker family—but Jefferson County knew and admired him for so much more.

After graduating from dental school, he returned to Monticello and practiced dentistry from 1953 to 1993. More than just a distant cousin, he was also my childhood dentist. Yet his most meaningful work may have been the one day each month he devoted to providing dental care for Jefferson County's indigent children.

He was a faithful member of First Baptist Church in Monticello, where he served as a deacon and Sunday School teacher for over 41 years. During his time as chairman of the Jefferson County Historical Association, the organization bought the historic Wirick-Simmons House, built in the 1830s, which now serves as the association's headquarters. He also led the effort to purchase the former Aucilla High School building, paving the way for the founding of Aucilla Christian School.

Yet perhaps people will best remember Dr. Sledge for his work in honoring his childhood friend—the late Sgt. Ernest "Boots" Thomas, who led the flag-raising on Iwo Jima and who was killed there three days later during World War II. To ensure his friend's legacy would never be forgotten, Sledge spearheaded the effort to create and dedicate the Boots Thomas Memorial.

A World War II veteran himself, Dr. Sledge gave generously of his time, knowledge, and heart. He leaves behind a lasting mark on Jefferson County—and on all of us who knew and loved him.

#

Table of Contents

Preface

Yankees in the Courthouse is the third book of the *Palmetto Pioneers* series. During the last book, Mary Adeline Walker witnessed the emptying of Jefferson County, Florida of its men and boys. In the Civil War, ongoing since 1861, Florida, the eleventh state out of eleven in population and the last great frontier east of the Mississippi River, seceded third and joined the Confederate States of America.

First, the state authorities sent its men and boys to the coastlines to protect the homeland. They stationed them at several of its busy seaports; but by 1862, the fighting in the North became more serious. Regiment by regiment, Florida sent its native sons to northern battlefields, drawing from a pre-war military age population of 15,000. This story picks up in July 1862, nineteen months after Florida seceded from the nation.

At home, though, were Florida's wives, daughters, sisters, and female cousins, as well as the boys too young to fight and elderly men too old. There will be sixty-nine military events in Florida during the Civil War, mostly near Jacksonville and Pensacola. The events ranged from a major battle at Olustee to raids, bombardments, and skirmishes in various ports and cities of the state, including but not limited to Tampa, Cedar Key, Key West, Marianna, and Apalachicola. All around Florida, a Union naval blockade patrolled.

Again, I used personal documents, letters, journals, and diaries to recreate Mary's family's wartime experiences. Since Mary's family did not own slaves, I searched for answers to questions that they may have had, such as: Why did they fight? Was it to defend their homeland against Yankee invasion, or was it something larger, like states' rights and maintaining the economy which depended on slavery? Or did some resist purely because they refused to be told what to do by the North?

Did joining require much thought and introspection, or was it peer pressure and a moment of quick decision? And what about the giddiness of being a hero? Did the boys fantasize about battles and how brave they would be?

Why did the South think they could win? Was it because agriculture in the southern lands was much more prosperous than in the rest of the country?

What was it like to be in battle? Were they first excited? And later were they frightened? How did one face death?

For the women and children: What was it like to be at home and feel powerless? How did everyone do their part? How did children react to the news from the front and losing their father and older brothers?

In compiling this story and its history, I uncovered past events by interviewing the eldest family members, listening as they shared tales, legends, and traditions handed down by word of mouth from grandparents to parents and from parents to their children.

The story mostly takes place in Monticello, Florida, the third-oldest historic district in the state of Florida. Many of the buildings in the story are well-known structures in the historic district and are on the national register of historic places. This national register listing signifies that a property is an important part of our nation's cultural heritage and was worthy of preservation.

In these stories and documents, I learned that Jefferson County, the last county in Florida today without a single stoplight, had a past, a prosperous one, as learned in the second book of the series. But it also had a disharmonious one that followed during the Civil War and Reconstruction. This is the story of the Andrews and Walker families and Jefferson County. And above all, a story about how Florida evolved.

How to Read this Book

Note: This is a regurgitation of the first two books' instructions.

This book, written in a genre called creative nonfiction, may be classified in a sub-genre called family history writing. It uses elements of creative writing to present a factual, true story. Palmetto Pioneers uses literary techniques usually reserved for writing fiction. I used dialog, scene-setting, and narrative arcs. It is rooted in facts. No part of the story is made up or fabricated unless the author signals otherwise.

To write this story, I used primary and secondary sources. The subject was extensively researched, and a bibliography follows at the end of the book. It is divided into time periods, such as "Life in Antebellum Florida" and "The War Between the States."

Because this book takes place almost two hundred years ago, the dialogue is almost always "composed." Dialogue only in quotation marks are simply created dialogue, dialogue I made up word for word. These conversations are from my imagination—what I think people would have said in a given situation. I wanted to give the characters more life, and the character's personalities reflect their descendants. One can hear my mother's voice in Mary's mother's.

True dialogue, not created or actual word-for-word quotes, is set in quotations marks and is also italicized. Mary's father was quoted in a newspaper article when he described his wife in her obituary. When a character reads aloud from a newspaper, the dialogue is set in quotation marks and italicized.

I created homes and businesses using written examples and photos from that era. Diaries and journals were used, as were local newspapers. For example, was there a photo of the inside of Palmer's store? No, but I recreated its interior using other period photos and newspaper ads that describe how he probably stocked his store.

I added scenes that reflect the realities of living in Florida or the South. I added them for interest and to give the reader a feeling of what it was like to grow up in territorial or antebellum Florida. Some of these scenes are stories from my life. I grew up in the Florida county where most of this story takes place. Other scenes I gleaned from diaries, journals, and family lore.

I also added letters sent home from those who traveled away for the war. These letters are what I thought they would have said to each other, using actual letters as a guide, from others who wrote during the Civil War. We have no letters from any of the Walkers or Andrews. The letters in this book are in italics with no quotation marks.

Following this part of my family's story, I discovered their place in Florida's history, and this became a secondary purpose of this book. Hopefully others will learn more about our state's history through the eyes of Mary and her family and can help us all appreciate who we are and where we came from.

There are genealogy trees in this book in the appendix, but they are single families from the book. The overall tree I created and used is online with Ancestry.com. It is a public tree, so anyone can take a look. The link below will take you to Mary Adeline Walker in the tree. A tree search (upper right-hand screen) will let you search for any other family members mentioned in the book, though there are many people in this tree, many beyond those mentioned.

The tree is entitled the Lightsey, Andrews, Walker tree. If you are a Lightsey, Andrews, or Walker and your ancestors have been in this state for a few generations, your ancestors may be in this tree. There are over 5,500 people in it.

It is at https://www.ancestry.com/family-tree/person/tree/23894133/person/1441730272/facts or you can use your cell phone to take a picture of the QR code below. While it is trying to focus, notice what appears on your screen. When you see a web address, click on it. It will take you directly to the tree. You will have to register to log in, and Ancestry will try to get you to join, but you don't have to join to view this tree. It is free to take a look.

\#

Chapter I
Florida's Sons Go North
July to September 1862

The Western Theater of the War

By July 1862, fifteen months into the Civil War, the southeastern Confederacy was under enormous strain. The Union blockade had tightened its noose around the coastline, cutting off ports one by one until almost none remained. New Orleans, Pensacola, Apalachicola, and Cedar Keys had already fallen, leaving Mobile as the last major Confederate port on the Gulf. It became both a lifeline and a symbol: a hub for blockade runners, a fortified military stronghold, and a much-needed boost to Southern morale.

To defend it, the Confederacy kept the 3rd and 4th Florida Regiments in Mobile instead of sending them north with the Army of Tennessee. Many of Mary's brothers and cousins served with the 3rd Florida, while her husband William was with the 4th. These were mostly homegrown units—local volunteers who had marched off to war carrying flags sewn by the women of their communities.

Mobile itself, a city of about 30,000 before the war, was transformed into a vast military post. Camps stretched across old lots and along the horse railroad west of the city. William, fifty-one and imposing with gray eyes and sandy hair, walked among the encampments bordered by oak-shaded streets and generous grounds. The city pulsed with wartime movement: 45,000 Texans passed through, Yankee prisoners traversed from the north, and new Confederate units arrived from the river routes that funneled conscripts from across Alabama. The war was no longer a distant rumor—it was everywhere.

Across the region, Southern families felt this upheaval. Mary's brother J.J., serving with the 1st Florida Cavalry under

General Braxton Bragg, was in Tupelo as midsummer approached. Other Florida units were on the move as well: on July 4, the 7th Florida left for Knoxville, soon followed by the 1st Florida Cavalry —and with it, J.J.

At Home in Monticello

In Monticello, a town eight miles below the Georgia state line in Florida, the family followed their men and boys' movements with the newspaper and more timely announcements from the telegraph office. Their home sat on a canopied street near the Jefferson Academy, a school for the town's children.

The family's home was a common four-room house with a wide central hall running through it, plus an attic room and a detached kitchen behind the house. Florida was hot much of the year, and a detached kitchen not only removed heat from the house but was safer.

Reading the newspaper wasn't like it used to be. Because of the lack of paper, the publisher Mr. Fildes printed a handful of copies and hung them on bulletin boards around town. Mary, forty, with her slightly faded navy calico full skirt, held it up lest she trip. Using the shaded, boarded sidewalks, she and their third-oldest son Vollie, fifteen, wormed their way to the courthouse so he could read to her there. Some of the townspeople, always hungry for any news at all, were there to listen to another reader.

Appalled, Mary listened to reports of barbarous warfare. Earlier, she had heard about a French-style bullet which killed more efficiently. The bullet's larger end had a small excavation containing a brass cap of powder, and in the tube-like aperture on the exposed side, it was filled with a thin piece of punk and a green, poisonous-looking substance. This punk was combustible when the gun was fired. She worried that the Yankees would use these.

She also knew her Confederacy was capable of its own diabolical weapons. In Alabama, the state armed their troops with a *"keen two-edged steel head like a large bowie-knife blade, about a foot and a half long, with a sharp sickle like hook bending back from its socket."* They mounted the blade on an eight-foot long shaft of tough wood. They used this "pike" to cut the bridals of Yankee cavalrymen, to yank them off their horses, or to retrieve an enemy in retreat.

What if they used these weapons on her William or their sons John and James? Then she looked at Vollie, fifteen, with his sandy hair and gray-blue eyes. He was taller than she, and she was not a short woman. He looked at her and she sighed. It was only a matter of time.

Places unheard of became familiar to them in both theaters of the war, such as Shiloh and Manassas. In the family's home, a map lay permanently on William's table in the parlor near a window. They marked the small towns and hamlets where serious battles occurred.

The war had reached their home, though Mary had felt its arrival earlier on the day her brother Henry died at the mill more than a year and a half ago, just days before Florida seceded and her husband William served as sergeant of arms in the Florida House of Representatives. The mill had been operating non-stop to fill the defense contracts from the state. This stressed the old boiler until it exploded. Henry died in the scalding accident.

For the past year, they stationed William, like most Florida volunteers, along the state's coastline, defending it from Union incursions. His service began on St. Vincent Island near the bustling seaport of Apalachicola and later moved to the even busier Fernandina. However, when Union forces captured Fernandina and enforced a blockade that crippled much of Florida's shipping, William's unit evacuated.

Mobile, a crucial hub as both a seaport and a river port, became a lifeline for the Confederacy. Mary felt a measure of relief knowing the Confederacy needed William in Mobile, far from the more harrowing battles in the northern theaters of war. Her greatest fear was they might eventually send her kin to the front lines of the Confederacy's most desperate struggles.

Days later, Mary, downtown at the courthouse again, smoothed her dark hair and listened this time to Zech read the *Family Friend's* July 1st edition. Though she had already given William ten children, nine of which survived, and helped him raise three more from his first wife, she was still trim and kept herself neat. Constantly busy and moving, her waistline maintained its shape.

With a tenseness in his voice, Zech said, "Mama, Lincoln issued an executive order calling for more troops. It reads, 'T*he enemy* (he means us) *has a formidable insurgent force at Richmond and can therefore threaten us on the Potomac.*' He looked at her. "Their Army needs more men. Lincoln called for 300,000 more." He had a stunned look on his face.

She said, "Well, I guess President Davis will call for more brave Southerners to answer," though she knew the South would run out of men. Because William was from Washington, DC and knew what was north of there, she knew the South began with few resources, human and otherwise.

She also knew the Confederacy had sent their son, John Slicer, and his unit north to Virginia to the current vortex of the war. Dreadful news came in a circadian rhythm. She thought, 'How could half again of our men overcome the north's "cowardly" army? And were they cowardly when so many of them repeatedly responded?' She massaged her right temple next to her brown hair, which she kept in a tight bun at the nape of her hairline, a nagging ache that wouldn't go away.

As they left the courthouse, they walked west on Washington Street past the town well. Monticello had grown into a handsome small city. The prosperous years of the 1840s and 1850s had been good to the family and the county. Horse, carriage, and wagon traffic circled the courthouse and flowed all four directions between buildings and homes. Gone were the log and planed wood buildings of her childhood, and in their place arose a new city.

Later, at home in her bedroom, she decided she needed to lie down, even if only for a few minutes. On a table by the bed was a sorrel-colored trinket box covered with leather and mounted with brass fittings. It had compartments for various objects. She removed the shell combs from her hair and put them into the box. Staring at it, she remembered when William gave it to her at Christmas years before. She could still see his smile. Shaking her hair down, she curled up in their bed.

The Western Theater

Meanwhile, a renewed pride took place among the 3rd and 4th Florida regiments in Mobile. In the days leading to Independence Day, the men polished buttons, brushed uniforms, and cleaned their weapons. William reminisced about this special day in Monticello and wondered if it was being celebrated there. He straightened his gray coat and brushed it one more time to make sure it showed no stains.

We have no photos of William, but we have several of his sons when they were older.

Valentine Andrews and James J. Andrews

William learned later that because of the war, July 4th came and went with little fanfare in Monticello. The town's former big Independence Day events were no more. They no longer entertained people from throughout the state for its special celebrations. For years this had been a tradition in Monticello, and people came from all over to celebrate with the descendants of America's founding fathers. When Mary and William were younger, President Thomas Jefferson's grandson lived in the town, as did several descendants of famous Revolutionary heroes. The year President Jefferson died, Jefferson County and Monticello received their names.

In Mobile, though, on the Fourth of July, the 4th Florida, along with other regiments, paraded its streets to celebrate their land's independence from England. Even though there came a downpour and the streets turned to mud, the soldiers never missed a step.

By July 12th, the North delayed its offensive in Tennessee. Union General Don C. Buell stalled to construct defenses and strengthen railways for the needed supplies and ammo. Meanwhile, the ghostly Nathan Bedford Forrest slipped in and wrecked the line near Murfreesboro, causing weeks of more delay. By the time General Buell was ready to invade Chattanooga, it was too late. The Confederate army had strengthened its hold there.

When General Bragg took command from General Beauregard, he sent William and his in-laws north by the end of July. The 3rd left Mobile on July 20th with eight of Mary's kin. Sent to the western campaign, they rushed them up the Alabama River toward Montgomery, but the ship grounded on a mud flat, losing a man overboard. Mary's brother George reported in a letter home, which Zech read to the family,

We even had to portage through a swamp while they loosened the ship. You know I've traipsed my share of swamps on horseback, but we privates were on foot.

What should have taken a little more than a day to travel from Mobile to Montgomery took over three days. Afterward, they boarded the rail cars in Montgomery and arrived in Chattanooga two days later to camp at the foot of Lookout Mountain near the Tennessee River on a large branch and by a fine cold spring. The Florida boys noticed immediately that this area was different. Instead of sand, it was clay; and because of the drought, the clay dust kicked up with any motion. Their daily rations were meager—a quarter pound of flour, one pound of beef, and one pound of bacon with a little salt. Because of all the marching, the energy constantly spent, George was always hungry.

The 4th Florida regiment experienced even worse problems between Mobile and Montgomery after they boarded the train on the 20th. William wrote home,

At the station, a long train waited. We marched past the belching engine to the platform and filled every square inch of its freight boxes, including flat cars and coal cars. Our overflow rode on top, where they tied themselves to the walk using their gun slings. Getting to Chattanooga took six days and nights, stopping long enough to cook and eat.

Civilians on Box Cars, Atlanta, 1864, Library of Congress

One night, the engine tore loose from the train and fell down an embankment. Because of an imminent wreck, men on top jumped even though several box cars never left the tracks. It bruised many, and several suffered sprained ankles and broken bones. It was a miracle no one in our unit got killed, but I can't say the same for other units. At 2 am, we were stranded in a deep clay cut with our injured and dead.

From Montgomery by train, William's regiment traveled through Atlanta and headed north. In Marietta, the local ladies at the depot sang to the soldiers. People threw apples, peaches, and miniature Confederate flags. William told his family,

Every time a female appeared, a roar of cheers came forth.

They detrained in Chattanooga on July 25th and camped near the 3rd Florida at the base of Lookout Mountain. Many felt they were in enemy country since the Yankees occupied parts of Tennessee.

The following day, William woke to a heavy smoke cloud hanging low overhead. He felt dirty, uncomfortable, and a bit ill. His tentmate Standley rekindled their banked and smoldering cookfire which had faded during the night.

Within moments, the camp pulsated to life with the voices and laughter of its men. Horses and mules neighed, and wagon wheels creaked by, cracking and squeaking under their loads. Drums thrummed, and somewhere nearby, he heard the lonely melody of a mouth organ.

He penned a letter to Mary. The censors blanked out all the locations.

July 26th, 1862
Chattanooga

My Dear Mary,

This will be short, but I wanted to let you know I landed in Chattanooga and am well but weary and tired. I am now 350 long miles from you and await orders to march north.

We marched through Chattanooga yesterday from the depot, and one can tell our arrival wears thin on everyone here. We're told they cheered and welcomed us when this began, but now we are only one more unit marching through.

Mary, our rations grow more meager, and the variety is less. The other night I dreamed about your kitchen and on the table was fresh butter, eggs, and oranges. Strange, because it is summer and we only get oranges in the winter, but I would give anything to taste butter, eggs, pork, and peas. These are left out of our diets now.

And I haven't seen moss since we left Montgomery. Who would have thought we could be homesick for moss. They don't have it up here.

Kiss all my babies and tell everyone I love and miss them. Of course, I miss you most of all.

Your Loving Husband,
William

At Home

Mary listened to Zech read the letter. Because she came to Florida at seven and because Florida provided no schools nor could the family afford to send her away, she could neither read nor write. Being the oldest of her parent's eleven children, all of which survived, her mother had needed all the help she could get. Mary was proficient at mothering and family care, but she always wished she had learned to read.

On August 1st, per a voucher for two days at $8 per day, one six-mule team transported the rest of the 5th Florida Regiment from Monticello to Station 17, the closest Georgia station on the LA & G (the Savannah) Railroad. They sent them to Richmond, where a drought ceased and the rains came. With the rains came chilly nights. With the 5th were the Aucilla Guards and more of her kin, fifteen cousins, her brother David, and her Uncle Littleberry, fifty years old. It appears her Uncle Littleberry joined along with three of his sons. They sent the Aucilla Guards to the Eastern Theater to Richmond.

The Eastern Theater of the War

In Richmond, the stalwart, bushy-bearded Dr. Thomas Palmer, their family physician in Monticello before the war, served as surgeon-in-charge of the Florida ward at Howard's Grove, a Confederate hospital. He wrote several missives to Florida's governor and Confederate senators about his deep concerns for the welfare of Florida's soldiers. He told them, "if the new 'Florida Brigade' did not return home, the "*entire aggregate may die of diseases such as colds, coughs, sore throats, typhoid fever, and measles.*"

The brigade was this small group of Florida soldiers composed of the 2nd, 5th, and later the 8th Florida regiments.

Richmond, 1862, National Archives, Wikipedia

While Dr. Palmer was in Richmond, the Monticello general store Denham & Palmer supplied the Confederacy with hogs, beef, bacon, lard, vinegar, much sewing thread, gallons of syrup, sugar, shovels, nails, spades, and buckets. William Denham signed several of the receipts. Dr. Palmer's first and second wives were Denhams before they married.

It kept raining in August, sometimes raining for days. The ditches remained half full of mud and water. On several miserable nights, the 5th

Florida and everything they owned got soaked. They lacked warm clothes and blankets because in Florida August nights are hot and sweltering. The Virginia nights were uncommonly wet and chilly.

The Western Theater

But southeastern Tennessee was hot. The Florida boys around Chattanooga learned about the cool, higher elevations; and they especially enjoyed the chance to see mountains. Many had never seen them. According to their journals, they explored Lookout Mountain and the countryside. With the Floridians, the south had upward of 80,000 men in this vicinity awaiting their next orders.

William may have written home.

On a clear day, one can see North Carolina, Georgia, Alabama, and Tennessee from Lookout Mountain.

Below were farms and a view that reached for miles. He also wrote about a large cave nearby. He spent his free time visiting family and friends in other regimental camps.

On August 14, Confederate General Kirby Smith's army slipped into the mountains southwest of Cumberland Gap, northeast of Chattanooga. With him were the 1st Florida Cavalry's three mounted companies, the 7th Florida, and the 6th. Mary's brother J.J. reported later they had no tents, only knapsacks, rifles, forty rounds of ammo, haversacks, canteens, and three days' provisions.

Three days later, William watched as the last of his in-laws marched away with Bragg. They formed into columns and left as a band played. Leaving with them were evenings sitting by campfires sharing stories of home.

Because he was in the 4th with none of the rest of the family, he sighed and turned, walking to his campsite. He remembered Mary's superstition about watching as something or someone disappeared in the distance. Though he doubted it, he thought it better to take no chances.

Three of Mary's tall, dark-haired brothers left with Bragg— George, Berry, and Archibald, not counting her Uncle David, who was like a brother, and three of her first cousins, Joel, William, and Jesse. Eight Walker men left over a three-day period, and William may have never felt so alone. He would never see all eight again.

Bragg and his army, including the 1st and 3rd Florida Infantries, crossed the Tennessee River. Lines of marching troops, mostly outfitted in short jackets, caps, and trousers of gray cloth, tramped in the dusty road. Of course, all were not the same. Among them were men dressed in every conceivable type of coat—some longer, some cutaway, and all types of colors. Some wore foraged Yankees clothes and hats. Most had let their hair grow long.

Though they appeared lean, unkempt, and entirely unsuited for military service, within their eyes one could see a determination and dedication for what had to be done. It was a look of inner conviction and steady fortitude. Plus, their guns were clean and well-cared for. Rumors followed about a Confederate offensive—that Bragg planned a foray into Kentucky to liberate Middle Tennessee and Nashville.

He moved northwest while Kirby Smith flanked the Cumberland Gap, forcing the North to abandon it. Later, the two generals planned to unite in Middle Tennessee, coming down from the unguarded north, to defeat General Buell's Union force.

The 1st and 3rd were part of Colonel John Calvin Brown's brigade, along with the 41st Mississippi, under Monticello, Florida's General James Patton Anderson's Division in Hardee's right wing. The 1st fought at Shiloh, but the 3rd remained untested.

Kentucky was neutral. Though its governor was a secessionist, its legislature was pro-Union.

A few days later, William got a letter from home with unexpected news. Vollie talked his mother into letting him join Company D of the 2nd Battalion Partisan Rangers, also known as Brevard's Partisan Rangers, a cavalry battalion under Major Theodore W. Brevard. Mary must have thought this a safer option. The unit's order were to keep supply routes open and safe. Vollie's unit would stay in Florida.

Vollie was their second son and William's third son. His full name was Valentine E. Andrews. We're not sure what the E. was for. He was popular at school and a good-looking boy. All the boys liked him, and the girls loved him. He was almost never in an angry mood. It took a lot to rile him, and he had a cool head when things got tough. William felt he would make a good soldier. He hoped he could stay away from the vices, mainly because he worried about their oldest James on the latter.

Valentine E. Andrews, possibly a school picture

James was their firstborn son. He did well in school but pestered his mother unmercifully until William took the bull by the horns and signed for him to join the Army. Mary didn't speak to William for days, and times were tough in the Andrews household for everyone.

James served on the east coast in the 3rd Florida Infantry, but thankfully the Confederacy sent him home when the unit went north. He arrived in Monticello mad with all kinds of vices learned in the Army. Mary was not happy about the new intruder in her home. He went away a mild-mannered boy and came home a hardened man.

General Braxton Bragg was *"a puzzling mixture of competence and ineptness."* He gained seniority during the Mexican War but would have trouble leading his officers in the Civil War. His ineptness would surface soon, and those under him would point it out in case President Davis missed it.

When Bragg's armies moved north into Tennessee, they ferried across the Tennessee River and disappeared into the foothills on the other side. Before long, most marchers relieved themselves of all extra items, leaving the road strewn with clothing, blankets, and extra knapsacks.

Farther north, they stopped and camped in the beautiful Sequatchie Valley for a week, waiting for the army to assemble before moving farther.

George's knapsack, a constant fixture on his back, carried underwear, soap, towel, comb, brush, looking glass, a toothbrush, paper and envelopes, pens, ink, pencils, a couple of photos, smoking and chewing tobacco, a pipe, and string and cotton strips, needed for dressing wounds. In addition, he also had needles and thread, extra buttons, a knife, a fork, and a spoon. On the outside of the sack were two folded blankets and a rubber cloth. Unlike many, his twenty-plus-pound knapsack weighed extra heavy, but he didn't jettison any extra items. As part of his body now, he seldom thought about it anymore. He thought he might resemble a pack mule.

With a full canteen, he fell in and marched for three dusty days on an old rocky, sometimes steep, wagon road. The tall, square-shouldered George topped a hill, and the marching columns before and behind resembled a great serpent in both directions as the long dark serpentine lines of men, wagons, and animals weaved through open fields and patchy woods. The men carried rifled muskets. All had knives of all shapes and sizes brought from their homes. George stopped to drink and wet a rag to wash the dirt and grit from his streaked and stained face.

Forward and behind him were voices. Men swore when they stumbled. Horse teams clacked their chains. Wheels creaked on rocks, and wagons loaded with big guns splashed through shallow streams. A moving army was a splendid spectacle, something he felt he would never forget.

Because of a drought in this area, the dust settled over everything. Creeks dried, and water stagnated where it pooled. Covered with a green film of algae, the water became a problem. He regretted using his supply earlier. The Florida boys decided this part of Tennessee was a hellhole.

After a brief rest in a village called Dunlap, they marched north, crossed the Cumberland River northeast above Nashville, and passed into Kentucky. On their first day in Kentucky, they marched until midnight underneath a scorching August sun. They moved ten to twenty miles daily through mountains, rivers, and streams. Many developed blistered feet, mountain breathing problems, and sore muscles. Their days were hot, but the nights were downright cold.

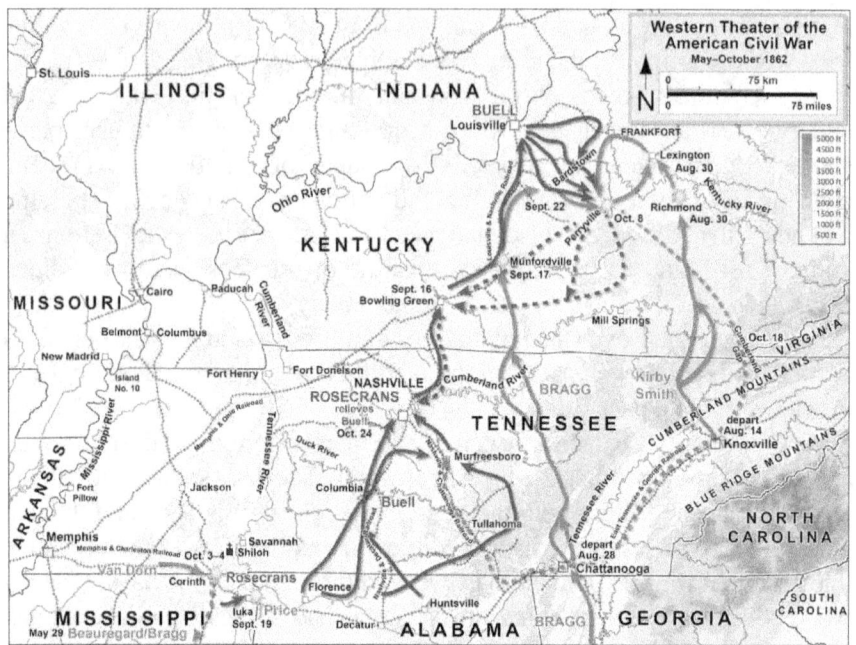

Perryville, Western theater of the American Civil War, Wikipedia. Drawn by Hal Jespersen in Adobe Illustrator CS5. Graphic source file is available at http://cwmaps.com/

In the mountains, the 3rd, who guarded the army's wagon train, pulled the wagons up mountains and worked against them on the declines by scotching their wheels with rocks to keep them from rolling backward out of control. George and his brothers, raised to work with livestock, were valuable with the horses and mules.

Bragg received word Kirby Smith had occupied Lexington. Undeterred, Bragg felt they could crush the Northern Army once the two armies met there, along with all the new Kentucky recruits. The Confederacy wanted Kentucky to join them.

Meanwhile, in Chattanooga, the 4th Florida, with only 483 privates, remained in camp near Lookout Mountain to form a base of operations and guard stores kept near Chattanooga. William received a ration of eleven pounds of bacon and four pounds of beef every seven days. He had learned he needed to protect his ration and everything else he had. There were thieves in the camp. He augmented his rations with peaches and apples, both of which were of a fine variety and plentiful.

They were available from 11 to 24 cents a dozen. Irish potatoes and green peas were also plentiful if you had money.

Still, the men knew their colonel and lieutenant colonel were both ill. Lieutenant Colonel Wylde Bowen survived, but not Colonel James Hunt. William noticed a summer haze hung over the area, a haze from all the dust the advancing Southern armies made north of them. It had been dry.

By the end of August, it appears from muster rolls David Walker was in Florida and reported absent without leave. We are unsure if this is Mary's brother, uncle, or cousin. The rolls report him the same through March of the following year (1863). An earlier muster roll reported him as having served with no pay for the same period. His compiled service records are hard to read, but one document dated 1864 mentions they may have arrested him in Florida in August 1862. It is almost unreadable, though, and there were several David Walkers in Jefferson County, so which one was it? And why did this David Walker feel like he had to get back to Florida?

The Eastern Theater

In Virginia, food became scarce. As a result, illness further weakened the 2nd Florida Regiment. Men at night conducted foraging expeditions, and some reported they killed anything in their path.

The Western Theater

In early September, the news about the South's victory at Second Manassas spread throughout Chattanooga and William's camp. For him, the problem was not knowing for days if his son survived. He told himself most people survived, especially on the winning side.

The resultant concoction of relief, worry, and fear made for long, restless nights of bad dreams and general sleeplessness. Sometimes, he woke with a sour stomach.

Though the Union blockade controlled many ports along the southern coastline, it still did not control those in Alabama and Texas. The war at sea was a continuous fight because the South's ships broke the blockade repeatedly. This rendered the blockade ineffective. War materials in significant quantities still slipped through where Florida alone had over 1,200 miles of coastline. In addition, Union forces could not take Richmond.

25

It wasn't all roses for the South, though. President Davis grew increasingly unpopular, as did his government. The aloof Davis rarely campaigned or tried to gain support for his administration or government. Small farmers, most of the population, were the first to speak against him and his cause. Most southerners owned no slaves and saw no need to continue fighting unless the Union armies threatened their state or homes. In addition, a prevailing sentiment against any strong central government grew in popularity while casualties and desertions caused chronic shortages in manpower.

In September 1862, the Confederate Congress raised the draft age limit from 35 to 45, and a month later, an officer review board caused a rapid and widespread thinning of 1,700 incompetent officers. Even less popular, the review board suggested a new mandate. Thereafter, the men elected only second lieutenants and lower. Any officer above that rank would be appointed.

In Florida, these changes and the impressment of slaves soured their owners, the planters/officers. Thousands of slaves served as laborers and cooks with the state regiments. At home, freed blacks and trusted men of color served in local state militia units, deployed for local defense. Otherwise, the young boys and old blades were utilized; they were all that was left at home.

Conscription was different, though, for the enlisted men in the army. It provided equity, but conscription was not something used for other American wars. The Confederate Conscription Act was the first in American history. It was a radical departure, but those who first volunteered thought the stay-at-homes should shoulder the burdens of war. They also knew the larger their army, the better their chances in battle. Mostly, they felt it might put an end to the war sooner.

At Home

One September afternoon in front of the courthouse, the local militia fell into line as the crowd pushed back to give them room. Monticello's courthouse stood in the middle of two main streets, and its traffic circled both directions to clear it. On its north side, its steps swept from the ground to its second floor, low-country South Carolina style.

At the foot of its steps, the boys and old men of the home guard executed a brisk drill as the audience cheered and applauded. Mary saw the coquettish moments between the boys and the girls in the audience. She remembered her youth and enjoyed the show. Let them enjoy it while

26

they can because marriage for her girls meant dull-colored clothes and dancing only with your husband.

As men deserted, Florida swamps and woods filled with deserters from both sides, the North and the South. Even though some had been part of the Confederacy, they became the opposite of partisans of the cause.

When they deserted, they belonged to no army and plundered all citizens regardless of their political sympathies. These first deserters were usually the rebellious ones that thought it was someone else's fight. Florida's swamps and wide-open spaces offered refuge for bands of men who roamed throughout the state in guerrilla units. As their numbers grew, they needed more food, clothing, and shelter. Therefore stealing, confiscating, ransacking, and raiding Florida's farms, plantations, and communities occurred. Often these men were citizens of the state, and oftentimes they set slaves free.

The early Union occupation of forts such as Ft. Pickens near Pensacola and Ft. Jefferson at Key West created places on Florida's coastlines for Yankee infiltration. Because of Florida's indefensible shoreline, neither army fought to keep control of the state. So until the end of the War, the North's navy controlled Florida's ports and rivers, while Florida's local home militias maintained its inland lands.

The Western Theater

When Bragg's army crossed the Cumberland River, marching north, it was a good day for all. The Florida boys got to wash away the dirt and dust from their bodies and clothing. Later, around the fire, with clothes steaming on a temporary rope line, they wrote home. Through their letters, George, his brothers, and cousins described the area's beauty with its changing leaves. They camped in a fine farming country with superior stock.

Bragg's army foraged the countryside, living off the nearby fields and orchards. If they passed a field of food, it got raided. They roasted ears of corn and later captured Federal supplies.

George and his brothers may have found a farmer killing hogs but offered to buy his meat. The farmer agreed, which resulted in a large pork pot pie later.

That evening, when alone, George told Arch, "I feel I will never see our home again." His brother frowned. George added, "But I push it from my mind and try not to think of it."

Uncomfortable because of his own thoughts on the subject, Arch let the comment drop. He didn't enjoy thinking about it either.

The next day, they entered even more fertile ground with great foraging, orchards filled with ripe apples, and water. People offered their food and cheered their passing. The 3rd Florida described it as similar to what the 6th and 7th under Kirby found earlier.

It didn't last, though, when they crossed into a part of Kentucky with a mixed welcome. From town to town, the people acted differently— one a Union town and the next a Confederate. They camped in Glasgow for two days to rest and received a hero's welcome. Afterward, in Barbourville, they paused again.

At Home

Early one evening in mid-September, everyone in Monticello gathered around the depot, as did people all over the southland, awaiting news from the eastern front. Mary sat in her buggy along with Florida and Ellen. Like everyone else, she held her breath as she watched Zech walk through the crowd. In his hand was a list of casualties from Sharpsburg, known as Antietam by the North.

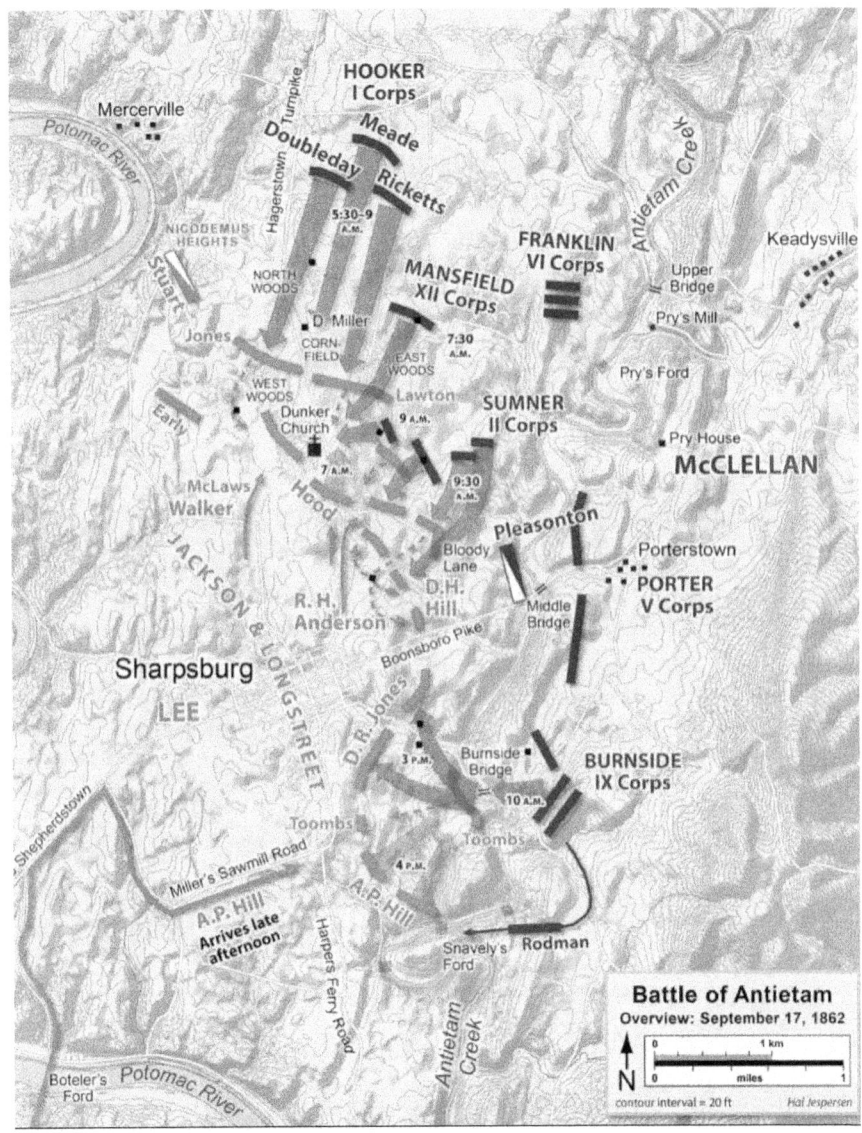

Battle of Antietam, Wikipedia. Map by Hal Jespersen, www.cwmaps.com

Standing next to the family, he read the list of wounded to his mother as she sat looking off into the distance. He spoke loud as others listened too, "George Bishop, Irvin Granger, John King, and Mama," he said as he looked up, "they wounded Uncle Littleberry, too." He saw his mama's shoulders quiver, even with her bowed head and eyes closed.

Seldom something he witnessed, he watched his mother sob. He couldn't tell her the rest; they killed her cousin John Adam Lightsey.

John Adam was Mary's first cousin, the son of her Aunt Mary Jane Walker Lightsey. He left behind his wife Amanda Sledge Lightsey, pregnant with their fifth child, and their four children, ages eight years and under.

He fought with the Florida 5th Infantry, Company G, the Aucilla Guards, who got into the worst of the desperate fighting. They killed five more Jefferson County men, including Eli Bishop, Elijah Bishop, Ira Ayers, James Gadsden, and James M. Johns. After the battle, one southern soldier said, "*the Yankey army is now as good as ours*." Everyone realized Yankees did not lack courage.

The Western Theater

While Braxton Bragg moved through Kentucky, General Lee drove north in mid-September. However, the Union turned him back to Sharpsburg in Maryland, where they fought an inconclusive battle with over 22,000 casualties, known as the deadliest day in American history. Over 10,000 were Confederates. In Chattanooga, when William heard they were fighting in Sharpsburg, he tossed and turned all night, because he knew John Slicer was there.

#

Chapter 2
Burnt and Barefooted
September to November 1862

The Western Theater

In Kentucky, the 3rd Florida entered their first line of engagement in a railroad town called Munfordville. It would be a brief skirmish before the Union forces there surrendered. George noticed as they watched the surrendered forces pass. "Berry, did you see their clean new uniforms?"

Frowning, his brother Berry said, "And they look well-fed, too." Both boys looked around at their cousins and brother Arch—bony, ragged, burnt, and a few barefooted.

During their days in Munfordville, General Brown's brigade clerk Samuel Pasco wrote in one of his reports about George W. Walker, Mary's brother. He reported the twenty-six-year-old boy as sick and weakening.

After the skirmish, the 3rd occupied the surrendered men's breastworks to make a defensive line and await the rest of Buell's army. Their officers reminded them to waste no ammo—to hold their fire until their aim was sure. George thought the reminder was similar to his father's advice when stalking deer. In the trenches, the 3rd Florida waited on a high hill where they sat and talked until dusk, but no Yankees came.

Four days later, Bragg's army moved closer to Kirby's army on September 20th, reaching Bardstown, thirty miles from Louisville. The town threw open its doors with a band playing Dixie. The 3rd Florida columns marched into town with their colors unfurled, their bayonets fixed, and a quick swinging step; but George W. Walker came into town in an ambulance wagon with Michael Raysor, also from Jefferson County, and another George Walker from Jacksonville, who was in Company A.

In Bardstown, they encamped for two weeks while Brown's Brigade encamped several miles from town on the Louisville road as pickets. Bragg's army lived on roasted corn and ripe pumpkins, which made many sick. Michael Raysor from the 3rd spent his time in a hospital housed in the local school, and this is where they probably sent the two George Walkers as well.

At Home

Meanwhile, a few days later, in early October, Mary bought in her own name 160 acres south of Monticello near the Nash community. She paid $1,280 for the tract of land. Even if the South lost, she could sell the land for cash or provide a place to live away from town amid any problems urban living might bring. She probably paid for it in Confederate cash. William thought it best to convert their assets to protect her and the children. If the South lost, many thought southern soldiers' lands might be sold to pay the North's public debt incurred during the war.

Mary probably got a male family member to help her read the documents and negotiate the sale, but it may not have been her father Jesse. Jesse disappears after the beginning of the Civil War. We know he was still living when the census taker took his information on the 13th day of July in 1860, but this is the last known document for Jesse.

In the census, he is still farming and living near other family members, with a personal estate of $200. After selling much of his farmland to other family members, he lists his daughter Jane as living with him, plus William, George, and David. However, the census enumerator lists George and David in the same census, living and working with their older brothers at Walker Mills, over five miles away. One wonders if Jesse was confused when he reported this. George and David were twenty-five and seventeen respectively in this census.

Jesse may have lost a third son. Joseph, sixteen, was in the 1850 census but disappeared by this 1860 census. There are no records that he joined any Monticello units during the war nor any other records about him. He simply vanishes, and several siblings will name their sons Joseph, including Mary.

There are tax rolls during the war, but they do not list Jesse. The next one, after 1860, was dated in 1863, but they excluded him. Neither was he in the 1866 roll.

Also, a David goes absent without leave from the Army of Tennessee earlier in February 1862. This David was arrested at home in Jefferson County. Could it be this David went AWOL to help take care of his ill father? David, nineteen was the youngest sibling.

Mary's father Jesse would have been sixty-one in 1862, and he may have been weakened by all the deaths in the family. In the past five years, we know he lost his wife, two sons, and a granddaughter. One of these deceased sons was his oldest, Henry, who successfully owned and ran two mills at Walker Mills.. Henry's estate in the 1860 census was valued at over $20,000.

The Western Theater

Leaving his brother George behind in a grave, Arch stood in line, ready to march from Bardstown with his other brother and their unit. Standing on its main street, their breath fogged the air. Arch shivered, hoping they could move soon to warm up.

His thoughts were on George, though. His head told him there was nothing more they could do, but his gut rebelled and every part of him felt sick at the thought of leaving his older brother behind. Arch was twenty-three, and the two of them were closest in age. They were more like twins, always discovering new things together.

He was glad his mama didn't have to go through this, but worst of all was letting Mary and the rest of his siblings know. Being the oldest, Mary had become like a mother to George, first when their mother had her hands full during the Indian war, and then later when their mother died.

The commands rolled down the lines, and they marched away, Arch beside his other brother Berry.

Arch Walker, family photo

They marched to Lexington, where the two Confederate armies converged. The third leg of the stool, the new Kentucky recruits, didn't materialize. Neither Bragg nor Kirby's armies could recruit the needed Kentuckians; and the recruiting efforts of the installed Kentucky Confederate government fizzled, too. Meanwhile, Buell's Union army rested and, moving north, itched for a fight.

After a feast the night before, the 3rd Florida made a quick march and stopped around midnight. The following day, Arch and Berry, with only two hours of sleep, joined their column and marched west to Perryville, where Bragg's army stopped. Unseasoned in combat, the tall, dark-haired brothers, twenty-four and twenty-two, were among the younger ones, joking and hoping to be first in the fight. They expected a battle the following day.

At Home

Meanwhile, unable to breathe, Mary reached for the telegraph. Her son Jesse, stunned and silent, didn't know what to say. He added, "Mama, I'm so sorry" as he dropped in front of her rocking chair and put his arms around her waist. He buried his face in her skirts, and they both wept as she ran her hands through his hair.

A telegraph from Sergeant Sam Pasco reported Mary's brother George had died. It came from the depot to her. After a moment, she disappeared into her bedroom to grieve alone; about fifteen minutes later, she sought Zech, who chopped wood at the woodpile. Crying, he had been there ever since she told the kids.

She stepped onto the back steps. "Zech," she said, "hitch the wagon. We need to tell everyone else." He dropped the ax and disappeared.

We aren't certain she received a telegram, but Monticello had a telegraph office at the depot. They built the railroad and depot in 1859, when her William became its first depot agent. We also know that Samuel Pasco of Jefferson County mentioned in his wartime journal that he wrote a letter to George's sister about George's demise. It may be another hint that Mary's father had passed away.

The Western Theater

In Perryville, the officers supplied lots of whiskey and plenty to eat. Before dawn the following day, Arch and Berry rolled their blankets and stacked them and their knapsacks in a safe place before forming ranks. Each had a little piece of paper pinned to their shirt with their names and addresses on them. They did it before they rolled their blankets. Their cartridge boxes and canteens were full.

On Wednesday, October 8, the firing began, and the younger ones got their wish. The Floridians discovered their place in the line of battle was not good. Artillery shots burst over their heads and flattened them to the ground.

Around 1:30 pm, they called the 1st Florida Brigade, the 3rd Florida, and the 41st Mississippi to stand shoulder-to-shoulder in a line. Under shots and shelling, they took their assigned positions and surged forward. Only the men without footwear remained behind because of the briars ahead.

The Shiloh-hardened boys of the 1st were detached and cautious in their demeanor, but the enthusiastic, untried boys of the 3rd were spirited and ready to go. As the 3rd moved forward, the shrill *yip yip* of the Rebel Yell surged ahead of them, and their trot turned into a run.

Collapsing into disorder under their red flag and flashing muskets, their line moved far ahead of the seasoned 1st and 41st. Their officers pulled the unseasoned boys from the line until the three infantries converged again. The lines of men and boys topped a knoll and faced their awaiting enemy one hundred yards away.

The first to fall was twenty-two-year-old Thomas Moseley from Madison with a bullet to his head. George Hartsfield fell, too. Dispirited by the occurrence, the 3rd Florida boys fired as the ferocity of the battle consumed them. All the while, shells fell upon them like rain. In the melee, northern snipers shot General Brown's horse from under him and wounded the general.

Farther down the line, the 1st Florida color guard became casualties, but a staff officer carried the regimental standard for the rest of the battle. They ran low on ammo, and at one point they withdrew to restock by rummaging through the dead and wounded soldier's cartridge boxes.

While restocking, Captain William Capers Bird got his second wound. The brass, though, thought he was dead. It would later cost him an elevation to colonel, something he would not learn until mid-1863, months after the North captured and exchanged him.

After they restocked and returned to the battle, they moved upon a weakened Union line while the 41st Mississippi and a Tennessee Regiment flanked them. The Union soldiers fled, kicking up much dust. The problem came when the unseasoned Confederates moved down and fired without checking their background and fired into the Mississippi regiment.

Again, the battle paused for Brown's Brigade, and the men learned the sad news—Monticello's Captain Daniel Bird had been shot through the heart. His men carried his body to a nearby farmhouse. The fight lasted until 4:30 pm. Arch, Berry, and their Walker kin and friends searched for each other at its end.

Night fell. In the silver moonlight, as ordered, Arch and Berry, along with the others, moved through the battlefield, removing the wounded from amongst the dead, who lay in every direction. They rifled the Yankee dead for rations, finding sardines, butter, and crackers.

They gained better canteens, tin cups, and pocketknives. The Union soldiers were better supplied. Someone found George Hartsfield injured but not dead. He survived the battle.

All the while, the wounded begged for help, the dying groaned, and both cried for water. With blood everywhere, the Floridians slept that night amongst the casualties.

Meanwhile, the rest of Buell's army closed in. Bragg ordered a retreat after midnight to Harrodsburg, where Kirby Smith waited. Florida's regiments didn't receive the word of the retreat until 2 am when they woke them.

Arch and Berry fell into line and moved like ghosts over the moonlit battlefield, retreating without their blankets, haversacks, and knapsacks, left at the previous night's camp. With no time for retrieval, they lost their clothing, food, and belongings forever. All they had were the Yankee confiscated items. A full moon glowed as they slipped from there, unbeknown to a Union picket only a quarter mile away.

Berry wrote home to his sister.

October 10, 1862
Kentucky

Dear Mary,

I guess by now you've received the letter about George. We are all so distraught, but there is no time to grieve in this war.

Shortly after we left Bardstown, we met the enemy on the battlefield and were victorious, or so we thought. The victory was only where we fought. Around 2 am, we learned this was only a tiny part of the enemy's army, so we vanished like ghosts in the night. All of us Walkers survived, and you would have been proud of our brave southern troops who fought to turn the Union's army.

I witnessed such immense courage—men who kept fighting even with a lost limb and those inflicted with mortal wounds, who took their last breaths, firing at their enemy.

This region is suffering from a drought, and we have had problems getting water. It has parched me for most of the campaign. Our fight was over a stream called Doctor's Creek. We had it, and they wanted it.

Mary, I can't wait to see Jefferson County and our Elizabeth community again. I miss you and everyone so much. Give everyone my love. I miss them.

There's the signal for lights out, so I need to close.

All my love,
Berry

The Battle of Perryville cost the Florida regiments dearly. Florida 1st left twelve behind on the battlefield and 53 wounded out of only 167 who entered the fight. The 3rd began with 275 soldiers and lost 14, with 86 wounded. Four more were missing in action. Twenty-six died later from their injuries, most from the lack of antibiotics, which didn't exist. Many officers were killed and injured, such as Daniel Bird.

The moving Union units captured 133 sick Floridians left behind in makeshift hospitals. Of Brown's Brigade, another thirty Floridians, including the two Georges, died of various diseases.

Thirteen more of the 3rd Florida were discharged for disability after Perryville. Sent home to Jefferson County were Charles Chase, Mathew Granger, William Grantham, John and Noah Hay, Whitfield Horton, Benjamin Johnson, Berry Lastinger, James McAdam, Henry Mershon, David Sauls, Fredric Sealey, and John Wetherington.

Beginning in Chattanooga, Brown's Brigade marched over 700 miles, while Kelly's army marched over 600.

In Kelly's army, during the battle, the 6th and 7th Florida Infantries and the 1st Florida Cavalry (with Mary's brother J.J.) lost forty men to illness, and the Union captured 170 more. J.J. survived and was not taken prisoner.

Overall, Bragg's army suffered 3,400 casualties of the 16,800 total soldiers. The Confederate Congress named them the Army of Tennessee. The Union engaged with 20,000 men and received 4,200 casualties.

Before their disabled came home, Mary may have gotten another letter from one of her brothers. She knew about the battle and read the lists of those dead, missing, or wounded and the corrected lists. Zech read the letter in her kitchen.

October 9, 1862
Kentucky

Dear Sister,

This will be short, but I write to let you know Berry and I are alive and well. We discovered yesterday they reported me dead on one of the earlier lists. It happens from time to time.

We battled in a little crossroads town called Perryville. After marching through woods, swamp, rain, and mud on the Springfield Pike, it was an awful time, but I thanked William for James's high-top boots.

Mine were falling apart before we left Florida, and James offered his. On the marches, I could stuff my pantlegs inside the boots and stay drier. I hope James got Mr. Palmer to make him a fresh pair using Father's cowhides.

In Perryville, the skirmishing took place all day long when we withdrew with heavy casualties. Though we gave as much as we got.

I'm sorry this is short. They've ordered us to move again.

Tell everyone I love them and think of them every day. It is our family and memories of Jefferson County that keep us going.

All my love,
Arch

Identification of bodies, difficult during the Civil War, caused many misidentifications. Fingerprinting was still many years away. When each man joined the Confederacy, he filed information such as his general height, build, hair color, skin tone, and eye color. This is all they had to go on, and the body was often too maimed to identify. The more destructive the battle, the more challenging to identify everyone. Sometimes, they misidentified and recorded a death that did not happen.

From Perryville, Bragg's army fell back, headed for Chattanooga, where they merged the decimated ranks of the 1st and 3rd Florida regiments. The newly merged unit stayed in Bragg's army and became a part of Breckenridge's division. They next headed for a place called Murfreesboro.

Because of the illnesses of his commanders, William and Florida's 4th missed Perryville and stayed in Chattanooga until they sent them, too, to Murfreesboro.

At Home

Bad news came from all directions. On the afternoon of October 16th, Zech ran into Mary's kitchen with news from the telegraph office. Federal gunboats had fired upon the civilians of Tampa. Many expected an invasion.

Later in October, though, they got a pleasant surprise. Arch came home on leave. Arch had the Carter height at 6 foot 1 inch, and he wore faded and patched homespun butternut clothes with a dark brown Yankee coat. With his skin bronzed and dark brown hair bleached, the skin around his mouth was fairer than his cheeks and forehead. Earlier, he had stopped in town and shaved off his beard.

In his flat-topped wool forage cap, with a leather brim in front and its crown high and draping forward, he stood military straight in his high boots and dull spurs. To the family he still looked wonderful, though skeletal thin. She noticed the change in his demeanor. He went to war still boyish, but he returned a man with square-set shoulders and a cool alertness in his eyes.

From the family the questions came nonstop, but Arch circled any genuine answers. In his eyes appeared a weary, haunted look. Mary noticed Arch talked, laughed, and did not stop to take a breath—as if he didn't want them to find out anything about his place in the war. Whatever he had seen, he kept it hidden, if not from all of them, at least from himself.

He told many funny stories about the other soldiers and the jokes they pulled on each other. There were jokes about the long marches, the rain, and their accommodations. He talked about the generals and the other officers but didn't tell them anything about the fighting.

At the end of his leave, he may have left with a thick gray wool coat made from the one large gray wool shawl she had owned and an oiled leather and felt slouch hat with a grosgrain band. They made the coat's lining of homespun fabric. He looked dashing, but Mary noticed there were lined spokes etched from his eyes and two lined furrows between his eyebrows where there had been none before. He looked older than his years.

By the fall of 1862, losing Missouri, parts of Tennessee, Kentucky, and Maryland left the Southern government in control of only 63% of its population. Subsequently, they attributed their weakness to a lack of manpower at the front and a lack of supplies. Shoes were a problem, as was exhaustion after long marches and lack of food. Even the Southern newspapers pointed this out.

On the flip side, it was still early in the war. The South controlled more than half its population, and General Lee continued his damage to the Union army in Virginia.

A few days later, in October, Mary got terrible news. John Kinsey, twenty-eight, passed away at home with his wife Sarah, seventeen, by his side. Sarah was Joel and Betsy Walker's daughter. Betsy Howell was a dear friend of Mary's long before she married Mary's Uncle Joel, who was Mary's same age. More a childhood playmate than an uncle, Joel had died in 1859.

Mary, who had her buggy ready for the ride to Elizabeth, went to Betsy's. Betsy joined her, and the two talked all the way out. Said Betsy, "I can't believe my seventeen-year-old baby is a widow."

According to family lore, they sent John home. John Kinsey never recovered from his illness. They buried him in the Kinsey Cemetery in Jefferson County and not on a battlefield far to the north. His unit, the 5th Florida Infantry Regiment, was in Northern Virginia.

His was a typical death among soldiers in this war. A soldier's chance of surviving was one in four. Over half a million soldiers died before it ended. Until the Vietnam War, the number of soldiers killed in the Civil War surpassed all other American wars combined. Over 60% of these deaths were by disease.

The Western Theater

By November, William had problems with illness. He wrote Mary.

November 1, 1862
Chattanooga, TN

Dearest Mary,
I wanted you to know I have been sick and am better. I got worse with dysentery until I was so weakened they sent me to the Newsom Hospital in Chattanooga. They named it for a nurse, a lady who took her own money and bought supplies for our sick and wounded. I am in camp, though, so there is no need to worry, though we hear we are soon to head northwest toward Nashville any day.

Zech stopped reading. "Northwest is Nashville, and that's where the Yankees are." Mary sighed. The letter was more than a week old. William might be there now.

William lay propped against a tree trunk with his left ankle stretched over his right. He thought about being in the hospital. He had never been the sickly type, but he was an older man now. Too old to be acting like a younger one. Fifty was old, and many mornings he felt it.

From October 31st to December 31, 1862, Major Boyd, Boyn, Bord, or Boid paid William. On a muster roll dated October 31, 1862, they showed him absent because he had been hospitalized. This is a muster roll from October 31 to December 31, showing payment for service. Because they dated it February 14, 1863, his hospitalization may have occurred anytime between those dates and only for part of the two months. These muster rolls are often incomplete.

A railroad runs through Murfreesboro from Nashville to Chattanooga, and whoever holds these rails or the Nashville Pike holds Tennessee. Nashville became the first southern capital under Union occupation, but the Confederates held Chattanooga at the other end of the rails. Murfreesboro lies between the two cities but much closer to Nashville.

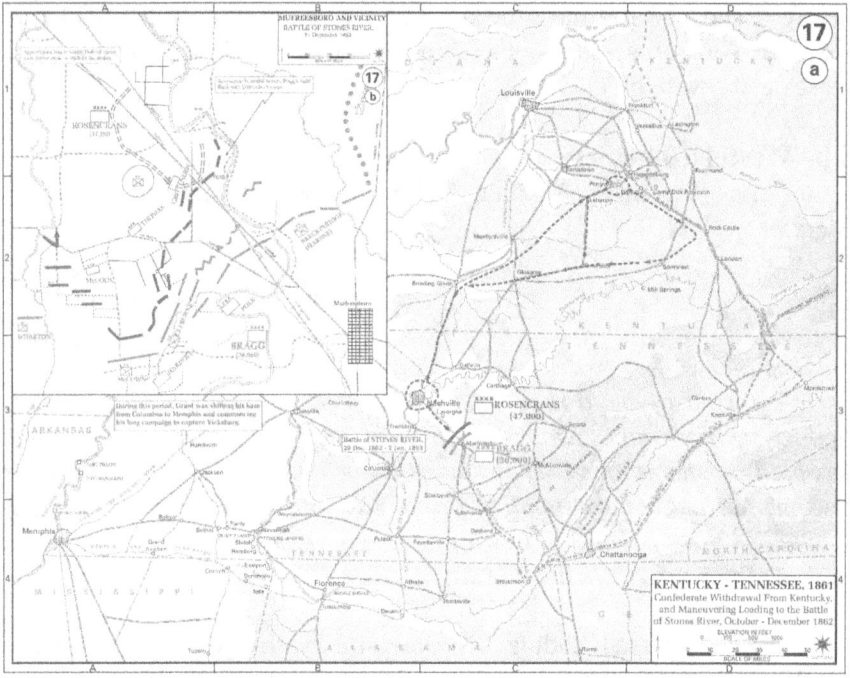

The West Point atlas of the Civil War. Source: West Point - Department of History (The American Civil War) and Library of Congress. Wikipedia

William reenlisted for three years or the duration of the war. All men over forty-five and under eighteen could withdraw from the army, but he did not go home. His devotion to his homeland and its southern rights trumped all else. He also must have felt fit for the job. This and several other instances show William Andrews as a vigorous man at heart and— he thought—in body too.

After the first of November 1862, near Chattanooga, he got a letter from Mary and read and reread it. Moving farther away from home, he grew homesick.

They were moving out because General Forrest, with a cavalry force, captured the garrison at Murfreesboro. William's company and the others of the 4th rushed to Forrest's aid to hold the position until Bragg arrived.

The road they took, the Nashville Pike, traveled northwesterly across Tennessee and for a ways ran beside the Tennessee River. There were mountains all around, and the road was canopied in many places. William thought it beautiful.

But many nights were already cold. Winter was coming quickly for Tennessee. Nights at home in Florida could still be balmy, thought William.

November 7, 1862
Tennessee

Dearest Mary,

In your last letter, you asked what camp life was like. I see a big, bustling city with a perpetual haze hanging over it from hundreds of campfires. In cold weather, you don't know which is worse: lingering smoke that makes you cough or the wind which blows away the haze but leaves you shivering in your blanket.

The camp bustles because of the rush, dash, and scramble of hundreds of people hurrying in no particular direction. The whole place, during the day, is full of activity. There are streets between the rows of tents. It is massive.

This is temporary, though. The only permanency we get is when winter comes, and I'm told we will lie in for "winter quarters."

Camp life is arduous. I have the threadbare blanket I brought from home. I will need another soon, as winter is almost here. I sleep under the stars. If it rains, I try to find a splendid tree and a suitable mate so we can use our blankets to make a makeshift tent. Standley suffices. The tent leaks like a sieve, though.

When leaned against a wonderful tree within the drip line, it can provide a sort of umbrella, and the ground there can be higher and drier. A good tree, though, can be difficult to find near an encampment, firewood being invaluable.

43

Confiscated pieces of canvas from the dead Yankees during the last battle make a better tent. They are white and buttoned together with another piece of canvas. We can stretch the two parts over a pole parallel to the ground and fasten the ends to the ground with knives or any sharp object. A few use the bayonet from their rifle.

The ends are open to the elements, but in a slight drizzle with no wind, it will keep you drier. The Yankees call them dog tents because they say only dogs can stay dry. At least they issued them tents. Most of us lost ours long ago, and no more are coming. The Yankees should have to deal with our camp life. They might appreciate theirs better.

Everywhere, one hears marching boots, chopping hooves of horses and mules, and creaking wheels of rolling equipment. Harnesses jingle, and officers bark. Nearby in a clearing, men practice marching. At night, all around me is a sea of tents and fires.

Best of all, though, are the rubber blankets the Yanks have. They make the best tent yet, but they are like gold. If you get one, protect it. There are thieves in this man's Confederate army.

The soldiers here come from every walk of life. There are farmers, gentlemen, merchants, mechanics, and students, to name a few. Somehow, they merged us into a band of brothers on the battlefield.

Mary, I think of you and how much I miss your love and care. Having to cook and care for our clothes makes me realize how much you do for all of us. Not to mention how much I miss your warmth next to mine. My bedroll gets chilly.

Eight of us have banded together, and we share a large camp chest containing our skillet, a frying pan, a coffee boiler, a bucket for lard, and separate boxes for coffee and salt, sugar, meal, and flour. This chest also holds knives, forks, spoons, plates, and cups. It rides in a wagon with other chests used by other groups of men. They carry our ax, water bucket, bread trays, and tents. Each company has a wagon.

I am much obliged for the buck gauntlet gloves your dad had. The long cuffs are a necessity I didn't realize I needed. My hands stay so much warmer. We are all beholden to him for his cowhides and willingness to have Mr. Palmer tool the leather. So many of our colleagues lack shoes and gloves now. I will miss my friend forever, as I know you will, too.

Speaking of shoes, I could sure use a pair of brogans. We more wealthy have noticed our less affluent comrades have it better. Their broad-bottomed, flat-heeled brogans hold up better in this environment. Because my thick-heeled soles have worn on one side, I've twisted my ankle several times. Also, when wet, my boots are difficult to remove and worse to get on in the morning.

They are always wet. I believe a pair of brogans are much more sensible. If you can get them, James and Vollie will need a pair, too. Tell James to have Mr. Palmer make him those for when he returns.

Hug and kiss all the kids for me, and tell them how much I miss every one of them. When this war ends, I will see all of you again, but if I can't, I'll be waiting for each of you with St. Peter.

All my love,
William

At Home

The kids giggled about the cold bedroll, but the last line made her shiver. She'd told him frequently—it's bad luck to talk about one's demise. Also, she noticed he included Vollie in the list for shoes. He thought it was only a matter of time before Vollie went north with the rest of them.

Several days later, her sewing circle worked on quilts. All their men needed them. They lined them with wool, but the blockade made it harder to get fabrics. Plus, money was scarce.

Their regiment bivouacked west of Murfreesboro in a massive camp. Days later, she received another letter.

November 15, 1862
Murfreesboro, Tennessee

Dearest Mary,

Moving since I wrote last, we are here. I am almost five hundred long miles away from you and our babies. The miles were hot and dusty while the nights were mostly cold. I marched with my home on my back on the last day in a driving rain. It is more than a man can imagine living through. I thought the rigors and demands of Indian fighting were rough, but being a part of a moving army, which moves the miles we do, is many times rougher. On our way here, our columns extended for more than a mile, a dense moving mass of soldiers.

At first, during a march, we preserve our place in the ranks and march in a good show of order; but within a short time, a lively boy starts a song or whistles a tune. The column breaks into jolly singing, laughter, talking, and joking until the regimental band plays and brings us all into order.

45

Good-natured fun and ribbing between men occur, but heaven help the young officer who passes by in anything new. The men say, "Come out of that hat," or "you can't hide in that shiny, fresh coat." They especially love to torment the cavalry. If anyone passes by and takes a moment to recognize someone in our ranks, he gets replies from everyone in the column. "Hey Bill, here's your brother. Bill, oh Bill, your Mama's back here. How de do! Glad to see ya!"

There are days the dust gets so bad that our nostrils fill and dry out. Our throats parch, and there's grit between our teeth all day long. On those days, I feel sawdust in my eyes. The other day it was sand. It got in my clothes and was incredibly irritating to my neck, wrists, and ankles.

My skin has toughened into a dark brown. My hands stay black, and my beard and hair are long. From the constant beating sun, my hair, which hangs from under my cap, has bronzed.

We march when told, even if it rains, snows, or hails. Sometimes my mud-caked boots weigh ten times their usual weight. These rainy days are the worst. When we stop, everything is wet, including the wood, which will not burn. Without fire, we eat whatever we have on hand. Soggy bread is not so palatable. We sleep on the wet ground under wet blankets. All this after marching all day, wading through swollen streams, mud, and a hundred other discomforts.

Night marches can be disconcerting. Heaven help someone if he gets lost. I'd wander in the wilderness instead, because you're doomed if you ask for directions. The men in the columns utter catcalls from every direction. "Aw, you poor thing. We're over here." "Have you lost your mother?" Roars of laughter follow. They make everything into a joke.

I've been lucky in the socks and shoe department, but many of these men have not. Many have their boots in their hands or hanging from their shoulders. Few have fitting or comfortable shoes.

The starts and stops wear us out, too. We hear "halt," so we sit or lie on the roadside, in the shade, if found. But when we get comfortable, we hear "forward on." Such an annoyance. Often, it isn't worth it because of the stiffness of my limbs. It is hard to stand and get going again.

A swollen stream on a hot day is a godsend—a joy to bathe your hands, feet, and face in the cool, clear water. It reminds me of swimming at Sandy Ford.

Mary, what I miss most are your pies. We have time to purchase a pie, but there's only a trace of sugar in it. Sometimes the lard is rancid and the apples of a crab variety. We eat it anyway because they still fill you up.

Later in the day, as the column tires, we talk less. A quietness falls as our minds take over. I find myself occupied with my thoughts. Sometimes I listen to our boots' steady tramping and canteens' rattling.

As evening closes and the road darkens, the questions begin. "Hey, captain, when are we going into camp?" "How long have we got?" "Seen our wagon?" The latter is a question because our wagon is our supper.

By the way, I need a pocketknife. Mine disappeared and to buy one here is no less than $2. Please send one.

Mary, I look forward to sitting with all of you on the porch, talking and reading. If I can get back there and the good Lord is willing, I'll never leave you again.

Please keep sending stories about you and the children and what you do daily. No event is too common. I long for news from all of you.

All my love,
William

The Western Theater

Vollie mustered into Company A of the 2nd Battalion, also known as Brevard's Partisan Rangers. He enlisted on August 8th in Monticello for the "period of the war" under Sergeant Hamilton, but they did not call and muster him until November. Commanded by Major T. W. Brevard, the company would become, by 1863, Company D of the 2nd Battalion.

Another letter from William arrived a week later.

November 20, 1862
Murfreesboro, Tennessee

Dearest Mary,

Winter days are long, and I miss you and the kids all the more. We built a log hut in winter quarters when six of us felled some trees. However, we went a long way to find them because our companies and regiments are collecting wood near Murfreesboro for a fight anytime the Yanks push forward. They need the wood to build ramparts and trenches.

We built the hut on stones as a floor and had no trouble finding them in the Stony River. We filled the gaps between the logs with mud. The hut even has a fireplace of dirt and sticks, and I often think of your dad.

He knew how to build a fireplace that wouldn't smoke a house. We may have to rebuild ours.

We made bunks for ourselves so we do not sleep on the floor. I wish we had good moss for stuffing our mattresses. We sleep on and rolled into our blankets. Speaking of blankets, thank you so much for the quilt you sent. Seeing all the pieces of fabric you and the kids wore makes me think of home.

Inside, our hut is austere. My only chair is a one-foot-long log sitting on its end by the fire. I use it outside and roll it back and forth each day lest someone steal it.

We decided our hut was so exquisite compared to our makeshift tents, we nicknamed it "The Astor House" after the grand hotel in New York City.

Now, we are here for the winter and the long stretches of boredom. At least I can read and find relief in my books. I could use a couple more if you can get your hands on any. Up here all we have now are the worn-out, dog-eared dime novels. We share and pass them around. I guess my library there is getting sparse. We love anything from Erastus Beadle and his eastern frontier characters.

Thankfully, though, I never thought I would say it, we now covet the drills. It allows us to work together, warms us up, and makes the day go faster. It is not good to sit too much. We drill both morning and afternoon, a blessed aversion to the boredom.

Several times, the friendly people of Murfreesboro invite us to eat with them. We feel like honored guests. Still, guards protect their smokehouses and barns. Our foragers sometimes get carried away.

Well, there's the cue. I have to line up.

Love,
William

For those whose homes were nearby, the Confederate officers relieved them to go home and bring a supply of warm winter clothing. William wrote home to Mary for his winter wear.

When he went to war, he purchased a civilian greatcoat or overcoat similar to what the officers wore. The difference was there were no turndown cuffs, nor did its cape have buttons. The cape reached to his waist. Its collar was a turndown collar, and they made the coat of heavy wool.

William sent word home for the coat, and it arrived in time for his new assignment in Murfreesboro. The coat had five cloth buttons on the front and two on the back for adjusting the belt. It had a heavy cotton half-lining to the waist. He wished he had gotten a full wool body lining, especially when they were sent behind the enemy lines with General Nathan Bedford Forrest.

#

Chapter 3

To Get There First
December 1862

At Home

Because William's letters came more often from a winter camp, Mary thought her people were safe for the moment. The children made Christmas plans as if nothing had changed. She relaxed in its normality.

December 2, 1862
Murfreesboro, Tennessee

Dearest Mary,

I guess you are preparing for Christmas while we wait in winter quarters here. Winter camp is boring, and though winter days are short, the days here are long.

For us Florida boys, the weather is harsh. The north wind blows, and the rain falls. Most roads are impassable for wagons, even the roads causeway'd with poles. Meanwhile, General Forrest creates havoc for our wretched enemy.

A soldier is a peculiar thing. Younger boys are eager to fight but never ready for camp chores. They see no need to support a well-run camp and shirk their responsibilities. There is constant conflict between them and our superiors.

Mary, please send two of my darker woolen vests and long underwear if you can find them. I heard clothing is scarce in Florida. They will help me stay warmer. I could use a couple of wool or flannel shirts if you can find them. I will ask my sister in Virginia as well.

People in Murfreesboro welcomed us warmly, and they have given many parties and events to our men, especially our officers.

Please do not worry; I am better, but they confined me to the hospital. Dysentery is a common thing in army camps. This is an accommodating two-story stone building called Bradley's Academy, but they should release me tomorrow.

Tell the children that Davy Crockett used to visit this city often. There are still stories here about him.

Mary, this place lacks your tender, loving hands. Male nurses' hands lack the care of a woman's hands. I miss you more every day.

51

My friends visit often. They tell me the camps grow monstrous as other regiments join, but my latest visitors brought me the most joy.

Yesterday, Bragg's army arrived, and Florida's 1st and 3rd came with them. Your family came at once to check on me. I enjoyed their company. They send their love. We are now called Preston's Brigade, and we're under the command of Breckenridge.

Your brother, Arch, had picket duty earlier today. He said they looked for liquor. Every little animal trail within three miles of the camp has a picket posted, and with every load of forage passing through, they search for bottles and jugs. The soldiers, though, are most clever in getting it into camp. Several get past the pickets with thriving businesses in their tents.

Well, it grows dark, and it gets hard to see my page. Our window overlooks the west, so I got a sunset to enjoy.
From my view, the ground looks flat in the distance. All the best, and kiss my babies for me.

Your always loving,
William

For the Confederate soldier, his lieutenant's directives for success were courage, endurance, and devotion. The soldier's recipe for defeat was sickness, starvation, and death. William survived whereas many, like Mary's brother George, did not.

The nation considered the rich farmland west of Murfreesboro the breadbasket of Middle Tennessee, which provided the Confederates with food. Murfreesboro, the former capital of Tennessee, whose early legislators included Davy Crockett and Sam Houston, functioned as a transportation hub with turnpikes and a railroad. Crockett was already a legend. The city is only thirty miles from Nashville, about as far as Monticello is from Tallahassee.

With Bragg's men, the army now numbered about 35,000, camping around a town of approximately 9,000 citizens. They hunkered east of the Stones River and expected no fighting until spring. William rested and enjoyed the lull, but his superiors were mistaken.

President Lincoln worried because the Confederate attacks in Kentucky and Maryland had shaken northern confidence. He felt his generals wasted their victories at Antietam and Perryville when they refused to advance quickly against the Confederates, giving them time to retreat and regroup. He felt the Union war effort had stalled.

And the news for Lincoln worsened. In Virginia, John Slicer and the 50th Georgia fought for their lives in Fredericksburg. William's oldest son fought alongside the 5th Florida Aucilla Guards and the 2nd and 8th Florida under Perry's Brigade in Longstreet's First Corps. William heard about the enormous battle and worried about his son, his nephew William E. Goff, David Walker, and Mary's cousins. The fighting in Virginia appeared more intense.

Because of the Confederate victory at Fredericksburg, Union morale plummeted. After Fredericksburg, the South thought both sides' armies, east and west, went into winter quarters to recruit and train for the coming spring.

More than ever, Lincoln felt he needed a victory soon, so he ordered a winter campaign for his Army of the Cumberland under General Rosecrans. They were located only thirty miles east of Murfreesboro, in Nashville. Lincoln demanded they quickly invade the Confederate-occupied Murfreesboro, an invasion which would cause almost 25,000 casualties, the sixth costliest Civil War battle. Each side would lose almost one-third of their men. The north would call it the Battle of Stones River, but the south called it Murfreesboro. For Mary, one of its casualties would rend her world.

The Western Theater

In the intervening period, though, Confederate brass ordered General Forrest to disrupt Major General Ulysses S. Grant's supply lines in west Tennessee. For over a week, William and his unit joined Forrest's men and marched a hundred miles southwest, behind Grant's lines, midway between Memphis and Nashville. Forrest's raids lasted almost a month, beginning on December 11th.

One night during this time, William, near Clifton below Double Island, stood on the banks of the flooded Tennessee River. He saw no way to cross, but he would learn nothing so minor stopped Forrest, the Wizard of the Saddle.

The following day, the raiding party found a hidden flatboat which they made into a pontoon. Using this, Forrest's 1,800 men and four cannons crossed the river by the 15th of December. On a frosty morning on the water, William, wearing his wool coat, tried to shrink into the warmth of it, creating a layer of air between his skin and its cotton lining. His gray coat's shawl flapped in the wind. He stood on the pontoon, surrounded by other Florida soldiers, and felt guilty because so many others shivered with nothing more than thin blankets draped across their shoulders.

To provide cover while his small army crossed the river, Forrest and his rangers moved like swarms of yellowjackets and stung the Federals for days. On the other side, William and the 4th continued to move away from the river until the following day, when they stopped and bivouacked to rest, dry their clothes, and prepare for the next raid. They discovered their ammo and caps were wet and of no use.

To Forrest, the 4th Florida Infantry came ill-prepared with only ten rounds of caps for their rifles. Their muskets lacked flints. Unknown to the 4th, Forrest foresaw the problem and had sent a raiding party behind enemy lines to scavenge for guns and ammo.

Later, William and his company got new guns and dry ammo. They even passed out coats and jackets. Forrest impressed him and all the men. They considered the general a wise military strategist. Pride formed in serving with the man.

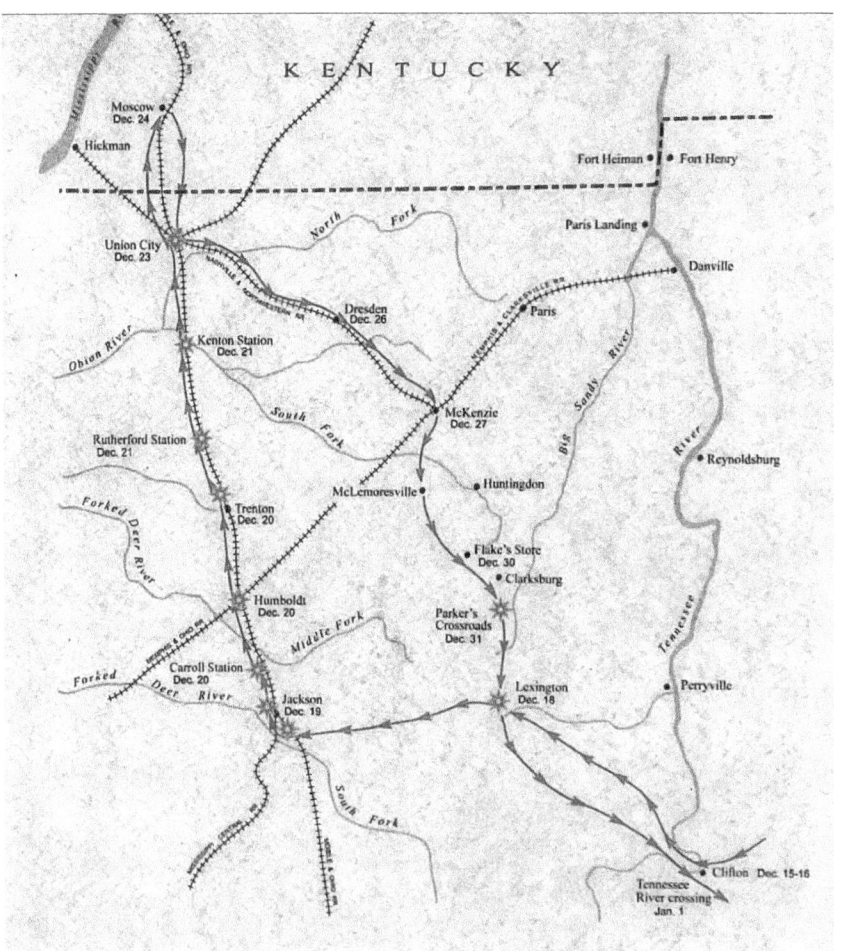

Forrest's Raids in Tennessee, Historical Marker at Parker's Crossroads,
Henderson County, TN, personal photo

William wrote Mary. As always, someone marked out the locations.

December 15, 1862
Somewhere west of the Tennessee River

My Dearest Mary,

We move, sometimes twenty miles a day. General Forrest is
tireless in the saddle, and our units trail on foot. Their dust is almost
unbearable. They cake their faces and ours with it. With the streaks of
perspiration, we are a fright.

The general is a military genius. In his former life he planted, raised cattle and horses, and traded slaves. A tall, striking man of commanding stature, he joined this war as a private with no military training. He rarely drinks and does not smoke. Though mild-mannered, he can be angered; when he is, his usually mild eyes flash with the glare of a wildcat.

I tell you this because I believe when we finish this war, we will remember this man and his successful tactics as much as we will remember Granny Lee and his. Forrest's success is because of his overall goal—to get there first with the most men.

With mobile warfare, he flanks and harasses our enemy. He disrupts their supply trains and communication. We have destroyed railroad tracks, cut telegraph wires, and made havoc behind our enemy's lines. When Forrest and his rangers get to a fight, they tie their horses and fight on foot as well as any foot soldier.

I hated to leave our warmer temporary cabin, but I've enjoyed watching this man operate. Now, though, we again sleep on the ground in tents.

Mary, I miss you and the children every day. Please send information no matter how trivial, because we long for anything about home.

All my love,
William

The next day they broke camp early and encountered a Federal force eight miles from Lexington, Kentucky. Part of Forrest's raiding party engaged in a quick skirmish and cut off their retreat. They captured 200 men, including officers; 300 small arms of mostly Sharps carbines; 200 horses; and many wagons needed for a Southern army short on everything.

William's adrenaline charged him. This was similar to rounding cattle with Jesse in the river swamps of the Aucilla. A great feeling. William felt young again. He wrote another letter home.

December 17, 1862
Western Tennessee

Dearest Mary and Family,
We heard good rumors about Tampa Bay and Captain Pearson, whom we hear is a local hero. I'm sure you listened to the same story.

Pearson used a wily ruse to defend the city, a ruse they cannot use again for a long time.
Your last letter asked me to describe my surroundings and camp life. Most of my fellow soldiers were once farmers and planters who had trouble taking orders. If you can imagine your father taking orders from anyone, you can understand what I mean.

When Zech read this to his mother at home, he looked at her and grinned. "Yep, Old Jesse taking orders—something I'd like to have seen." He continued reading.

Theirs was a lifestyle spent alone except for family or slaves. They took orders from no one. Now they take orders from men younger than their younger sons. It causes problems.
One day in camp, my company spent the day clearing the ground for drilling. Last week, I spent another peeling potatoes. I hate it, but it makes the time go faster. I'm still following Forrest, but they should relieve us soon.
Could you send me letters describing how home life is for you and the children? I treasure them. I enjoy hearing about your most mundane routines. It transports me home, even if only for a few minutes.

All my love,
William

In Tampa, disgusted when the Federals fired on his civilian town, Captain Pearson sent a detachment of men to meet them. These men painted themselves black and posed as slaves fleeing to safety in a small boat. When the boat was within earshot of the ship, they called for help. Thinking they were what they appeared to be, the ship sent a party of twenty-six men in a yawl for rescue. With a successful ruse, Pearson proved to be a creative guerrilla fighter.

Far to the north, though, Forrest headed for Jackson, Tennessee, only a hundred miles northeast of Memphis. They arrived on the 18th and took another Federal force, capturing 150 Union soldiers. All around Jackson, they raided and disappeared repeatedly. They seized the nearest stations, captured approaching trains, and destroyed Mobile and Ohio Railroad tracks in many places.

Forrest sent another group to Bolivar to do the same. Again, they captured men and supplies which Forrest distributed to his troops.

William, well-outfitted, left his inferior supplies with the locals. They always needed them.

A rumor of a Federal force exceeding 15,000 circulated in Jackson, but it did not deter the Wizard. William became part of a master-minded ruse. On December 19th, Forrest spread his forces thin over a wide area. He ordered drums beaten to sound as if a heavy infantry force had surrounded the city. The Yankees thought the general had many men.

The men he had worked in a radius, captured forces here and there, but never one after the other, as the enemy might guess his direction. In the end, his men captured more rounds of small arms, ammunition, and many supplies.

His guerrilla raids ranged to Trenton, thirty miles north. He attacked its depot. Trenton surrendered, and after Trenton and all around Jackson, the raiding parties captured a thousand mules and horses, seven caissons, 20,000 artillery rounds, 400,000 small arms ammunition, over 100,000 rations, cavalry equipment, quartermaster stores, thirteen wagons and ambulances, and at least a half a million dollars in American cash.

Late one afternoon, William wrote another letter home. Military censors blackened out its date and place.

December 19, 1862
Murfreesboro, Tennessee

Dear Sons,

Life in winter camp was boring, but not while serving under General Forrest. Our directions are clear, and our goals exceed our expectations. Though he has no formal military training, he is a natural commander and relentless pursuer. Our cause is better for it.

Today we captured a large group of Yankees. After the day-long fight, they rose from their trenches with a white flag and surrendered like lambs, including their subdued officers. Forrest captured so many Union soldiers we paroled 1,300 officers and men on the spot because the captured prisoners overtaxed our ability to manage them.

The miles have been cold and wet. Sometimes I march with everything I own in the driving rain, but it is many times exhilarating. General Forrest is the best at moving an army, and the Confederacy needs more officers like him.

Yesterday evening, a man in our unit recited a poem that spoke to my heart, "All Quiet Along the Potomac Tonight." Its words remind me of Virginia.

If the good Lord sees fit to see us through this unending conflict, I hope to take you there to see the beautiful Potomac River where I became an adult. Listening to the song brought many memories, yet it made me sad because if the Potomac looks like this area, sadness prevails there, too. I fear this widespread devastation will change our beloved Southland forever, a scar that will not soon heal.

Kiss your mother and sisters for me; I hope to be home before this letter arrives because we hear they are giving paroles in the winter camp.

All my love,
Father

At Home

As Mary rolled out her biscuits, she sang, "From angels bending near the earth, to touch their harps of gold: Peace on the earth, goodwill to men...." Earlier, they were at the courthouse for an early parade. She thought it odd. Instead of seasonal music, the band played the "Bonnie Blue Flag" and "When Johnny Comes Marching Home." She thought, wasn't war enough without songs to remind us during the holidays?

Stephen Foster's dreamy songs gave way to music written for the war. Songs such as "The Battle Hymn of the Republic," "Dixie's Land," and "Maryland, My Maryland," became popular.

As she pinched off dough to roll her first biscuit, she thought, not only is it a sad Christmas, it is especially dismal—Joel and Mama's passing, with Henry, less than a year ago. William was hundreds of miles away and Vollie was not home either.

Still, the children brought their spirit home. Inside, they decorated the parlor like William was at the station instead of 600 miles away. Worst of all, though, James would soon leave—another thought pushed back into her mind. But it was getting crowded there. The worries kept spilling out.

After dinner and her nap, she visited Ann Lightsey. Earlier, she had sent Hattie to let Ann know she planned a mid-afternoon visit. Since losing her mother, Ann became a mother figure to her. Mary took Laura and Joseph with her, and they played outside while the two women talked.

Said Mary, "Ann, you didn't need to serve real coffee for me."

Ann smiled and winked at Mary as she parted Mattie's hair with her fingers and pulled it from her face. Smiling through her blue-gray eyes, Ann said, "Well, if I serve it to you, I get a cup, too." When she finished, Mattie took off and joined the others outside, chaperoned by seven-year-old George Henry. Their father had left with the 1st Florida long ago and saw action in Shiloh and Perryville. He too waited in Murfreesboro.

The Western Theater

With Forrest, William's unit captured or destroyed Union supplies for several more days, traveling as far west as the Mississippi River. They burned bridges, trestles, and bent rails until Forrest reached and captured Union City, sixty miles north of Jackson, destroying its railroad lines. He reached this on December 23rd, but William's unit he had sent earlier to Murfreesboro.

William walked in the evening air to the in-laws' camp. It lifted his spirits to have so many friends and family close. Their conversation around the campfire centered on family and home, especially Elizabeth. William listened to their stories, some of which he heard Mary tell. War had taught him—home isn't a place but a sense of belonging. These stories made him feel at home even though he was hundreds of miles away.

Changing the subject, Arch said, "I heard Forrest and his men cut timbers to reinforce an impassable bridge, and Forrest himself led his men across the rickety thing in the dark."

Added Berry, "I heard the road was so frozen, his men had to fill its potholes with coffee and flour so they could pass over it."

A conversation lull followed when William said, "Many times we were waist-deep in mud, water, and sleet, but nothing stopped us." He paused as they listened to the sounds of the fire popping and cracking. He added, "I've met no one like him. I believe his men would follow him into the gates of hell itself."

At Home

Days later, after James, seventeen, reenlisted in Quincy and left to rejoin his unit in Tennessee, Mary sat in her parlor darning socks for Henry. She had taught James and Vollie how to mend and darn their clothes and socks earlier. Neither boy wanted to do it, insisting it was women's work, but she stood her ground, something now regular.

Sitting in her rocking chair to the right of the fireplace, the fire warmed her. It flickered lightly throughout the room. She had a view of the street outside, through William's window, where he once sat and deciphered. The kids napped, and the older ones visited friends outside the home. In the quiet, she heard footsteps and a knock.

The postman had a letter for her. It was William's writing, so she put it in her pocket for later when a kid could read it to her.

The Western Theater

Christmas provided a respite with many boxes received from home which contained good edibles and useful presents. William especially missed Mary and the children, this being his first Christmas without them. Later, staring at the fire, he remembered how they sat around the fireplace—his memories were vivid and painful.

He spent his evening with family and friends from Monticello, members of the 1st and 3rd, including his son James. They put their dinner rations together and passed around a bottle or two of brandy brought from home. For several, it would be their last Christmas.

He could not help worrying about his son. For James, there would be his first battle, his first exposure to the singing of flying lead, his first time to see a man's guts spilled or half a face destroyed. William knew it was something James would carry for the rest of his life—the anxiety of waiting and watching the lines advance as his sergeant yelled, "Hold your fire; shoot low!"

He knew this would be when terror gripped James, when his heart pounded so hard it felt like it would rip from his chest. He also knew the green boys, fresh from their parents' homes, lacked training and the discipline it instilled. This was when some cut and ran while others kept firing in the face of an enemy.

The following day, William wrote again.

December 26, Friday
Murfreesboro, Tennessee

Dearest Mary,

Christmas wasn't the same without you and the children. I couldn't help being melancholy all day, though James was here, and our officers did their best.

They prepared a feast and played many games. I even let James talk me into a foot race. It felt good to feel young again. There were horse races and boxing matches. The band played off and on all day.

Yesterday, one of my campmates found a lost kitten. He nursed it to health. A little touch of humanity feels good. It hangs around the tents, and the men grow fond of it. Though we must leave it behind when we next march. A few fellas have dogs following us, but a cat will not usually follow.

We woke to clouds and mist this morning, but it was raining almost incessantly. Everywhere is mud because a campground this size is nothing more than bare dirt.

I miss you, Mary. There are so many of your kin here. I'm sure our women and children are as melancholy. Christmas is not the same without our women—your cooking, decorating, and the children.

There's the bugle announcing retirement. Give my Christmas love to all my babies.

Your loving husband,
William

Forrest and his men, behind enemy lines and outnumbered, turned to flee the increasing, fresh Federal brigades until they were surprised and trapped. Then Forrest alone turned and surrendered.

After a conversation, they allowed him to gallop toward his troops to lead his men to them. But, like a ghost, he and his men disappeared in the confusion. Later, around a campfire, William listened to one lieutenant tell the story; William again felt proud to have been a part of Forrest's legacy. With a twinkle in his eyes, the beaming lieutenant added, "Forrest surfaced twelve miles away—regrouped, rested, and watered." The man's eyes danced, and he slapped his knee. "The pursuit was on again."

From mid-December to the end of the month, Forrest's campaign of guerrilla tactics frustrated and exhausted the pursuing Union army. He fought three well-contested engagements, demolished fifty more large and small bridges. He destroyed so much trestle work of the Mobile and Ohio that the railroad remained useless until after the war.

During his foray into west Tennessee, he captured and burned almost two dozen stockades, captured or killed about 2,500 Union soldiers, took or disabled ten pieces of field artillery, seized over fifty wagons and ambulances with their teams, ensnared ten thousand stands of small arms, and detained over one million rounds of ammo.

William later told his family how his unit initially joined Forrest's raiding party, insufficiently armed and supplied, but returned to Murfreesboro, thoroughly armed and equipped, including blankets and tents. Forrest armed every man with supplies, including 500 Enfield rifles, blankets, and knapsacks.

When they were with Forrest, William said they never rested a full night because they averaged twenty miles daily. As exhilarating an experience as he had ever known, William added, "Forrest got an inexperienced group of men, but he returned us to Murfreesboro, a well-prepared fighting force." They would need this additional conditioning because Murfreesboro would test their resolve. William returned to Murfreesboro with white fibers he gleaned from a cotton field they passed through. He thought they might give him some ear protection from shells bursting and shots fired. Battlefields were terribly noisy.

At Home

In Monticello, Mary ran her household and waited on the letters. She learned to depend more on Zech who, at thirteen, became the man of the house and who would become a young man overnight. She pondered what life was like for William, which made him distant.

The Western Theater

In Murfreesboro, it rained torrents for days through freezing nights, turning the roads to slushy mud. Every morning, William woke to damp bedding, where he and two cabin mates spooned three to their blankets for warmth. Glad for the morning, he put on his boots, went outside, and listened to ice crunching as he walked to the latrines. The smoky air stung his nostrils.

Meanwhile, Rosecrans's Union army of 43,000 soldiers in a grueling forced march tried to reach Murfreesboro, but the conditions slowed them. General Rosecrans, who had been an architect, mining engineer, and inventor, rejoined the Union army as soon as the war began. He was impulsive and excitable, which served him well with his men. He was popular.

On December 28th, on the Stones River, William and the others built breast-high barriers of wooden rails and stone designed to stand behind and shoot. On his prancing horse, General Bragg rode by and looked fierce, as any commander-in-chief should. It raised their spirits, and William wondered if Bragg would make his stand on the river's east side.

On the same day, the Union Army of the Cumberland traveled the turnpike to Murfreesboro within miles of the entrenched Rebels.

On December 29, 1862, Monday, the enemy crept closer until Rosecrans's army filled in a line across from the Rebel army in an area filled with rocky outcrops, clumps of forests, and rolling ground. By nightfall, two thirds of Rosecrans's army was in position. The enemies were in parallel lines, four miles long, with only a narrow river between them.

By evening, a brief skirmish ensued as a wing of the Union army tried to cross the river, but it ran into a hornet's nest of grays. William wondered if it had been a reconnaissance.

Later, after the blues retreated, in the dark musicians played songs from their different regions. William's mind would not quit, knowing a significant battle was imminent. The days of waiting, doing little or nothing, left him anxious. It was hard to pass time in boredom while waiting for something to happen. He tried to push it into the recesses of his mind and fell asleep listening to the sounds of the camp's quieting for the night. Thousands of soldiers thought this night could be their last as the two armies bivouacked only 700 yards apart.

On Tuesday the 30th, a midnight bugler sounded, bringing everyone from a midnight slumber. Fires started, and they cooked all their flour, meal, and bacon on hand and stored it in their haversacks long before daylight. William thought a northern attack must be imminent.

At daybreak, the rain continued. Rosecrans's army advanced to better position themselves along the Wilkinson Pike, and the final third of his army arrived. His army now numbered about 41,000 while Bragg's was 35,000.

Both armies took their places in defensive lines. William waited in the rear with the rest of Preston's Brigade. They reserved them on the right at a river crossing and well away from the point of attack.

William heard sporadic fighting, shelling, and shouting, especially to his left, evidence of a skirmish. With the rain, it was hard to see anything.

Everyone awaited the Yankees' attack, but none came. They waited, and time passed.

As the sun dropped, darkness came fast. Preston's Brigade and William were relieved to a position where they could build fires and dry their clothes. Their officers sent a barrel of whiskey.

After a day-long wait, they got their supper about midnight in heavy rain; after eating, William retired in his line of battle with his gun in his hand to catch a few hours of sleep. He believed by the next morning, he would meet his enemy. Over 81,000 soldiers went to their camps to await what would come the following day.

Night came, and intermittent icy rain showers rolled through as temperatures plummeted. The men of the 4th did what they could to stay warm. William had a warm wool blanket with a hole in the top for his head. He wore it, and with his head wrapped in a scarf and his hat on, it kept him warm by the fire. William noticed many sat silently looking into their campfires, contemplating morning and the coming fight.

Later, thinking of Mary, the kids, and Monticello, William sat, listening to his army's band play a rousing version of Dixie. In reply, the opposition's band played "Yankee Doodle." The melodic sounds clashed and echoed through the darkness as the two bands engaged in their battle with songs. It helped him to forget everything for a wonderful moment.

One band played "Home Sweet Home"; as if led by a common conductor, the other side's band joined them when it got to the refrain. Men on both sides joined their choral voices to sing the melancholy lyrics.

William noticed Standley held his hat to his face lest someone see his tears. For a moment, men on both sides of the river found something to agree upon—the prospect of a peaceful home. William mentally moved throughout Monticello, street by street. Thinking about how each house and business looked and remembering the faces of its occupants. He did this sometimes to help him quell his homesickness.

At Home

The next day, Wednesday, on New Year's Eve, Mary felt something foreboding, deep inside, like a shadow of impending fate cast upon her. She arose earlier than usual to a warmer December day. Christmas had passed, but she had trouble getting into the spirit. She blamed this on her melancholy, but William was on her mind.

How could she celebrate a holiday season when William and the boys were so far away? She reminded herself again: they were in winter quarters. They were safe.

Moving through her typical day, always trying to keep busy and forget when worrisome thoughts appeared, she scrubbed the floors in the hall and worked on another pair of socks each for William and her boys. Later, a knock came at the front door as she pulled her bedroom curtains down for wash day.

There stood Ann Lightsey with a letter in hand. It was from William. She knew his handwriting.

With a smile and hug, she said, "Ann, please come in. It is so good to see you." They had a wonderful chat, but she hoped she didn't let on. She couldn't wait for Ann to leave so she could get Florrie, William's daughter by an earlier marriage, to read the letter.

This letter, though, worried her, especially William's mental state. His lack of spirit showed in his writing. Plus, this letter was out of turn. It was older.

December 20, 1862
Murfreesboro, Tennessee

My Dearest Mary,

I'll never get comfortable again, but I hear this is a warm winter at home. I guess Florida thinned my blood because I cannot stay warm.

We had torrential rains last night, and the wind blows strong from the north today. We thought we camped correctly, taking advantage of a small bluff to diminish the wind and rain, but the wind shifted during the night. Thus, we are at the mercy of the elements this morning.

We camped a couple of miles from the slow-moving Stones River, once surrounded by much flora, but an army of this size needs wood. The forests are gone, and nothing stops the wind. All once planted in cotton, the fields are brown and dug into furrows by the many military movements.

They tell us the Yanks are west of here in Nashville, and if they are anything like before, they will sit there until we bring the war to them, which I feel confident we will do as soon as winter is past. Still, we built battle works. This is in case the Union comes to us after all.

The countryside is barren, Mary, and the old once-stately mansions need repair, though they are the lucky ones. So many were burned. If they left their empty barns standing, fences and everything else disappeared to some far-off campfire, where scarcity prevails. It is cold, and the damp winds whip through the entirety—nothing to break their fury.

Mary, I so miss you and all the children, though it comforts me you are so far from this carnage. When we pass through these little towns and homesteads, I cannot help wondering how frightened these women and children must be.

Christmas makes all of us homesick. Our officers try their best to keep our spirits high. We sing Christmas carols, and local people come to camp with homemade baked goods, though most are made with nothing sweet. Best of all, though, my good brother Jesse brought a Christmas box, and we had a wonderful visit.

I need a bath, but it is too cold, and the river is icy. Since we left Chattanooga, the men have been in good health and have high morale. They fight like men, though many are mere boys. I worry about John and Vollie. James is coming, and I hope he gets here by Christmas.

Mary, we especially enjoy the boxes from home. Please tell everyone their generosity keeps us going. Kiss all my babies for me and tell them I love them more daily. Tell Florida and Sarah I relish their letters. And Mary, you cannot imagine how homesick I am for you. Merry Christmas, my love, and Merry Christmas to everyone at home.

Yours for eternity,
William

William's older brother Jesse lived in Bluff Creek, Tennessee in Smith County, which was about forty-five miles to the northeast of Murfreesboro, a long day's horse ride. Family lore says Jesse visited the family in Florida, maybe after the Civil War, according to William and Mary's son Henry. Jesse, too old to serve, had sons on both sides.

At Home

In reply, Mary got Zech to write a letter to William. What Mary would not share with William, though, was how difficult living had become in Monticello. She had retrieved her mother's old spinning wheel and enlarged her garden with flax and peas for clothing and food. Using okra and chicory substitutes, they had no real coffee left.

Spinning Wheel, Thomasville History Museum, personal photo

Most likely, William sent most of his paycheck home. He received $3 a week for his service, but families, hard-pressed because of inflation, barely existed on such a sum. Because of the blockade, the price of flour per barrel had risen exponentially, as had medical supplies.

State governments pleaded with their planters to grow less cotton and more food. Georgia made it a crime to grow excess cotton.

The Western Theater

Meanwhile, west of Murfreesboro, it was a bitter wintry New Year's morning, and their officers greeted the 4th well before daylight with a whiskey ration. William took a sip and felt its warmth in his throat but noticed others who did not drink a drop. His officers hoped it would bolster courage—because the men would need it. Standing in the morning twilight, William found the combination warmed him after a long night of rain and cold. He dunked his hardtack in the whiskey to soften it.

A fire and good, hot coffee would have been better, but their orders were to have neither. Everyone moved about in the gray morning mist with only a little early daylight to light their way. In the camp, otherwise quiet except for murmurings, the officers watered their horses in a nearby stream while the quiet regulars dressed and awaited further orders. The horses stamped their feet, their nostrils making white steam in the air. Meanwhile, a long line of silent grays from other units swarmed toward the unsuspecting Union right wing at dawn.

The firing began, and people at the line dropped on both sides. Here, the Confederates drove the Union through the cedar woods to Wilkinson Pike, where they struggled to penetrate the forests made of splintered trees splattered with blood. Smoke clouded the battlefield. Though they surprised the North, Bragg's disorganized men sometimes left their support artillery behind.

The fighting continued throughout the morning until the Union's right-wing and center gave way.

From ten in the morning until mid-afternoon, waves of gray advanced on the north's left wing, facing volley after volley from Hazen's men on the Union side. A Mississippi unit went first, followed by the Georgians. One regiment sent in 280 men, but only 58 returned.

Around 3:30 in the afternoon, Bragg ordered Breckenridge's division forward into the fray. William's unit followed in a line, crossing the shallow river at a natural ford. Ahead, he heard the volleys and the cannonading of a raging battle.

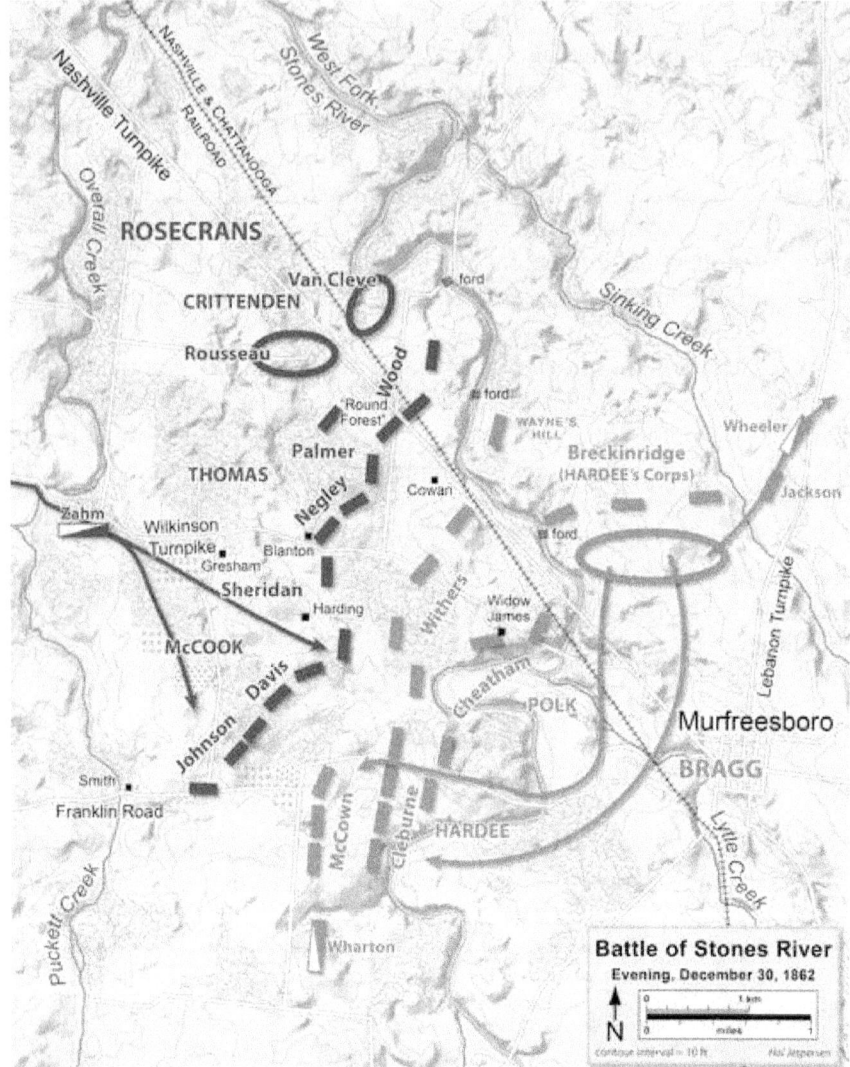

Battle of Stones River, Evening of December 31, Wikipedia, Hal Jespersen, creator

When they first arrived, they found the devastation unimaginable and eerie. Through the smoke, they saw stunted trees torn to shreds by gunfire as men retreated through them. William asked one, "How is it there?" and the reply was, "Awful!" They stopped to set their bayonets.

Washington Ives of the 4th Florida wrote in his diary, "*I saw a Confederate soldier walking away from the fight with a bloody stump where his arm used to be. The walking wounded man yelled to the*

Floridians, 'Pay them for my arm.'" Lieutenant General William J. Hardee moved his brigades forward, and Colonel Bowen followed suit with his 4th Florida regiment.

They passed through a picket fence and broke ranks. Some got crowded out of the space because the 60th North Carolina advanced too quickly and fled. According to Ives, under the hottest cannon fire from a half mile distant, his company halted and fired into the cedar thicket to drive out the Yankee sharpshooters, though the thicket's trees were as thick as hair on a dog's back. William saw Ives and his unit from Lake City get the worst of it because the Yankee batteries got their range. Their men dropped in their tracks.

Through the late afternoon, Florida and Georgia units and other states had fought hard over this little piece of ground, later called "Hell's Half Acre." It lay between them and the round cedar thicket forest, a crucial position for Rosecrans's army. It anchored the left side of his Union line. William didn't know that Rosecrans had ordered his men to *"contest every inch of ground."*

The Rebs tried four times to cross this half-acre piece between the Nashville Pike and the railroad. They advanced, retreated, wavered, fell back, and advanced again, but Hazen's Brigade under Sheridan did not retreat while Sheridan sent waves of men to relieve the ones who fell. Hell's half-acre cost both sides dearly.

William's unit moved forward late in the day, but the fighting subsided at dusk. The half-acre and other fields lay silent, covered in the dead and wounded. Injured soldiers on both sides streamed into their field hospitals, where a different type of horror existed.

Hell's Half Acre, personal photo

Men from both sides checked their wounded and aided the dying. William walked between the bodies which littered the ground. Several groaned and moaned while others shrieked with pain, especially when they were moved to stretchers.

William noticed one man had crawled to the foot of a tree and laid his head on its roots to take his last breath. A number lay upon their backs with their arms and legs outstretched. A few doubled into a fetal position.

Interestingly, the expressions on their faces were similar. A portion stared into eternity with their eyes open, and some were closed as if they wished to pass looking within. Several died with their mouths open and some closed. He questioned if those who died with their mouths opened slept that way. Only the disfigured faces were distinct; the difference was the injury itself. All of them were thin, worn, and pale.

From a distance, he watched the burial details, which were makeshift and hasty, yet dignified. Buddies showed genuine sorrow as they made the proper gestures toward their colleagues.

With water in his canteen and a little brandy left from the holiday, William administered until both were gone. He walked to the creek for more water and returned many times until late at night. Walking amongst the bodies required careful steps to keep from trampling them. Eventually, they were all either moved, asleep, or dead. The field fell quiet, and he and the others retired as the temperature plummeted. Their officers ordered no fires. It was New Year's Eve.

At the end of this first full day of battle, there were over 23,000 casualties. In all of Shiloh, there were 24,000, but the Battle of Stones River was far from over.

Too anxious to sleep, William wrote again to Mary. "We had a tremendous battle today, but I fear it is not finished. I'm afraid we merely stopped to take care of our wounded. My company was not in the heart of the battle, like others of the 4th, but we will most likely be when we begin again. From where we are, we can hear their camps on the other side of the river and can see their fires." William fell into a deep sleep.

In headquarters, with over 3,000 Union soldiers taken captive and thousands more dead or mortally wounded, Bragg sent a telegram to President Davis to claim a significant victory—so sure he had.

Still, the Federals captured or destroyed nearly 200 wagons and ambulances, and the South did not breach Hazen's line.

At Home
By day's end, Mary and all of Monticello knew the men in the Army of Tennessee were fighting. Even though their letters were weeks old and written when they were safe in their winter quarters, the information at the telegraph office was timelier. All of Monticello waited for news from the front. In the Battle of Murfreesboro were the Jefferson Rifles and the Jefferson Beauregards, with hundreds of husbands and sons from the county.

#

Chapter 4
When a Man's Belly is His God
January to March 1863

The Western Theater

Thursday, on New Year's Day, William awoke to an aching back and howling wind but no sound of rifles or cannons. Though difficult to move, he knew he must seek relief. He stood and leaned back, bending his spine. The sooner he got moving, the quicker his muscles would stop their aching. He looked at Standley, wrapped in his blanket like a mummy.

William sought the edge of camp to relieve himself. The wind cut through his coat like a knife. Chilled, he could see other people stirring in the awakening camp which would soon pulsate with life.

It surprised the men that there was no attack at night or during the early morning. There was no reveille at dawn, a common occurrence in camp whether or not the enemy was on your doorstep. Nothing jerked William from his sleep.

Walking through the wind, the quiet unnerved him. He watched the woods around him for any movement, worried the Yankees might make a surprise attack like his side had done the day before.

Afterward, he joined his mates and cooked breakfast on an open fire, not speaking much. There was nothing to celebrate. They received word it would be a long day tending to the wounded. Although his group remained uninjured, many boys from the other Florida units were. He thought he could help there and so spent a rather quiet first day of the new year moving between camps, doing what he could. He sought the others from Monticello.

As he walked through the fields between the dead and wounded, he could feel his heart beating, occasionally skipping a beat. A wave of sadness and loss gripped him, and he stopped and closed his eyes to the panorama. For the moment, thoughts of his impending separation from Mary and the children overwhelmed him, but he pushed away the feelings and buried them deep into his mind. He continued on.

Both sides sought to retrieve their dead, bury their comrades, seek better ground, and await further orders. Bragg thought Rosecrans was finished and viewed his change of position as a retreat.

Amongst Bragg's men, though, the grapevine ran. They talked to each other from camp to camp and even side to side, especially as they roamed the battlefield searching for survivors. Several times, William met his enemy, and they discussed the war. Most on either side felt sure an attack would happen the next day.

On one deceased Yankee, William noticed a wad of papers hanging from his pants pocket. He pulled it out and noticed it was a small stack of blank military forms. The man was not an officer but may have been carrying them for someone else. Still, it was valuable to William, and he pocketed them. Paper was scarce in Florida, and he could expect no more paper to come from them. William kept the dead man's papers, thinking he might need them later to write home.

That evening, William lay in his bedroll and listened to the soft, distant voices of those still awake and wondered how many would survive after tomorrow.

He pondered his thoughts. He wasn't frightened about getting killed. No, he always believed the end was peaceful, like being asleep and never waking. His terror was losing an arm, or especially a leg. He tried to push it from his mind, but sleep didn't come quickly.

Meanwhile, President Lincoln issued his Emancipation Proclamation in William's home city of Washington, DC. Lincoln understood that freeing the slaves on paper meant little without the military success to enforce it. Yet his proclamation instantly freed 60,000 slaves in Florida. Seventy percent of them lived in Middle Florida, which included Jefferson County. Word of their freedom, though, would not reach these slaves until the war ended.

As the war dragged on, well-thought-out imperatives pulled Lincoln and the North toward abolishing slavery to undermine their Southern opponents. Lincoln's proclamation changed the conflict from a war between the states to preserve the union into a war to free America's enslaved people.

On the second day of 1863, a Friday, the Union at Murfreesboro was ready for the South, and they killed or wounded 1,800 Confederates in less than an hour in the last fight of Stones River. William would be in the middle of this battlefield clutch.

It was a calm and freezing, bitter day as 4,500 of the South's men waded through the crystal clear running river, two to three feet deep and full of stones. With a man on each side of him and his rifle in hand, William could see his breath as he silently crossed, moving through a thick smoky mist generated by all the campfires made by the combined armies. The cold water shocked his calves and knees.

Stones River, personal photo

Bragg was taking the offensive, but there would be no surprise this time. A soldier, Lieutenant Spencer Talley of the Tennessee Infantry, wrote of the river, *"We made no halt but plunged right through it, and soon after crossing, our pants were frozen and rattled like a rawhide."*

They quickly ascended a hill on the Union's left flank when the bullets began, and in the distance, the big Yankee batteries above belched shells and shrapnel. In front of him, it turned the field into smoke and fire. William smelled the sulfur from the shot, saw the line of cannons on the ridge, and realized Rosecrans was ready for them this time. Colonel Bowen turned towards his men and, with a saber in hand, pointed toward the fifty-seven cannons.

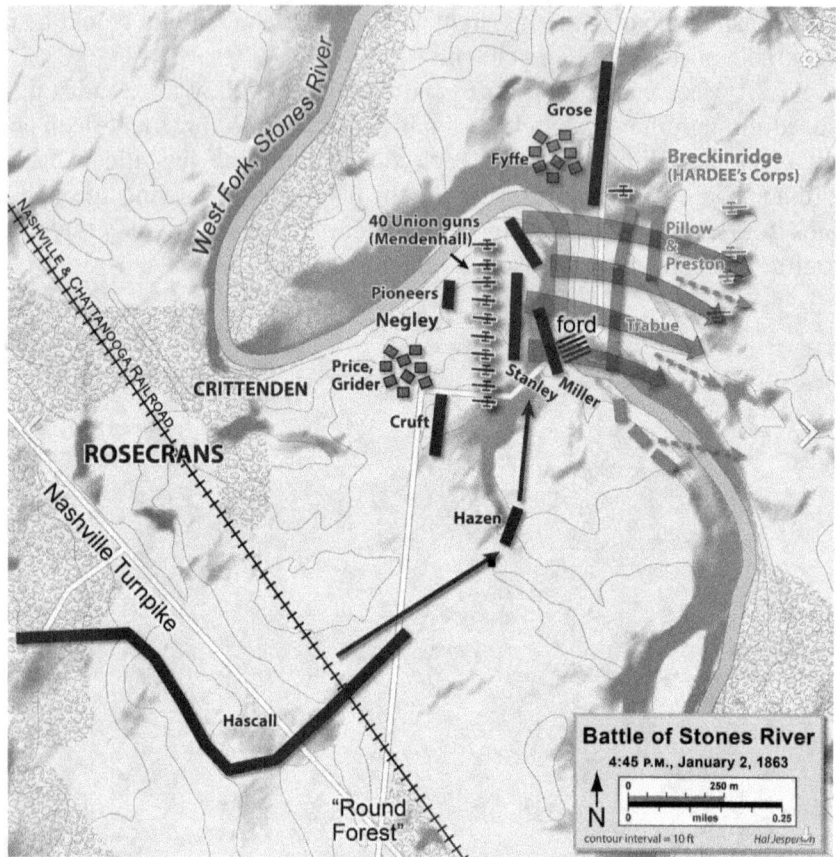

January 2nd, 1863, but later in the day when the North attacked. Map by Hal Jespersen

In his mind was his captain's earlier good advice. "Keep your head down, no talking." He and his unit moved forward in a line, shoulder to shoulder. Their pace quickened, as did his breathing. As they grew ever nearer, he heard bullets hitting around him. He feared getting shot at every step, and to his right, he heard one strike Standley, who groaned, staggered, and fell. He glanced at his friend on the ground but could do nothing. William kept going as ordered because he was within no-man's-land, between two closing armies.

Wild yelling erupted around him, and he roared himself, half in anger for his fallen friend and half because it empowered him. Even with cotton in his ears, the cannons deafened him as he ran toward them. They killed or wounded 1,800 men within minutes. By this time, he felt a surge of energy and did not think of anything except shooting the enemy.

Until he felt stinging, searing pain, and nothing. For a moment during the continuous shelling above, he felt his heart pounding against the ground, but nothing again.

Later that morning, a supply train with infantry rolled into Union camps on the west side of the river, and the battle was over when the Confederates retreated that afternoon. William's company in the 4th Florida Infantry suffered over 40% casualties, with 34 men killed and 129 wounded. Breckenridge had earlier ordered them and other regiments to take the hill occupied by the Union troops. The result was eighteen hundred casualties in less than an hour.

The number of killed, wounded, or captured from both sides was over 23,000 soldiers, nearly 29% of the total fighting force. The North suffered over 13,000 casualties, and the South suffered over 10,000. The total casualties would be the highest percentage for all Civil War battles. Many of the wounded later died.

One can visit the fields at Stones River National Battlefield Park near Murfreesboro. One park ranger had an ancestor who fought there, and he was knowledgeable about its fields and skirmishes.

With this park ranger's help, he located where William's unit started the day he was wounded. The problem is the area is now in a settlement of homes. It is eerie to stand at the edge and look at the space between the ridge and the river. One can imagine the hell William and his comrades faced.

The 4th Florida lost its flag. A soldier from the 78th Pennsylvania reported five color-bearers fell before they gave it up. He also added when they had the Rebels on the run, they yelled, "Fort Donelson." When the Rebels chased them, they replied, "Bull Run."

Breckenridge's unsuccessful charge is where Floridians suffered heavy casualties, but Colonel Brown reported the 4th Florida did not retreat until "almost totally abandoned by the rest of the line." Of the 468 men who engaged from the 4th at Murfreesboro, 42% were casualties.

The North killed over 300 men of the 1st, 3rd, and 4th Florida regiments. At home, when they posted the list, Monticello mourned Lemuel Dixon and Theodore Kyle of the 3rd and George Hartsfield, who had been wounded earlier in Perryville. George's brother Jacob Franklin Hartsfield, who would survive the war, would marry Sarah Andrews, Mary and William's oldest daughter.

Several maps depicting troop movements and positions throughout the day are available on the park's webpage. The most brutal charge appears around 4:45 pm, much later than William's earlier charge. By 4:45, they had probably taken William to have his head wound attended to.

William probably remembered the overwhelming pain next as the jolting stretcher or ox cart moved toward the field hospital. His biggest fear was coming true. No one even talked about the field hospital. The camp surgeon, Dr. John Davidson's abode, was not a place anyone wanted to go to. William probably heard men say people who go there go to die. His mind turned to nothingness again.

In France, between 1860 and 1865, Louis Pasteur experimented and formed his germ theory. His work, though, would be too late for the Civil War. Few battlefield doctors, North or South, practiced medical hygiene; most of their patients died of infection rather than their wounds. For every three soldiers who died during the war, two died of disease and/or infection.

Head wounds bled proficiently and often looked worse than they were. Most likely, a shell or shrapnel caused the injury. William only suffered a slight head injury, though, which may have left him addled, confused, and with a horrible headache.

Field Hospital, Savage Station, Va. after the battle of June 27, Wikimedia Commons

At the field hospital, he watched men come and go with loaded stretchers or propping staggering men, too wounded to walk by themselves. Around him was every form of mangled humanity. A boy came by with a bucket of water, and William felt the cool water slide down his throat. His head throbbed with an intensifying headache.

After a while, because others' wounds were more pressing, William waited and felt almost good enough to leave. He tried to stand but staggered and collapsed back into his place. Next to him, another soldier offered him a drink of whiskey. At first he thought maybe he shouldn't, but his throbbing head made him feel otherwise. He said, "Don't mind if I do." He sipped it, and it burned in his throat and belly, a good feeling. It took his mind off his headache.

The man next to him said, "Another swig will help." So William obliged. They struck up a conversation, but William's thoughts dwelled on something else. They both had stories to tell about their fighting. The man came from near Macon, a plantation city similar to Monticello. As William relaxed, his headache relieved itself.

The field hospital was akin to a modern-day emergency room, except for open air and without the implements of modernity. They were usually located behind the lines. A triage method was used to help those who could be saved as dozens of wounded soldiers arrived on hand-held stretchers. They gave little thought to hygiene, mainly because it was hard to practice hygiene in these places and circumstances.

There were soldiers with all kinds of injuries. William worried they would move him to a more permanent hospital full of soldiers with illnesses like dysentery, typhoid fever, pneumonia, mumps, measles, and tuberculosis. All diseases spread among the poorly sanitized camps, where men lived weakened by fierce fighting and their meager diets.

His head wound most likely coagulated, and the bleeding may have stopped. He watched as they brought in 3rd Corporal John Gary with a leg wound. It was more serious, and they took him in immediately. It would be for naught, though, because Gary died less than a month later. They brought in Corporal Richard Morgan, who lost an arm.

Later, William worried the bad news might reach Mary before he wrote her, and it was likely he wrote Mary either in the early evening or the next day.

At 10 pm, Bragg retreated through the freezing rain, a retreat to Tullahoma, Tennessee, thirty-six miles south. Not pursued by their enemy, they camped the first night south of Murfreesboro on the Shelbyville Pike, which is present-day US 231. Rosecrans occupied Murfreesboro two days later and did not pursue.

Joel P. Walker, Mary's first cousin through her Uncle James, had recently enlisted in the 3rd Florida Infantry, Company H. They sent him north to Tennessee. William Berry, Mary's brother, survived the battle, and he and many other family members welcomed Joel.

Rosecrans took Murfreesboro and claimed victory. The town's location offered him protection, and he used the town as a vast supply base. He used it as a launching point for campaigns farther afield which would slash through the heartland of the South, paving their way to Chattanooga, Atlanta, and Savannah. With the victory at Murfreesboro and the Emancipation Proclamation, the North's spirits soared. The North's strategy to control the railroads, rivers, and ports was working.

At Home

To Mary, most of her loves were in Murfreesboro. Like most of Monticello, she went to the depot to await news of the battle. Weeks later, though, she received a letter from William, though she already knew he was a casualty.

January 3, 1863
Murfreesboro, Tennessee

Dearest Mary,

I saw fearsome combat and received a slight head wound, but do not worry. I can duck and weave with the best of them, even though I am much older than most of these boys, most of them young enough to be my children.

As ordered, we crossed the river to its western side and assaulted the Federal center, though we were unsuccessful. My company suffered injuries. Jacob Dykes and Joe Edenfield shared a hospital tent with me. Their wounds were more serious, and I left them there. They left Robert Regan there.

We fared better, though, than the rest of our regiment. On the day of fighting, we lost fifty-five souls, including 1st Lieutenant S. D. Harris of Company I.

As Zech read the letter, he looked at his mother and siblings. "They blanked out the totals, too."

Later, Zech told her, "Mom, he must be fine, or he wouldn't have been able to send us a letter or leave the hospital. He must be OK." She agreed but also knew wounds, even minor scratches, could be fatal, especially if not cleaned properly. And even it may be beyond one's control. In her room, she prayed extra for God's help.

Mary found it increasingly hard to accept William's decision to leave the family to her while he opted for the military when he didn't have to do it. He was over the required age, but he signed the contract anyway. In her opinion, men readily became soldiers whenever they could. She had watched her brothers and sons in their zeal to play war. She had noticed how their eyes danced when they talked about it.

Another letter arrived a few days later, and Zech read it, too. It was a letter out of turn, meaning someone delayed it somewhere between Murfreesboro and Monticello, and it arrived before the family received a later-written letter.

December 28, 1862
Murfreesboro, Tennessee

Dear Mother,

I am with my unit here in Murfreesboro, Tennessee. Mama, I wish you could have seen the mountains around Chattanooga. Our train wound around and through them. There is nothing like them in Florida.

Camp life here is hard, but we survive. Christmas, though, was better this year with Dad in camp and so many Walker kin. Still, I missed your cooking!

Speaking of food, we long for a Christmas dinner fixed by our mother's hands. I miss your table set with your dishes of red and bone, with the pictures of Gothic ruins.

I fondly remember the last time I had milk or buttermilk. It was at your table only a few weeks ago, but it feels like forever. If we got milk here in camp, it would disappear quicker than frost in Florida on a sunny morning.

Well, there are taps, and a man needs his rest. Kiss everyone for me, but I miss you most of all.

Your loving son,
James

Mary looked at Zech and said, "He had little to say, didn't he? I wish he had described the mountains more. None of us has ever seen one." Zech realized his mother longed for these letters which seldom came. James was not the type to write. Neither was Vollie. Zech hoped the letters would increase in frequency if the war lengthened. He wrote to both brothers to let them know.

The Western Theater

Several days later, William could feel something tickling in his shirt. He scratched, and a nearby Union officer noticed. All the men under this officer were scratching.

According to Northern records, a week after the battle on January 10th, the Yankees captured William somewhere near Murfreesboro. How William fell into the hands of the Union army is unknown, but his head injury could have played a role. He could have had a possible concussion that can sometimes alter one's judgment.

Bragg's army retreated, and it took a lot to feed an army. Maybe William foraged, or perhaps another skirmish occurred, unmarked in history. In Confederate records, it shows they captured William at Stone's River as a prisoner of war of the Department of the Cumberland and sent him to Nashville. In others, both Federal and Confederate, they show they captured him eight days after the battle ended.

Thankfully, though, the Union army didn't want their lice, so the officer told William and the other men to remove all their clothes and put them in the boiling pots provided. William thought the remedy would be short-lived, though, as the annoying pests would reappear as soon as they returned to their prior quarters.

Returned prisoners of war exchanging their rags for new clothing, 1864, Library of Congress

After his capture, he spent time in a Union hospital in Nashville. His Confederate unit's winter quarters were not far away. They were in Shelbyville, Tennessee, less than sixty miles from Nashville.

A Confederate company report dated December 31, 1862 to February 28, 1863, listed him as absent and wounded in the Battle of Murfreesboro on January 2, 1863. It lists him as a casualty of Preston's Brigade with a slight head wound. The report was written after February 28, almost two months after the battle. The North's incarceration of him is not mentioned in this record.

This card is unclear when he was absent. We know, though, he was not absent or even captured as early as December 31, 1862. Another card shows him as wounded in battle on January 2nd. The conflicting cards may result from clerks who marked the cards at the end of a period when memories were not as reliable. Other Union records report that eight days later, they captured and arrested him.

All William knew was the death rate of prisoners of war for both sides was high, as high as going into battle.

At Home

Later, at home, Mary laid the notice on the parlor table. She studied its lines, though she couldn't read, and ran her finger over the writing. Tears stung, and she quickly retired into her bedroom. She didn't want the children to see her cry. With telegraph technology, William's family may have gotten the news within a day or two after he was captured, and any letter written earlier may have arrived afterward.

For weeks, Mary moved quickly through her chores without talking. Daily she waited for further news. She struggled to remain normal, whether standing in the kitchen, knitting in her chair in front of the fireplace, or combing her hair at night. Her emotions alternated between abject fear and relief—fear that unknown people held him in an unknown place, yet relief because no one was shooting at him.

Eighteen sixty-two was a long and cold winter, and 1863 appeared no better. The war grew larger with both sides swapping victories and defeats. Any earlier hopes of a quick war were now gone. Both sides underestimated the strengths of the other. The North underestimated the South's powerful will and ability to fight. The South failed to understand the Northern strengths—its abundance of human resources and materials.

Later, at the courthouse, she and the kids went to a benefit concert to raise money for the effort. A man read the poem, "Weeping Sad and Lonely."

When he got to the refrain, Mary reached for her handkerchief, and thankfully the dimly-lit room hid her tears. He read, "*Sighs and tears how vain, when this cruel war is over, praying to meet again.*" A split oak basket circled the room, and everyone gave what they could.

But it was the latter words that did the deed. "*If amid the din of battle, nobly you should fall, far away from those who love you.*" Mary left the room; Florida and Sarah followed with Laura and Joseph in tow. It was too much. She knew Zech would make sure the rest got home safely.

She thought to herself: for all I know, William could be dead.

A few days later, she got an "out of turn" letter from William. She listened as Jesse read:

You cannot imagine how much I miss you. There is much drinking, drinking to excess, in this army, or maybe it is only in our unit, but my experience says otherwise. Several of our officers drink heavily. I'm afraid it is not a good example for the men.

They wounded Major Badger again. With all his wounds and the horses shot from under him, he'll be a Florida legend if he survives.

Midway through, Jesse realized his mother was crying. He stopped and stared at her, adding, "He'll be alright, Mama. At least he's not fighting. He'll be safer where he is." Though she nodded in agreement, Mary wasn't so sure.

Lately, she had noticed Zechariah's depression, and she heard his threats to "go whup some Yankee arses." She never had to say a thing, though, because Sarah one day quickly told him, "Hush! The last thing Mama needs is to have you getting shot at, too."

Zech's worried glance at his mother was the end of it. He never broached the subject again, but Mary could see the frustration on his face. It was there when he woke up and there when he retired. She knew at only two years younger than Valentine, Zech was almost grown and would leave her, too.

After Jesse finished, he refolded the letter, put it in its envelope, and handed it to his mother. She tucked it inside her blouse next to her heart. Several times she sat down, took it out, and stared at William's script, running her fingers over it, trying to imagine him writing it, wishing to feel closer to him.

More than ever, Mary wished she could read and write. These letters could be so much more personal, but she knew William knew someone would need to read them to her. This was the second time she had taken it out, and it was the second time she wept.

Ever since William's capture, she worried he was cold and hungry. What if he got sick? He mentioned several times this was no old man's fight, and lately his letters reflected that he thought himself old. Not knowing was awful, yet she could do nothing except worry and pray, both of which she did incessantly.

Eventually, a dark pall descended upon her home. Even little Laura didn't run around as before. The children played too quietly while Mary moved throughout the house with the letter close to her heart. Everyone acted as if their father had died. She realized this and knew it wasn't good. But what could she do about it?

She had lost her mother, Julia Ann, Joel, and Henry within two years. Though she felt better now, this tore open the old wounds. This war sucked the life of everyone, whether or not they were fighting. In her house alone, William, James, and Val were all gone. She tried to remember that other homes had it far worse.

Distressing news about John Slicer followed quickly after William's capture. She thought about the stormy afternoon when William and Elizabeth's frightened children jumped into their bed. Four-year-old John Slicer had hesitated before receiving special permission from her.

That is how she would always remember him, standing by their bed, though now he was a man who had contracted consumption, an illness that would shorten his life. Still, it wouldn't keep him from fighting. Consumption or not, he remained in Virginia in his winter camp.

The Union kept their records on William's whereabouts and gave clues about him. Union prisoner of war cards described him as 5' 8" with gray eyes, light skin, and light hair. Because the average man in the mid-1800s was 5' 5", people considered William tall.

His listed age is hard to read; at first glance, he appears to be twenty-two years of age, but upon closer inspection, it could be fifty-two, which would be a match. They moved him to Nashville.

Meantime, another Confederate muster roll for March 1 to April 30, 1863 shows 3rd Corporal W. H. Anders enlisted for three years for the war by Captain Wallace. This action occurred in his absence.

While William remained in Nashville, Mary's letters to William probably described the widespread rumors at home fueled by Lincoln's Emancipation Proclamation. Local rumors predicted the slaves in Jefferson County planned an insurrection. The community patrolled more, but no uprising occurred.

When freed, all the three million slaves of the South had to do was run away to Federal lines, a line getting closer daily. If the slaves could reach an advancing Federal army, they were offered paid jobs as laborers, cooks, laundresses, teamsters, and later even soldiers.

However, Monticello and Jefferson County were a long way from the Mason/Dixon line; most slaves probably did not know about the forts in Florida held by the Union. Most slaves in Middle Florida were most likely kept in the dark.

William's sons got another letter out of turn from their father. Posted before his capture, it came by a soldier on leave on a Tuesday, a cold day even in January and especially by Florida standards.

Stoking all the fires in the house, Jesse answered a knock at the door, and a young boy handed him the letter. Jesse saw William had addressed it to him and his brothers, so he called them to the parlor. His sisters came, too. He read it to the family.

December 22, 1862
Murfreesboro, Tennessee

Dear Sons,

Assertions from your mother describe how much you're doing at home. She says you take good care of her and your sisters, and for that I am thankful.

You boys might be interested in learning about our games. There is much free time in winter quarters, but not so much when we are actively moving or fighting. I usually spend my free time reading and stay away from card games, though there are games where no money exchanges hands. Right now, there is a card game right outside our cabin.

Most boys are competitive, but many here play cards like it is an incurable disease. I pity their families because I feel certain little of their money finds its way home to take care of their misses and children.

Zech interrupted, "I feel a sermon coming on." Mary cut her eyes from one son to the other and caught a furtive glance between Zech and Jesse. She wondered if her two oldest sons had yet yielded to the card games. Jesse continued:

There is always a game of horseshoes going on, and the Yankee prisoners taught us this new game. You boys might be interested in it.

They play a game called baseball with two groups of men playing against each other with a small hard ball and a stick of wood called a bat. One person throws the ball to another, who tries to hit it with the stick.

If he hits the ball, it is the job of people behind the person who throws the ball to catch it and tag the person who hit the ball. Meanwhile, the person who hits the ball must run past three bases before returning to the place where he hit the ball, which is called home.

If he runs home without being tagged, it is called a home run, and his team gets a point. But if he needs to, he can stop at any base and is safe. No one can tag him unless he steps off the base again.

*Union Prisoners at Salisbury, North Carolina. Lithograph by Otto Boetticher,
New York: Sarony, Major & Knapp, 1863, Prints and Photographs Division,
Library of Congress (013.00.00)*

*Meanwhile, another person with a stick comes to the home base
to begin the entire process again. They continue this until they strike out
or are tagged out three times.*

*Next, the team in the field comes to bat, and the team who batted
goes to the field. I know this sounds as clear as mud, but it is fun to play
and watch. Get the men home on leave to show you how it's done.*

Jessie added, "Mr. Chase is home. Let's get him to show us." He
continued to read.

*We Floridians have been playing the ballgame we learned from
the Indians. We've learned other states' soldiers gained a similar game
from theirs.*

*Up here, each team comprises twenty to thirty men. Players score
a point if they hit the goal with the ball and two points if it lands in the
nest on top. The first team to score eleven points wins. Someone made a
ball of pigskin wrapped around dried mud.*

*They play it rougher here, so I've refrained from playing. It is not
for old men. These players will do anything to get the ball. Players often
trample and kick fallen players, particularly good ones.*

If a player has a ball, he is fair game. They kick him, sometimes in the face, pull on his arms and legs, and I've even seen them stuff mud in his mouth.

Thank goodness the poor guy can't stuff the ball in his mouth. He is liable to get choked and maybe even kicked in the stomach, anything to make him cough it up. To stop further broken bones, the officers stepped in and introduced new rules.

When actively moving, we have no time except for sleep, cleaning uniforms, and writing a letter or two.

I miss you, boys, more than I can say, and I might not even recognize some of you when I get home. Your mama says several of you have grown half a foot since I left.

All my love,
Father

Jesse looked at his mama, wiping away tears, but she quickly smiled at him and the other kids. She watched as the kids happily talked about the games their father described. They forgot, if only briefly, he was somewhere in prison.

The family waited for every letter until the first letter, written after they captured him, arrived. Zech read it one cold February around the dinner table.

Nashville, Tennessee
January 15, 1863

My Dearest Mary,

I sincerely hope you receive this letter. This letter should inform you that I am not badly hurt but that Union forces captured me. I keep passing out from my head wound. I guess I fainted at the wrong time on a foraging expedition. The countryside crawls with bluebellies, so you can surmise the rest.

It is not too bad here in Nashville. I've never been to this metropolis. This is Old Hickory's city. Therefore it cannot be so bad, though it teems with Yankees. I am not sure he would appreciate an invading army, though this one was his own at one time. These are indeed confusing days in which we live.

Mary, we did not own nor want to own slaves. I especially appreciated your dad's perspective on this, but when my home state of the Old Dominion seceded, I knew the die was cast. I could not use arms against my people. Old Hickory might have felt the same way were he still alive.

Could you tell the children we have entertainment here? Someone who was here before us managed to tame a little mouse. He is our pet and provides us with joy.

Grinning, Mary interjected, "At least this means he's eating well." Everyone looked up, a confused look on their faces.

Florrie said, "Ewww!" Mary laughed, and Zech continued reading.

Daily they say they will send us farther north to a prisoner of war camp. I don't have the foggiest idea of where it will be. People tell me the hospitals provide better care, but my stay here is short because I'm not as sick as most patients. They will soon release me.

Be of good cheer, Mary, as our skies will brighten again soon. Colonel Dilworth's family will tell you how to forward your letters to me in the interim.

You can also send letters to my sister in Leesburg, only a ferry away from Washington, DC, where the rest of my family lives. She will take it to them. The mail runs better in the North. They can mail me your letter.

In reverse, I can mail letters to my family in the city, who can carry them to my Leesburg sister, who will mail it to you. In this way, we are lucky to have family living on both sides of this war.

Also, my brother Jesse lives only fifty-six miles from here in Smith County, Tennessee; he knows where I am, though neither of us is sure how long I will be in Nashville. He visited me while I was in Murfreesboro.

My dearest love to all our children and affection to my friends and family. And I miss you, Mary, every minute of the day. Oh, to see your face again. It is what keeps me going.

Love,
William

Two days later, Mary caught Henry making a trap for a mouse. She asked, "What are you doing?"

"Making a trap to catch a mouse."

She frowned. "Henry, the last thing this household needs is a pet mouse; Tomtit will kill it, anyway." Tomtit was their kitty, who kept the place free of rodents and other critters.

"Mama, why can't I do it? I'll keep it caged so Tomtit can't get to it."

She put her hands on her hips and squared off, facing him down. "No way; I won't have a pet mouse in this house." He slumped and walked off. She added, "And pick up all this mess." He returned and retrieved the pieces of wood and wiring. He knew better than to cross her.

The Western Theater

Weeks passed while William was in Nashville. For prisoners of war, especially those imprisoned near Confederate fronts, letters did pass through enemy lines. Samuel Pasco, who fought with the 3rd Florida, kept a journal and described how he sent mail to Monticello with the help of exchanges at the front. Later, when his prison camp was far away, he sent correspondence to Monticello with the help of his family, who lived in Massachusetts. It is probable that William's letters from Nashville got through to his in-laws in the Shelbyville winter camp, after which they were sent to Monticello.

When they captured William, Mary received a letter that they had mustered his nephew William E. Goff from the 5th Florida, Company K on January 1st, 1863. They reenlisted him into Company A of the Florida 8th. She had Jesse write to his father, but he probably would not receive it because the Union had moved William before the letter got to him. Someone may also have carried and passed it through the lines.

On the freezing dark morning of February 25th, William and other prisoners marched in a line to the Louisville and Nashville Railroad depot. As he passed through the hospital gate, they handed him his daily rations, a piece of bread and meat. At the depot, he boarded a train headed north. He pocketed his rations and nibbled on them throughout the day.

Before midnight, tired and weary of riding, he reached Louisville, and they took him immediately to a prison near the depot. Again, they gave him a piece of baker's bread and mess pork in the icy darkness. They marched him and the others into a dining hall with no forks, knives, spoons, or plates, but he got an old oyster can full of hot coffee. Afterward they lined up and marched to their barracks. At supper, there was bean soup, tasteless but filling.

It was freezing cold, and the wind blew constantly. Thankfully, he still had his coat, but it was getting threadbare and worn. He hadn't ordered the coat for this kind of daily wear, and he'd worn it almost constantly since mid-November.

While in the Louisville camp, all they burned in the chimneys was coal; but the chimneys didn't draw well. The coal smoke hung in the air and stifled them. William coughed constantly. The gray ashy substance covered everything and everyone.

Thankfully, it was temporary. Within days, they moved by train farther north and eastward through Cincinnati to Columbus. Again William marched in a single file two miles west from Columbus to Camp Chase, an earlier training camp for the North's volunteers. Once he arrived, the authorities ordered William to give up his valuables and money. They gave him a receipt, promising to exchange it for his items later.

Camp Chase, Ohio

William did as he was told, a good thing because they searched him. The prison had a high board fence around the low cabins built directly on the ground. The earth on which it sat was like "*a hog pen*," according to one prisoner, and there were no boards to walk over the mud. It was a gloomy scene, even with the faint glimmer of lanterns at night.

Many of Florida's soldiers made this trip north as prisoners of war. Almost half never returned or came home wounded and broken. Many died of starvation and diseases, some caused by poor diets.

At Camp Chase, they ordered William to a cabin with a rickety stove and rusty, greasy cooking vessels. He squeezed in with twenty other men and quickly claimed himself one of the twenty bunks. He spread a blanket he still had on his bunk, and he noticed other men without theirs. For them, they slept under nothing more than clothing and the clean shirts issued. Prisoners were also issued a bar of soap and ordered to bathe. He tried to dwell on the blessings here—the bar of soap, the closeness of people to keep them warmer, and the absence of the horrors of battle.

The cabin was twenty-four feet square, and their bunks occupied seven feet on one side of the room. The stove was in the middle, with shelves and tables beside the wall on the other side. Each man had a chair, stool, or box to sit upon. Shortly, William tried his best to secure an upper bunk where it would be warmer. On top, he learned he could keep his blanket cleaner. Plus, it was less crowded and more private.

Camp Chase, Columbus, Ohio—Prison of the Rebels captured by U. S. forces February 6, 1862, Library of Congress.

Because they feared theft, they piled their wood stock here and there. One soldier said, "*If every bunk was occupied, it was about as thick as we can be to stir with a stick.*" Every man was always in someone's way.

If you want mules to fight, put a few in a stall together; but if you want peace, crowd them in as many as it will hold. William realized it was the same here. There were little quarrels.

For clothing, they issued him one change of undergarments and a suit of ordinary gray pants and coat. The coat was warmer than the one he wore. He could buy from the prison supply writing materials, tobacco, cigars, combs, hairbrushes, toothbrushes, clothes brushes, scissors, thread, needles, towels, soap, pocket looking glasses, and matches, but money became scarce. It was almost impossible to send cash through the mail as it often disappeared before they received it.

Outside the cabins, the ground was soft and loamy. It stayed continuously damp and muddy, lacking drainage. William thought this ensured the infestation of rats in the cabins. No one complained about the conditions, though.

The water was good, cold, and clear. It came from a well that was limestone below. The next day, they got their rations. The endless days began. He read what he could find, wrote letters home, and played cards. Authorities permitted mail from home, but mail did not flow consistently between the North and the South.

At Home

For Mary, the days turned into weeks until an entire month passed; there was no further word from William.

Finally, in mid-February, a letter arrived.

January 28, 1863
Camp Chase, Ohio

Dearest Mary,

Well, I am certainly becoming a great traveler as now I'm in Ohio, near Columbus. Camp Chase is full of fellow southerners. At night we sing old familiar songs such as "Home Sweet Home" and "The Girl I Left Behind," and I fondly think of my girl who is keeping my home sweet home waiting for my return.

During the day we amuse ourselves by gazing at the passing clouds, as our fence is so high. At night, I look at the stars; and I wonder if you might do the same, looking at the same stars. I feel so alone that I will seek anything to feel closer to you and our children.

It is not so bad here. Yesterday, they let a few go into town for a shave and haircut. I also got a much needed bath, but now I'm almost out of money. I felt so much better and felt like a new man. It was the first hot tub bath I've had since I left home last July. It took a second change of water to rinse reasonably clean as the first turned into mud. I even kept falling asleep in the tub.

Mary, do not send money or anything of value. So much goes missing as it passes through to the North. Thankfully, Sister sends a little now and then.

I miss all of you. Give a kiss for me to my children.

All my love,
William

Around the end of February came a letter from her brother Berry (William B. Walker). Initially, it alarmed her; but when Zech read it, she realized her brother wrote to make sure she was well.

Winter Camp
February 10, 1863

My dear sister Mary,

Samuel Pasco returned after his Jefferson County leave and brought me your letter. It was wonderful to hear from you and the children. Please keep writing even though I am a poor correspondent. Your letters mean so much to me.

First, please know, Mary, we all think they will exchange William soon, so you are not to worry. We hear rumors every day about the exchanges. His incarceration shouldn't be long.

Sergeant Pasco stayed a while in our camp and smoked a pipe at our fire. It is always good to hear about home, so he was a welcomed guest. He says our county works hard to support us. Please extend to the ladies of the Soldiers Relief Society our appreciation for the socks, blankets, and other items they sent.

Sergeant Pasco came through Atlanta and says it was much changed. Where there were once cotton gins and general buildings along the railroad, now it is the junction of four railroads going in all directions. Through Atlanta travel all the stores and supplies of the Confederacy. There are now great factories to make saddles, tents, ammunition, and pistols. The city also houses enormous hospitals, and the railroad lines are continuously bringing in the wounded and convalescents. Much has changed since we came through last year on our way to Kentucky.

The state of Georgia is one vast granary now. Plus, they make cotton and most of our woolen wear. Compared to our own state, this war has made Georgia rich.

Mary, keep the home fires burning. I can't wait to come home to our little part of this big old country. I've seen enough for a lifetime, and none of it compares to our Florida.

Respectfully, your brother,
Berry

William Berry Walker

Mary's brothers may also have written letters to William.

February 12, 1863
Winter Camp

Dear William,

    Though we all worry about your treatment, it is better you are safe from the daily vagaries of war. We are in winter quarters, and the 3rd regiment was so devastated after Murfreesboro they combined us with the 1st. Henceforth we will fight as a merged regiment. Where we go next is any man's guess.

    I cannot help but think about George all alone in Kentucky soil. I'm glad Mama did not live long enough to see it happen. To fall in this war because of sickness is a sad thing. On another note, though, they promoted Jesse Allen to full 4th corporal. Heaven help us all if they make him sergeant!

I'm wondering if you are being treated well? We hear rumors about the mistreatment of our men who are prisoners. We hear of the meager rations, insufficient clothing, and blankets. The diseases passed around. Daily we hear someone has died of smallpox and another of pneumonia.

The Yankees entice our boys to sign an oath of allegiance to the Union; in return for signing, they release a boy for two years of Indian service in the west. Something like jumping from the pan and into the fire! We Floridians know about fighting Indians!

Well, there are taps and the end of our day. You take good care of yourself, and I hope to see you again soon

Your brother,
Arch Walker

Probably, both Arch and Mary wrote about the earlier occupation of Jacksonville in February, only 130 miles east of Monticello. Everyone worried because the Yankees were again so close, but Middle Florida breathed easier when they left. The Yankees burned the city before evacuating. Vollie still rode with the 2nd Florida Battalion in East Florida.

Camp Chase

While William was a prisoner, the Confederate army still kept records on him. A later record showed him absent on February 28th, 1863; they promoted him from private to 3rd corporal on March 1, 1863. His northern records show he is still a private. William may not have learned they had promoted him.

William's diet was bread, meat, and beans. Frequently, they made soups and did the cooking themselves. Some days, the camp cook made dinner, which was comprised of roast beef, light bread, and two rations of Irish potatoes. Still, the portions may have been meager.

He may have seen a rat cooked, as recorded in their journals, which reported it as good meat. Others wrote about a cat which took up amongst them. It gave enjoyment, but it died of starvation. One man wrote, "*A man's belly is his God.*"

With his rations short, his stomach empty, his clothing scarce, and his feet cold, William probably weakened. Several soldiers wrote about how they sought the sunbeams through the door to keep warm. Daily he heard rumors of moving again, though he didn't know where. Like all the others, his most earnest prayer was for an exchange.

William hadn't seen Mary and the children in over ten months. He had little to remember them by—only creased letters which were read until memorized and a locket of Mary's hair in his Bible. At night, he played in his mind the last night and morning before he left. He wondered when he would return—and how many birthdays and special moments in the children's lives would he miss? Would the littler ones remember him?

And how would Mary do without him? He thought often of her brown wavy hair with its red highlights. He thought of her in her kitchen, always industrious and holding the household together. Frequently at night, before he drifted away to sleep, he pictured her face as she smiled and looked up from her rocking chair in the parlor. But sometimes he tried to remember her and could remember nothing but her hands.

At Home

At home, Mary went to the depot again to see another relative leave for war. At thirty-eight, her brother J.J. re-enlisted the first week of March with another unit Company E of the Florida 11th Infantry Regiment. They reported him as 5' 8" tall with a dark complexion, gray eyes, and dark hair. That the state did not raise the Florida 11th until 1864 confuses the records. Also in the 11th in Company G was James Goff, William's brother-in-law.

Mid-19th Century Locomotive, Keystone Genealogical Library, Monticello, Florida

March dragged on, and they sporadically received word from William. Mary wrote, hoping her letters got through.

One day at the depot, the clerk handed her a letter which had been dropped off by a soldier passing through. They sat in the buggy under the oak trees which shaded the yard by the depot as Jesse read:

February 25, 1863
Camp Chase

My Dearest Mary,

I'm still in Ohio, though the talk of exchanges continues to give all of us hope. Still, it ends as hopes dashed on the walls that imprison us. I sincerely hope this letter finds you and our children well. I have had several days of disagreeable health. Dysentery makes its rounds again.

Our captors coerce us to swallow the dog, the demon oath. It is tempting because they promise I'll get to see you again soon. I cannot do it in good faith, though, especially to my sons fighting on distant fields and your brother George, who lies six feet below the ground of Kentucky. I could never bear to face him at the feet of Jesus, let alone my old and dear friend, your father.

Jesse felt the buggy quiver and looked up to see his mother with her head bowed. She didn't want him to see her cry, but it was no use.

It was a relief to hear from William, but all of it today was too much with William detained in Ohio, her brother George buried far away, and J.J. leaving for war. When would it all stop? Jesse folded the letter, took the reins, and headed for home.

Lately, Mary carried daily a feeling of dread and doom. Every morning it manifested itself anew as she remembered William's plight. It crawled on her skin like a spider. She was sick and dispirited. Sometimes in the evening she felt herself sink into moments of despair.

She tried to hold away the wolves in her mind, to keep them walled off in a room deep in its recesses, but she was frightened. If something happened to him, how would she ever raise the rest of their family alone?

Who would want someone her age with a house full of children? The thought made her ill. Even the idea itself made her feel guilty for having thought it to begin with. She kept her thoughts to herself, and she instructed the children to write to him on her behalf.

March 15, 1863
Monticello, Florida

Dearest William,

The home fires are burning here, and we continue to miss you, Val, and James every day. We hope this letter finds you in good health, warm, and treated well.

A few days ago, we sent off J.J. with Florida's 11th Infantry. He is going to Virginia with Company E, primarily men from Madison. Now I have family all over the southeast—and with you in Ohio, well, I guess I should say throughout the country.

In an interesting occurrence, our county commissioners wrote the governor of Georgia to see the possibility of buying cotton cards to make thread in our homes. Wouldn't my mama enjoy this? All those years of making her own cloth, which was something my sisters and I never had to do; but here we are again. Thankfully, she taught me how. I hope I can remember all that is needed to do it.

Earlier, they had a real scare near Elizabeth. A man named Wheeler contracted smallpox. The county quarantined Mrs. Humphreys's house, and it became a hospital. Anyone staying with her who did not have the pox, they quarantined in Mrs. Scott's house. No one could leave or enter either house except for doctors and nurses. They posted guards on the houses and kept the roads to them closed. It is all over now, but not before they burned everything Mrs. Humphreys owned, including her home. The county paid her for it.

The reports of casualties keep rolling into our fair community. It has taken a heavy toll, and the fanfare of military service wanes as battle after battle takes its reckoning. The earlier battle at Perryville hit us hard, and I thank God every day you weren't there. Losing George was devastating, and our town is filled with men shot up and missing extremities. Now, worse, you are a prisoner of the North. When will it end?

We have no more cooking soda (baking soda), but Ann Lightsey remembered how they made it when they first got here. They took ashes from corncobs and put them into a jar, covered them with water, and let it stand until it was completely clear. When we need it, we mix it with sour milk (buttermilk) of one part to three parts.

Fortunately, we still have milk, thanks to Dad hiding Matilda in the swamps every time the requisitioners came. He always knew when they were coming because Uncle James's messenger system worked like it did during the Indian War. Uncle James takes care of her now.

Regardless, the children and I are well, and we await your return every day. I long for you, too. I miss you, my love.

Longingly Yours,
Mary

Camp Chase, Ohio

Examining the paper containing the letter, William wondered which of his books had lost another flyleaf. The tiny writing filled every part of the page, with little space between the lines.

During the spring of 1863, the North continuously squeezed the South through a trade embargo. In Richmond, a mob of Confederate housewives took to the streets with axes to protest the rising prices of flour, now at $100 a barrel. They pillaged shops, seized a wagon of beef, and stole over 500 pounds of bacon. After President Davis threatened to bring in troops, they dispersed. By the end of the war, though, flour rose to $1,000 a barrel.

GRAND REAPING.

SOUTHERN WOMEN FEELING THE EFFECTS OF REBELLION, AND CREATING BREAD RIOTS.

Southern women feeling the effects of Rebellion, and
creating Bread Riots, April 2, 1863, Frank Leslie's Illustrated Newspaper,
Wikipedia

The Richmond ladies were not alone. In Atlanta, women rioted over the cost of bacon and broke into shops to steal food. The South lacked an adequate welfare system. The prices of grain, meat, and salt inflated exponentially.

William and his cabin mates overheard the Yankee wardens discussing it. Because most prisoners had women at home, they talked until way into the night. They were worried about them. William wrote home again:

March 10, 1863
Camp Chase, Ohio

Dearest Mary,

I hope you and the children are not suffering from hunger. We received word women in our cities are rioting over food. Hopefully yours and your uncle's gardens are doing well.

Here we have enough to eat but suffer from boredom. To relieve mine, I write letters. I sincerely believe I have found my purpose in this war. I write letters for those who cannot. Sometimes I write for someone who knows they will not see another sunrise. These are missives to their loved ones—final entreaties to their family to remember them after they are gone.

Over eighteen months ago, when I first left Monticello on the train, I thought my purpose was to protect our home and our way of life. But after Murfreesboro, God has another plan for me. My task is to make sure these young men who cannot read and write send their departing thoughts and words to their homes—to let their parents, spouses, and children know where they were and what they were doing until their life's end.

My days go faster reading and posting letters. I am one of the few who have a Northern family. My sister is tired of reposting letters, but others know I'm a channel to the South.

Please keep sharing what is going on in Jefferson County and elsewhere. You are my best source of information. I appreciate all the letters from home.

On March 27th, dear Mary, please go outside at exactly 8 pm. and stare at the sky. I will do the same. Hopefully the stars will be out for each of us; and hopefully my letter will reach you in time. Take a few minutes to think about me as I will about you. As we both view the same stars, I'm hoping it will help us feel closer to one another and less homesick. I miss you so much.

All my love,
William

March 27th came, but the letter did not make it in time. It didn't matter, though, because that evening William couldn't stare at the sky either. He was in a railroad car, one of several, transporting over six hundred prisoners of war. He and his fellow prisoners talked in the dark, sitting on the floor, while the mass of their bodies shifted with the roll of the train. In his mind, he saw Mary outside their home, looking at the stars.

#

Chapter 5

Clouds of Dust & Ashes
March to July 1863

Camp Chase, Ohio

A day or so before March 28th, William rose as usual, but the day turned into anything but normal. He was sick and had not slept well that night. His throat was scratchy, and his head felt like it would explode.

It was a relief to walk around, but he could tell he wasn't well. He had been sick off and on for weeks and was weakening. Still he carried on, as to do otherwise was not good for his constitution.

They had a quick breakfast before someone ordered them to gather their belongings. The burly red-headed Yankee warden sitting behind a table in a corner of the dining room handed him a package of his belongings confiscated when he arrived. He leaned over and signed for it. Leaning over caused his head to throb more.

Leaving, they marched two miles into the city, where he and many of his Confederate countrymen were loaded onto a train guarded by a Union company of soldiers. They marched single file into the cars, and a door closed behind him. Daylight filtered through its sides as the jolt of the train couplings clanked and the mass of men shifted. He did not know where they were sending him.

The ride was crowded. They were in the cars for days. He had a splitting headache, and he burned with a fever. They loaded 618 prisoners on to several cars, but when they opened them, only 617 were still alive.

Because it was early enough in the war to make exchanges but still not late enough to prohibit them, the two sides exchanged their prisoners of war. The Union exchanged them at City Point, in Virginia, also known as Aiken Landing, almost 500 miles from Columbus, Ohio, but less than twenty-five miles from Richmond. Today, City Point is called Hopewell. It sits on the James River southeast of Richmond and northeast of Petersburg. Upon the exchange, William rejoined the Confederate army.

Petersburg, Virginia

William woke in the hospital and at first did not know where he was. He thought he was in a Union hospital. His memory was cloudy. He remembered fading in and out of delirium on the train coming from Ohio, but the last people he thought he remembered were Union soldiers. Finally, though, he regained consciousness, and there was a fellow Reb talking to him.

He asked where he was, and the Reb answered, "Petersburg." His next question was if the city had fallen.

"No!" came the reply with a grin. "You're safe now and home." William relaxed and went to sleep.

Records show on March 28th, 1863, they traded William at City Point and admitted him to the General Hospital in Petersburg, Virginia, eight miles away. They recorded him on April 2nd in the register there. The records listed him as Sgt. William Andrews. He may have been surprised to learn they promoted him while he was in prison.

It may have been days before Mary learned about the exchange, or it may have been later that day. We're unsure, but there was the telegraph, and Dr. Palmer was a chief surgeon stationed in Richmond less than twenty-five miles away. Someone may have sent word home that William was in the South.

When she received word, she may have been momentarily relieved that he was safely in a hospital, away from both Camp Chase and the battlefield.

It is a pity that they did not send William to the general hospital in Richmond, where Dr. Palmer practiced his craft. During the 2nd Florida Infantry's Richmond encampment, Palmer boosted troop health by supplying rations of *"40 gallons of whiskey, 20 gallons of molasses, 77 pounds of dried apples, 401 pounds of bacon, and 153 pounds of flour."* Palmer took good care of the men in his charge.

In Petersburg, William's Confederate records showed he spent ten days in the hospital before being discharged on April 18th. Another hospital record, though, shows him in the hospital on April 2nd, and none of these records coincide with the union records.

When they released him, he boarded a train heading to Monticello, probably because of a stipulation in the parole agreement that he would not bear arms again against the United States for one hundred days. However, since many exchanged went immediately back to war, they may have sent him home to recuperate and regain his strength.

At Home

During the days preceding the exchange, Mary wrote often, not knowing if William got any of her letters, while a letter here and there from him may have trickled down to Monticello. All the while she worried about James and now Valentine, too. Because of the rumor mill and the imminent danger of Yankees being in East Florida, it was common knowledge that Valentine's battalion fought repeatedly in skirmishes all around Jacksonville. She may have started a new daily routine to pray for him, his brother, and his father maybe sometimes as much as four times a day, at meals and at bedtime. She probably sought the quietness of her bedroom behind a closed door for any such ritual.

On April 25th, Isham J. Walker, thirty-one, Mary's first cousin through her Uncle James, reenlisted in the 5th Florida, Company G. He was 5' 8" with gray eyes and light hair. On the same date, Jesse Allen and William J. Walker, two more of Mary's first cousins through her Uncle Littleberry, also reenlisted. Meanwhile, at home, Mary received word that her brother Archibald Jesse was serving as a nurse in the Buckner Hospital in Cherokee Springs, Georgia somewhere between Chattanooga and Dalton. That seemed safer, and the news gave Mary relief.

She was trying to compartmentalize her worries. With this good news, she spent the morning trying to only think about Arch and William, both of which were safe for the moment. She remembered the good times when her brothers were little and she herself still young and vibrant, her mother still alive. It gave her solace to count her blessings, and she tried to keep the negative thoughts deep, deep in the back of her mind. She thought, "I'll think about George later," but she knew it would come roaring back maybe sometime that night when something awakened her. Best of all, though, William was safe and coming home on leave. It was a wonderful respite to the sorrows of this war—William home safe and sound, if only for a hundred days.

Later that afternoon, Mary could not help thinking about her Aunt Mary Ann Kinsey Walker, who was only a few years older than Mary herself. Though aunt and niece, they were close in age and in spirit. Mary Ann's husband, Littleberry, and two of their sons were at war. Also in common, the two women had many children at home as young as five years of age. She mentioned to Zech that she needed to visit Mary Ann, and the two of them planned an outing the next morning.

A trip to Elizabeth was what they and her other children needed. As they drove through the Bellamy lands, they talked about the problems with the droves of deserters who hid in the Florida swamps and who now numbered in the thousands. They both had heard about the lack of food amongst the troops, the fatigue, filth, disease, and their irregular pay, all hardships which played heavily into the reasons that men left their units and joined the droves of deserters.

"Mama," said Zech, "it's no secret that blockade runners are enticing them to raid our local farmers and steal whatever they can carry off. That band in Taylor County grows more menacing by the moment." Deserters banded together in small groups and lived in desolate areas for protection against recapture. They operated as bandit gangs preying on lesser protected farms and plantations. Added to their numbers were those who engaged in criminal activities. Mostly, deserters were detached from other human societies, without homes, wives, and children or the elderly. By living this way, they became radically individualistic and scornful of the ties that bind humanity together. Their detachment was a choice, and they lived with audacity and no certitude of a day after tomorrow.

Why did they desert? Some did it out of revenge against an officer, seeking to leave the authority they encountered. These detested any strict moral order meted by their officers. Others liked the career choice, a payment that was a share of their plunder instead of a periodic wage. For some, it was a means of survival for an infraction. A few were killers, but not most. Others came for the lazy life and love of drink. In the army, there were low wages, hard labor, and strict command. In the swamps of Florida, there was pleasure, ease, liberty, and power—and sometimes plenty. It was a merrier life for the time being.

Sometime around the last week of April, William probably came home a weakened man. He had had pneumonia preceded by a head wound. His injuries may have crippled him. After several days on the train, William rolled into the depot in Monticello. It was April, and he marveled at the green of the forests and flowers all along the way. Florida was always pretty to him, but even prettier after seeing how war makes the soil a wasteland. He was thankful it had not reached his home county. It was good to be going home, but he itched and was miserable the entire trip.

It had helped to while away the hours of travel talking to the other soldiers who were coming and going from the front—the fronts being both Tennessee and Virginia. He stepped from the train, but no one recognized him at first. He thought he must be a sight, all thin and emaciated with ragged clothes and the constant itch. Then he saw Mary standing on the masonry platform, looking at the passengers. He knew they had gotten his telegram but still wouldn't know exactly which day he would get home.

She saw him, and she and the children rushed forward. Laura would have been six and old enough to remember her father, but Joseph hardly knew him and certainly didn't recognize him. They both clung to their mother's skirts. Mary and the older ones went to give him a hug, but he held them at arm's length. He had been riding for days with people who probably had lice. He didn't want her or the children to get them. With his itching, he wasn't sure if he had them or not.

She reached with her right hand, though, and laid the pads of her three warm fingers on his left cheek and longingly looked deep into his eyes. She noticed the tension around his mouth and a perpetual frown creased into his brow—something not there when he left. There was also a stoop in his bearing.

When she touched his left cheek, there it was. With one soft touch, the love of his life welcomed him home with all their children around her, the little ones with their upturned faces taking in the scene.

He likely led the movement to the buckboard and insisted on taking the rear seat. Facing backward, he rode home with the kids in front, some walking or riding close by. He forgot about his itch, and it was a good drive passing through the well-known streets, though everything needed maintenance and painting.

Monticello, a thriving and upwardly mobile city when he left, now needed the help only its men could offer. He wondered how many would make it home and be in shape to do what needed to be done. So much had been lost. So much so that in distant fields, where no battles raged, the clouds and ashes of war had changed even those places where no fighting befell.

His next to the youngest son remembers his dad coming home from the war and that his dad was in terrible shape, with a limp and a severe case of the itch all over. The itch was probably a skin fungus.

If William injured his leg, neither Confederate nor hospital records mention it. Records reflect William stayed in at least three war hospitals, the last of which was in North Carolina, but there was no record of a leg wound. The limp may have been from fungus on his feet.

The rumors came from Texas where Henry settled, and Henry would be William's longest living offspring, who died in 1932. The author had the pleasure of talking to one of Henry's sons who also lived a long life and said he remembered his father talk about "his father" William coming home from the Civil War. Henry was ten years old at the end of the war.

Not known is which time Henry remembers him coming home since William may have come back more than once. It is certain he came home this time because the authorities recorded it. The question remains: did his homecoming this time coincide with his son's memory? We cannot be sure.

Everything we know is family lore, which says that William came home to recuperate. We do not know if the Texas story about his returning from the war was this spring in 1863 or later at the end of the war.

All we know for certain from his service records is that he received a head wound at Murfreesboro, spent time in a northern prisoner of war camp, had pneumonia by the time they exchanged him, spent time in the hospital in Petersburg, and came home on leave for one hundred days.

There is also no record of him signing an oath of allegiance to the Union. The situation that Henry remembered may be when William came home after being exchanged and after serving time in the hospital in Petersburg, Virginia. He would be home for over three months until late in July 1863. The following moments in William and Mary's life, after he returned from the War, were recreated.

Mary peeked in. The room reeked of rotting flesh and the chemicals brought in by the doctor. She checked to see if William was sleeping. In the early morning daylight, she could see him lying on their bed with his back to the door, curled into a fetal position under the light muslin, all of it barely noticeable in the dim light. They kept the room darkened because he wished it that way. She didn't want to disturb him because when he was awake, the pain was worse. He had been like this almost all the time since he returned from the war.

The fungus that he brought back on his skin was bad, but the lye treatment he endured was worse. The area between his legs and under his arms never healed but continued to erupt into sores and blisters, itching and burning and cracking and peeling into more sores and blisters. Mary daubed turpentine on the broken skin to help it heal faster. William was in agony most of the time. It had been more than a week since his return.

He may have had it almost during the whole time he was in the war, and it probably spread while he was in Camp Chase and the hospital in Petersburg. She sat and listened for long periods as he explained the horrid conditions in those hospitals, the bedbugs, lice, the screams and groans of agony, sometimes his own.

The itch would almost disappear in the winter and then return with a vengeance in the summer. She frequently took cool water and tried to pat a cool rag on it to give him relief. The doctor suggested keeping it clean and pat it with vinegar, which burned and caused more pain.

One of the old-timers told him that in the old days, when someone got the itch, they would find an old burned-out tree and use it to rub themselves against its ash. Ash was also used to make lye soap. William did this, and the cure almost killed him. William told her about the trip from Virginia, how most of it was by train and comfortable enough; but there still was no train between Georgia's railway and Florida's, and he had had to leave the trains in Georgia at Troupville and take a stage from there to Walker's Mills. Troupville is now Valdosta.

The stage came down on what is today the Old Grooverville Road. It stopped in Grooverville, a trading center and stagecoach route with its gristmills, churches, homes, tavern, and a general store on each side of its crossroads. He was as good as he had been for days, but the ride weakened him again.

William told Mary, "Crack went the whip from the driver above, and he shouted to us 'Hold on by your teeth and nails!' The buggy lurched forward as we found neither of any use. We crashed into each other and each other's valises and boxes. I thought I would not live long enough to see Florida again."

He described the coach as having three seats on each side, like those commonly used throughout the country, the middle seat equipped with a broad leather strap. William said that they decided he should ride in the middle with the chance of hitting something softer than the hard wooden sides, though he said that all three of them were skin and bones and it was like sitting between two bags of bones the whole way. "I'm sure I felt little better to them either," he added. "I may have been better sitting by the driver."

Mary grinned and said, "No, you might not have made it at all. They might have lost you somewhere south of Troupville."

He continued, "Anyway, often the driver would yell 'throw your weight to the right' or 'throw your weight to the left' in order to balance the coach and prevent it from turning over, like when it was sinking in on one side in a deep rut. And thankfully sometimes he made us all get out and walk alongside.

"One of those times I thought about telling him to go on to Walker Mills and that I would walk the rest of the way to Monticello. I even thought about getting off in Elizabeth." William grinned when he said it. "But I didn't. I got back on each time, and when his whip cracked, signaling another jolt, I wished I had stayed behind. Several times we bounced on logs in the road, and any sleep at all was impossible. We rolled incessantly from side to side even when the road was clear, making it no better. Mary, I had never noticed how badly a stage rolls you around until this time. As an old man, I am too infirm for such movement."

William improved quickly and loved rejoining his family on the porch in the evenings. This was something he longed for while away at the war, these peaceful moments. Visiting around the campfire with his fellow soldiers wasn't quite the same, but neither was it the same on the porch either. *The Family Friend* was simply a printed paper on the bulletin board at the courthouse because there was no paper to print it for its subscribers. Its once-a-week news had to be read, remembered, and repeated to the rest of them on the porch. This evening, however, James Sanders Walker, Mary's distant cousin, joined them with additional information.

James, a county commissioner, came by to see how William was doing. He said, "I guess you've heard, but word is we are outmanned and out-provisioned at this place called Chancellorsville." Mary and William exchanged glances as James proceeded. The glances were two-fold, for it portended truth to William's earlier fears that the South did not have enough people to win this war—but more importantly, the glance was for their son John Slicer, whom they knew was there.

The battle lasted from April 30th to May 6th, and William got a taste of Mary's life and the long periods of uncertainty as they waited for news. Besides John Slicer at Chancellorsville, there was also the Florida 5th and the 8th. Within the 5th Florida were the Aucilla Guards, and many of their family and close friends fought in this company. Besides Mary's first cousins and uncle, there was William Bailey, J. S. Walker, John Joseph Kinsey, William A. Kinsey, Berry Walker, George R. Walker, James A. Walker, Stephen J. Walker, and Archibald Lightsey, Mary's first cousin through her Aunt Mary Jane Walker Lightsey. Many of these men were Mary's first cousins, either full or once removed. William's nephew, William E. Goff, was there as well.

Just like that, she could feel waves of worry where she had spent a day mostly without them. That night the two of them went to bed and hardly slept, worried about John Slicer in the 50th Georgia Regiment who was in Bryan's Brigade under Brigadier General Joseph B. Kershaw in McLaws's (old) Division. In the darkness, William said, "Mary, he is not in harm's way during the nighttime. They run too low on ammo to fight during the night. The fighting always stops. He is most likely resting, so we can rest, too. That's how I try to think of him and our other two boys. It sometimes helps me sleep better." She thought about that and drifted off to sleep.

Fought over multiple days, the battle's news from the telegraph added to their concern. General Stonewall Jackson suffered a serious wound. Casualties were heavy. After six days of hard fighting, the north retreated. Chancellorsville was a Southern victory, but the family each day sent someone to the railroad station to check the casualty list.

Unfortunately, the casualty lists received in Monticello did not list Georgia regiments, so they would not know for even longer about John Slicer's fate, and they needn't have worried about the Aucilla Guards and Perry's Brigade because they somehow missed the worst of it. William's nephew William Goff also survived.

Not everyone in the nation was so lucky, though, because out of the 50,000 men at Chancellorsville, there were over 30,500 casualties. With 13,000 of them Confederates, Chancellorsville became the fourth-costliest land battle of the War. At home, there was joy over the victory, but losing so many boys overshadowed it—as well as what was publicly the South's most beloved general, Stonewall Jackson, who died of his wounds a few days later.

A pall hung over Monticello and the rest of the South. Luckily, only one person from Jefferson County suffered a wound. He was from the Aucilla Guards, Corporal W. E. Bolen. Though the battle's worst fighting did not involve the 5th Florida Infantry, the people at home remained unaware of this until the battle ended. People were weary of the constant foreboding and worriment.

In June, the consolidation of parts of the 2nd and 4th Florida Battalions created the 11th Florida Infantry. General Finegan assigned the new 11th to the Florida Brigade alongside the 2nd, 5th, 8th, 9th, and 10th Florida Infantry Regiments. Later, while William was still home,

115

Valentine's Partisan Rangers unit became part of the Confederate regular army, joining Company D, 2nd Infantry Battalion on June 24, 1863. At sixteen, they both thought Valentine was going north soon, especially since they had heard about the new 11th. Lieutenant Colonel T. W. Brevard and Major John Westcott commanded the new battalion, but they did not move Vollie for the time being. Also, while in Richmond, they mustered William Goff out of Company A, 8th Florida Regiment and into Company G of the 11th Florida. Their son James transferred to the 11th Florida Infantry, Company K. His records said he was an average height of 5' 6" with gray eyes, black hair, and a dark complexion.

William noticed Mary developed a new habit of pacing. She couldn't keep still, and welts covered her hands and arms. It was hot and at first she thought it was the heat. She took a break and sat on the front porch with a fan William brought her from Tallahassee. With its ivory and hand-painted paper, she fanned and rested. After a while, she went inside and applied cool compresses. Repeating it often, she even went to the spring and plunged her arms deep into the cold water.

She gave up. Pressed for time, she cleaned and cooked without pause until William suggested another trip to Elizabeth, a recurring activity for them. Ultimately, Mary fought the urge to scratch, eventually forgot about it, and the welts disappeared.

At dinner several weeks later, Jesse, who was the most studious of the lot, asked his dad, "Why haven't the British stepped in on our behalf? I thought their factories and mills depended upon our cotton."

William replied, "Well, I'm not sure. I know we have been sending emissaries, but Britain remains quiet. I guess they're waiting to see who is the strongest." The South made a grave error in believing its cotton would make Britain support them. During the war, India and Egypt took advantage of the blockade and increased their production, replacing the American South's. In addition, there was no embargo of Northern products, and the North, even at war, exported significant quantities of food to other countries, including Britain. As a result, there had been no formal recognition of the Confederacy internationally.

Only once did England and the United States government come to blows. The US seized two Confederate diplomats aboard a British ship, but the diplomatically astute Queen Victoria quickly interceded to negotiate a peace. The tension dissipated like a fog before the morning sun. Neither Britain nor any other country appointed diplomats to the

Confederacy, though they sent military observers. Internationally, they also saw the Confederacy as a serious attempt at nation building.

Meanwhile, in William's unit, Captain Wallace listed William as present from April 30 to June 30, 1863, though this was when he was home on furlough for one hundred days. During this time, William's regiment remained in the western theater, and Mary realized how fortunate they were that William was safe at home. His unit was in Vicksburg as the North continued to move southward.

Meantime, West Virginia joined the union. Because it comprised small farms, no slavery, and a populace who nullified Virginia's ordinance of secession, President Lincoln proclaimed their admission to the Union on June 20th as America's thirty-fifth state.

Only Confederate-controlled Vicksburg remained as the last Confederate command on the Mississippi River, the control of which was a strategic objective for both sides. A battle was eminent, as the city had been under siege since the middle of May. Within the city was Florida's 1st/3rd and 4th Infantries.

However, everyone's attention turned on July 1st to the war in the east as the entire South held its breath—or at least those with a telegraph office like Monticello. On the eastern front, there arose a great battle at a place called Gettysburg. The family waited over three days for the dreaded news. Fighting there was Perry's Brigade with Florida's 5th, 2nd, and 8th Infantries and again the Aucilla Guards. Also, there was John Slicer.

Each day, people waited outside the train station for any news that trickled down on the telegraph wires, and news arrived. By the battle's end, they had captured Captain William J. Bailey, a Jefferson County casualty who later died in prison. William A. Hamrick of Elizabeth was seriously wounded and, like William, sent home on parole to recuperate. Samuel N. Johnson, Lemuel Lang, L. Long, James Milton, J. P. Strickland, K. Ward, F. M. Woods, G. W. Cole, and James Bryant also suffered wounds and remained on the field. George Dice lost his right arm. Killed was 1st Lieutenant George R. Walker, Mary's distant cousin from the second group of Walkers.

That evening William and Mary talked about George and how he left behind a young wife and two little baby boys, ages one and two—two little babies who would never know their father. They also killed John Baugh. They captured several more and sent them to Fort Delaware, a Northern prisoner of war fortress set on an island, where they joined

13,000 other prisoners. Joseph E. Blackburn, H. W. Morris, Charles W. Roach, and William M. Woods joined Captain Bailey. The Battle of Gettysburg took many of Jefferson County's sons, causing shock and sadness throughout the county. Following the wounding and capture of William Bailey, they promoted George D. Raysor to captain.

Sadly, a day later, they got word that Vicksburg fell, ending the South's access to the great river, a strategic loss for their war effort. Towering on the heights overlooking the river, Vicksburg had been under siege for months; it ended on July 4th. The Jefferson Rifles and the Jefferson Beauregards were in this siege, as was their son James, several of her brothers and uncles, and many cousins from Monticello. William's regiment was there, too. The news was an enormous blow to the Southern people.

With the fall of Vicksburg, the Confederates' channel to Texas cattle abruptly closed, but the large herds of Florida grew in importance. Bragg's army alone required an average of 400,000 meat rations a month.

#

Chapter 6
A Gift from William
July to September 1863

At Home

Until the loss of the Texas cattle supply, the Confederacy had forgotten about Florida's beef supply. In pre-war Florida, according to the 1860 census, approximately 388,060 head of cattle grazed in the state. A 600-pound animal typically yielded about 300 pounds of beef. This means that Florida at the beginning of the war could supply over 116.4 million pounds of beef to feed the South's armies.

Upon the loss of the Texas supply, the Confederacy developed a system of five commissary districts in Florida. They built supply bases at Albany, Georgia and Quitman, Georgia, Quitman being less than thirty miles from Elizabeth and the remaining Walker cattle operations. Mary's uncle began supplying beef to the Confederacy, driving the remaining Walker herds to Quitman.

The Confederacy wanted 3,000 head a week. The expectation was that this district would move 1,000 head weekly.

But winter was coming, and the Confederate authorities didn't understand that moving those numbers in winter was an impossibility. In the winter, herds from farther south came to Lafayette and Taylor Counties to be held until the spring for finishing. Herds moving north had less forage to feed themselves. They needed to gain weight for the rest of the trip.

Likewise, herds were driven up the east side of the state to places like Baldwin and later shipped by rail to Charleston and Savannah stockyards. By the winter of 1863, Floridians had moved over 30,000 head of cattle, and even more illegally.

Though Florida kept a considerable number of Confederate soldiers fed, it wasn't enough.

At home, William learned his regiment had escaped capture and immediately marched from Vicksburg. They marched eastward toward Jackson for the siege of Jackson, Mississippi, which lasted from July 5th to the 25th. After waiting again for word about James in Jackson and Vollie near Jacksonville, they learned their sons survived.

About the same time he learned his regiment safely left Vicksburg, he also learned that the Yankees captured John Slicer west of Gettysburg near Cashtown. The bad news hung over the Andrews household.

For Mary, she felt like she was constantly walking through a hot, humid fog. But the days slipped by, and William's one hundred days dissipated like a memory. She constantly worried about William's return, which was now only weeks away.

One night while he and Mary sat on the porch alone watching the kids on the street, they discussed army life. "Mary, I don't think being a soldier is good for a man's mental direction, and it certainly engenders laziness. There is so much time with little to do."

Mary said, "I thought they kept you busy with camp chores."

"They try to fill the time, but there are too many minutes in a day with little to do, particularly in a winter camp. It is demoralizing, especially to men who were productive and efficient. Plus, there is the hardening of our minds to the blood and gore. I'm afraid it has changed me and will change our sons. We walk on ground strewn with bodies and soaked in blood. I've become hardened by it. I was worried about coming home and not being the same. Military life breaks down all ideas of status and identity. One's image of oneself is threatened." He looked at her and saw questions in her eyes, but he decided he had said enough.

By July 12th, John Slicer had been sent to Fort Delaware. One wonders if he would have survived the war if he had remained with his unit, who later fought at Spotsylvania and Richmond. Although the family feared he would die of consumption in prison, they also knew that many men died on these battlefields. Either way, his life hung in the balance.

The information about John came from a pension application (#14118) filed by his widow Emily in 1909 after he passed away. Her claim was approved. John's son A. D. Andrews would be the state legislator who introduced and helped pass the Special Act Confederate Pension bill which would help take care of Florida's war widows.

As for William and Mary's other family in the 3rd Florida at Vicksburg and Jackson, they would later describe it as a time of starvation and survival.

At home with his family from April 18th to mid-July, a little over three months, William regained his strength. By the time he returned to his unit, he would leave Mary pregnant again.

During the third week of that hot, humid July month, all of them made the trip to the depot, riding on the same street as before. It was a beautiful morning, though the humidity was rising. Clouds billowed like white towers in the sky, and they all knew that by the afternoon a thunderstorm would provide relief.

Dogwood Street today, personal photo

As before, William and Mary sat in the carriage with six-year-old Laura sitting between them. Walking alongside were the rest of the children except for Zech and Jesse, who rode their horses. Joseph and Henry walked with their sisters, Sarah and Hattie. William looked at each of them, trying to freeze their faces in his mind.

At the depot, he pulled around back. She watched him descend from the buggy. He turned to help Laura and when he reached up to circle his hands around Mary's waist, he said, "Your waistline is thinner than I remembered." It had been five years since their last child was born. She glowed, wearing her green calico dress. He may not have known she was pregnant.

She had told Ellen and Florrie earlier that day that the green dress was the best one she had left, but it was threadbare in spots. There was no fabric to be found anywhere. No one was raising cotton as the entire South had become subsistence farmers.

She turned her face toward the morning sun, temporarily closing her eyes to its glare. Then she looked deep into his eyes. She may have known she was with child, though she may not have been one hundred percent sure. She may have kept the fact to herself. No need to add any more worries to a mind crowded with worries. The last baby had been hard on her, and they had decided to have no more.

She knew he wanted to stay. They talked about it last night. He asked her to walk with him, his warm hand in hers, as they strolled through Monticello's streets. All the while, he watched her, a small smile playing around his lips.

But vows were given and promises sworn. William, in his thoughts the night before, thought about those vows and promises not only to the Confederacy but to her, too. Yet even as strongly as he felt duty-bound to her love and their home, he knew he had to leave. Desertion would bring with it even more problems.

At the depot, he took her by the hand and kissed her a quick goodbye since the long goodbye had taken place earlier the night before. They held each other tightly as if this might be their last. The children hugged in to surround both of them in a family hug. Even the stoic fourteen-year-old Zech was tearful.

They walked into the depot waiting room and heard the train whistle echo through the woods to the south. Later, outside on the platform, they replayed the moments again as the conductor called everyone aboard.

She watched as William finally turned his head and stepped onto the steaming train. He was in his short-waisted, single-breasted gray jacket with the new soft felt hat which he now preferred over his earlier soldier's cap. He no longer wished to wear his longer tailed coat, and it was worse for the wear, anyway. She would try to mend it into shape in case he needed it later that winter.

William found a seat near a window to catch one more glimpse of his family, waving. He waved as the train moved backwards on the spur to Walker Mills.

She gathered the children, and they all turned their backs to the departing train. He knew what she was doing, but Little Laura looked again and waved before Mary turned her back around.

He felt a little mirth. Mary still believed in the superstition that if one watches someone leave, it meant that one would never see them again. He frowned and looked away as the train moved south.

It was hard leaving Mary again. Though there were people to talk with, she was on his mind as he moved north, feeling bereft of his responsibilities to take care of his family. They needed him at home, but going AWOL was not an option, not to an Andrews and not to him.

Worried that the war would come to Jefferson County, he knew what happened to local people when overrun by an enemy. He did not want that for his family. He decided he needed to fight the enemy far north to protect his home. Thankful he was that Mary was in Monticello with a home guard to maintain peace and order, though the guard was just old men and young boys, including his own sons Zech and not quite twelve-year-old Jesse, who was tall and looked older than his years

Meantime, the South's shortage of soldiers continued to expand exponentially. President Davis and his cabinet called for more. The Confederacy revised its conscription to include men up to age forty-five. The South was running out of soldiers. In reply, Texas's governor refused the state troops needed in the east because of Texas's problems with Plains Indians and Union forces that threatened Kansas. In addition, North Carolina's governor opposed conscription, which limited the success of recruiters there. Their governor repeatedly opposed Davis because of its perceived state's rights. States' rights were the reason many fought, and now in irony many felt the Confederacy was infringing upon their states' rights as the North had done earlier.

The North had its own problems, too. The South conducted a raid into Ohio called Morgan's Raid, and there were draft riots in New York City. During an earlier four-day standoff, white rioters attacked federal buildings as well as black employees. The draft in the North was hugely unpopular, but the raid in Ohio failed; and Lee's failed strike into Pennsylvania at Gettysburg was still on everyone's minds.

Newspapers in the South claimed a stalemate at Gettysburg, with neither the Rebels nor the North winning. The northern papers, though, said it was a victory, a glorious rout. The North needed a victory, especially after Chancellorsville.

Once at Walker Mills, William took a return stage from there to Troupville in Georgia to catch a train going east to Savannah. In Savannah he caught another train heading west and north to Macon. From Macon he boarded again, going north through Atlanta to Chattanooga, completing a big circle to where he began before his capture in Murfreesboro.

William returned to the 4th Florida Infantry by the end of July 1863. He missed Vicksburg completely (May 18-July 4, 1863).

Western Theater

After losing in the Battle of Jackson, William's unit arrived in Chattanooga by train on September 1st along with the other Florida units who fought in the western theater. William arrived by train later and was glad to see all of them, especially his son James in the 1st-3rd whose leader was now Monticello's own 'Colonel' William Dilworth, who never forgot Mary's plea to watch after James. It was a joyful reunion between William and James, especially with all the questions from everyone—including the rest of Mary's family—her uncle, brothers, and cousins. All were hungry for news from Monticello.

The 1st-3rd and the 4th Florida units, along with the 47th Georgia (the counties around Savannah) and the 60th North Carolina (counties around Asheville) made up Stovall's Brigade under Breckenridge's Division of Hill's Corps. The other Florida units were in Preston's Division under Trigg's Brigade.

From the others, William learned that his brother-in-law Arch had entered French's Division Hospital in Enterprise, Mississippi around mid-July. So many places they had never heard of, but this one appeared to be east of Jackson.

Gone was William's knapsack. He had long left it behind with his change of clothes. He realized the inconvenience and that battlefield opportunities always existed for obtaining new clothes. The dead did not require theirs, and if need be, he would send home for more. It was too inconvenient to carry around a change of clothes. He would wear what he had until they were no longer needed. Washing with hot water was not to be, and a cold-water wash was useless. It did not clean, nor did it get rid of the vermin.

He was down to one blanket. Two was inconvenient. This blanket he kept rolled lengthwise with his rubber cloth rolled around it. He tied the ends together and made a loop, carrying it on his left shoulder and hanging under his right arm. He still had his haversack, and it carried what used to stay in his knapsack. Now he kept his caps and cartridges in his pockets.

He noticed and had taken under his wing, though, a young recruit that had joined his unit while he was in Monticello. The boy from Gretna near Quincy was lost, inexperienced, and lacked proper clothing and other necessities. They nicknamed him Coon because he was always scrounging and foraging for his food. Somehow he survived, but William started making requests of Mary and his family for help. Coon needed socks and so much more. Hattie knitted him a pair of socks, and Sarah made him a scarf for when it grew cold again.

Also new in camp was much cursing. Earlier there had been some cursing, but most southern men refrained, probably because of their mamas. Well, ladies were no longer around, and swearing became universal. Nearly every man cursed now.

While William traveled to Chattanooga, his friends and family of the 5th Florida fought in another battle at Second Manassas in the eastern theater, again on the stream of Bull Run. The Aucilla Guards must not have seen as much action this time, but some came home maimed while others never came home at all. William's nephew William E. Goff was there but in another company. He survived, too.

William's big news, though, was about his nephews Napoleon and William, his brother Jesse's sons. Both boys joined the Union's 5th Tennessee Cavalry, Company B, which was raised locally. William knew this was not what his brother wanted, but Tennessee was occupied. People had to do whatever they could to survive.

These weren't his family's only sons to fight for the North. His sister Julia's son John F. Pic had joined the North's navy.

Why was Chattanooga so important?

Earlier, Union officers noticed "Atlanta" stamped on many confiscated articles from Confederate armies. In addition, Chattanooga, called the gateway to the deep South, was a vital rail hub with rails going north to Knoxville, west to Nashville, and south to Atlanta. Besides its role as a Tennessee River port, Chattanooga manufactured iron and coke. It sat between Lookout Mountain, Missionary Ridge, Raccoon Mountain, and Stringer's Ridge. William thought it a fine town, though by this time of the war it was full of military units and hospitals, food shortages, and rumors of a spy around every corner.

The Union General Rosecrans' orders were to push into Georgia, but first he had to take Chattanooga. He sent three infantry corps by three separate roads, the only three suitable for such movements. On the right was McCook's division, who moved into southwest Alabama. In the center was Thomas' division, who moved immediately below the Tennessee/Georgia line.

On the left was Crittenden's division, who moved directly toward Chattanooga around Lookout Mountain. This is how the north planned to take Chattanooga, but Bragg evacuated the city ahead of the three corps. William and his unit evacuated, too. The Army of Tennessee fled south early in September.

At Home

Elsewhere, battle upon battle on the high seas intensified, and Mr. Lincoln's naval blockade began to prove effective. The scarcity of supplies (due to captured munitions and the blockade runners) left the South's armies minimally supplied. Southerners suffered reduced rations, lack of medicines, shortages of uniforms, shoes, and boots; but at home the shortage was worse for Mary and the children as prices steadily rose.

In April the southern authorities made Major E. C. Simkins responsible locally for collecting the Confederate Tax in kind. In fact, the US Marshal Elias Blackburn was from Jefferson County, too; he was appointed chief collector of the taxes for the entire state. The taxation, though, caused many Jefferson County merchants to cease doing business. Those who remained open were Marvin Bros, John S. Divine's store, J. B. Collins & Company, Bird & Co., J. T. Budd's Store, and Partridge & Randolph. Denham & Palmer still hauled freight for the county from Station #17 on the Savannah Railroad to Monticello.

The farmers in the county now mostly only grew corn, rice, sugar cane, potatoes, and peas. Their government asked them to grow what they needed. Unlike food, the government did not need cotton. Though a common practice was to distill corn into corn whiskey, the state legislature banned the manufacture of private whiskey without a permit. Still it continued because the Confederate Navy was the biggest buyer of Florida's brewed corn liquor. Also, Rebel doctors needed it to offer the wounded in field hospitals to ease their pain.

Many, like Mary's Uncle James, also raised hogs and cattle. If you lacked cash, the Impressment Act provided for transferring large quantities of supplies from individuals to the Confederate government at prices below the market rate. Farmers paid their taxes in corn, beef, pork, rice, potatoes, peas, molasses, sugar, and hay. Commissary agents took control of the in-kind payments. They shipped some of these immediately to the war department, but they also kept some in commissary warehouses, including one in Monticello.

Meantime, the Confederate government adopted a tariff on imports of fifteen percent, but the money it raised was negligible. The Union blockade minimized commercial traffic, and people seldom paid the taxes, especially on the smuggled goods. Lacking the money to fight a war, the South began printing money, which simply led to higher inflation. Its economy was being strangled by the blockade and the raids from the north.

Transportation was being stymied. Where the South's waterways and coastal access usually made for cheap transportation of its products, the North systematically took those away. Now gone was the mighty Mississippi River and its avenue of commerce.

Railroads in the South did not all use a standard gauge. This disparity required freight to be portaged into wagons to connect with other railroads. Delays were frequent and lost freight common. This was the norm in Vicksburg, New Orleans, Montgomery, Wilmington, and Richmond even before New Orleans and Vicksburg fell. Also, there were few parallel rails, so using the railroads to get around the blockade was useless. Losing the South's cotton, their primary source of income, caused the railroads to suffer economically. By mid-1863, the railroads in effect came under control of the South's military.

Western Theater

Unfortunately, William got to his unit immediately before a great battle, the first major battle of the war fought in Georgia and what would become the second highest number of casualties for the entire war. Georgia was now a major target, and the South knew what it had to protect.

Many would describe this battle as a bloodbath, the most significant defeat for the North in the western theater. Of Mary's family, over twenty family members of various kin, including her husband, a son, cousins, and a brother, would fight in it. One would not return home.

When Bragg surrendered Chattanooga, the Union thought the demoralized general was gone when in fact Bragg camped south of

Chattanooga less than twenty miles away in Georgia. Rosecrans guessed wrong and ordered his three corps south—McCook to break Bragg's railroad supply line at Resaca, Georgia; Crittenden to turn south in pursuit of Bragg; and Thomas to continue toward La Fayette where, unknown to Rosecrans, sat Bragg's army waiting like a spider in its web.

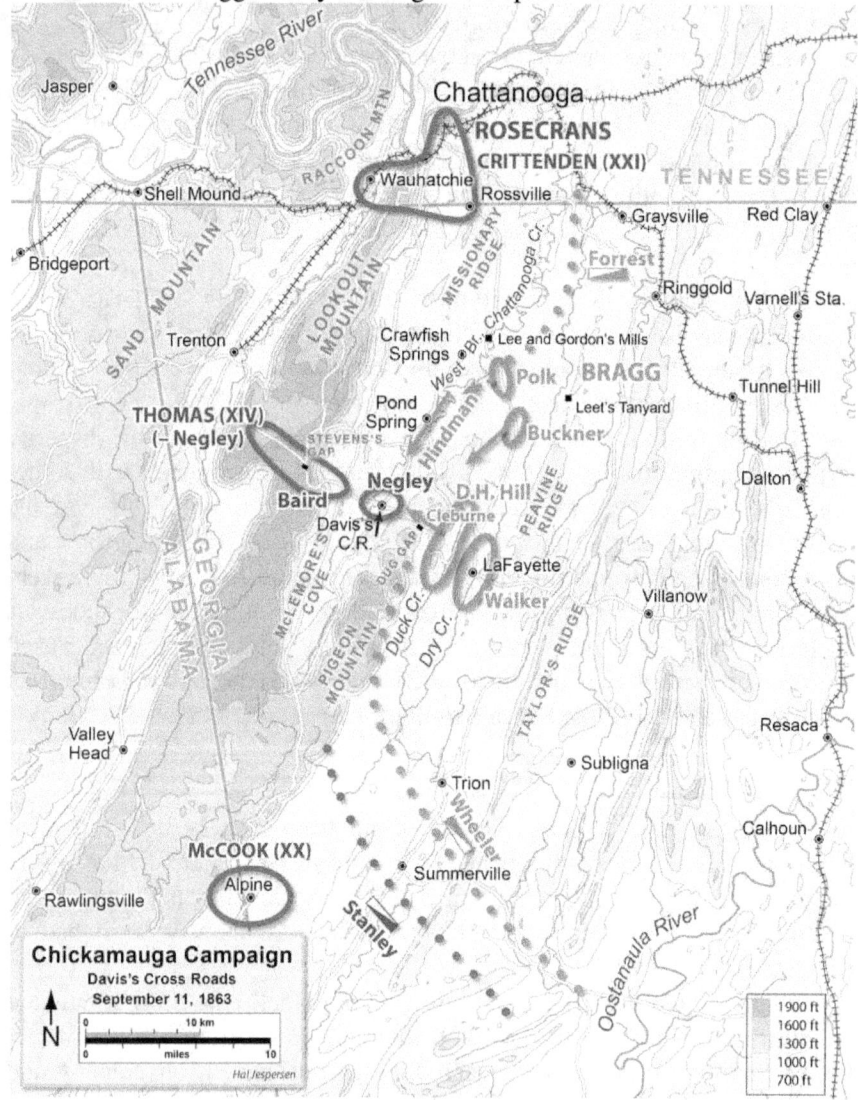

Chickamauga Campaign, Wikipedia. Map by Hal Jespersen, www.posix.com/ CW

In the meantime, Bragg received new orders to reoccupy Chattanooga, an order so important that General Longstreet came down from the Army of Northern Virginia to provide aid. General Longstreet brought none of the Florida units from the Virginia front.

As Longstreet made his way south, Bragg, who commanded 69,000 men, marched his army north on September 17 where together they engaged the enemy near a stream called Chickamauga Creek. Many marched barefooted.

Again, Mary suffered the torture of the damned, expecting any day to hear she was a widow, her children fatherless, or that she was the mother of a dead son.

#

Chapter 7

Smoke, Bedlam, & One Continuous Din of Noise
September to December 1863

Western Theater

At first Thomas's corps pursued Bragg, but Bragg was twelve hours ahead. What was missed, though, was an opportunity for Bragg to turn and take Thomas' corps. But through miscommunication, illnesses, and a general failure to follow orders by his officers, the Confederates did not do it, and Bragg lost a great opportunity.

On the next day, the Army of Tennessee crept down Chickamauga Creek, which ultimately meanders up to the Tennessee River near downtown Chattanooga. Some say Chickamauga is a Cherokee word meaning "river of death," possibly named after a smallpox epidemic among the area's former inhabitants. Lines of soldiers, like they were moving through a maze, passed through the hills, mountains, forests, thickets, and along the creek.

William was in one such line. Ahead was the 3rd Florida Infantry and his son James. It was fall, but most of the colorful leaves were gone. A brisk breeze moaned through the pine woods and across the rolling hills and thickets.

Later, their officers ordered them to stop, and both the 3rd and 4th Florida spent the rest of the morning constructing breastworks near Glass Mill on the extreme left of the entire Confederate army. They worked and were not quiet.

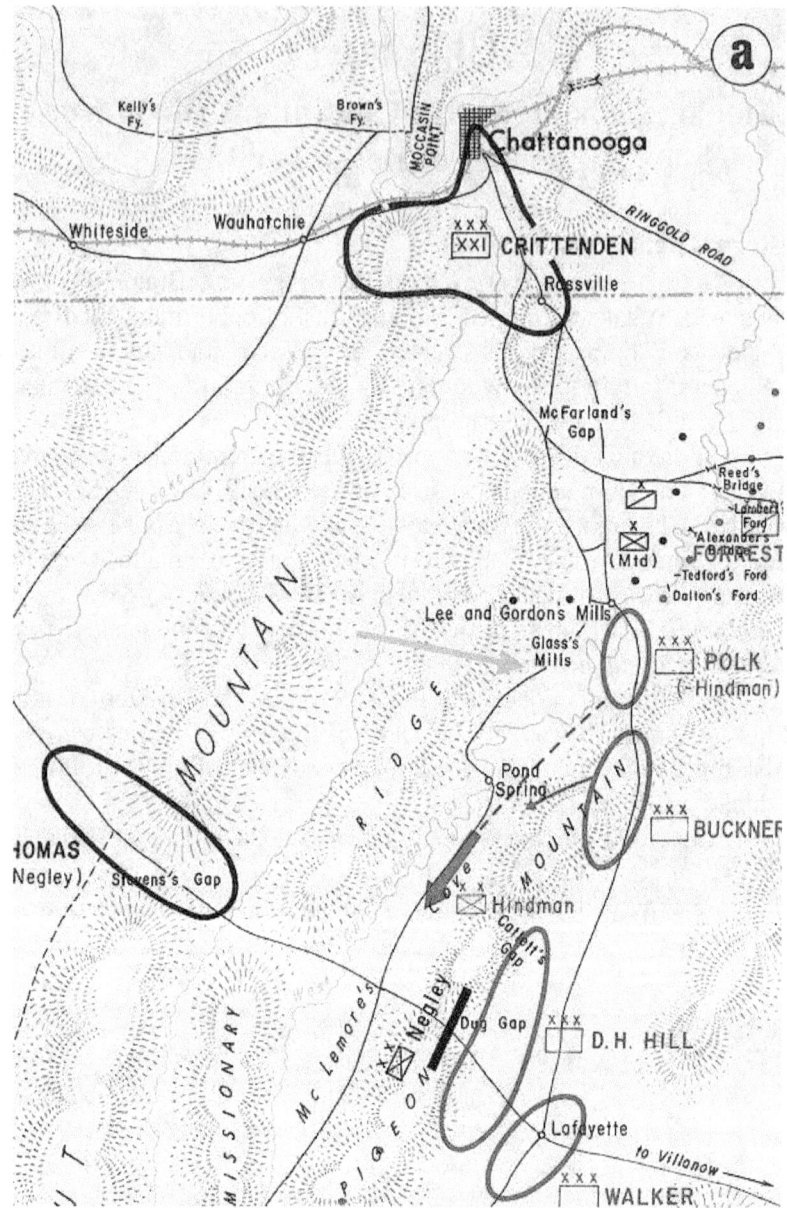

Glass Mill is indicated by a green arrow. The West Point atlas of the Civil War, West Point - Department of History (The American Civil War) and Library of Congress

William spent the morning pushing logs into place along the banks of the recently dug trenches. All around him, the men worked to form a line in the woods. His mind wandered to stories about food shortages at home. That night around their fire, the discussion went to their womenfolk. Said Arch, "They pray for us constantly and shower blessings on our heads. Prayers for our welfare and safety."

Added Berry, "I'm always amazed how they anticipate our wants."

Another said, "Mine writes so that I can see her smiles and words of cheer."

Added William, "While in the hospital, I appreciated my male nurses, but it was the women who cooled my fevered brow and took moments to listen." The male nurses were all business.

One man raised his coffee cup. "Here's to the mothers and daughters of Florida!"

"Here, here," added their collective voices. They fell into a silence, a silence as they missed their womenfolk.

Morale was low. William and his campmates struggled to keep their spirits up. There had been bad news all summer for the South. Gettysburg was a debacle, Vicksburg fell, and Union gunboats now controlled the Mississippi. Forthwith, Bragg fled Chattanooga, leaving Tennessee to the Federals, which demoralized William and the rest of the army.

The 4th Florida heard somewhere else the beginning of a battle. First came the tatting of skirmishers, and then a crescendo that only meant they were fighting elsewhere in earnest on the creek. Bragg's first engagement in battle began by hammering the North's left front, but the Federal line held.

Bragg renewed his assault the following day on September 19th, the first day of the actual battle. Light skirmishes developed into an artillery duel, but casualties were light.

Late that afternoon, William's unit received orders to move to the right toward Lee and Gordon's Mill. Later, after the movement, William's company rested near the mill until Breckenridge ordered them to move again, this time even farther right past the mill far from the breastworks they had just built.

Bragg would hold them in reserve the entire day, but William could hear the carnage elsewhere. It was cool but not cold. The sounds of the skirmish reverberated through the hills and forests while the 4th waited their turn and William worried James was fighting.

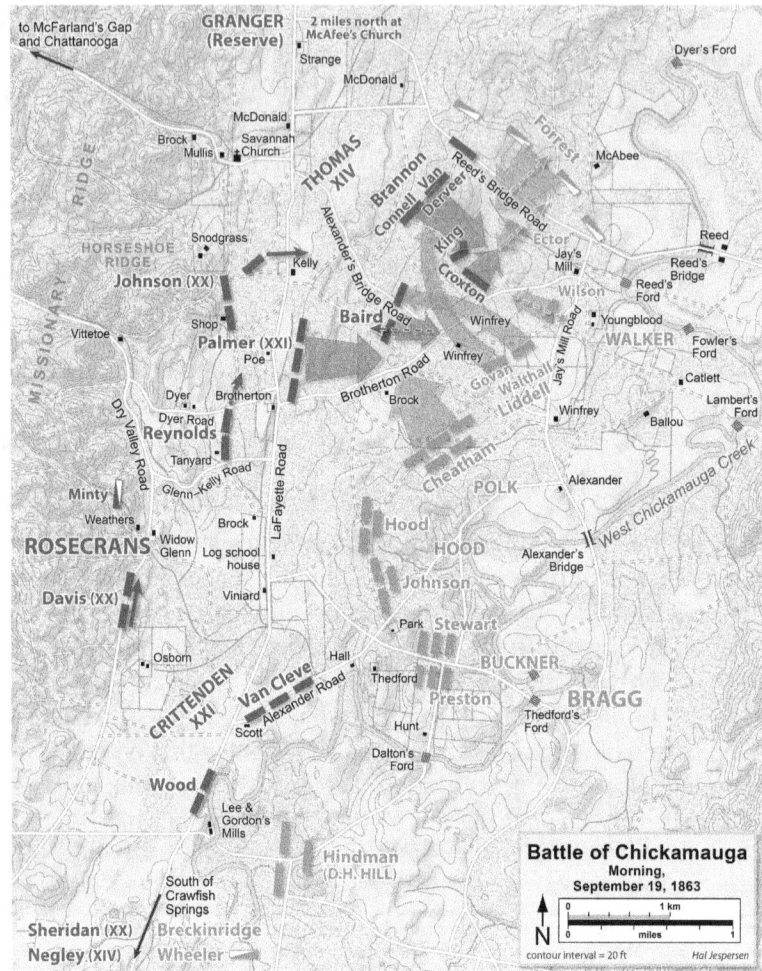

Battle of Chickamauga, Morning, Wikipedia. Drawn in Adobe Illustrator CS5 by Hal Jespersen.

William looked around him at his comrades-in-arms, some with arms grounded leaning against trees or prone and resting with their guns right at hand, waiting for their next command. He and his tentmate sat on the ground with their legs stretched out, leaning against each other's backs facing in opposite directions, each using the other for a backrest. William faced woods smoky from the firing, and the smoke stung his nostrils. He felt his friend sigh.

The gently rolling hills and deep woods of Chickamauga Creek posed a problem because no officer above the brigadier could see all of his command at once. It would be a battlefield where not only did a commander not know exactly where his enemy was, but he even lost track of his own men as soon as they entered a forest or rounded a hill. By the end of the day, the fighting tore and smoked the woods, making visibility even worse. Like Antietam, Chickamauga would be a soldier's battle.

With the North's superior numbers and firepower, they pushed the Southern line back. The cannons thundered, and plumes of smoke slithered into the sky. Added to it was the crack of trees as they snapped and burst. Fallen trees posed problems for troop movements.

Around 11 am, the rumbling stopped, and a hush fell over the pines. William heard the cries of the wounded and the rustling of moving units. Under orders, he and his unit remained where they were.

They held them to fight another day. William and his unit even thought that others had overlooked them. During the evening of the 19th, Rosecrans rushed to send troops to his embattled left, creating a real breach in his line. Breckenridge camped near the Lee and Gordon's Mill that night, close to the breach.

In contrast, Bragg was pleased by the day's end that they had held the ground, though the enemy outnumbered them. What he did, though, was give Rosecrans an opportunity to locate the Rebel positions. And there were more missed opportunities.

If Bragg had sent heavy reinforcements to Walker, he could have rolled up the Union's left. Instead, Walker lost over twenty percent of his strength while Stuart and Cleburne lost thirty percent of theirs. Also gone was any opportunity of a surprise blow to Rosecrans.

That evening, Bragg reorganized his Army of Tennessee into two wings, the left led by Longstreet, who had recently arrived, and the right wing by Lt. General Leonidas Polk, who was also called the "fighting bishop." Under Polk was General John C. Breckenridge and William's unit.

Meanwhile, at the camp that night, William's thoughts were in a dark place. He and several of the Monticello boys from the 3rd talked over their campfire, sharing rations and mentally preparing for the job to do the next morning.

Mostly there was much laughter, and it helped him. He noticed soldiers laughed far more than they wept. Because they were in reserve today, they knew their time to move to the front would come tomorrow. In the distant firelight, he could see Dilworth and the other officers huddled over a map. Couriers and orderlies rode in and set off at full speed with verbal orders and reports of unit locations.

William and the other men talked about home, women, news from home, anything to pass the time and keep their thoughts away from the job before them.

Unfortunately, William bedded down with his mind still troubled. He wondered if it portended his own demise, or would it be one of the other Monticello men? He slipped off to sleep as he reached to make sure his final letter was safe in his pocket.

That night, William and his mates were to the right of General Patrick Cleburne's division and the extreme right flank of the Confederate line of battle. What he didn't know was Breckenridge received orders during the night to begin the battle with an assault on Thomas at first light.

While William's regiment rested, Bragg moved men and increased his firepower to the North's right flank, opposite William's flank, adding the recently arrived Longstreet's men.

At Home

Mary awoke to sobbing in her bed. Laura had an earache. Six-year-old Laura, who often slept with her, was crying in her sleep and pulling at her ear. The night was warm, and Mary got her up, lit the lamp, and the two of them crept out to the kitchen. In her long white cotton nightgown, she set Laura at the table in the pale golden light and handed her a rag.

She told Laura, "Take this and gently blow your nose several times." Laura did as she was told. Mary took a small tin and sat at the table.

In the tin she spooned a little bacon grease and set it over the lamp to warm it. Laura in her white muslin nightgown kept blowing her nose.

Mary took a little of the warmed grease on her little finger and gently pushed it into Laura's ear. The warmth provided relief. She put the tin near Laura and said, "Now you put some on your own finger and do it yourself."

Laura looked up at her mother as she pushed her index finger into her own ear, "Mama, it's already stopped hurting."

Meantime, Mary pushed her finger into some cotton batting to make a depression. She replied, "Good. Now we need to do one more thing so your earache doesn't come back." Mary took a pinch or two of pepper and added it, filling the depression.

After rolling the batting into a ball, she dipped it into the oil and inserted it into Laura's ear. She said, "You hold this in your ear, and let's go to bed."

Holding the lantern as they walked onto the dogtrot, she said again, "Don't let it fall out. When we get to bed, I'll wrap a scarf around your head to keep it in."

In her bedroom, sleep didn't come. Mary had heard earlier they were fighting near Chattanooga, and she knew both the 3rd and 4th Florida regiments were there. After a while she got up, wrapped herself in her woolen shawl, and walked to the back porch. The moon gave just enough light to lay the backyard in shadows. She sat on the porch and sighed. Sometimes the peacefulness of the outdoors gave her a relief not found otherwise.

Western Theater

On September 20th, the plan called for fighting to begin at dawn, but miscommunication again prevailed, and the Confederates lost the opportunity. Once more, Bragg showed he was a skilled tactician, but his inability to lead men impeded his maneuvering. His officers failed to follow his orders.

The delay was good for Rosecrans because it gave him time to build more defensive breastworks in the few hours after dawn. With Longstreet's reinforcements arriving during the evening, the South now outnumbered the North. Rosecrans knew he must remain in place on the defensive.

So William awoke to the tatting of axes and hammers far off in the woods. His tentmate stoked the fire under a pot of boiling water for coffee. William crawled from the tent to brisk mountain air and fog along the banks of the Chickamauga. A thick frost lay on the ground. The fog was extra thick because of the lingering smoke from the previous day's battle. It filtered through the trees surrounding their camp. Using his cloth-sided canteen, he cupped its cold water in his hands and washed his face.

When his unit lined up later to receive their rations, Colonel Dilworth, in the center, spoke a few words of encouragement to his men. He reminded them that there were thousands of Southern people praying for them this morning and that God was listening. He said, "I want you to remember that God loves every one of you no matter what, and let us pray for ourselves now."

Dilworth removed his hat and dropped to one knee as his unit followed suit. Instantly every uncovered head bowed in reverence as their hands clasped their rifles. Their bayonets gleamed in the morning sun, and their ragged flag drooped because there was no wind. Dilworth's voice in prayer drifted through the surrounding forest.

It did not escape William that for some of these boys they would never again hear words of prayer upon terrestrial ground. He wondered if he himself would hear it again. When Dilworth finished there followed a low murmured "Amen." Dilworth had them stand, then told them to go forth, be brave, be men, and remember their purpose: they were defending their motherland from an invader who might push all the way to Florida, splitting the heart of Dixie. He dismissed them and they went to their tents and fires, awaiting further orders.

Later that morning, the first brigade to engage the bluebellies in battle was Brigadier General Benjamin Helm's Orphan Brigade of Kentuckians, forming the left of Breckenridge's division east of the Kelly Field. His brigade moved forward in search of their enemy when the battle opened with great fury.

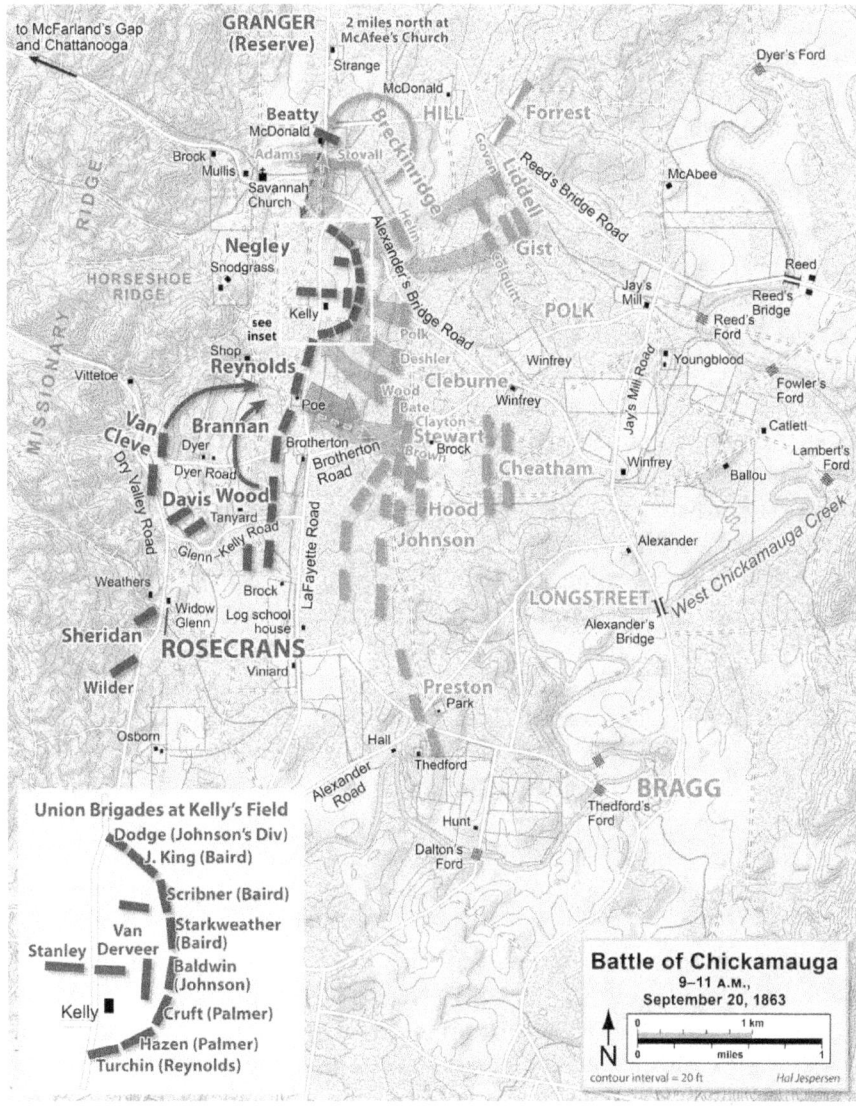

Battle of Chickamauga, Day 2, Wikipedia. Drawn in Adobe Illustrator CS5 by Hal Jespersen

The enemy was behind breastworks, strongly fortified with three lines of entrenchments made of fallen timber and rocks and concealed in thick undergrowth. Helm's men could not break through, and it was a third attempt that took Helm's life.

Still, Helm's Brigade was only the center, and the left and right were more successful—two brigades which flanked the enemy and caused the

Yankees to shift their fire 180 degrees because their enemies were now in their rear.

Right of Helm's Brigade, William in Stovall's Brigade moved forward about 9:30 am. Embedded within one of two Breckenridge brigades, they reached the La Fayette Road when Breckenridge realized his division was beyond the Union's left. He quickly faced his two brigades from the west to the south on either side of the road and led them to assault Thomas's left flank and rear. William was in this position.

They were to move into action following the unit on their right against the lone Union brigade of Negley's division, which was quickly moving to Thomas's increasingly fortified far left flank, a position east of La Fayette Road and near its intersection south of Reed's Bridge Road.

Though William's brigade faced increasing numbers of blue coats, they didn't have to push headlong into action. The northern fire was fierce, but Stovall and Adam's brigades avoided tremendous loss of life.

Negley's division at the rear of Thomas's position had been quickly moving into place when the fighting began, but Stovall's and Adam's brigades seized the opportunity and attacked around 10:30 am before Negley got into position. The two Confederate brigades advanced to a tree line bordering the north edge of Kelly Field, catching Negley's unsuspecting men and tearing them to shreds.

William heard the singing sounds of shots and shells—the whistling of bullets. Focused on his task, he never even thought about the one in wait for him. It only lasted a few hours, but to William it was an eternity. Everywhere, men moved forward through the smoke, dust, and bursting of shells.

By this time in the war, William had become adept at eying his surroundings, keeping an eye out for fences, trees, ditches, and rocks, all valuable in providing cover. All around him were the sounds of roaring Napoleon twelve-pounders and the whiz of minis flying by his head. As any good soldier, he had learned to guard his life and yield it only at the call of duty.

Battle of Chickamauga, Confederate line advancing uphill through forest toward Union line, by Alfred Waud, Wikimedia Commons

Within an hour, in the middle of the incessant roar of artillery and musketry, William and the others noticed that the Northern line was fading into the woods and hills. They were retreating.

Somehow, he heard the order to move forward as Stovall's Brigade, along with two others, flanked Thomas's Corps, rolling up the Federal line. He told Mary in a letter later that the musketry was not in single shots or even repeated volleys but one great fearful continuous din of noise; he did not know how he heard anything above the roar.

He and his division, though, did as ordered, while most of the battle still sounded off to the south of them. He and the men at a run pushed the retreaters into the forest, slowing to a trot, trodding over bodies, and every so often the enemy turned to pepper them with bullets.

Unfortunately, for several of the units, the terrain was unsuited for this flanking movement. The thick forest made it impossible to see where the enemy retreated. For the 4th, it was smoke, bedlam, and a wall of thick timber. They hardly saw beyond their rifle barrels.

At Home

In her living room with several ladies sitting in a semicircle before the fireplace, Mary listened to Ann Lightsey. "Those deserters from Taylor

County continue to terrorize folks. Mostly the planters are getting involved because of the number of slaves they carry off,
but they've been stealing cattle, and no farmer is safe from their bands."

Added Rebecca Sledge, "We heard yesterday that Finegan has ordered Marshal Blackburn to offer them amnesty to join Florida organizations."

Blackburn was unsuccessful, though, so the governor sent state militias to rout them out; but they discovered what the Indian fighting militias did twenty-five years earlier: Florida's dense swamps and jungle-like hammocks proved impenetrable. Taylor County's dark swamps held millions of places to hide. And just above the swamps, the flatwoods were immense stretches of lowlands covered with pines, gallberry, and palmetto. Travelers often found trouble securing a spot of high, dry land on which to camp.

Western Theater

The two armies traded round for round until the Confederates had positive results, but new Federal troops came to Negley's rescue. A surge of bluebellies with fixed bayonets emerged into the frenzy of the battle. Breckenridge's line collapsed, and the enemy chased them all the way to Reed's Bridge Road. Thomas's line had held after all.

Quickly, they brought forward Gist's Brigade, a brigade that marched all night and whose colonel thought it was in no condition to attack. They placed his brigade where Helm's Brigade had crumbled. They were there to aid Stovall and Adams but were unable to penetrate the Union line. In the melee, they killed Colonel Peyton Colquitt. By this time, Breckenridge had fought himself out on this portion of the field; and it, too, was an opportunity lost.

As the northern part of the line was failing because of the heavy fighting there, Thomas continued to pull units from the southern part to aid them. By noon, Longstreet had his part of the Northern line on the run.

Together the opposite flanks drove a third of Rosecrans's army, including himself, from the field back toward the city of Chattanooga; the two-thirds left in the center under Thomas held strong as the South rolled up the North's left and right flanks to tighten the noose.

Later, William again found himself in reserve, four lines back, as they moved toward La Fayette Road to flank Thomas's corps once more. By noon, the attack on the Confederate right flank fizzled, but William could hear spurts of hot battle along the line in the distance, where there were onward dashes of artillery and mounted men, distant shouts, dust, smoke, and the fire of arms, whistling balls, grapeshot, and bursting shells.

Now, like all good Floridians, William sought the shade of the forest and gazed upon an open field flooded in sunlight. He learned to rest and still his mind when he could. His troublesome thoughts for the moment, though, were: when would this horrid battle end? He listened to the pounding of the cannons, knowing his enemy and brethren were getting pounded beyond.

Where he was, the woods were still lush and unbroken. There was a breeze; except for the hell beyond, it was cool and comfortable here. He tried to still his mind and take a moment to admire nature's beauty, sucking in his surroundings. Except for the cacophony of pain and suffering beyond, he could imagine himself just on another outing. He thought about Mary's latest letter and how Hattie longed for her own separate page, a separate missive from him just for her.

Mary thought their daughter needed to better understand the price of paper, but he thought he could accommodate his daughter another way. Maybe a separate paragraph all her own. Maybe he should do it for all his children. Thus he tried to still his mind with these thoughts of his family far away instead of worrying about what was to come here on the battlefield.

Still, there was this sickly smell in the air, the smell of blood with its stench. This meant there were bodies, bodies to be taken care of later. He tried again to quiet his mind.

He received word that George Walker had fallen. Someone thought this George was his brother-in-law, but this was George Walker, son of James Sims Walker, a distant cousin of Mary's. Still, he asked for temporary leave from his unit and moved back and parallel of their lines. He heard the cries and screams and met the walking wounded retreating. A few required his help walking on their own.

Still, he tried to keep moving. Men running with stretchers rushed past him and, as always, the worst injured were shot through the chest.

He found George in a hospital near Alexander's Bridge too far gone to be moved into surgery. The house's yard and hallways near the bridge overflowed with injured soldiers. It took him a bit to find him and, blessedly, George was unconscious. He asked the doctor if there was any hope, but none was given, so William checked George's pockets for any letters, sat with him the few minutes until he passed, and returned to his company to look for the rest of the men from the 3rd Florida.

What he did not see on his way was a center that was holding and a southern wing that was winning. Longstreet had the bluebellies on the run. Most of the Army of the Cumberland was fleeing to Chattanooga, including General Rosecrans himself.

Only the north side in the middle was still holding, but by 4:30 pm on the union side, General Thomas received orders to take command of the army and begin a general retreat. On the Confederate side, Preston's division surrounded three remaining Union units and took them prisoners, forcing the surrender.

William's comrades in the Southern army pushed until that night when the rest of the Northern army of the Cumberland slipped away, retiring into the city and leaving the Confederates to occupy the surrounding heights of Lookout Mountain and Missionary Ridge.

What William or any of the rest of the Army of Tennessee failed to understand was that the Union army had slipped from their grasp. They did not pursue and failed to inflict the significant further damage that could have been done, but also the South stayed put mainly because of inadequate supplies such as wagons, horses, and pontoon boats needed to cross the Tennessee River.

What the Confederates seized, though, was the opportunity to reorganize and gather equipment left by the Union army. Found were large quantities of ammunition and arms left behind.

Later, it was big news that the Confederate Kentucky brigade lost their leader, Helms himself, who was the brother-in-law of President Abraham Lincoln, the brother-in-law who fought for the South. William also heard that Helm's first brigade continued fighting until later in the evening. They returned to camp with prisoners. Only darkness stopped the day of fighting—a bloody day.

Earlier that morning, the confusion on the Confederate right reflected the failures of command; overlapping formations and exposed gaps betrayed a lack of coordination. Later, to rescue survivors from Gist's Brigade, someone brought forward the Walker Corps after Colquitt and the rest of his brigade suffered heavy casualties during their failed advance—Colquitt himself being among the casualties. Their advance resulted from a gap between Breckenridge, under whom William waited under Stovall.

Unfortunately, the Confederate victory cost them over 18,000 casualties—2,312 killed, over 14,000 wounded, and 1,400 captured or missing. Several Confederate generals were killed, including Helms, James Deshler, and Preston Smith. All the enlisted men and the officers were casualties that the South could ill afford. The Union's losses were less at over 16,000.

William that night probably penned a letter to Mary, asking her to ride out and tell George Walker's family that he was there as George slipped away. (See Appendix 4 for information on the four George Walkers.) Added to the letter, he also told her they gravely wounded Michael Raysor. The Raysors too were from Aucilla. Because of his wounds, Michael Raysor passed away by the following January. They also wounded Howell Wolfe.

The next day came an assessment of the men left on the battlefield. There were quick burials, with bodies being wrapped in their blankets and laid in shallow graves. It was the kids of eighteen and younger that got William the most—those boys who never lived their lives to sire children and to grow old with all the wonder that life offers.

William knew, though, that something else went missing on that battlefield. Though they won this battle, there was a sullenness that followed, resulting from the loss of hope. He knew that though the Army of the Cumberland had vanished north, it would return repeatedly, and each time with reinforcements from the vast numbers of Northern men, numbers far greater than what lived in the South.

That night, while in the trenches, rats crawled over him and the other soldiers. The floor of the trench became like glue from the earlier rain. Still exhausted, he somehow found comfort and slept.

Chickamauga was an empty victory, and for the first time William questioned if it was worth it—especially for all the lives lost, this George, Standley, Archibald, and his brother-in-law the other George, who left neither a wife nor children to remember him.

He added to a letter he had started earlier. Trying to keep things light and thinking maybe humor or good news was in order, he wrote:

September 20, 1863
South of Chattanooga, Tennessee

Dearest Mary,

Today we finished a long battle, and our enemy is on the run back to Chattanooga, and I have good news to report. We have a plan to obliterate that demon pest, the lowly lice. Someone discovered that all we need to do is stretch our garments by inserting a stiff brush into them and hold them over a blazing fire until almost hot enough to burn. It took us a little time, but we may have exterminated the vermin. Sleep is so much easier without the biting buggers.

He stopped writing and looked away, where he could see the flicker of fires in the trees above and hear the soft murmurings of his brigade. Exhausted, his age got the better of him, and he slipped off to sleep thinking about his children long before the camp quieted into slumber. He failed to finish his letter.

The Union army retreated within the strong defensive works of Chattanooga built earlier by the South, a tight three-mile-long semicircle around the city. Meanwhile, the South weighed whether to outflank, directly assault, or starve out the Federals. The flanking option wasn't possible because of the Tennessee River and a loss of pontoons, wagons, and ammo. A direct assault was not possible either for the same reasons and because the enemy was well-fortified thanks to the South's earlier work to defend the city. Therefore the Southern army established a siege line around Chattanooga, trying to starve the Union forces into surrendering. Problem is, the South's rations were poor, too.

William was about to enter what became known later as the Chattanooga Campaign. His regiment in Bragg's Army of Tennessee occupied the high ground around Chattanooga, where they sat for the next two months. But it was two months of poor rations and no hope for better food.

The high ground here included both Missionary Ridge and Lookout Mountain, both of which had excellent views of the city. In the distance, William could see the Tennessee River flowing north out of the city, as well as the Union supply lines. He couldn't remember the last time he had had beef.

One problem that William couldn't see was the trouble existing between Bragg and his leadership, who quarreled amongst themselves. In late September, the distracted Bragg relieved both Hindman and Polk from command. Subsequently, on October 4th, twelve of Bragg's senior generals sent a petition to President Davis, asking for the removal of Bragg himself.

The campfires were becoming even more important in the cool crisp north Georgia mountains. One evening in early October, several of Mary's cousins, her brother Jess, and other Monticello men sat around the fire, passing a jug of rye mash.

The liquid warmed William's throat as it slid down, taking the chill off. Jess Walker, his brother-in-law, said, "Did any of you see the president? He was here today. I heard he looked tired and thin." No one had seen him, for they had all been building breastworks.

Jess added, "I heard he was here to check on Bragg, as Bragg's reputation is being questioned." William looked at Jess and around at the circle of men, each one with their blanket around their shoulders, but most of them were looking at their shoes or staring at the fire. No one wanted to look at each other or to face what was becoming obvious.

He looked at Samuel Pasco, and Pasco met his gaze. Jess looked at Pasco, too. Quietly Pasco broke the silence, speaking in a lowered voice: "Davis was here all right, and there is trouble in the ranks." All eyes were on him because he always had more information, though they knew he didn't always share it.

Jess added, "I heard that Hindman and Polk have been complaining about Bragg's inability to command and the lost opportunities."

Pasco added, "The man has been ill lately, but who wouldn't be? This war is relentless in its savagery."

After that, the conversation died, but morale was low even here amongst friends and family. William couldn't resist thinking about Mary and the children, who were probably sitting at home in the warmth and comfort of the house he had provided for them.

Someone broke the silence and raised his cup in a toast to George. He said, "To George, who is in heaven tonight, who got there in good company." Of course, he meant the Generals Helms, Colquitt, and Jackson.

At his own camp, William noticed a change in his men, a change to an attitude of defeat. Defeat and retreat. That was the problem. As their corporal, he worried about them and felt that what they needed and needed soon was a victory to bring them back.

Lately, he frequently slept under the same blanket with two other men for warmth. The days shortened and the frosty nights lengthened.

The next morning, William crawled out of his tent before daylight and walked nearby to relieve himself. Chilled, he got busy right away, stoking the fire from the banked one the night before. He put on a pot of coffee as his tentmate crawled out of the tent. "Good morning," said William. His colleague stretched and silently headed away from the camp.

William crawled into the tent looking for his "housewife." He had a tear in the seam under his arm, and he planned to repair it. He was getting quite good at using the little tin of thread, pins, buttons, and needles that Mary put together for him.

His mate returned and sat down before the fire, which was already going well, and said, "I've been thinking about the rumors we heard last night about Bragg and his generals."

"Me too," William said. "It's worrisome when leaders bicker."

"Hard to put your confidence in them," replied his colleague.

The plea for the removal of Bragg was for naught, because after visiting the army, President Davis kept Bragg. In retaliation, Bragg relieved Hill and Buckner of their commands. Bragg was losing the confidence of his men from his generals to the lowest rank.

It was no better on the other side, either. Stunned by his army's defeat, Rosecrans seemed unable to take decisive action to lift the siege. The army was feeling its effects, and many horses and mules died. Rations were low.

The only problem, though, for the South was that the Army of the Cumberland still had a supply line that remained open to the southwest. This supply line was not controlled by the Confederates, though it was a tortuous line that stretched nearly sixty miles long into Alabama.

Heavy rains in September washed away mountain stretches of this road, and on October 1st a Confederate cavalry unit intercepted and damaged a train of 800 wagons. By the end of the month, a typical Union soldier's ration in Chattanooga was "four cakes of hard bread and a quarter pound of pork" every three days.

The month of October and most of November was a game of skirmishes and waiting—for both sides. Meanwhile, the 1st/3rd and 4th waited in a makeshift winter camp. They probably steadily worked on their residences there to make them more permanent and livable.

Meanwhile, at home, Vollie's 2nd Battalion kept him waiting. Impatience best described him during these days. In his mind, he was a man, but everyone else knew better. However, the same record listing his age as sixteen and his detachment at home also stated "Manassas Oct. 25, 1863." Since they fought 2nd Manassas earlier, this notation is confusing.

Battle of Missionary Ridge

Rosecrans was relieved of his duties and replaced by a new commander of Union forces named Major General Ulysses S. Grant, a stolid and unemotional man. Grant gave General Thomas the Army of the Cumberland as the North gathered reinforcements, arms, and supplies. Their plan was to seize the lower high ground south of Chattanooga, including the area below Lookout Mountain.

Meanwhile, the quick, nervous, and volatile Major General William Tecumseh Sherman planned a surprise attack against the South's right flank on Missionary Ridge.

In response, Bragg counseled with his leaders on whether to retreat or stand and fight. William's commander advised retreat, but the other leaders disagreed. Bragg ordered more troops to dig in on Missionary Ridge.

Late that afternoon, William's division received its orders to remove themselves from the base of Lookout Mountain and march to the far right of Missionary Ridge, south of Tunnel Hill.

Marching again, thought William. Someone constantly gave orders to move, but the men mostly didn't understand the where, when, and why of it. These were always their questions, but generally their questions went unanswered.

They were a mass of men orderly on the move, but their minds kept pace with their feet. Shrewd guesses were exchanged among the men, and any piece of gleaned information added to the rumors, though these guesses were often wrong.

Initially, though, there was simply the order to "get ready to move." And so it began. The sergeant shouted, "Fall in, fall in!" and there was no time to lose. They quickly rolled blankets, found frying pans, and decided what to leave behind and what was necessary, discovering that one man's junk was another's treasure. In the end, they discarded little. Some camps were easy to leave, but some were not. Those were the ones with straw upon which to sleep, a good spring, firewood nearby, and cool shade. The area around Lookout Mountain provided all four.

Having little word about why or where they were moving, Florida's regiments made the journey in about six hours. At its completion, the men quickly set up camp and fell asleep, exhausted from the night's movement.

Before they left Chickamauga early in November, the 4th Florida was issued pans, jackets and superior army goods, especially the new

English blankets, large enough to cover a full bed. William thought the caps and underclothes miserable, though. He slept better rolled inside the blanket.

Early the next morning on November 23rd, Grant's army seized the lower high ground south of Chattanooga and pushed around to the south of Lookout Mountain in the early hours of dawn. They pushed through the area that Stovall's unit, under William's command, had camped on days before.

Meanwhile, on Missionary Ridge, William woke to dark, low clouds. Everywhere he looked, the fog obscured the forest and rocky outcrops which appeared through differing shades of gray. A drizzle also chilled him to the bone. Better to get up and get moving, he thought. It always warmed him quicker.

The day progressed quietly for them, though they could hear battles elsewhere. This was the hardest part—even harder than making a charge in battle—the sitting around waiting. He knew the fear always left him the minute they ordered him to engage.

Because the battle was so far in the distance, his comrades decided they were tired of all the mundane rations, and several left to forage for something different—maybe a farm woman's well-filled table. One can dream, but the unhappy foragers returned empty-handed and realized that they had traded a certain supper for their uncertain plenty.

Now they were hungry, and the rations were gone. The whining began as they explained, "Well, we have walked over nine miles of these mountains and haven't found a morsel to eat." But the rations were gone. There were none left to share.

They did not know it, but below in the valley, more of Sherman's men crossed the Tennessee River for better position and sat on the hills at the north end of Missionary Ridge. It wasn't long, though, before William's entire camp knew and was making ready for battle. Far south, he heard the battle on Lookout Mountain, a battle that the North would win by the day's end.

Below, Sherman was dug in on the foothills of Missionary Ridge. Opposite Sherman, Cleburne dug in around Tunnel Hill, a hill next to a railroad tunnel for the Chattanooga & Cleveland Rails. William and his unit were a few hundred yards down from Cleburne. Everyone bedded down for the night.

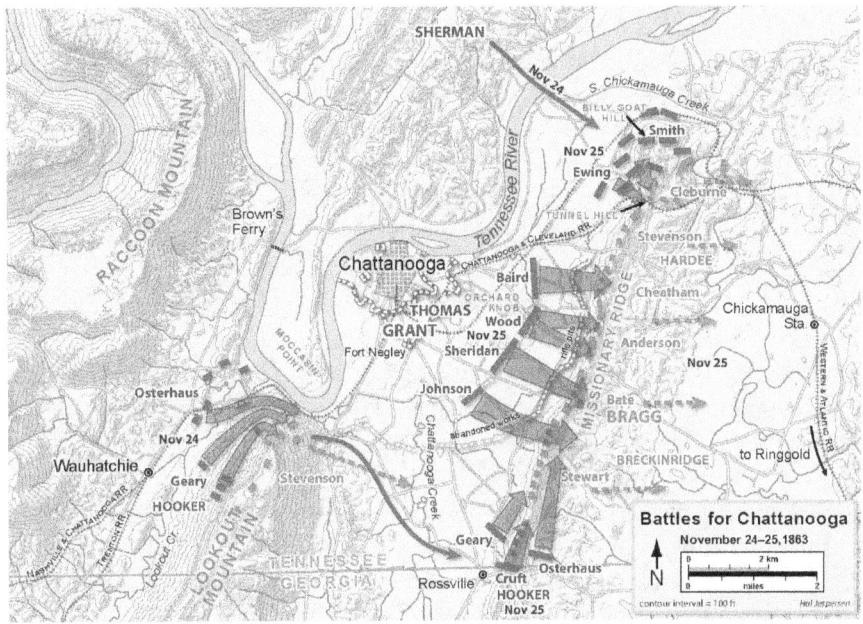

Missionary Ridge, the battles for Chattanooga, November 24–25, 1863, the culmination of the Chattanooga campaign of the American Civil War, Wikipedia

The next morning on November 24th, immediately after they heard the first cannons on Lookout Mountain, Sherman struck, pushing hard toward Tunnel Hill. All along the ridge, the firing began. The skirmishes continued throughout the long day. The battle, though, to William's right on the South's right flank, was the hottest where Sherman was.

Around 4 pm, William heard Cleburne's men routing Sherman's as they charged down the hill from Tunnel Hill. Sherman's men were too tired and low on ammo to resist, and the South took several Federal prisoners. Sherman's attack was a tactical failure, and he lost a little under 2,000 casualties. The North badly miscalculated the terrain.

The South's boldness stemmed from their unawareness that Sherman still held back forces. In the center at the bottom of the ridge, General Thomas's units continued to push. From his left down below, William heard shouting, and the Northern advancing tide yelled "Chickamauga! Chickamauga!" The Union army captured many Confederates in the rifle pits at the base of the ridge; the rest, fearing shots to their backs, started their 300-400-foot climb to the ridge top.

As the Northern soldiers took the Confederate rifle pits, over one hundred Confederate cannons to William's left above on the ridge zeroed in on them. Seeing that it was suicide to stay in the rifle pits, the Northern soldiers began their climb to the top of the ridge, following the escaping Confederates all trying to get away from the cannon fire.

All of this took place while Cleburne skillfully made the terrain work for him to William's right at Tunnel Hill. William and his unit realized they were in the middle of it yet well away from the thick of the two battles.

By the end of November 24th, Sherman had secured a section of Missionary Ridge while Union forces dealt a decisive blow to the Confederates at Lookout Mountain in the center of the line. Only the Confederate left flank at Rossville and the rest of Missionary Ridge, where the Florida regiments waited, remained.

The next day, on the 25th, William woke to a beautiful day with the normal smokiness of the mountains in this region. From their current position above a rocky outcrop, he could see for miles. Rather than think of the carnage to come, he dwelt instead on the beauty of the moment of a sun rising to a new day with new possibilities.

There was little to make ready as they rolled out of their bedrolls in the same soiled clothes they had worn for over a week. He rolled his blanket and used it to sit under his butt on the hard ground. He leaned his gun against the makeshift breastworks they had made the morning before and breakfasted on hardtack and water. With a touch of homesickness, he thought of the smells of Mary's breakfasts and missed her all the more. Sherman's attack on the South's right flank began again, but it would be Thomas's men who would finish the job this day by surging to the top of Missionary Ridge, routing the Army of Tennessee by midafternoon. What looked to be impregnable was simply a narrow ridge top, and Bragg did not have the tactical reserves to protect it. Bragg's defenses were simply a thin crust.

The thin Southern line fought at their front and would eventually fight on their flank. It was about 5:30 pm when Stewart ordered a retreat, and William saw the ridiculousness of the situation. After penetrating the ridge, the Yanks swung their regiments right and left, rolling up the Confederate line.

William's unit was to the south of the breach, and that is where the North turned first. William, caught in a swirl of pandemonium, quickly realized that he and the entire unit were in danger, and they turned and quickly rolled down off the ridge.

Like his other comrades and their leader, they simply melted away down into the woods, running, hopping, and descending. Bullets whizzed through the trees, and William kept running. Adrenaline miraculously gave him the youthfulness needed to keep up and sometimes pass younger men, though he worried about falling and getting trampled. Noticing a fallen man in his path, he reached down and pulled him to safety before others could trample him.

William felt demoralized that they had to turn tail and run again. Cleburne's unit was the last one down, and they fought off the pursuing Sherman, who gave chase until late in the night.

During the evening, they withdrew toward Chickamauga Station on the Western and Atlantic Railroad. (This is where Lovell Airfield is now located.) That night, as the Florida men regrouped and counted themselves, they sadly realized Mary's little brother David was missing.

The family would pay its own price for Missionary Ridge when authorities later sent David to Rock Island, Illinois via Louisville, Kentucky, where he remained for the rest of the war.

The next morning William thought about David and that the North had taken Samuel Pasco, whom he learned was missing and a prisoner. He also heard from the 3rd that they killed Charles Ulmer as he carried the colors of his regiment.

So many Jefferson County lives lost in this war, and when would it end? Those were weary questions he pushed far into his mind as he followed his unit in a single line on a gravely road going south—a movement he would repeat many times in the months ahead.

Eastern Theater

Meanwhile, the Aucilla Guards in the 5th Florida Infantry were fighting near Bristoe Station in Virginia. The Bristoe Campaign lasted from October 9th to November 9th, a full month. The campaign followed the Orange and Alexandria Railroad line that reached north through Washington, DC and down south to the west of Chancellorsville through Charlottesville, Virginia. Bristoe Station itself was south of Manassas Junction on this line.

Mary only saw one positive outcome from this battle: her cousin Isham James received a discharge for disability, probably occasioned by a serious wound. He was twenty-seven years old and listed as 5' 8" tall, with light hair and gray eyes.

Confederate losses during the campaign amounted to over 1,500 casualties.

Western Theater

In late November in the western campaign, the Rebels yielded Chattanooga, the gateway to the lower South. The rout on Missionary Ridge launched a retreat as far as Dalton, with only Cleburne's unit protecting the South's rear by fighting off the Union pursuit at the Battle of Ringgold Gap. The South's defeat by the winter of 1863 eliminated their last significant control of Tennessee and opened wide the door to an invasion of Georgia.

The Union army returned to Chattanooga and readied for its next movement, using the city as a supply and logistics base for Sherman's later Atlanta Campaign. They would winter there until March 1864, when Grant would receive command of all the Union armies. For the rest of the war, all the fighting was south of the Mason and Dixon line. The noose was tightening.

The casualties for the Chattanooga Campaign were 361 killed, over 2,000 wounded, and over 4,000 missing, who were mostly prisoners. About 100,000 men in all took part, but the Union had more men and suffered more casualties, with few missing. The Confederates won Chickamauga, but their victory was short-lived since the North won the Chattanooga Campaign at Lookout Mountain and Missionary Ridge.

After Chickamauga, the senior Colonel William Scott Dilworth fell ill, and they sent him to his home in Monticello for a forty-day furlough. While on leave, there was a long-awaited consolidation of the Florida troops. Because of the heavy losses on Missionary Ridge, they combined the 1st Florida Cavalry and 4th Infantry. Bragg's orders created Finley's Florida Brigade, which grouped the Florida regiments of the Army of Tennessee together.

It simply said that Finley would take command until they appointed a brigadier. Because Colonel Dilworth was on furlough, the leadership of this new Florida Brigade fell on Colonel Jesse J. Finley, who was later appointed brigadier general. The Marianna, Florida resident remained in command, and people forever called his brigade Finley's Florida Brigade.

The maritime blockade of the South, though, was still not a complete success. The Northern blockade's weakest links were Wilmington and

Charleston, where there was now more shipping than before the beginning of the war. Also, the South had other blockading successes. Their cruisers disrupted Federal commerce at sea, destroying several of the North's civilian commercial ships. Northern shipping insurance rates increased by 900%.

Commerce, though, in Savannah remained affected even when Commodore Tattnall attempted to break the blockade on the Savannah River; the blockade by this time meant that military stores were increasing in importance. Civilian stores were now less valuable to the blockaders.

While with the 4th, William was promoted to sergeant. His promotion included increased pay, which William sent home. Mary pondered how God always provided. The extra money was so much needed because the cost of stores had increased. Inflation drained her coffers. They learned to live simply and use only what they could make or grow. She thought a lot these days about how her parents survived when everything was so meager after they first moved to Florida.

Men of the various regiments elected their own company and regimental officers by ballot. This could mean that a man who enlisted as a private, such as William, could find himself commissioned even as high as a colonel and in command of an entire regiment.

Such a man was Private William S. Dilworth from Monticello and Private Jesse J. Finley from Marianna. They rose through the ranks because of these elections until they found themselves colonels. Again, we realize William must have been a respected man for his men to promote him. Then again, William was fifty-two years old and probably considered a clearer thinker than many of the younger men.

At Home

William and Mary were lucky to have the extra cash, but there were many indigent Jefferson County families by the winter of 1863 who were not as lucky. Florida's general assembly again decided there was a need for relief for these families in the state. The local officials had reached the limits of their local budgets, and men were deserting.

The state appropriated half a million dollars to be paid semi-annually to boards of county commissioners for distribution. With the help of their local justice of the peace, they prepared lists of soldiers and their family members who were destitute. These listed families received clothing and provisions such as corn, spinning wheels, and other necessary family supplies.

Found in the county commission minutes for Jefferson County are reports of who received corn. These lists provide a sign of the challenges faced by Jefferson County families and other Florida families.

Mary spent more time in Elizabeth. She pondered the need to move closer to her family, and she considered it again one warm December afternoon as she walked to her sisters through the pines on a little trail. Her sister had recently moved back to Elizabeth.

Overhead, the sound of the wind in the boughs moaned above her, swelling gradually and dying away as the breeze rose and fell. Her long faded blue calico skirts billowed in the wind. It was a beautiful day, and she felt good. She grinned to herself and thought, "Well, William's gone again and left me with another little present."

Mary had moved her top hoop a little higher so no one would notice her pregnancy. Usually, one stayed in and away from people by this time, but that wasn't possible with a war going on. So many conventions were being pushed aside for the war. It had changed everyone and everything.

The trail popped out next to her sister's kitchen back of their home, and Mary went right in. She quickly joined in to help Sarah prepare dinner.

Sarah, also called Susan, had married Isaac Pillans, who was a widower. Isaac passed away before the war.

Their oldest, John, was away fighting, currently in Florida's 5th Cavalry Battalion. Sarah needed him at home, but the war got him and her second born, too. It seems they named William Henry Pillans after William.

Her third born, though, was still at home like Zech and ran the farm in the absence of his older brothers. Mary donned an apron, and she and her closest sister gabbed while fixing dinner. It felt good to talk to her, and Mary realized that this was simply good for her soul. She needed the Elizabeth community even though her father and mother were gone.

From November 11 to December 31, 1863, Captain McKay paid William and listed him as present. Meanwhile, continuing to form in the swamps below Perry was the band of deserters who now formed a new union and called themselves the Independent Union Rangers with a constitution that called for the death penalty for any member who deserted the band. Within sixty miles of Tallahassee, there was now a union company of volunteer soldiers, all with prior knowledge of the area.

When it merged with the 1st Florida, the 3rd Florida Infantry Regiment had initially organized with 950 officers and men. They lost 26% of their remaining 230 men in action at Chickamauga. By December, they totaled 240 men with 119 arms. The 4th was in even worse shape. Out of the 200 men who had fought at Missionary Ridge, only 33 men were still effective.

Florida newspapers mostly ceased to exist. Paper was not to be had. The *Family Friend* continued with its two copies each week, and the Tallahassee *Floridian and Journal* was still being published. The *Florida Sentinel* in Tallahassee, though, ceased publication in December.

Down the Gulf Coast to their west, Federal ships shelled the town of St. Andrews because they believed it to be the headquarters of several Confederate companies to protect Confederate saltworks there. St. Andrews is now a part of Panama City, between Frankford Avenue and Lake Caroline. The Union shelling destroyed thirty-two homes

Though the Union army held or controlled various coastal railroad terminals in the state like Fernandina and Cedar Key, the Confederacy still controlled the internal rails and used them to move materials and commodities. Key inland ports such as Baldwin became more important to the South's commissary agents. Far west from Baldwin, the railway bridge over the Suwanee River became more important as well.

There is no certainty from where the casualties came, but the Bond House in Lloyd was converted into a hospital during this time. Lloyd sat on the railroad, and the road was probably used to bring in the casualties.

Meanwhile, the South continued the impressment of cattle in Florida for the war effort, and the Confederacy now looked primarily to Georgia and Florida to feed its troops. It was rumored that over 2,000 head of cattle a week were being sent north, half of which came now from middle and lower Florida, as the easy pickings of North Florida cattle were already gone. If Georgia was still the Confederate's food basket, then Florida was its stockyard and barn.

Meanwhile, Jefferson County became Florida's manufacturing center for the war effort. William Bailey's existing cotton mill contained 1,500 spindles and was the only cloth factory in the state. Near Monticello, before the war in 1856, Bailey and other citizens had formed the Southern Rights Manufacturing Company. He established it on land donated by Martin Palmer near Palmer's Mill. The factory was under contract to Palmer to furnish wood for its furnace for five years.

William Bailey was the promoter and largest stockholder. He realized the potential of a cotton factory in a region in which cotton was a staple product. The directors of the company were John Finlayson, William Denham, James Scott, and John Johnson. William Bailey was the general manager. With the mill was also a small shoe factory which also made wool cards.

Though the Confederacy commandeered the cotton mills throughout the South to furnish clothing for the army, they exempted this mill because it was, at William Bailey's personal expense, clothing two companies of the 5th Florida Regiment. His two sons, Captains William Bailey and Abram Bailey, commanded the companies.

The state purchased the other two-thirds of its output, and its militia guarded these enterprises closely. Historians speculate that because of Bailey's other stocks in Florida's railroads and the State Bank, Bailey may have been the Sunshine State's first millionaire.

Palmer's Mill still produced leather, and Walker Mills cut and shipped timber from the county's vast southern flatwoods, but it appears Palmer's Mill also sawed timber, too.

In Tallahassee, Governor Milton proclaimed December 24th a day of fasting, humiliation, and prayer for all the citizens of Florida. That Christmas Eve, Mary probably gathered all her children and maybe several of her extended family members, like her sister Susan, her Aunt Mary Jane Lightsey, and her Aunt Betsy Walker and their children, for a Christmas Eve feast and prayer meeting. These women and their children may have left the table and knelt for this special prayer, their faces illuminated by the lanterns and fireplace as they bowed their heads.

#

Chapter 8
The Beginning of the End
January to May 1864

That winter, both the South and the North remained in winter camps. Meanwhile, Lincoln made major changes. Congress revived the grade of Lieutenant General, which was previously held by General George Washington. On March 9th, at the White House, Lincoln commissioned Ulysses S. Grant as Lieutenant General, giving him the entire command of his armies. For the first time since the start of the war, one man commanded a concerted effort for all union armies.

Grant changed the strategy to pressure the Confederacy in several coordinated areas—Virginia, Georgia, and Mobile. He turned to his favorite general, William T. Sherman, to invade Georgia, the first prize being Atlanta.

Though not Grant's only objective, Atlanta, the deep South's major transportation and industrial center, was significant. A powerful symbol, next in importance only to Richmond, Atlanta's fall would be a heavy blow to the Confederacy's morale. With heavy casualties and morale low, Atlanta's loss would be a double catastrophe—material and symbolic. Grant ordered Sherman to destroy Johnston's armies and capture Atlanta.

Sherman devised a secondary strategy to reach his goal—a strategy of destruction and psychological warfare to crush the will and capacity of the Southern people to make war. As he planned to move through Georgia and the Carolinas, he would destroy everything in his path, later known as a "scorched earth" invasion. His goal, like Grant's and Lincoln's, was to hasten the restoration of the Union and the abolishment of slavery.

Confronted by superior enemy numbers, Confederate General Johnston could only use what he had available. He aimed to catch his enemy in a mistake and felt his primary responsibility was to keep his forces intact. Secondarily, he set a goal to defend Atlanta. Meanwhile, his plan was to stall for time, hoping Northerners would tire of the war.

Western Theater

First, Sherman planned from Chattanooga a southward series of moves between the two great armies that, if needed, could last for months.

Johnston would take nine successive defensive positions, but Sherman would flank him each time, causing Johnston to pull back again and again to thwart him. Only once would Sherman's patience wane, and only once would he fall for an unsuccessful frontal assault.

Unfortunately, Johnston, who led the Confederate's western theater, considered the loss of his army more important than the loss of Atlanta. Some would later say he couldn't see the forest for the trees.

Because of a lack of reserves for battle, though, he and Lee's generals could not exploit their advantages. While fresh numbers of the enemy would arrive daily, the South's troops would become exhausted and diminished. Added to this, the South was outmatched in military equipment, industrial facilities, railroads, and wagons. The Southern people wouldn't have a chance. William's prognostications would become true.

Except for the ghostly Forrest, Sherman would prove unstoppable. As a threat to Sherman's rear guard, General Nathan Bedford Forrest would conduct cavalry raids and play havoc with the Union's lines of communication, but these raids would be little more than annoyances to the decisive push of the North.

As the South's armies dwindled, the cry for a rich man's war and a poor man's fight led the Confederate congress to abolish the substitute system. Until then, the Confederate Congress had allowed substitutes, but they banned them by the end of 1863. Regardless, the South simply ran out of men.

Companies evolved and became decimated by disease, wounds, desertions, and death. As the South's soldiers became fewer, the need to merge regiments arose. This was hard on the men as until now they had fought with men from their same neighborhoods and villages. Some had been schoolmates.

Because poor food rationing occurred, North Florida's beeves were driven toward supply bases at Albany and Quitman, Georgia, some as late as Christmas. Winter necessitated holding the beeves until spring, when grazing could resume. That the Confederacy demanded Floridians keep driving cattle north in the winter showed a lack of understanding of the conditions in Florida. By December, stockmen moved north around 30,000 head during 1863. Too bad that the beeves that made it were lean and provided little meat.

It was about this time that William realized one could distinguish between the old warrior regiments and the newer ones simply by observing their flags. The older warrior regiments marched under flags with many holes through them and the names of from three to twenty hard-fought fields of battle. Beneath some flags, only fifty rank-and-file soldiers remained in the regiment, and some of these flags carried the numbers of three and four merged regiments.

The Army of Tennessee spent the winter in the valleys near Dalton, Georgia. It was good to not be in the mountains where the cold was colder and the wet wetter. Still, the winds howled through their makeshift cabin.

A Winter Camp - Union troops mill about the Union lines during the Battle of Nashville, Tennessee, in December 1864, Library of Congress

The Florida Brigade first camped north, near Dalton, but their superiors moved them about a mile farther north along the railroad tracks between Dalton and Chattanooga. Again, the thousands of men denuded the land of trees and any other wood they could find. Gone were the farmers' fences, and scoured was their land. Luckily, the Florida Brigade occupied huts built by the Bates Brigade, comfortable huts of logs and chimneys weatherproofed with chinking.

William and three other men had a new Astor House, and he remembered his old friend Standley and missed him. Unlike their chimney at Murfreesboro, this one drew better.

They laid out the beds like spokes on a wheel, with their feet pointing toward the middle. They propped their 'mules' against each other in a center tower. (They called their guns mules because they kicked so hard.)

That night, one of William's roommates said, "You know this is useless. They have more men to fight, more iron, more supplies, and even more food. It is hopeless." No one engaged him. Silence ensued. They hadn't played taps yet, and they heard wonderful music in the distance.

In camp were some hill people, what they called the men from the Appalachian Mountains. Some played the fiddle and were very good. Joining them were men who learned to play banjos from the slaves. Together, they made fine music. William said, "I guess the hill people practice so much, they've gotten skillful at their craft."

Another roommate added, "They are the best in camp."

Winter Camp, Library of Congress

Drinking was always available in the camps, but alcohol was becoming scarce, like everything else. The officers tried to keep the men entertained. There were jumping contests, wrestling matches, and boxing matches. Of course, card games were universal. They celebrated the Christmas holidays, and the officers donated their whiskey for the event.

Joining them were young men, scarcely sixteen and barely old enough to go to war. Many had rarely traveled from the fields in which their families farmed, and many came in from their first ever train ride. Some were beardless boys, and the youngest they used as drummer boys.

Still, three quarters of all the men were between eighteen and thirty years old. William knew what the officers knew, though, that young boys made better soldiers than old men. He also knew that most of these new recruits would die of disease rather than a bullet.

Poor education characterized most privates. Illiteracy ran as high as fifty percent in some units, but in the Jefferson Rifles and Beauregards it was closer to fifteen percent. Mostly, these latest recruits signed for the same reasons as the earlier ones did. Their friends and neighbors enlisted, and they thought it would be exciting to get away from their family's responsibilities and restraints, especially the daily mundane repetitiveness of farming.

Though a high percentage were illiterate, many of these boys were quite literate in survival, especially in the woods. Life hardened these backwoods boys, making them resourceful. They were better able to bear bodily fatigues. Life had not been easy for them, and they were more seasoned.

These were the boys who hardened easier into men, who built better huts; hunted rabbits, raccoons, and turkeys for their sustenance; and who could build a sled to haul in the firewood. They were more compatible with the patterns of camp life. Many gentlemen's sons, though literate, lacked experience with manual labor and the hardships of military life.

Around the camps, humor was still at play. There were still pranks and horseplay, especially with the new recruits. Sitting around the campfire one evening, William joined Mary's brothers and cousins in the camp of the consolidated 1st/3rd. Jesse Allen was instructing a new boy from Aucilla and said, "Now, whatever you do, stay away from the 5th lieutenants. Tomorrow you'll need to report to your supply sergeant and get your umbrella. You don't want the 5th lieutenant to catch you without one if it rains." The boy hung on every word.

Laughter aside, though, the men in camp knew that the war had decimated their ranks, and to leave would be to abandon their fellow men to bear the full responsibility. They knew everyone's help was crucial, especially during these days. They became honor bound to their comrades in arms and consequently ashamed of their situation, their clothes, their lack of supplies, and especially their lack of bathing.

William may have lain in his bedroll many nights, thinking about his revolutionary ancestors and what they did for later generations. His upbringing instilled in him a sense of duty to his cause and country. His revolutionary father had often mentioned Washington's sufferings at Valley Forge.

By now William wore a short-waisted single-breasted gray jacket, but Mary may have patched the overcoat and sent it to him. He noticed the cape was shorter than before, but it still afforded warmth.

He wore his soft hat and never again donned the earlier cap. Mary and his daughters spun and wove the rest of his clothes that he received for Christmas from home, colored a butternut color with homemade dye. He may have even had a poncho confiscated off a dead Yankee at Chickamauga.

Drums and bugle calls regulated daily life in camp. He rolled out of his blanket to reveille at dawn. He and his mates made breakfast after roll call and a brief drill. A third call was for the infirmary and fatigue duties. He picked up the grounds, cut wood, and kept the Astor House clean. By now it was 8 am.

After breakfast was another signal, when their first sergeant inspected his detail and marched them to the parade grounds. The sergeant lined up the men, inspected them, and dispatched them to their guard posts. Those not assigned to guard duty were kept for drilling.

Lunch followed with a little free time and more drilling. After drilling, they were free to return to their quarters to clean up. One more call for another inspection and parade, and then the call to supper. Free time followed, usually around the fire. Soldiers sang a lot. In the distance he heard a mouth harp and a voice singing, "When This Cruel War is Over." Others joined in. His heart hurt when the music turned to, "The Girl I Left Behind." Someone said, "Play something faster," and the band of songsters turned to "Tenting on the Old Camp Ground."

They could also hear hymns. He especially liked "Rock of Ages," "Nearer my God to Thee," and "How Firm A Foundation." Then he heard the lonely taps, three drum taps which signaled all lights out and talking extinguished. It was routine and industry that kept them in line.

One day when the snow fell extra damp and deep, someone from another company threw a snowball. It hit one of William's officers, and the contest was on. The rest of his officers scooped the damp snow and returned fire for a big snowball fight. William got soaking wet and chilled, but it was exhilarating.

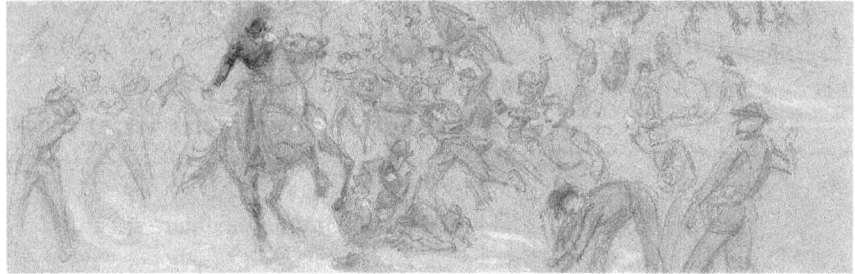

Confederate troops engage in a massive snowball fight at Dalton, Georgia in March 1864, sketch by Alfred R. Waud, Library of Congress

Christmas came and went, as did New Year's Day. The highlight was a box from home with two shirts, six oranges, and a cake.

Every day was so cold that William's ink and every other liquid froze. He was especially happy when a pair of gloves arrived from his sister in Leesburg, Virginia. Sadly, though, wood was scarce. He expected them to move any day, seeking an area closer to more forests. In the distance he could see mountains to their east, mountains with woods.

Down in the bare valley, though, the winds howled through with little to stop it.

He heard the 1st and 3rd Florida Consolidated were on post guard duty in Dalton and were being blamed for an incident. Someone stole a box off a train but left it behind when they discovered it contained a corpse. He worried because the perpetrator remained unnamed, and that was James's regiment.

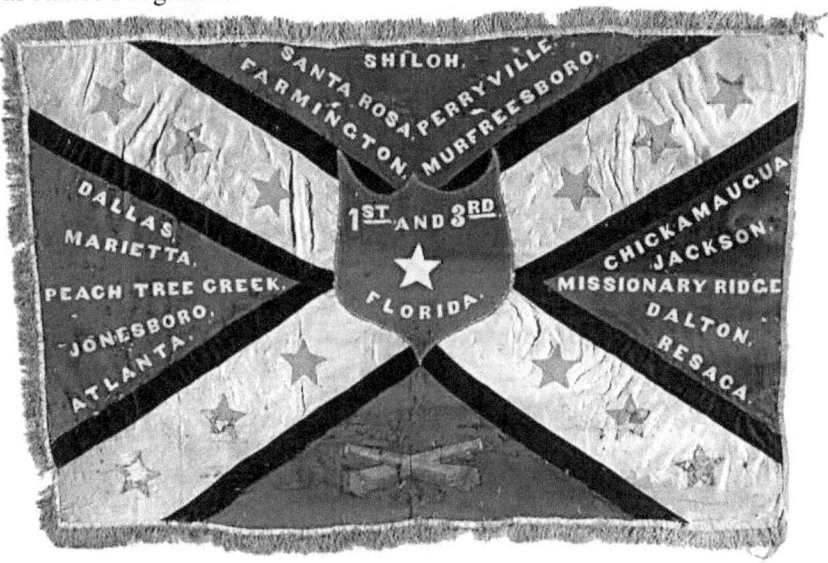

1st and 3rd Florida Regiment Flag, WikiTree

By February 1864, because of combat losses, William's 4th Florida Regiment all but disbanded and was consolidated with the 1st Florida Cavalry. By that date, the age bracket for the Confederate soldier was seventeen to fifty. Also, the Confederate Congress conscripted all Southern men under eighteen and over forty-five still at home for state defense inside state borders. This home defense became the men and boys who would later fight at Natural Bridge south of Tallahassee. Monticello's William Capers Bird received a promotion to colonel.

William did not go with the rest of his unit in February and found himself mingled indiscriminately with many men previously unknown to him. Mary may have noticed a change in his letters, which now seemed demoralized and drained. Thankfully, it did not last long. William easily made friends and gained people's trust.

They transferred him to Company H of the 5th Georgia Infantry. Most of the men in Company H were from Bainbridge or nearby. By this time he was a sergeant with the 4th Florida but reverted to a private after the transfer, a common practice used to avoid extra expenses and additional pay. Later, he received another promotion.

The 5th Georgia Infantry had been in Cheatham's Division under Jackson's Brigade with Colonel Charles P. Daniel. Jackson's Brigade comprised the 1st, 2nd, and 5th Georgia and the 5th and 8th Mississippi.

Elsewhere, the authorities combined William Allen Walker's 3rd Florida Cavalry Battalion with five Alabama independent cavalry companies to create the 15th Regiment Confederate Cavalry. They remained in the Mobile and Pensacola area.

We know that on February 19, there was a notice on the bulletin board in Tallahassee saying that the Confederate Congress had passed an act conscripting all companies and regiments as they now stood. One wonders if this was an extenuating circumstance of a recent change or impending change? We're unsure.

We know it was a common practice for soldiers to transfer from one unit to the other when regimental numbers dwindled because of deaths and captures. They also combined regiments as needed.

We're unsure why William didn't go with the rest of the 4th Florida to the First Florida Cavalry. Maybe he had had enough of the cavalry when he fought under General Forrest near Murfreesboro. Maybe his superiors felt he was too old and infirm to ride again. With William's injuries and the time he was out on sick leave, one wonders if he could ride with a cavalry regiment. Maybe he was closer to the men in the 5th Georgia Infantry, where he transferred. We do not know why they moved him into the 5th Georgia, but he would remain there.

A cousin through William's son Henry who moved to Texas provided all of this information. She spent a considerable amount of time and money having someone trace William's service record during the Civil War. Our cousin Lynette Andrews saved us considerable efforts and expense.

The 5th Georgia Regiment originated in Macon, Georgia on May 11, 1861 and had previous experience in Florida. They were first posted at Pensacola under General Braxton Bragg, where they received their training. Their first combat assignment was on Santa Rosa Island off the coast of Florida.

Because each company of the 5th represented a town or county in South Georgia, their communities well equipped and nicely uniformed them. Because no two companies dressed alike, people nicknamed them the "Pound Cake Regiment."

Men often enlisted in a company recruited in their county where they lived, and this was the case for Company H. Most of the men came from Bainbridge and the surrounding area in South Georgia called Decatur County, which was only about twenty miles north of the Florida state line and less than sixty miles from Monticello. Their company nickname was the Hardee Rifles. They fought alongside many of the companies from Florida in various battles, including Murfreesboro, where William's Florida unit was earlier assigned.

At Murfreesboro, they received thirty-two percent casualties along with the loss of their Colonel William Black and their regimental flag. Again, at the Battle of Chickamauga, it cost them fifty-five percent casualties. By December 1863, before William joined them in February, the entire regiment was down to only 161 men. There are records that show a company muster roll dated June 8 to August 31, 1864. It also states William received no pay. The Confederacy was running out of money.

William may have written home in February.

February 22, 1864
Dalton, Georgia

Dearest Mary,

I know you tire of hearing it, but I long daily for the comforts of home and your arms. We are still in winter camp and continue our defense of Atlanta; but I'm glad you cannot see me now as all of us are an emaciated lot, though I still have much energy. I'm unsure why.

Yesterday, there was a break in camp life, and different ones of us struck out to forage. I was luckier than the others. I happened upon a farmhouse and wife who needed cord wood and other work done around her home. She repaid my help with corn, a little hog meat, and turnips. Mary, if the fighting ever gets close, try to strike a bargain with whomever comes to your door. They're mostly hungry, and they can do most anything around the place. It sure left me feeling better than just begging.

Yesterday, by happenstance, a wild hare got too close to our camp, and the race was on. Throughout the woods came the wild yells as the boys chased the poor straggler. On one occasion, it scampered through our camp and my cabin mates joined the melee. I'm sure the winner got a tasty meal.

Speaking of something tasty, I told my cabin mate yesterday I would give my eyeteeth for fresh cream. I want the soup you make with the creamy broth. That plus real coffee, though the coffee we make with dried, mashed sweet potatoes is sufficient. If we only had fresh cream to make it more palatable? I guess you can tell I'm homesick...

When William joined the 5th Georgia, it served under Brigadier General John K. Jackson called Jackson's Brigade, which was under Major General William H. T. Walker in Walker's Division. Walker's Division was under Lieutenant General William J. Hardee or Hardee's 1st Corps, who was under General Joseph E. Johnston.

One night around a campfire, William listened as several talked about soldiering. One said, "It was the old ex-soldiers with their previous Indian fighting experience who got us through those early days. They were the ones who told us what to watch for, what to dodge, and what to do. So many of us boys were weedy, sallow children, frightened if you know what I mean." William realized these men he was with had been through a lot and had bonded much like he had bonded with his former unit. He also kept quiet, though he was one of the old ex-soldiers with Indian fighting experience.

At Home

At home, Zech and Jesse were chopping wood for the next cold front. Today, though, it was pleasant. Zech said as he placed a piece of wood on its end: "I have to admit, I've been thinking a lot about what I'd do if the Yankees made it this far."

Jesse let go of an armload of short logs and piled them on the ground at his feet. "Well, we'll have to fight, what with all the men gone and nothing left but us boys and the old-timers to defend the town. Some men say that one of us can lick a dozen Yankees any day."

Zech stared at his brother. "Can't you tell from their letters that ain't true?" He added, "Do you think you could kill someone?"

Both stood in silence, their dark eyes thoughtful. Between them, a jenny wren streaked through. Jesse said, "I don't know. They teach us at church the commandment about killing someone—that it is wrong."

*Northern Occupation of Jacksonville, Florida, Library of Congress.
Photograph Taken in February 1864. You can see the military wagons
traveling up Ocean Street from the corner of Bay Street on the St. Johns
River. Notice the sentry on the roof of the building.*

East Florida

Though it was cold in the mountains of north Georgia, it wasn't in
North Florida. There was no winter camp there. On the 20th of February,
three Florida regiments under Brigadier General Joseph Finegan, along
with other reinforcements under Brigadier General Alfred H. Colquitt,
came from Charleston to a place called Ocean Pond near a railway station
called Olustee.

Hardly anyone in Monticello knew where Ocean Pond was, but
rumors had run rampant throughout North Florida ever since the Union
General Truman Seymour landed in Jacksonville on Sunday, February
7th. His chief orders were to sever the Confederate's food supply, but he
wanted a bigger prize. He wanted Tallahassee. The next day, Camp
Finegan fell eight miles west of Jacksonville near the railroad.

Meanwhile, to help with the Confederate's food supply in Florida,
Mary's brother J.J. now rode with the 1st Florida Special Cavalry
Battalion which had earlier been organized near Plant City and was based
out of Fort Myers. They drove cattle north from central Florida to

Baldwin, where rail transport took them to the Southern war front. J.J. was in Company A and was thirty-seven years old. On his enlistment papers, he was described as 5' 8" with a dark complexion, dark hair, and gray eyes.

With the area around Baldwin now in enemy lines, the South's food supply of beef was partially severed. This made the area around Lake City more important for defense. Also, they had to deal with threats posed by the Union army and navy while dealing with deserters and draft evaders. They even worried about the Seminoles as the last uprising, the 3rd Seminole War, had ended only six years earlier.

Seymour's expedition, a force of 5,500 Federal men, began making raids into northeast and north-central Florida following the Florida, Atlantic and Gulf Railway, the railroad that led straight through Lake City and Jefferson County to Tallahassee. He met little resistance along the way, capturing small bands of local militia and freeing slaves. By the following Wednesday, he took Sanderson. His next goal was to remove the Columbus Bridge which crossed the Suwannee River near present-day Ellaville, to stop crucial communications and cripple another transportation corridor for cattle sent north to the Southern armies.

In Olustee, fifty miles west of Jacksonville, at 2:30 on a Saturday afternoon, Seymour's troops encountered Finegan's entrenched force of 5,000 Confederates at Ocean Pond. Seymour thought this group was simply one more small band of militia, a crucial mistake. The fighting was in open pine woods where the South ferociously attacked until the Union lines broke and fled back to Jacksonville. During the Union retreat, the 35th United States Colored Troops, mostly slaves and the 54th Massachusetts Volunteer Infantry Regiment, mostly freemen, provided cover as the Union soldiers fled. Confederate troops killed and captured most of the wounded colored troops, and they sent some to Andersonville.

Soldiers of the 8th U.S. Colored Troops advancing against Confederate entrenchments, lithograph by Kurz and Allison, 1892, Florida Memory Project, Wikipedia. The image is inaccurate and reveals the artist's ignorance about the events. During the battle, Confederates operated well in advance of their prepared positions. Neither side fought from behind fortifications; the fighting took place in a pine forest, and there were few large, cleared areas.

No one ordered the Confederate units to pursue the fleeing Federals, another opportunity lost. The Union soldiers suffered over 1,800 casualties, about thirty-four percent of the original force. Confederate casualties totaled 946, about nineteen percent.

The ratio of casualties made this the Union's second bloodiest battle for the entire war. Letters and journals kept by men from both sides showed that the war veterans who had fought in earlier great battles in the east and the west thought this battle their worst fighting experience.

Trains carried most of the battle's dead to Lake City, where they were buried in Oaklawn Cemetery. Someone hastily buried about 125 Union soldiers in shallow graves on the field. An army detachment returned in 1866 and reinterred the scattered remains in a mass grave. In 1991, workers erected a more permanent monument on that spot near the railroad tracks.

At Home

Within hours after the battle, some of the wounded arrived by train in Monticello's depot. We know they took others to Lloyd. Probably

Mary, along with most of the town's women and older men and boys, met each train to help with the maimed men from the battle. Workers transformed the empty cotton warehouse at the depot's north end into a triage waiting room, and from there they loaded the men onto wagons bound for the school.

The shaded Dogwood Street became a thoroughfare as the wagons passed through town headed to the southwestern side, where the school provided an ideal temporary hospital. Its large, cavernous rooms and lofty ceilings provided healing airflow, though this was February, and February can get quite cold in the winter when the fronts move through. Zech, Jesse, and maybe even eight-year-old Henry may have labored to keep the fireplaces in the schoolhouse stoked.

Laura, at seven, was old enough to help. She and her siblings probably spent time in the high school toting water and pails to and from the school building. Young unmarried women like Sarah and Florrie could only work in the convalescent wards.

Older married women could nurse in the hospital. One day, Mary worked with a surgeon, holding a basin while the man cut away green flesh. She tried to be gentle and sympathetic, but with a cheerful countenance. She felt her nursing was the best she could do to volunteer for the South. The patient later thanked her and called her an "angel of mercy." She cupped his cheek and said, "It is the least anyone can do for your sacrifice." He was a Yankee.

The men were crawling with lice and smelled terrible. Many apologized. She spent a morning picking maggots out of festering flesh in hideous wounds amid groans, delirium, and many smells, some a sickly sweet. Mary wore a blood-splattered apron that covered her from her neck to her feet. Because it had warmed in the afternoon, the hospital crawled with flies and gnats which tormented the men. One man weakly sobbed.

Even though Mary may have been heavily pregnant, conventions were waived out of necessity. If needed, she probably did what she could. Plus, she wanted to be there because engagements came about so quickly now. She wanted to protect her girls. And who knew? At that moment, William might be in a Union hospital. She hoped the nurses there treated him as well.

The school building was only a little over ten years old, but it still stands today 167 years later.

Keystone Genealogical Library

Both the Confederate and Union soldiers who succumbed were buried in the Old City Cemetery northeast of town. One can still find their marked and unmarked graves there.

Graves of Civil War soldiers (in the fenced area above), personal photos

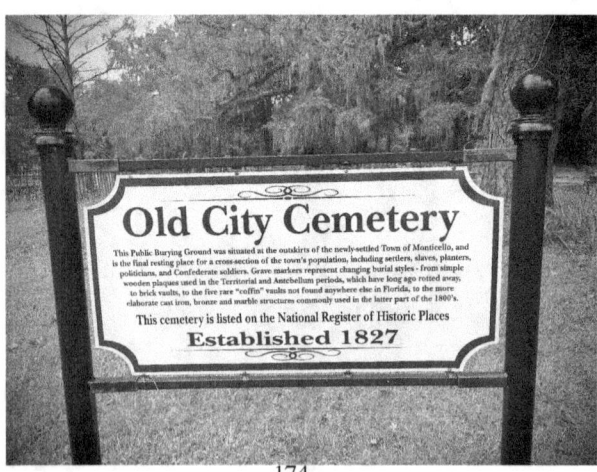

They buried the soldiers underneath the trees in the back, personal photo

In late winter or early spring, William got good news from home. He had a new daughter, and Mary and baby both were healthy and well. He worried about Mary having another child. She was about forty years old and had already had ten children, but his girl was strong and delivered yet again.

They named the baby girl Virginia, and one wonders if the name was because it was where his mother's people were from or if the name was from the state where, as a prisoner of war, William had again gained his freedom. We're unsure, but the name was uncommon for either of their families.

At home, Mary found herself in the old familiar routine with a baby at her breast, but this time William and the older boys were far away. Ellen was gone, but thankfully Florrie was still at home. She and their oldest Sarah were there to help.

Henrietta, also known as Hattie, was ten, and she loved helping with the new baby. She was only four when Joseph was born and was hardly old enough to help. "Eighteen fifty-eight," thought Mary, "the last year everything was fine." Now it seemed as if that had happened in another life.

175

Her thoughts went to poor Florrie. She was twenty-four and still living at home. She had discussed staying with Ellen in Marion County, but prospects there were even slimmer. This war had changed everything. The only ones left behind were old men and boys just out of the turnip patch.

She sat in her bedroom nursing little Virginia. Outside, everything was so pretty and green. Spring was always so grand in Florida when everything puts on a new dress. The camellias had almost stopped blossoming. She longed for a drive to Elizabeth, where the pines and oaks are so much greener against the red clay and white sands of the roads. The dogwood would begin their show soon.

The Western Theater

While all the changes were being made during the winter of 1863-64, the Army of Tennessee waited for the North to push south into Georgia. William's letters home increased as time moved slowly in winter camp. One of his letters described a phenomenon. He wrote:

March 20, 1864
Dalton, Georgia

Dearest Mary and family,

...You should hear how these men talk about General Lee. He is almost becoming an ethereal character. They say his command surpasses all expectancy and unnerves the North, as if he could read their minds.

The men here sit around the fires at night talking about Lee's military career during the Mexican War and the standard of conduct there that he set for himself. An honorable man, as they say, he granted his officers wide latitude to follow their own instincts. Apparently, it is an honor to serve under him. They also say he is a good husband and family man and that the North asked him to lead them first, but he refused to turn his back on his beloved Virginia and resigned his thirty-two-year commission.

They say he is very handsome, a man's type of man; during battle, he stands like a lofty stanchion. People describe him as gentle, especially with his children. He even has a pet chicken in his personal camp. As you can tell, he is truly taking on the ethereal persona of a gentle white knight of the realm. I look forward to hearing about him from Valentine, who has had the honor of serving under such a courageous and skilled soldier.

There is taps, so I must close. Give hugs and kisses to all my children, dear Mary; and I hope you remember me in your dreams as I do you.

All my love,
William

While both sides were still in winter camp, the North reelected Lincoln, who gave his second inaugural address to one of the largest inaugural crowds in history. Word of his speech reached Confederate soldiers in Petersburg, leading two South Carolina soldiers to desert. One said he "*could not stand the idea of hardship of four more long years of war.*" Desertion was now a common problem for the South. Their family loyalty was proving stronger.

Hardee assumed command of the Hindsman Corps in March. Most uncomfortable for all the Florida boys, though, was a big snowstorm on March 22nd. William noticed some boys thought it was grand that it snowed so much, but it didn't take long for them to tire of it. Their long stay at Dalton bored everyone silly, but a winter camp was better than desperate fighting. The newbies thought otherwise, but they would learn soon. Everyone spent their days practicing at targets and doing camp chores.

A week later, Federals on the St. Johns River in Florida took Palatka. The Confederates only had a small force at Gainesville and Starke.

It appears the North recognized Florida's value to the Confederacy. One Union general estimated Florida had been shipping north an average of 2,000 head of cattle a week to the Confederate military during the past year, but those shipments dwindled during the winter. The Confederacy's food needs and Sherman's march through Georgia would completely deplete Florida's food supplies.

The Eastern Front

In Virginia, Vollie heard the terrible rumors and worried about his mother and siblings. Two days after Cold Harbor, he heard the Yankees left Jacksonville to capture Tallahassee. They burned Lake City on the way and had overrun the areas between there and Tallahassee. Of course it was not true, but it worried him for several days before he heard otherwise.

By April, the Confederate Navy scored a major victory against Union gunboats. The aftermath of the engagement cleared the Roanoke River in North Carolina for commerce for six more months as the North struggled to close its blockade noose around the throat of the Confederacy.

In Florida

Meanwhile, the Confederate Bureau of Conscription for the Southern District of Florida and Alabama wrestled with the increasing number of deserters and refugees who hid in Florida's woods, swamps, and on its abandoned farms. Subsequently, on May 4th, three hundred cavalrymen raided East Bay east of Pensacola Bay to gather all the deserters and refugees hiding there in the river swamps of the East Bay River along with its adjoining woods and abandoned farms.

Most likely, they sent in the men from the 15th Confederate Cavalry. Formerly R. H. Partridge's Magnolia Dragoons, they became Company A in the 15th Confederate Cavalry. Union sympathizers organized to help the deserters in the area. All this was more evidence that the Southern effort was falling apart.

The effort came under General Beauregard, who had been in Florida for some time. Within a few days, over two hundred refugees and deserters gathered in the woods and swamps near St. Marks. With the United States gunboat *Mohawk* patrolling the Spanish Hole, the entrance to the St. Marks River, everyone worried the deserters were conspiring with the enemy.

Map of Florida by J. Lee Williams, 1837. The red dots show Delegate Locations for Florida's General Assembly, but it also is a good map showing the Spanish Hole near St. Marks.

Under orders, General Anderson merged all available troops in East and West Florida into one brigade under General Joseph Finegan and sent all troops to Richmond. He complied promptly, sending a brigade north, but motivated by duty to his native state, he held one regiment and two battalions of cavalry, among lesser units, to protect the flow of beef to Virginia.

Throughout Florida, men grew tired in body and sick in mind. Desertion increased as they joined the numbers of increasing swamp holdouts. They led frequent raiding parties against the civilian population of the state. Throughout North Florida, rumors persisted of the destruction of dwellings and property of those suspected of disloyalty to the Confederacy. This caused an increase in vindictive deserters who wished to avenge the wrongs. The whole countryside reeled in these turns of events, especially in areas around Taylor County and in northwest Florida.

War attracts those who live by the sword—men eager for vengeance and reprisal. They get carried away by the fury. Some seek to get even with those who disagreed with them while others seek to gain profit. Still, there were those who felt compelled to not fight for the Southern cause. Because of the former, though, there was much lawlessness in Florida's woods and swamps.

Mary worried about what her children heard, and she felt more and more powerless to protect them. The discussions on the porch became strained as she tried to maintain order in their little heads.

Because everyone was worried about the civilian population, increasingly those at home, older men like her Uncle James and younger men like her Zech, were constantly doing local militia duty. The countryside was no longer safe. Deserters infested the swamps—deserters communicated with the enemy.

In Quincy, they assigned Captain John Day Perkins as an enrollment officer at the conscript camp. The South and Florida tried to keep soldiers from desertion, but Florida had too many places to hide. The entire area was collapsing into lawlessness. Mary was now glad she had stayed in town, though she worried about her elderly Walker uncles, aunts, and young cousins who were still living around Elizabeth and Aucilla.

The Eastern Theater

Under the newly named Union General-in-Chief Grant, the North began with two different offensive moves against the South in May 1864. In the eastern theater, the Florida regiments were in the Battle of the Wilderness in Virginia, and in the western, the rest of the Florida regiments were about to fight for a place called Rocky Face Ridge near Dalton. The former was the first clash between the two great Generals Grant and Lee and the first battle of Grant's Overland Campaign. The latter was General Sherman's march to the sea through Georgia.

The Battle of the Wilderness raged from May 5th to the 7th in a dense, tangled forest west of Fredericksburg, Virginia. Lee fought there in order to neutralize the advantages of the stronger and better outfitted Northern Army. He used the dense forest to eliminate Grant's visibility and maneuverability. It was dark, with visibility sometimes only a few feet. A dense second growth of trees and underbrush, a result of earlier cutting of larger trees for iron processing, rendered the area impassable. While Grant tried to avoid it, Lee took advantage of it.

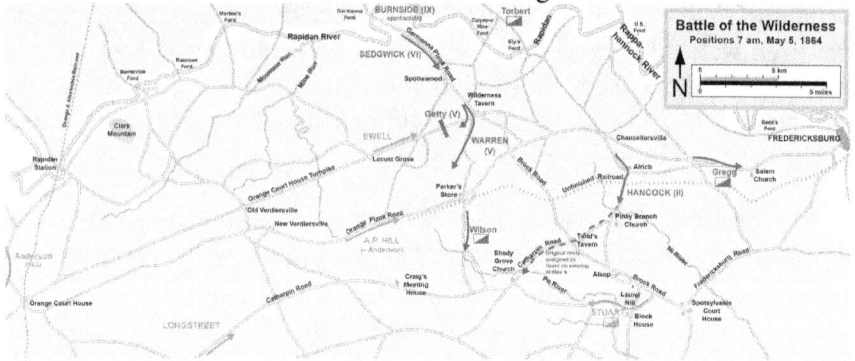

Battle of the Wilderness, Wikipedia. Map by Hal Jespersen, www.posix.com/ CW

The South had fought here earlier in the Battle of Chancellorsville as this forest covered about seventy square miles. This was where the late Stonewall Jackson concealed his men in the thickets of the massive forest and where 30,000 screaming Confederates emerged and surprised an entire corps of the Union army along a two-mile front. So the South knew the advantages this forested area held.

The fighting began late on the morning of May 5th for Perry's Brigade (the 2nd, 5th and 8th Florida Regiments) under Longstreet, but most of the Florida units were not on the front line. The 5th Florida Regiment, Company A, would never get into the thick of it, but Company

G would. Raysor's Aucilla Guards saw significant action, and it continued until the evening and erupted again before dawn the next day on May 6th.

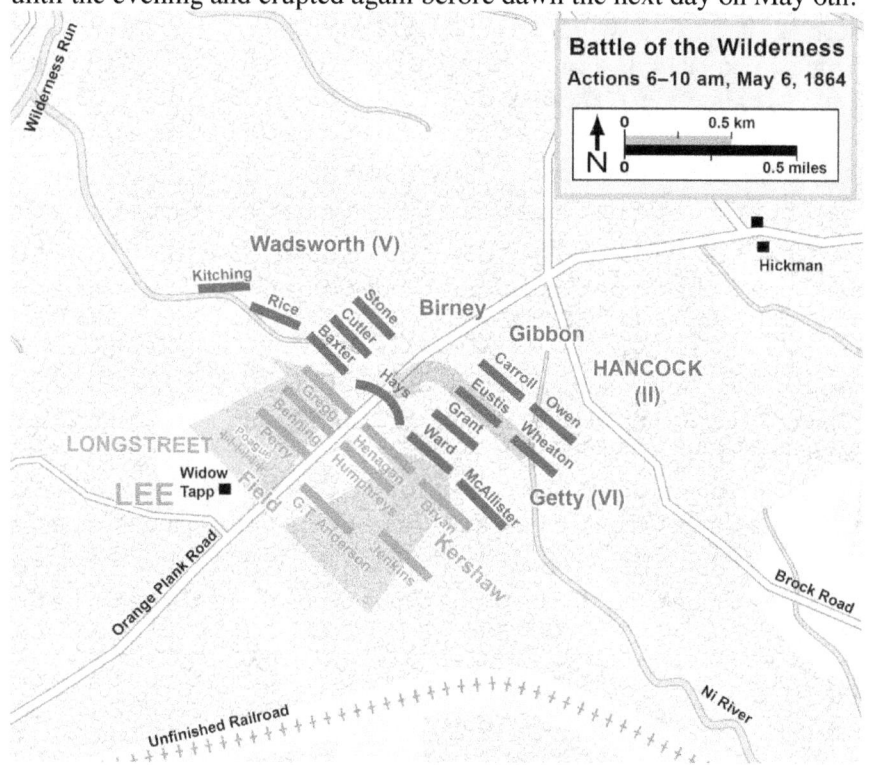

Map by Hal Jespersen, www.posix.com/CW, Wikipedia

The Confederates held until reinforcements under Lieutenant General James Longstreet arrived in time to prevent the fall of the Confederate right flank. In the confusion, one of the general's own men wounded him. The South kept pushing, but Grant held until he fell back to the sleepy village of Spotsylvania on the morning of the 7th with a new purpose—to get between Lee and Richmond. The little town was little more than a few stores and houses around a small park. However, it was an important crossroads.

Both armies suffered heavy casualties, including the Florida Brigade under Brigadier General E. A. Perry, which lost approximately 250 men. Anxiety filled many Jefferson County homes as they waited for news at the depot of another town in Virginia no one had ever heard of. Colonel Thompson Bird Lamar suffered wounds to his left hand and leg.

Its men would later tell stories about how fires started in the Wilderness during the fighting and trapped wounded soldiers. Raysor's

Aucilla Guards left the battlefield with four wounded and one killed, James Duncan; W. J. Cole, one of the four wounded, died later in the hospital at Charlottesville, Virginia. He lies buried in the University of Virginia Cemetery. The battle itself was the fifth costliest land battle of the War, with almost 29,000 casualties.

At Home

Meanwhile, in Jefferson County, a curious event happened. Mary's Uncle James's grandson Wesley Hezekiah Bishop enlisted in the 2nd Florida Cavalry, Company D as a private, a Northern unit. He enlisted at Cedar Key, joining the same group, which was mostly made of deserters and Unionists who had been raiding throughout North Florida. Most of the Walkers and Bishops were speechless. This unit began a vigorous campaign of raids and reconnaissance against Florida's shipments of beeves.

People speculated years later that maybe Wesley joined the North when Martin Bishop, his father at forty-seven, enlisted a little over a month later for the South. Others said that Wesley said his father suggested they need someone on both sides of the conflict. Martin Bishop was 5' 5" tall, fair complected with gray eyes and dark hair. He enlisted in the 1st Florida Reserves, Company F of the Confederacy.

#

Chapter 9
Fading Determination and Heart
May to Mid-Summer 1864

Eastern Theater

At Spotsylvania, a small village along Brock Road, General Grant pressed forward, determined to wedge his forces between Lee's army and Richmond, the heart of the Confederacy. However, General J. E. B. Stuart's job was to prevent this occurrence. His cavalry battled the Union's cavalry throughout the Wilderness for this road. It appears Lee had sensed what Grant might do.

Thus, parts of Lee's army were between Grant and Spotsylvania when Grant fell back and withdrew to a place called Laurel Hill. Some of Lee's army had reached the courthouse before Grant and entrenched themselves on the higher ground. This standoff for Spotsylvania and the road would last thirteen days, during which the rest of Lee's army quickly caught up and joined Stuart's cavalry. The clash began on May 8th.

On the first evening of the battle, Perry's Brigade spent the night building trenches near the left end of the battlefield line. That night, the Florida men could hear their enemy building their trenches immediately in front of them, and the Florida troops slept a short way from the enemy's entrenched line. However, the Union army did not attack their end, and by the next serious day of battle, someone moved Perry's brigade back from the front line.

On May 12th, the two armies fought through a torrential downpour; the fighting was essentially a point-blank slug fest, especially on the right side of the line. Both armies lost 17,000 lives after twenty-two hours of fighting. Captured at Spotsylvania was Mary's first cousin through her Uncle Littleberry, Jesse Allen. They sent him to prison in Elmira, New York.

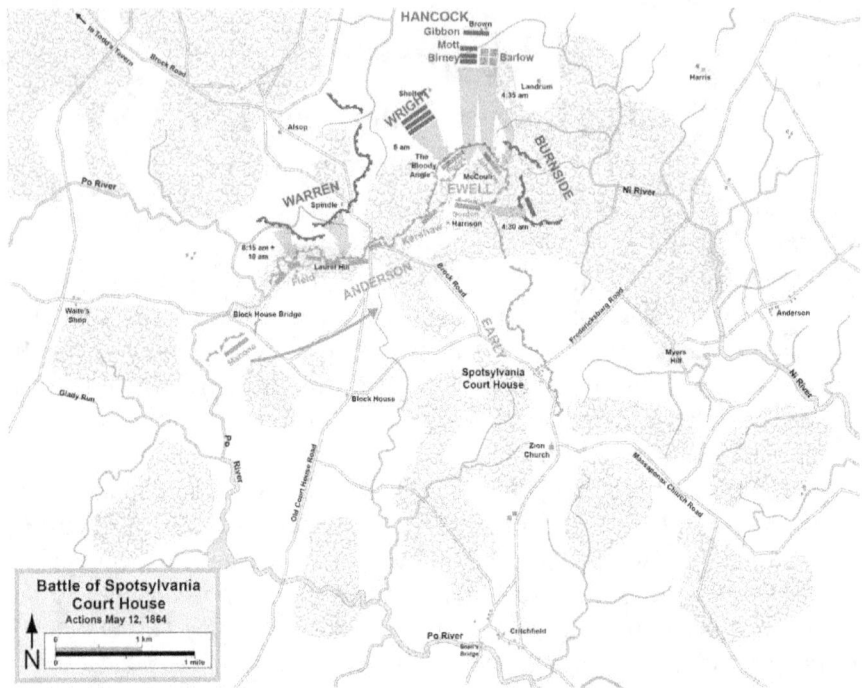

Battle of Spotsylvania Court House, Wikipedia. Map by Hal Jespersen,
www.posix.com/CW

Grant shifted his lines again and attacked on the 18th, but Lee's lines held. On the night of the 20th, Lee stealthily withdrew to fight again on the North Anna River. Like Grant before him, he was seeking better ground for his army.

These running battles would be called the Overland Campaign. At Spotsylvania there were 152,000 men in the battle, of which there were only 52,000 Rebels. Total casualties were 30,000, of which 12,000 were from the South, but none appear to have been from Jefferson County. Still, there were the missing.

Additional Florida regiments (the 9th, 10th, and 11th), sent north after their Olustee victory, reinforced the Florida regiments already at Spotsylvania. Brigadier General Joseph Finegan, the Olustee commander, took command of the overall Florida Brigade, which then became known as Finegan's Brigade. Mary's brother J.J. and her son Vollie would fight in this same brigade, though not in the same infantry. Both were now in the east fighting under General Finegan. At this time, fighting with Finegan were the 2nd, 5th, 8th, 9th, 10th, and 11th Florida Infantries.

Meanwhile, Union General Sheridan hit in guerrilla raids all around Richmond, and General Stuart was killed. Sheridan advanced next to a place called Cold Harbor, where he would be the first to attack.

The 1st Florida Cavalry was initially in the western theater. Mary's brother J.J. was there, but they merged his unit too and sent him to Petersburg, where he joined the 11th Florida Infantry, Company F. Also in the same regiment was William E. Goff, William's nephew through his first wife Elizabeth. Vollie would be in the 10th Florida Regiment, Company K, also known as J. L. Dunkin's Light Artillery, Battery A. All the newly merged regiments would get to fight at Cold Harbor. Records reflect that J.J. and Vollie's companies merged and fought at Cold Harbor, but other records indicate that the merging of companies also happened near Petersburg on June 8th.

Western Theater

While the Overland Campaign continued in Virginia, Sherman continued his mission to destroy the Army of Tennessee and capture Atlanta, subsequently pushing through Georgia and the heartland of the south. His orders were to "*move against Johnston's army, to break it up, and to get into the interior of the enemy's country as far as you can, inflicting all the damage you can against their war resources.*"

While Grant and Lee fought in the Wilderness, Sherman moved south from Chattanooga, the city called the "Gateway to the South." He used mobility and surprise to his advantage, employing a game of cat and mouse, a maneuver designed to force Johnston to attack him and his army of over 110,000 Yankees.

On Saturday, May 7th, William awoke to what seemed like an ordinary day in the Confederate camp at Dalton, Georgia—though he and the 55,000 men of Johnston's army had braced for a full-scale Union assault. Johnston's strength was his defensive skills, and north Georgia's terrain would be his only advantage—its rugged mountains, swift rivers, and narrow passes. Through an area with few roads, the Western and Atlantic Railroad's single track, which ran between Chattanooga and Atlanta, supplied both armies and ran close to William's camp.

On May 8th, Sherman struck first near the little town of Dalton, Georgia where William, the 5th Georgia, and Johnston's entire army sat waiting in their winter camp, dug in for fifteen miles along Rocky Face Ridge, a height protecting a pass twenty-five miles south of Chattanooga through which the railroad ran. Sherman had no intention of running the gauntlet, a direct assault, so he pushed against Johnston's center and right with the main body of his army while another major portion, a mobile force, went on a wide arc to a pass ten miles south of Johnston to take the railroad there in Johnston's rear.

While the battle ensued, William and his unit, entrenched south of the pass in the Crow Valley, heard galloping hooves as ghostlike figures of horses and men appeared and disappeared behind curtains of smoke. Ahead, the constant report of gunfire and cannons reverberated through the pass.

In the distance, the fields were crisscrossed by narrow lines of trees, their treetops hidden in the dense smoke. These tree lines offered refuge from which to shoot, but sometimes they offered death because the enemy hid in their foliage and waited. William glanced there frequently to study the foliage for any movement. He wondered if the gray in his jacket would afford him enough camouflage amongst the tree line. Meanwhile, smoke stung his nostrils, making him cough.

Ahead of his unit, haunting images appeared in the smoke, and William wasn't certain of what was real and what was not. When gray uniforms appeared, he and his nervous colleagues held their fire. It was their own men pulling back. All around him, men kneeled, stood, or lay upon the ground, all awaiting their turn.

While Sherman's men attacked the ridge, the other arching part of his army flanked and popped up at Resaca, miles south of Dalton. Johnston, though, discovered Sherman's movement south, so he evacuated Dalton by May 12th. William's 5th Georgia left Dalton the next day at 9 pm and marched nine miles before resting beyond Cleburnes's division near Resaca. Two days later, his unit heard Lee had repulsed Grant in Virginia.

Thus began a dance between Generals Sherman and Johnston that would last for months. The two armies skillfully maneuvered. Johnston chose strong natural positions in which to build elaborate entrenchments.

At Home

Casualties at Spotsylvania prompted an order for Florida to organize all existing troops there and send them to Richmond. The companies, over 1,200 men, met in Madison on a rainy day. The army commissioned Stephen J. Walker, son of Mary's Uncle David, as a second lieutenant in Company F on May 13th. He was seventeen years old, 5' 6" tall, with hazel eyes and dark hair. That young Stephen attained the rank of second lieutenant was normal, especially this late in the war.

The next day, more than 600 of the 1,200 marched north from Madison, headed to Quitman and Richmond, a seven-day journey. They left homes unprotected from deserters, leaving an area from which they had never strayed, adding their time and energy to a cause already lost. They marched twelve miles to catch the train to Savannah, arriving in Quitman at 4 pm and boarding the train at 5 pm.

The following morning, they arrived in Savannah by 5 am, where they boarded another train for Charleston, arriving fifteen hours later that evening at 8 pm. The men were hungry and exhausted. Many years later, they said they did not know where they were being sent, but in Charleston they received the grave news. Their destination was Virginia. As they marched through the streets of Charleston, ladies chased them all the way. The hollering, they said, was deafening, and they stayed there that night. Many said they were well in body but sick in their mind.

The next morning, on May 21st, they left Charleston at 6 am, again by rail, and changed to another car in Fair Bluff, North Carolina. They said they spent a restless night in the depot there. At 9 am the following morning, they left for Wilmington and traveled throughout the night and the next day, when they finally arrived near Petersburg. Because the enemy had destroyed the tracks, the travel-weary regiment walked the remaining fourteen miles to Richmond, Virginia, where they passed between fields and little plots of woodlands. They also passed fresh graves as they got closer to their destination.

On May 26th, the 9th Florida rested on the "green" of the Capitol Square in Richmond, awaiting orders. The 10th and 11th arrived later. The 9th had had no meat in their diet since Charleston. Finally, at noon, orders sent them to Hanover Junction, twenty-four miles north of Richmond. At Hanover Junction was General Lee and the front. At Hanover Junction on the 28th, the consolidation of the remnants of the 2nd, 5th, and 9th under Brigadier General Edward Perry began.

Western Theater

Meanwhile, on the same day at Dallas, Georgia, a gunshot wound to the left thigh injured Joel E. Walker. He was Mary's first cousin through her Uncle Littleberry. They sent him first to Black's Hospital in Augusta, then to another hospital in Lake City, Florida. The wound must have been bad.

At Home

A couple of days later, Mary's son Jesse, fourteen, stepped into Mary's kitchen. She was cleaning up after breakfast. A fear gripped her heart as she could tell something was wrong.

"Mama," said Jesse, "The Yankees captured Cousin Jess." She stared at him as the news took hold. Then she took her apron off and dropped what she was doing, handing it to Ellen to finish. "Get the buggy ready," she told Jesse, "I need to go to Mary Ann." Within days, the enemy had wounded or captured two of Mary Ann's sons. Next, Mary turned to Florrie, who was also in the kitchen, and added, "Go tell Laura and Henry to get ready. I need them to go to Uncle Littleberry's with me. Tell Henry to help Jesse get the buggy ready."

Within minutes, she put herself, Jesse, and Laura in the buggy and headed to Elizabeth. She took Laura because Mary Ann's Sealey was the same age, and their Edward was the same age as Henry. The four younger children could entertain and comfort one another. Probably Cousin Jess's young bride of less than two years would be there too. Mary Jane Hamrick Walker was pregnant or had recently given birth to a daughter named Ella.

In her heart, Mary knew that war was hard; and this war was long. Not all men survived, as attested by the daily news from the front. Day after day she walked to the depot, where the daily news, if it arrived, came by telegraph.

Western Theater

It was always on her mind that William was in this theater of the war, and reports came daily, though seldom good. Seven-year-old Laura often tagged along on Mary's daily walk to the depot. The walk on Dogwood Street was always a lovely walk, but she could not help noticing how shabby everything had gotten. Even the Presbyterian Church needed repainting.

Meanwhile, because General Joseph E. Johnston's philosophy appeared to prioritize the survival of his army over the defense of territory, he purposely avoided full out battle with Sherman, though he tried to slow the North's advance as much as possible.

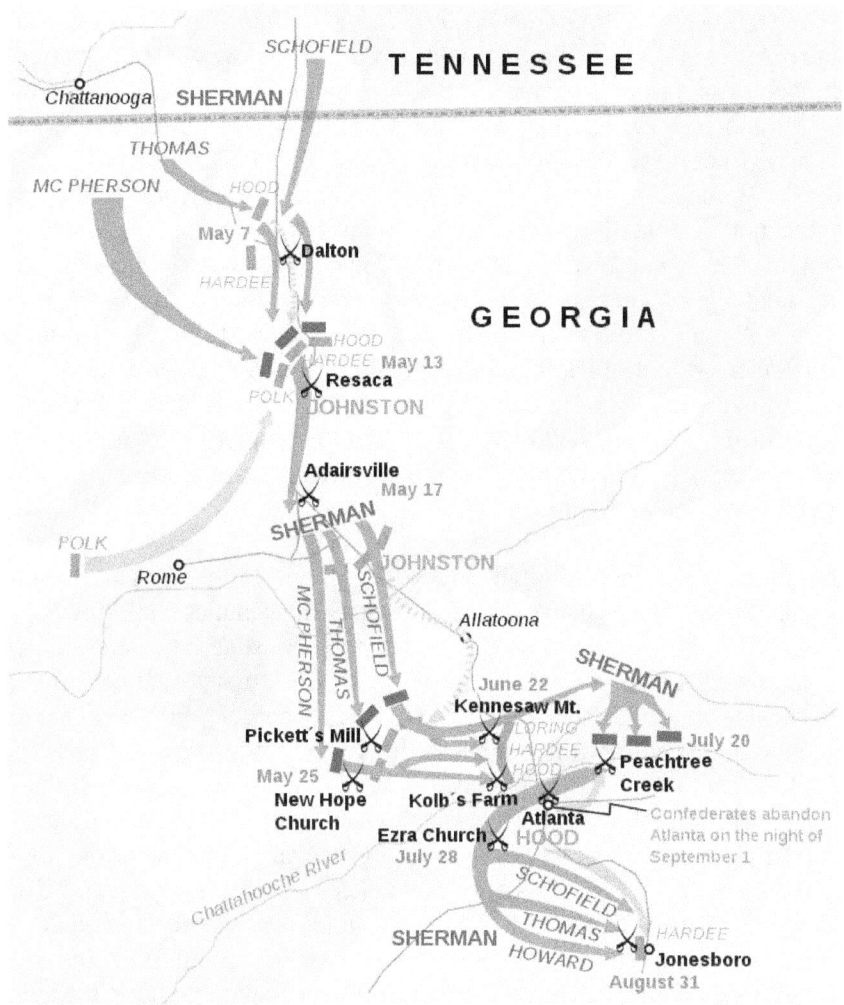

Sherman's March to Atlanta, National Park Service, Kennesaw Mountain Battlefield Park

Before Sherman could reach the railhead at Resaca, seventeen miles south of Dalton, Johnston established a four-mile defensive position west and north of where the railroad trestle crossed the Oostanaula River. William was part of this position. Johnston's excavations and embankments ran through the open fields along a slight crest. At first, the 110,000-strong Federals were a quarter mile away, but each night moving like a cat, they hunkered down and used the darkness to advance and assemble ever closer to their earthworks. Nocturnally, the distance between them and their prey narrowed.

189

By May 12th, Hardee's Corps with William's company and the entire Army of Tennessee now numbered a little over 50,000. Finley's Brigade was present, including the remaining members of William's family and friends. The battle would be the only one during the Atlanta Campaign where the full might of both armies faced each other.

Hardee's Corps quickly took their place in the center of the line, which ran next to the tracks. In his company's field of entrenchment, William felt as comfortable as anyone could. The Confederate engineers again did a good job of constructing shelter from which to fight.

A map of the Battle of Resaca shows that Lt. General Leonidas Polk's men were in the left center of the line, which ran along the west of the railroad tracks. In Hardee's Corps, Major General Patrick Cleburne, nicknamed the "Stonewall of the West," had Brigadier General Lucius E. Polk under his command. Across from their position, the ground was boggy, a kind of wet prairie.

It was a comfortable day with a cool morning, but the day warmed by 1 pm when the Yanks began their attack on May 14th. Sherman's men, according to Sherman's notes, pushed hardest at the left center to test Johnston's army. William worried about a retreat because the Oostanaula River loomed at their back. There would be little room to run, but at least he could swim, though swimming amongst drowning men was problematic too.

Still, they held their ground. That night they bedded down, wondering where the battle would begin again. The next day they awakened to quiet, but they knew the Yankees weren't gone. Later, before noon, the Yankees attacked their right flank—a full-scale assault on Johnston's right. The battle lasted for several days, and William's unit probably saw action as Hardee's Corps was now in the middle of the line.

One of those days, William foraged with his unit in little towns as far afield from Resaca as Redbud and Ranger. He felt sorry for these people. This was poor soil here, and these people had so little to begin with. All they had were their mules, and he knew that the North's policy was to shoot all local horses and mules they did not need in order to keep them from Confederate hands. So much death and destruction, it saddened him.

This cold, indifferent war, he thought, men fighting half-starved in threadbare clothes and enduring privation, toil, and contempt. The

190

constant toil for food and raiment now replaced the initial toil for glory and fame which was beaten from even the most vain now.

The food situation was no better for civilians, either. Food shortages were terrifying, especially in the cities. Food panic and public uprisings took place in Richmond and Mobile. Even corn was scarce, which limited bread. What little meat there was often spoiled because of lack of salt.

The fighting was especially fierce. On Sunday the 15th, it started at 7 am and lasted all day. The artillery on both sides added to the rattle and roar with deep, earth-shaking explosions. All around William the air was full of screaming grape. Sherman's columns threatened to flank the Confederate forces, pushing them farther north by 4 pm. Neither position was decisive, especially when Johnston realized that a division of Federal troops had crossed the Oostanaula, flanking the Southern army again. In the end, Johnston called a retreat, and they withdrew and marched seven miles south in the night.

On the move again, William had little time to write home. They reached Adairsville at 4 am, but they kept going. It rained when they stopped to rest at 2 pm the following day. The Yankees caught up again and skirmished with them.

On the 18th, his unit left again and marched all night, reaching Kingston bone tired but in good spirits. They camped a couple of miles southeast of the town.

Ten days later, northeast of Dallas, on May 28th the combined 1st and 4th of Florida saw heavy fighting about forty miles south of Kingston, Georgia. Commanders ordered Finley's Florida Brigade to charge the enemy breastworks, but heavy losses resulted in the brigade's repulse. The fighting claimed the lives of Lieutenants Roddie Shaw and James Kilpatrick as well as Major William Gorman. William, saddened by the tattered remnants of his former unit, learned that someone had removed and reburied Roddie's body in an easily accessible location along the Dallas-Marietta Road, ensuring his family could easily find it.

May 28, 1864

Dearest Mary,
    ...I have a sad task, for I must write a letter to Elijah's wife and family. He was killed yesterday, and I have been too full of thought to put

anything on paper. I thought I would write to you, and maybe it would ease me enough to write his widow.

We fought side by side; he was a brave, selfless, and loyal man. I trusted him with my life more times than I can count. As is often the case in battle, we got separated, and when the smoke cleared, I found him on the ground. Though we have only known each other a short time, he was my trusted and kind friend—my brother in arms.

I'll remember him forever. I wept for the price he paid—that his wife and children will pay.

Mary, it is times like this when I need you by my side; but I'll have to carry forward knowing you are in my heart.

All my love,
William

At Home

In June, Mary felt like she was walking through a maze of bad news. The men in the east were near Mechanicsville, Virginia while William and other family members were between General Sherman and Atlanta.

The day was hot—humid hot—the kind that clung to her skin with every step. Headed to the depot, she decided that no news would be good news for now. That would soon change. She received a letter from William, which was weeks old and out of turn. She returned home quickly to engage a reader.

Dalton, Georgia
May 10, 1864

My Dearest Mary,

You have asked again if camp life is different now. Here we mostly camp amongst the trees and talk all night about home and kin, who we fought, and where we've been. There is hardly anyone from home in this unit, so most of my campmates know little about my life in Monticello.

I speak of you and my friend, your father. We talk about our children and our sons who are in other units. I describe your cooking and how your family helped me get along in our strange land.

All of us here love to talk about our springs, rivers, and lakes; we even miss the palmettos and moss. It is a different type of woods here, though not less pretty—only different.

My tentmate Elijah likes to talk about his wife and children too. Like me, he has several old enough to fight. He talks about his wife's hair and his children's laughter.

Our nights can be so peaceful—serene—and yet our days can turn into hell at the drop of a hat. Cannons explode amid the smell of gunpowder, but the odor of death lingers most.

As you can tell, the latter creeps into almost every thought, and I am far past the ordinary camp life you asked me to describe. Kiss my babies. Tell them I love them, but it is you, Mary, that my memory dwells upon.

Yours forever,
William

After Jesse read the letter, Mary withdrew to her bedroom, where tears fell freely for a man—and a family—she had never known.

Meanwhile, on June 3rd, she received word that another battle was raging in Virginia. Word came to Aucilla and Monticello via the telegraph offices in each town. The 5th Florida Infantry was there again with the boys from Aucilla. As mentioned before, so were Vollie and J.J., with the 10th and 11th Florida Infantries, respectively. Everyone waited for news through the thirteen long days of fighting in this unknown place called Cold Harbor.

Eastern Theater

It was hot, and the land was flat and barren. As they marched in formation, J.J. asked Vollie, "I wonder how this place got its name?"

"I wonder, too. There doesn't seem to be a harbor, and it's more like walking in a baking oven." They marched ankle deep in a powdery dust, their feet in low, choking clouds of it. They both heard the command to halt. They stopped by a run-down tavern with the same name.

That evening, Vollie wrote to his brother Zech, who was at home.

May 30, 1864
Cold Harbor, Virginia

Dear Zech,

Hello, Little Brother. I sure miss you and the rest of the family. People exaggerate this man's war.

It occurred to me I might need something like a will or at least some sayings of how I want my thoughts known on the matter. In case I do not finish this war, I would like for my stone to read my name, company, regiment, and my battles. I should have enough money saved for the expenses.

Now don't be uneasy about me. I am not thinking I am gonna get killed, but I know that life is uncertain. I want to be prepared.

Kiss everyone for me, and say a prayer for all of us. I guess you get enough news to know we get closer and closer to Richmond. It is not a good thing. Please, especially, give Mama a big hug for me and tell her I miss her biscuits.

Your loving brother,
Vollie

Later, with the smaller Southern army entrenched, the larger, better-armed Northern army, led by General Phil Sheridan, attacked across an open field. The attack came amid a shroud of dust hanging in the air like a gritty cloudbank.

The Florida boys fought nobly at Cold Harbor. When General Breckenridge evacuated the Confederate breastworks in the face of a Yankee assault, Florida's brigade, supported by a Maryland infantry and artillery, jumped into play and stalled the Union surge forward. The Florida and Maryland boys occupied the three-foot-wide, two-foot-deep trenches made by Breckenridge.

Yankee sharpshooters kept up a steady crossfire and made it impossible to surface or show one's head even for a moment. At last, General Finegan ordered Monticello's Major Pickens Bird, commanding the 9th Florida, to lead a line of skirmishers to drive off the sharpshooters. It was a suicide mission but was carried out as ordered. The enemy wounded Pickens.

Over 13,000 Union soldiers were dead, wounded, captured, or missing by the end of the battle, compared to only 5,000 Confederates.

A bullet wounded Hilary Bishop again, but he was the only soldier from the Aucilla unit injured. However, two days later, Howard's Grove Hospital reported the death of Captain Pickens Bird, who had suffered a thigh wound. Pickens Bird had raised a group of men who joined Company K of the 10th Florida Infantry. He reportedly told his men when wounded, "Tell them I died like a Confederate soldier." They also wounded Hiram Henderson.

Cold Harbor was a much-needed Confederate victory, though, as much for morale as anything else. What the Florida and Maryland boys did to help retake the Southern lines at Cold Harbor was important. Confederate Brigadier General Bradley Johnson said that "*It was a most brilliant exploit, for it saved Lee's line and probably a serious disaster, for Grant had massed troops to pour them through the opening made by Hancock.*" It appears the Floridians and Marylanders may have saved Richmond. Sadly, it also prolonged the war for another ten months.

Still, a pall hung heavy over Monticello as waves of bad news continued to reach the town. In battle after battle, both on the eastern and western fronts, the South continued to lose control of its territory.

As a result, John Slicer and Archibald J. (A. J.) were waiting in prisons. And, because the South was running out of men, Valentine's battered and broken Battalion of Partisan Rangers merged on June 8 with Companies A, B, C and D and was transferred to the 10th Regiment Florida Infantry. Vollie's new company was Company K, and he was still only seventeen years of age. Other companies went to the 11th Regiment.

The other new Florida regiments were on their way, marching until dawn for Petersburg. They got there in time for the merger, which took place at Hanover Junction, Virginia. Finegan's Florida Brigade of Anderson's Division of the Third Corps received them. The boy's cousin Stephen J. Walker arrived and brought stories from home for their campfires.

Vollie may have written home to his mother.

June 14, 1864
Petersburg, Virginia

Dearest Mother,

We are safely in Petersburg, Virginia, which is only 25 miles south of Richmond. Rations up here are feast or famine. I believe we all would have succumbed long ago if it were not for the moldy crackers they sometimes provide. I guess you can tell that I most miss your cooking.

If I ever get home, I'll never leave your table again. Speaking of your table, what I miss most is to sit at a table and eat my food like a civilized man. Instead, three times a day, if we have food, I sit on the ground or a log or rock and balance my food on my lap.

I haven't had a grain of sugar or a lick of honey in a year, and my coffee is always black and lacking. Sometimes we march for a day without stopping to eat. It is not uncommon to go for two days doing the same. I have gone for three before.

I am not the size I used to be, but I still have plenty of energy. Did you know that one can live on corn that was meant for the horses, as long as there is fresh water?

You ought to see hungry men when they finally get to eat, especially biscuits and the grease from a frying pan. Using the biscuit to wipe the frying pan clean, his face wrinkles into a smile and his sunken eyes glisten in delight. By the way, many times we eat squatting around a fire with nary a thing on which to sit.

Afterwards, the tobacco bag opens, and they knock the ashes out of their pipes to fill them. But I stray from my original thoughts.

I do a lot of picket duty here. I was on last night. All was quiet on our lines and still is this morning.

Mother, I miss all of you so much. Family is precious, and I look forward to seeing all of you again, soon.

Yours,
Vollie

At Home

Safely in Petersburg, thought Mary. Lord, how can children be so clueless? She knew exactly where he was and what being in Petersburg meant. She had been following a map of the area William had made for her when he was home. He had explained the major towns of Virginia and why they were fighting in those areas.

Petersburg was a gateway by railroad to Richmond, and her boy was right in the middle of it. She took the letter and placed it in a small wooden box with all the other letters she received. Then she sat in her room by the empty fireplace. She didn't feel much like doing anything even though there was always much to do. The hall needed sweeping again, as did the front porch. Knowing what she needed to do made her blue. Where had her energy gone? She rocked and fell into a deep sleep. It was not even noon yet.

Vollie joined into what is called trench warfare. The Rebels who were there first prepared their forts and pits for the upcoming battle. They built forts and dug pits and trenches with walls of logs and dirt banked up behind them. The South's engineers dug ditches six feet deep with embankments piled six to eight feet high. They built bombproofs, which were square holes roofed with logs and dirt. It was miles long, but Grant would position his army opposite their front and eventually extend it to five miles long to take advantage of Lee's thinning army. Lee would have to match Grant's line, which meant less Southern men to every foot along the five miles of front.

Western Theater

By June 1st, Sherman retreated again to a position in the Allatoona Mountains, never straying too far from the railroad which was his supply line.

On June 10th, sitting in an entrenchment, William felt discouraged and tired of it all, and he certainly wasn't alone. They had their backs against the wall, every man. Johnston again had them repairing trenches and readying for the next attack despite the rain—weeks of continual rain. Mud ran everywhere. William had not been dry in days. His blanket was wet, his tarp, his socks. He had marched an entire day through muddy roads to get there.

June 17, 1864
Kennesaw, Georgia

Dearest Mary,

...There is a grayness of fatigue I cannot describe. Defeat is muddy and stained. Our beautiful South has turned into a silent, faded, and torn terrestrial life.

We are a ragtag lot. Our once shiny uniforms are rags. Many of us wear Yankee jackets, butternut homespun pants, and any piece of clothing one can confiscate after a battle. Stains, wear, and holes mark everything. Some can darn, but with the heat of summer almost upon us, what is the point?

Hopefully this war will end soon, and I can return to your arms....

Yours,
William

Waiting for the enemy, Johnston and the Confederate engineers built elaborate trenches from which cannon and rifle fire could hold the enemy's approach from any direction. At least it wasn't stinking hot, and the ground was easy to mold into the trenches they needed. Almost too easy. Sometimes, if built in the wrong place, the sides of the trench would melt back into the earth. That's why they had to be repaired, continually repaired.

Sherman, though, shifted south, flanking the Confederates, and Johnston sent Hood and 11,000 men to meet the threat. The result was Kolb's Farm on June 22nd. The dance continued.

After the hard-fought successive battles at New Hope Church, Pickett's Mill, and Dallas, the Confederates retreated toward a mountain called Kennesaw on June 17th, a position north and west of Marietta, which was the next important railroad town north of Atlanta. Johnston used the natural position to build eight miles of entrenchments for an eight-mile line of troops. Kennesaw, said one union soldier, "*swelled up like a bulb on a plain.*"

Then it rained off and on for days. Making breastworks as ordered was difficult, let alone making them all hours of the day and night.

Skirmishing and cannonading continued for days, as did the rain. It was hot by June 22nd.

By the morning of June 27th, William, with the 5th Georgia, rolled off his blanket and crawled backwards from his tent. It wasn't quite daybreak. The evening before, they had been getting ready for battle. Everyone knew the bluebellies were near. Johnston's army of 65,000 men stretched several miles in an arc on the north side of Kennesaw.

William walked a little way through the woods to relieve himself, past a colleague who was squatting, trying to start a fire. William had noticed lately a look on a man's face and in his being just before any battle. It was his compressed, firm lips with fixed and bloodshot eyes. A man's muscles were rigid and his veins corrugated and knotted. He wondered if he looked like this, too, a fiend going into battle.

On the way back, he said, "Joseph, I noticed you got a letter yesterday. Any news from home?" They chatted until they both heard the unmistakable scream of an incoming shell. They scrambled into the closest trench, along with all their comrades. Men came from all directions, and the bombardment began.

Within an hour, they could hear the heat of battle to their right and farther up toward Kennesaw and Little Kennesaw. William's unit was south of where present-day Old Mountain Road dead-ends into Burnt Hickory Road. One can see where they fought by taking the Noses Creek Trail. A marker in the woods shows where Walker's men camped and fought that day. One can still see the craters left by the Federal guns.

Next, they moved and marched the 5th Georgia over a mile south of its position. The heat caused William to wipe his face so often that his handkerchief soaked and became useless. Sweat got in his eyes, but thankfully his part of the line was not being attacked, though sharpshooters made it difficult to move.

Hood's offensive at Kolb's farm and heavy rains had cornered Sherman into a frontal assault at Kennesaw. It would be his only mistake. The strike at Kennesaw was on Hardee's part of the line. In front of Hardee was a creek, tangling undergrowth, and an open field, a stronger position. Sherman's men stormed anyway and got within five feet of Hardee's men, but the Rebs gave a Union slaughter. They mowed them down with gunfire, and some hand-to-hand combat ensued.

At one point, they called a two-day truce to bury their dead, mostly to get rid of the sickening stench of decaying bodies in the summer

198

heat. They buried them together, both Yankees and Rebels, in long, deep trenches dug for the purpose. William watched as they made hooks from bayonets, bending them to drag bodies which they then threw helter-skelter into the trenches.

Hot and weary, he slipped away to the shade of a stream to bathe his face and drink from his canteen. As he lifted it, he found his arm and shoulder battered, bruised, and sore. *Why not?* he thought; *I've shot more than a hundred times today.* His gun got so hot he took his dead friend's and continued. He sat in the water and turned to his side to vomit. Later, he removed his shirt to wring it out and realized there were holes shot through it.

Sherman was trying their center line, but the Confederate cannons drove them under cover. That night when everything quietened, William heard that their soldiers even rolled rocks down on the Union soldiers from atop Little Kennesaw and Pigeon Hill. Sherman had both misread the terrain and Johnston's defensive works.

Sherman lost the Battle of Kennesaw Mountain.

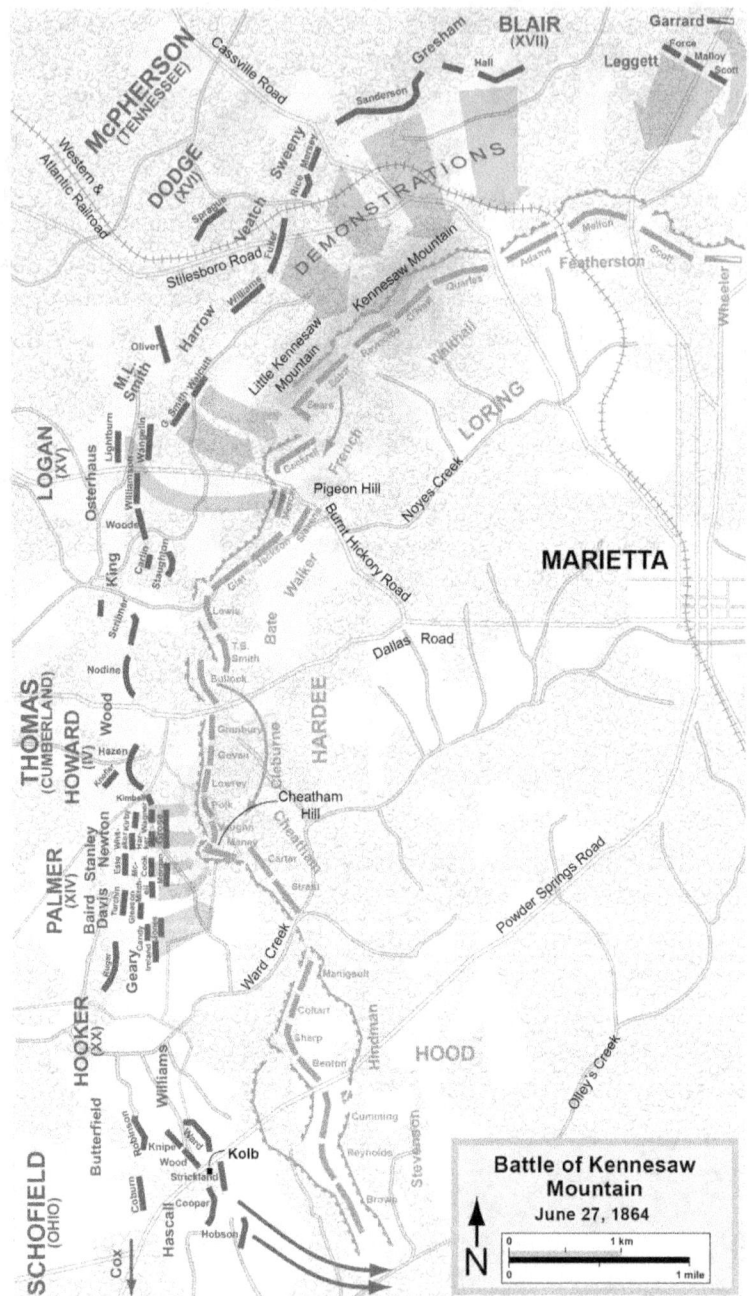

Battle of Kennesaw Mountain, National Park Service, Kennesaw Mountain
National Battlefield Park

At Home

For Mary in Florida, her daily trips to the depot held wretched news. Along with the news about Kennesaw and other towns, she listened to local reports about how the Union had again occupied Jacksonville and areas around it. They demolished a Confederate camp to its west, heavily protected by log and earth breastworks. This removed one more barrier between the Federals and Tallahassee.

Rumors ran rampant across North Florida into Middle Florida. Mary saw the fear in her children's eyes and worried about their little minds. Zech was doing well with the load of being the man in their family, but she worried about all the younger ones, especially Hattie, Henry, Laura and Joseph, ages ten to six. All were all old enough to know that unbridled danger lurked nearby.

On June 15th, Florida's Governor Milton received a letter from Monticello's William Bailey stating that he had kept his cotton mill in operation through the help of disabled soldiers which were discharged from military service and men who were not subject to military service. Finding enough employees was a universal problem throughout the south.

A few weeks later, an armed Federal boat landed about ten miles above Dead Man's Bay on the Gulf Coast and destroyed a saltworks there. Steinhatchee, meaning Dead Man's River and located less than seventy miles southeast of Aucilla, is the name people use for Dead Man's Bay today.

The escalation in rumors and reports increased everyone's nervousness. The Federal Navy even pillaged and burned the residence of former US Senator David Levy Yulee on the Homosassa River. Later in June, Federals burned many saltworks along the Gulf shoreline, resulting in many visible fires.

At Goose Creek (Wakulla Beach), the Union destroyed over 2,000 bushels of salt, three corn cribs containing about a thousand bushels of corn, a large quantity of hay and fodder, a blacksmith shop and tools, a carpenter shop and tools, 165 kettles and pans, forty-three large 800-gallon capacity boilers, ninety-eight brick furnaces, nine wagons and carts, and twenty sets of mule harnesses.

During this time, Florida was important to the Confederacy. It was hard for the North to bottle up Florida's twelve-hundred-mile-long, indented coastline. All along the coasts, blockade runners tried and tried again. Union records document sixty-three similar incidents in 1864 alone, including one vessel attempting to enter Indian River Inlet—and another making the same attempt later that very day. Both were British schooners with cargoes of salt, liquor, coffee, and dry goods. Earlier, another British sloop tried to enter Mosquito Inlet. She was supposedly bound for Key West from Nassau but was far off course. In the spring, the Union seized a schooner loaded with 132 bales of cotton and two barrels of turpentine on the Gulf. On the St. Johns River, the USS *Pawnee* captured the Confederate *General Sumter,* a river steamer on Lake George carrying passengers to the Ocklawaha. Mary heard rumors the city of Palatka would soon fall to Union hands again.

Salt became a scarce commodity even in Florida. Years later, family lore told how locals scraped dirt from the floors of their smokehouses to collect any salt they could glean. Salt before refrigeration was vital for more than just seasoning. It preserved their meat and fish. Otherwise, there was no way to preserve their food for leaner times, which were already upon them. People also needed salt to tan leather.

Mary put the dirt in her big iron pot, as she did for soap-making, and boiled it until there was a residue of salt at the bottom. Still, it would not be enough, and she probably remembered how the Indians preserved their meat with little or no salt. She showed Zech and Jesse how to cut their meat into pieces suitable for drying, the thinner the better. Next, they suspended the meat from rods up high near the column of smoke that disappeared through the hole in the smokehouse's ceiling. The fire had to be maintained continuously throughout the process for twenty-four hours. Summer sun on the smokehouse roof provided the conditions for this process. Beef and venison were easier, and she remembered pork was oily and was more difficult to cure. They depended less and less on pork. Mary noticed that all the activity needed to keep the smokehouse going kept the children busy and their minds off the horrors of the impending war.

Yet she always kept in mind what William's lot was like. Jesse read her his last letter, and William described their food situation, which mirrored their own. He wrote, "Sometimes we get meat but no bread. Later, we might get flour but no meat. Sometimes we can find coffee in abundance, but there's not a grain of sugar. Then we get sugar, but not a drop of coffee."

By the end of June, it was like an oven in Monticello. There had been little rain since earlier in the month when the heavy rains had destroyed the entire corn crop. Her family in Elizabeth were having a hard time of it, and she would too since they were her lifeline. Mary sat on her back porch in the shade, trying to cool off as best she could. She watched her two last settin' hens peck below around the back steps. Thankfully, she thought, William had left her with good advice. The gold they invested remained hidden. She traded using the Confederate money, and she had used the Floridian currency to pay taxes.

Good news came. On the last day of June in the eastern theater, the Florida Infantries reached Reams Station in Virginia by daybreak where, along with Lee's army, they attacked, driving the enemy back in a running fight. The Floridians captured seven pieces of artillery, several horses, and prisoners. Mary made good use of the communique when she and Zech made sure the children dwelled on this little piece of good news.

The next afternoon she sat on the back porch watching Henry along with other neighborhood boys replay the battle, as always taking turns being the Yankees. Nobody wanted to be a Yankee, but they needed an adversary to replay the battles.

A few days later, Mary and the younger kids picked blackberries. It was a great day to get away from Monticello, but they were careful not to venture too far. The woods of Middle Florida were full of deserters. The family may have used the Palmer Mill Road, being careful not to drift too far into the woods on either side. One can still see the old Palmer Mill roadbed behind the homes on the south side of East Washington Street, to which it ran parallel.

She added blackberries to her biscuits that night for a special treat, and she also made a sauce to serve over a beef roast the following night. Later she cleaned the rest of the blackberries well and added them and three quarts of water to a demijohn. To the water and blackberries she added two spoons of sugar, corked it securely, and put it in the sun on the back porch where it set for two weeks. It would make an excellent vinegar.

Western Theater

The South's biggest advantage, their determination and heart, faded as its men diminished during the summer of 1864. Sherman, with an army of more than a hundred thousand men, pushed south down the Western and Atlantic Railroad line. He continued his assault for days when General Johnston at last abandoned Kennesaw during the night of July 2nd.

At Kennesaw, Sherman's frontal assault cost him heavy casualties. Johnston's army lost 800 men, but Sherman lost 1,800. Again, the North's advantage of men and arms was their dominance.

After Kennesaw, Johnston sent men to guard the railroad bridge, but Sherman surprised him again, sending a small force across the river upstream. It was truly like watching a waltz between the two armies, a three-step gyration—a battle, a flanking movement, and a withdrawal before turning to fight again—always leading to Atlanta, this time all the way across the Chattahoochee River within a day's march of the city itself. The river was the last major natural barrier shielding Atlanta.

Once Sherman's army crossed the Chattahoochee, it was only a half-day's march to the outer trenches that protected the city. They crossed it on July 17th, the same day President Jefferson relieved Johnston of his command and replaced him with General John Bell Hood. The Northern forces advanced toward Peachtree Creek, where William waited.

Eastern Theater

Meanwhile, in early July, Vollie walked through the hot, dusty trenches at Petersburg. Journals reported 110-degree heat and four inches of dust. A dull, yellow-green, gray dust coated everything—trees, shrubs, uniforms, hair and faces. Added to the ugliness was the stench of unburied bodies. Sunstroke was common, especially on the northern side.

By the end of August, Monticello learned that Colonel Thompson Bird Lamar of Jefferson County had been wounded at Petersburg, and this wound subsequently caused his death. He was married to one of the Bellamy girls who grew up near Elizabeth.

Opposing sharpshooters were always alert with intermittent firing, always watching for any movement in the opposing firing slits. Every day, this method killed men. The two fronts were barely 150 yards apart. The firing made everyone try to dig deeper and hide in the trenches every moment of their days and nights.

That night, Vollie lay in the quietness of the early, sultry evening, thinking about home with its springs and shaded swamps. He knew if he ever got to see it again, he would never leave. He was sick of cowering in this God-forsaken ground.

At Home

While in Florida, Mary and the children listened to news from the west. A unit of the Second US Colored Infantry and the Second Florida US Cavalry, a unit made up of deserters and Florida Unionists, with 700 mounted soldiers, attacked areas around St. Andrews Bay. They would continue moving up into Florida and by the fall capture Cottondale and Marianna, home of Florida's Governor Milton. Though the home militia barricaded its main street entrance, the Union troops successfully entered Marianna and burned the Episcopal church, where the local militia headquartered. It drew panic in Middle Florida.

#

Chapter 10
A Relentless Grind
Fall 1864 to February 1865

At Home

By the spring of 1864, the nature of the war shifted dramatically. Before then, major battles typically unfolded in the spring, summer, and fall—pausing during the harsh winter months. But General Ulysses S. Grant changed that. Determined to wear down the Confederacy, Grant kept constant pressure on the Southern forces. Confederate soldiers found themselves under fire for eight hours a day, day after day, even through the winter of 1864. There would be no winter camp. He knew the South was running dangerously low on men and ammunition. From this point on, the war became a relentless grind—with little rest and fewer letters from William.

Death didn't always come from battle, though. After a deep night's sleep, Mary lay in bed, still not fully awake. In this moment of not asleep but not quite awake, she heard the birds rendering their good morning chirps, and a breeze came through the window. The broadcloth curtains undulated. In that strange borderland between dreaming and waking, the unwelcome thought slipped in. Her father was dead.

There it was, greeting her new day with a realization all over again. It didn't seem true. He had left this earth for a heavenly calling. She knew his spirit still lived, but she missed him. She needed him. He had been her rock, especially when William left for the war.

There had been a special bond, a bond of a father and his oldest daughter. Since her mother died, he had depended more and more on her thoughts and recommendations. But over the past couple of years, she had watched him decline physically and mentally. It was the weariness of this war, the toll on their family.

Tears rolled down the sides of her eyes as she stared at the ceiling in the early morning light. An aching emptiness, she felt, would forever remain in her heart. She tried to placate herself with the thought that she too would answer this call someday to cross over. It gave her comfort to know he would be there at the beautiful gate to meet her, and behind him would be the rest of her family, chatting and laughing. There would be Grandpa Walker and Granddaddy Wilson, whom she could hardly remember. Grandma Walker and Granny Wilson would beam, but the one with the biggest grin and best hug of all would be her mama. Oh, what a day that will be!

It comforted her now that her father's life had not vanished like a shadow, that his and the others' memories would live on far beyond their time on this earth. She slipped into a deep sleep.

We are uncertain when Jesse passed away. It is as if he vanished. We know he sold all his land by 1847 after mortgaging a lot in 1842. The last record for Jesse was in 1861 when he still owned a lot of livestock, but he does not appear in the 1870 census. We're unsure why he sold his land, but we wonder if he already struggled with malaria. For some, malaria creeps in slowly, stealing strength by degrees, one fever at a time. It is called the slow thief.

No death certificate exists, nor can anyone find one from that period. There was no register of deaths, nor was there a funeral home, anyway. There was no obituary, but the *Family Friend* ceased normal printing in 1862 because of a lack of paper and paying customers. No editions after this survive.

They buried him in the Walker Cemetery, which has no existing records. However, long-deceased descendants claim he is buried there. There is no tombstone. There is no family Bible that we know of. We searched for probate records but found none. Few probate records existed during the war, anyway. It almost appears as if families did not want to leave records during and immediately after the war. There are no church burial records either. We found no journals, diaries, or letters.

However, he lost so much in the four years between 1859 and 1863. His wife of thirty-eight years died, and within six months he lost his brother Joel. The next year, he lost his oldest son Henry and during the Kentucky Campaign his son George. His son Joseph disappears from documentation and may have died, too. With all his six other sons away at war and at sixty-three, it may have been more than he could take.

Eastern Theater

Meanwhile, after his overwhelming defeat at Cold Harbor, Grant quietly pulled his troops from the area and moved them across the James River toward Petersburg. Earlier, because Lee realized what Grant was doing, he had quickly ordered troops to fill the gap.

Grant swiftly attacked the industrialized city of 18,000, but because of delays, Lee scrambled more troops in time to hold Grant off. This is when Grant entrenched around Lee's entrenched army.

Meanwhile, as Lee's popularity soared, Grant's waned, but Grant wasn't finished. At the end of Grant's unsuccessful Overland Campaign, he put forth a new strategy. Whereas his Overland Campaign was to defeat Lee's army, this was no longer his immediate aim. The siege of Petersburg began on June 15th and wasn't exactly a siege. His army's goal was not to cut off the city's food supply but to eliminate the supplies and communication to Lee and the Confederate capital of Richmond, twenty-four miles to Petersburg's north. The prize was to control the Richmond and Petersburg Railroad.

Petersburg was a supply depot much like Atlanta, as war supplies arrived from all over the South through one of its five railroads. Since the North had cut off many other supply lines feeding Richmond, Petersburg was its last resort. The city's strategic importance had prompted the construction of a ten-mile, U-shaped trench line around it as early as 1862. Confederate forces built walls forty feet high and erected fifty-five gun batteries. It was a trench line Grant would batter for days, weeks, and even months before he could break through.

At Petersburg, Valentine's unit had joined the Confederate earthworks, which stretched for miles across the Virginia countryside, ending about six miles southwest of Petersburg. Joining the 10th was the 11th, including James Goff and Vollie's Uncle J.J. The Florida 5th Infantry was also at Petersburg. So many of Vollie's uncles and cousins were there.

The siege was a series of battles and raids as Grant repeatedly attacked in various skirmishes. The fighting would be repetitive and deadly.

On June 22nd, Valentine was in the Battle of Jerusalem Plank Road where Major General William Mahone received command of Anderson's former division. It would be the first in a series of skirmishes and battles around Petersburg.

Western Theater

North of Atlanta, Sherman's army crossed the Chattahoochee, and the Confederate army withdrew into the fortifications of Atlanta, where they would remain for almost two months. William was in another siege with the Confederates' backs against a wall. War colleges all over the world teach a basic premise that without proper food and clothing, not only does the body suffer and begin to die, but so does the spirit.

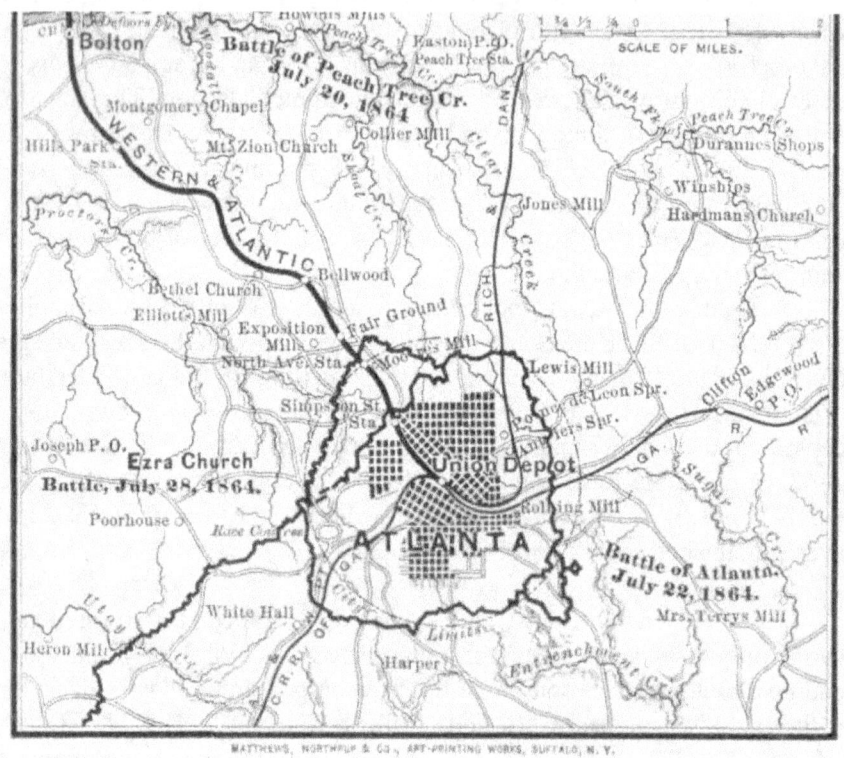

The Battles of Atlanta—The Battle of Peachtree Creek, followed by the Battle of Atlanta on July 22nd and the Battle of Ezra Church on July 28, Matthews, Northrup & Co., 1887, Library of Congress

Sherman attacked because Atlanta was too important. Atlanta sat at the heart of a still intact belt of manufacturing communities which stretched from Augusta to Selma. In Atlanta alone were its arsenal, foundries, magazines, and stores. It was the heart of the Confederacy. It was a vital Confederate rail junction of four roads, but it had not always been so. Founded in the late 1830s, it had begun simply as the terminus of the Western and Atlantic Railroad which ran from Chattanooga. By 1845, less than twenty years before the war, it contained only fourteen families and three general stores. Then came the other railroads and growth.

Sherman came down the one from Chattanooga, but the three others were still viable. One line ran south to Macon to the breadbasket of the South, and another ran east to Augusta, where it transported manufactured arms and ammo and connected with rails to Charleston, Raleigh, Richmond, and the port of Savannah. The third railway ran west into Alabama, connecting with Birmingham's iron and Selma.

When Johnston's army retreated into Atlanta after Kennesaw and after more than 2,500 Confederate casualties, Confederate President Jeff Davis was livid. Johnston and Davis had had their problems earlier, and Davis had no faith in him. He believed Johnston would surrender Atlanta. Davis relieved him of his command and replaced him with General John Bell Hood. In time, the replacement would be shown to be useless.

Davis's demoralizing change in generals created transfers of authority and responsibility reaching to the privates. They reassigned William's regiment to Taliaferro's Brigade in the Department of South Carolina, Georgia, and Florida.

In Atlanta, Hood, hell bent for leather, took Johnston's plans and formed his line on a ridge along today's Collier Road. There he waited for Sherman to cross Peachtree Creek, which he did on July 20th. The heaviest fighting occurred the following day.

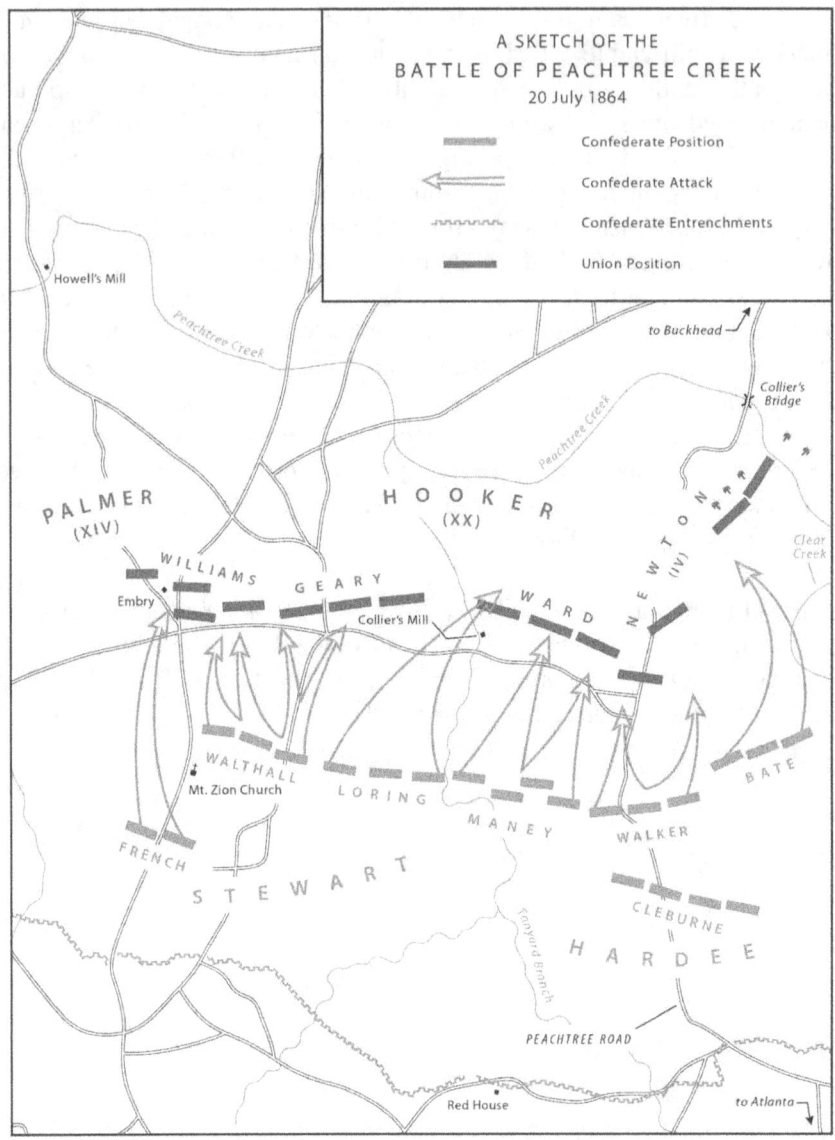

A Sketch of the Battle of Peachtree Creek, July 20, 1864, McCarley, J. Britt, United States Army Center of Military History, 2014.

Today, on Collier Road east of Peachtree Road, there are historical markers showing the place where the different units fought. Collier Road runs near Buckhead. Here William and his unit, under General Walker, were in elaborate entrenchments built earlier for the last defense of the city. William and his unit crouched in a trench behind rows of palisades, stakes made of tree trunks split into rails and slanted towards their enemy. Pointed at the top, they provided additional defense.

All around him, every tree of less than twenty inches' girth was taken down. This provided enormous areas with little understory.

Palisades and chevaux de frise in front of the Ponder House on Peachtree Road, Atlanta, 1864, Wikipedia

A fierce, stand-up fight raged all afternoon before the South retreated with heavy losses.

Today, near the site of this battle is Tanyard Creek Park. William was near the current intersection of Collier and Peachtree Road. Across the street, where Union soldiers struck, stands Piedmont Hospital, where William's fifth-great-grandson would be born over 160 years after he fought here.

Sherman thought he could take Atlanta in less than a week, but later he said, "*These fellows fight like Devils and Indians combined, and it calls for all my cunning and strength.*" After Hardee pulled his shattered divisions back to the safety of the outer defenses, estimates placed Confederate losses at 4,706. The North's loss was only 1,779. Hood suffered a bitter defeat, but he wasn't finished.

That night after the battle, General Hardee, under orders, quietly rallied his men. Tired but ready to move, William under Gist's Brigade marched fifteen miles around the left flank of Sherman.

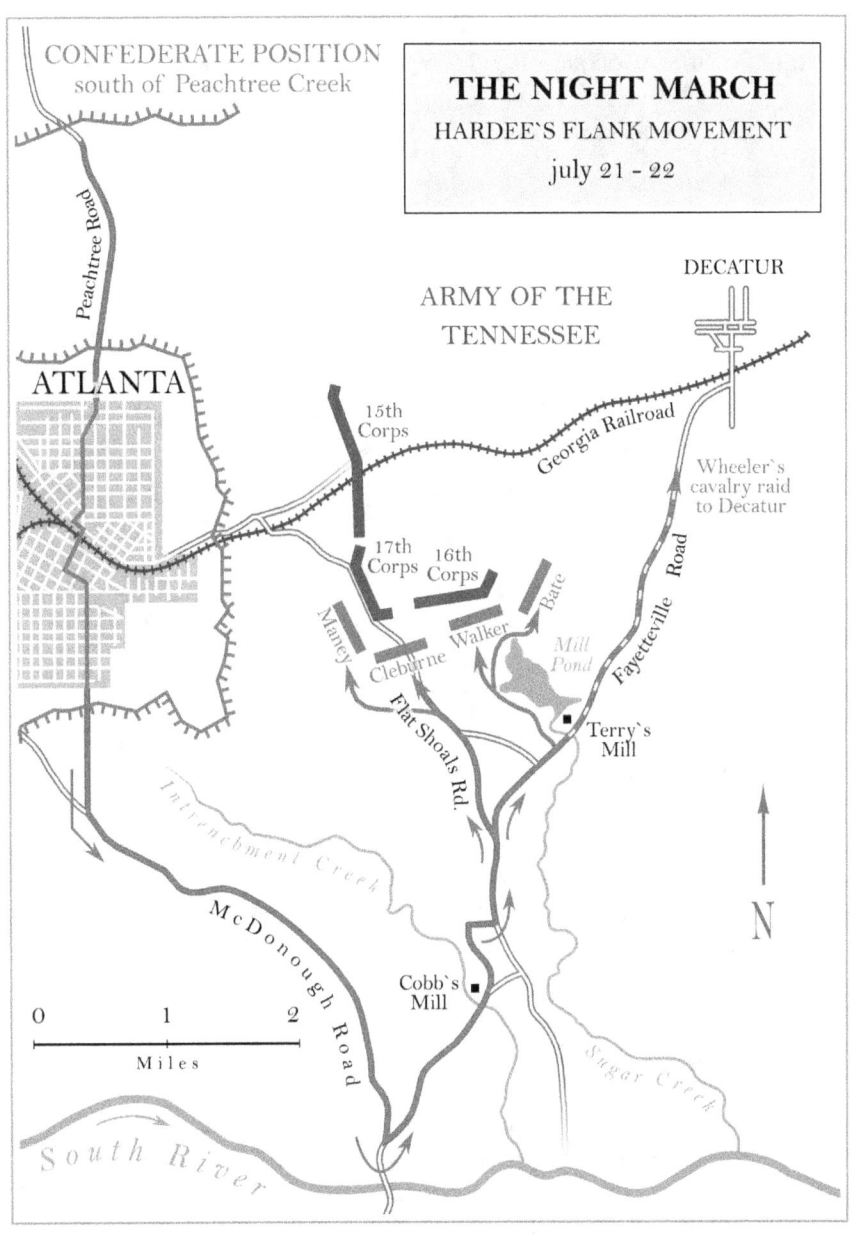

Hardee's Flank March, Bonds, Russell S. Wikimedia Commons

He was glad to leave the entrenchments near Tanyard Branch. It was good to stretch his legs, though the night-long march down Peachtree Road (now Peachtree Street) through Atlanta would weary even the youngest man. They marched through the heart of Atlanta, which

Sherman had shelled for two days. William's unit moved through more shelling down McDonough Road. By daybreak, they turned and ascended Sugar Creek. When they stopped, to William's right were the boys from the Florida units under Finley.

City of Atlanta, 1864, Peachtree Road, photo by George Barnard, official Army photographer during the war, Library of Congress

William's next battle would carry the name of the city. In the Battle of Atlanta, Hood's plan was bold. He expected Hardee to execute a great flank attack, but it took Hardee longer than expected to get his men in position. He attacked around noon on the 22nd, when he struck the Union Major General James B. McPherson's flank. The fighting was fierce near present-day US 23, now called Moreland Avenue and Flat Shoals Road. It occurred fifteen miles south and east of the Peachtree Creek Battle and centered on a hill known as Bald Hill.

In battle, they killed William's commander, General Walker—but the Union also suffered a major loss when General McPherson fell. Yet despite this, the South bore the heavier cost—casualties it could ill afford with an already weakened army. Hood was living up to his name and using his human resources far too quickly.

At Home

At home, it was hotter than usual. From 4 to 5 pm every afternoon, it rained. The moisture in the air was heavy, and Mary tried to move slower than normal to conserve her energy. The house could wait. No need to have a heat stroke. Sitting on her front porch watching the kids play in the front yard, she noticed that her hand-held paper fan was disintegrating.

She would make a new one and create it out of cloth. They lasted so much longer. For staves, she needed tender juvenile palmetto stems. Later, she asked Jesse to find her eight to ten young palmetto fronds cut off at the ground. She would begin drying their stems tomorrow.

Eastern Theater

On the evening of July 24th, in the cold and rain, a strong summer wind whipped through the Petersburg trenches where Vollie hunkered down. He thought about Monticello and how balmy their night would be, and he longed for the safety of his family's home. He had learned earlier that a hand wound had sent his friend, William W. Blackburn (a fellow student), to a hospital in Lake City, Florida. Vollie had been in line for battle since 3 am and expected to remain in line until sunrise.

In the dark morning, he heard a loud explosion to the north of Johnston's Division. All he could find out later was that the 22nd South Carolina was the regiment blown up. The worst of "The Battle of the Crater" took place about 4:30 am to their north. Vollie sought to find out if these boys were from Colleton District, his mother's birthplace, especially since so many of her kin were still there. Killed in the Petersburg mine explosion were 216 South Carolinians, all mostly from Edgefield and Oconee Districts.

Though the Southern boys knew they had scored a victory, it was short-lived. Stuck near Old Jerusalem Road, Vollie emdured the heat and hunger. The air was stifling, and whenever he could stand it no longer, he would break cover and risk the bullets of waiting sharpshooters.

After the disastrous loss at the Battle of the Crater, Grant never again attempted a direct assault on their position. Meanwhile, Vollie tried to settle his mind by reminding himself that sweltering in the trenches was still easier than enduring the long, punishing marches.

In the third week of August, Vollie left the ditches and marched down the Weldon railroad line toward a place called Globe's Tavern, where his regiment unsuccessfully assaulted a Federal position there. Southern casualties were heavy. Joining them were other recently arrived Florida regiments.

The skirmishing around the southern perimeter of Petersburg lasted for 292 days, a gradual wearing down of Lee's army. Plus, the Union destroyed a short segment of the rails before being driven off.

Later in August, to Vollie, it seemed it rained all month. Their trenches were half full of mud and water. Food rations steadily diminished. Through the sliver of emptiness high on the walls of the trench, Vollie stared up into the night. He missed the stars and moon, which were a welcome sight. He liked to think his family was looking at the same stars. It made him feel closer to them and to Monticello.

From August 18th to 21st, in the Battle of Globe Tavern (which is also called the second battle of Weldon Railroad), the Union army attempted again to sever the rail line. They destroyed miles of track this time while being attacked by the South. It would be the first Union victory in the Richmond-Petersburg Campaign.

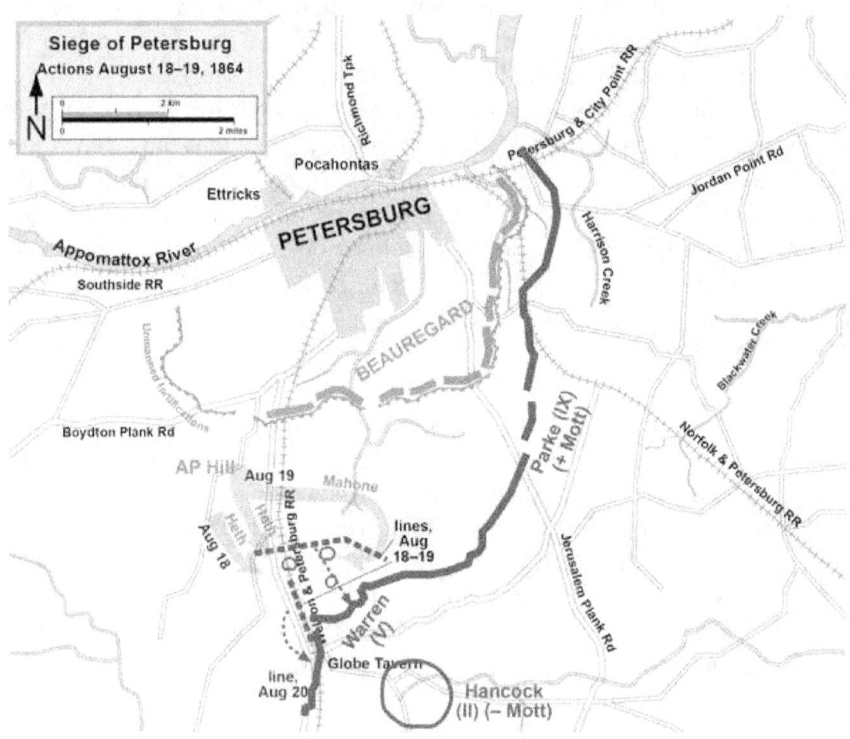

Siege of Petersburg, August 18-19, 1864, Hal Jespersen's Wikipedia Civil War Maps, 2011

At Home

At home, Mary heard of these places not on her map, but she felt they must all be near Petersburg. With some of her men fighting near Atlanta and the rest near Petersburg, she kept her habit of walking to the depot once a day to check in with the telegraph office. It was good to stretch her legs, and she also used it to fight off the melancholy. Besides, it helped her escape the hot house and kitchen. There was a breeze, but it was humid. She took her time walking and walked in the shade.

At night, on her knees in her bedroom, she prayed for God to help her be more faithful in her prayers and example. She prayed for all her family, wherever they might be.

While highly inconvenienced, the South could still bypass the destroyed rails by portaging their supplies by wagon to Richmond. So, still looking for a way to sever this same railroad which led south to Weldon, North Carolina and connected to the Port of Wilmington, Grant again struck near a place called Ream's Station, where the Florida Brigade was entrenched. They pursued and fought off the Northern soldiers. At the end of the battle, the North's casualties were over 2,700 and the South's over 800. The siege at Reams Station on August 25th resulted in the capture of Jefferson County's Benjamin Whitfield.

Civilians who had been enthusiastic in 1861 and 1862 had lost faith in the future of the Confederacy by the Fall of 1864. Instead, they simply fought to save their homes and communities. And this is how people in West Florida pulled together to defeat the Yankee invasion in their area. The superior Yankee force proved unable to hold what they had gained in Marianna and Cottondale.

Using Tallahassee's working railroad, the Confederate forces shifted enough troops to defeat the enemy from the east. Also, Marianna's proximity to Georgia, which had a large home guard and a more expansive network of railroads, threatened the Yankees' northern perimeter in West Florida. So wounded in action, their leader General Alexander Asboth, the Union commander of Florida, withdrew to Pensacola, taking with him approximately 400 slaves, 200 horses, and 400 head of cattle. Jackson County had been a supplier for Confederate beeves.

Mary, downtown with Ellen, listened to the news. She was in Palmer's store, making a much-needed single purchase, all they could afford. Upon walking home, she noticed everyone and everything looked haggard, from the old men to the buildings. A lack of money and labor force prevented any repairs, and the only young men available were physically and mentally scarred.

Hard to maintain one's spirits, she worried about her children, even though they were far from the battles. Children were more than skin, muscles, and bones. Their little minds were delicate and impressionable. She thought about her own mother and grandmothers and how they sowed such good seeds in her heart when she was young, and how those good words came to her when she needed them most. She thought, "How blessed I was to have had them in my childhood."

Early the next morning, she met with her sewing circle, who met early now because of the heat. Florida had an extra-long Indian summer this year. The days were hot. She started the conversation, and the ladies reminisced about their parents and grandparents.

Later, in bed and restless in the heat, she could not get something out of her head. If William did not return, Laura and Joseph would hardly remember their father. She sighed and turned over. They would most likely never know what it was like to live in better times. Poor little five-month-old Virginia was weak, weaker than her other children had been. The entire household was sad and lonely without him.

She wished she could read or write. Many times William got up when he couldn't sleep and read by oil light in the parlor or wrote at his desk, but she didn't have that luxury. She slipped from her bed, tiptoed down the hallway, and stepped out onto the back porch. Sitting on the steps under the half moon in her white gown, she stared at the stars and wondered if William might do the same. Sleepy, she went back to her bed, but her dreams were troubled.

Eastern Theater

With the cold of the Virginia fall coming on, Vollie wrote home for socks, gloves, and a new pair of boots. Finegan's Brigade also focused their efforts on building huts for their winter quarters, though they would remain unused. They were in reserve near Fort Gregg, south of Petersburg. They were suffering from want of proper winter clothing.

Enemy action was light and the front quiet. At Petersburg, the mood around the campfires had changed. It was quieter now—less jovial, with fewer jokes and stories. The usual yarns were rare. Many attributed the shift to the men who remained. They were sober, steady, and focused. Vollie noticed they spoke with less self-pity and rarely complained.

At Home

Mary and the rest of the family worked to get their men what they needed, but they still had to meet their own needs. She guessed they were better off than most. They made their own fabric, tanned cowhides and deer hides for their own shoes, and even used the buds of the palmetto to plait for their own hats. They had their own cotton and a spinning wheel for making thread.

Zech, with the help of family from Elizabeth, worked on a common acre of cotton so they would have it for making clothes. Then Mary ginned the cotton on a hand gin, spun it into thread, and wove the thread into cloth—a job that took weeks. By this time in the war, she and the other ladies of the South spent a significant amount of time clothing their men and families—several hours of every day.

Western Theater

A muster roll dated May to October 1864 reports Mary's Uncle David was absent because of illness. As Sherman drew his perimeter closer to Atlanta, he turned to Atlanta's southern side toward the end of August in a two-day battle near Jonesborough.

William was elsewhere, but Finley's Brigade was there with Florida's 1st-3rd, the 4th/1st Florida Cavalry (dismounted), and Florida's 6th and 7th. The Confederate corps, through desperate fighting and an onset of darkness, extended their lines east to protect the South's right flank and retreated south in good order to Lovejoy Station. The Battle of Jonesborough was the last battle for the city.

Regardless, though, Sherman cut Atlanta's last rail link to the outside world, the Macon and Western, Hood's supply line. At Jonesborough, they wounded Jefferson County's Major General James Patton Anderson in the jaw; however, he recovered.

With Atlanta's rail lines and roads blocked to the outside world, Hood ordered all public property destroyed and the city evacuated, including eighty-one rail cars of ordinance. He abandoned the city that night, escaping with his army, including William's Georgia 5th. William spent the rest of September near Lovejoy Station.

Subsequently, on September 2nd, Sherman triumphantly entered Atlanta. He telegraphed President Lincoln, "Atlanta is ours, and fairly won." In William's birthplace, people celebrated in the streets of Washington City. Atlanta's fall was a morale changer for Grant, Lincoln, and the North. Lincoln needed it because of the coming presidential election.

Unfortunately for the South, though, the Battle for Atlanta was simply a steppingstone for Sherman. His sights quickly turned to Savannah. Sherman wished to break the backbone of the South.

Meanwhile, Lieutenant General William Joseph Hardee assumed command of the 5th Georgia Infantry and took command of the Department of South Carolina, Georgia, and Florida. Hardee immediately aimed to strengthen the defenses of Savannah and Charleston. He organized his 12,000 troops.

Simultaneously, Finley's Florida Brigade, under Bates's Division, marched to Middle Tennessee for Hood's Tennessee Campaign, along with the 4th/1st Florida Cavalry (dismounted), the 6th Florida and the 7th. William Scott Dilworth served as the 1st/3rd's colonel, and William P. Moseley, the son of Florida's first governor, served as quartermaster sergeant.

Hood's goal—to sever Sherman's lines of communication and create disorder in the Union-held central Tennessee—caused Sherman consternation. He took the bait briefly but returned to Atlanta and began his "March to the Sea," leaving Major General Thomas and General John Schofield to deal with Hood. Before leaving Atlanta, though, he destroyed all of Atlanta's factories, railroads, and commercial buildings. He finished what Hood had left behind.

Because Sherman felt his supply line was too long and tenuous (it ran from Chattanooga to Atlanta) and because he could not hold Atlanta, he divided his two armies, sending half to Nashville and the other half to Savannah. He used a scorched earth strategy to scour the breadbasket of the South, which was Georgia, and began his march to the sea.

In November, James Andrews and his uncles and cousins moved deeper into Tennessee through rain, sleet, snow, and freezing cold. Their officers planned a frontal assault on the forces of Major General John Schofield, a classmate of Hood's at West Point. The two classmates met on a battlefield in Franklin, Tennessee.

It would not help when Abraham Lincoln won the reelection in November, though. Southern morale throughout the South plummeted even more. More desertions followed.

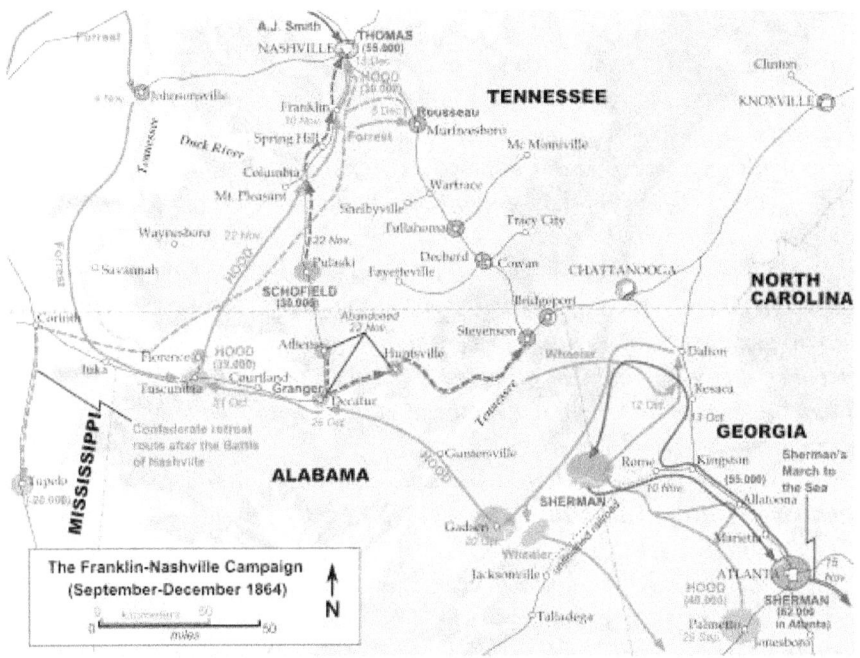

Union and Confederate Troop Movements during the Franklin to Nashville Campaign, October-December 1864, 2008, Andrein, Wikipedia

Meanwhile, William marched somewhere between Savannah and Atlanta. Military records from November through December 31, 1864 show William present and earning additional pay as corporal from January 1 to July 31, 1864. From November to December, they again assigned his regiment to Harrison's Command, Taliaferro's Brigade. During this period, it appears he got back pay. He probably sent this pay home with a letter.

October 21, 1864
Springfield, Georgia

My Dearest Mary,

Most of your family, including our James, is again in Middle Tennessee, but I fear it will not be as pretty as the last time I was there. Sadly, what was once beautiful, rolling fields are now worn and deeply rutted, eroding away. This war is a scourge on everything it touches.

223

Mary, I am now with General Hardee and the Department of South Carolina, Georgia, and Florida. Sherman is somewhere in central Georgia, and we have our backs against the seaside. I suppose after they are done with us, they'll advance into South Carolina; the rumor is that Sherman especially wants to punish your home state for its inflammatory rhetoric and bellicose attitude. I'm afraid your family, in and around Carter's Ford, will experience some type of occupation.

For all the bad, though, I have good news. Coming from a trusted separate courier is my back pay from January to July. Fortunately, it is a corporal's pay, which is more than I expected. The South is truly running out of money. Unfortunately, I know what with the cost of flour, milk, and eggs, it will not get you much.

I received the warm clothes you sent because of the clothing allowance received during October. It is not as cold here as it was in the mountains last winter, but I'm especially thankful for the new woolens because it could change at any time. I thank the good Lord every day that I married a woman whom her mother taught how to weave and sew, when some women never learned.

As to the Confederate bonds I received in October, I understand they are of little value. Buy what you need and get rid of them quickly. They will only decrease in value.

Mary, words cannot express how sorry I am that you and the children have had it so hard. This is a man's war caused by men's words, but it is the women and children who suffer, especially those whose provider never returns. I must say that if the good Lord sees fit to get me back home, I will never leave your arms again until He calls me to live on that opposite shore.

I miss you and all the children. Please kiss each of them for me and know that it is your face and smile that keeps me sane.

Always yours,
William

In the Second Battle of Franklin, James fought on November 30th in a disastrous defeat for Hood, who lost 6,000 men, including six generals.

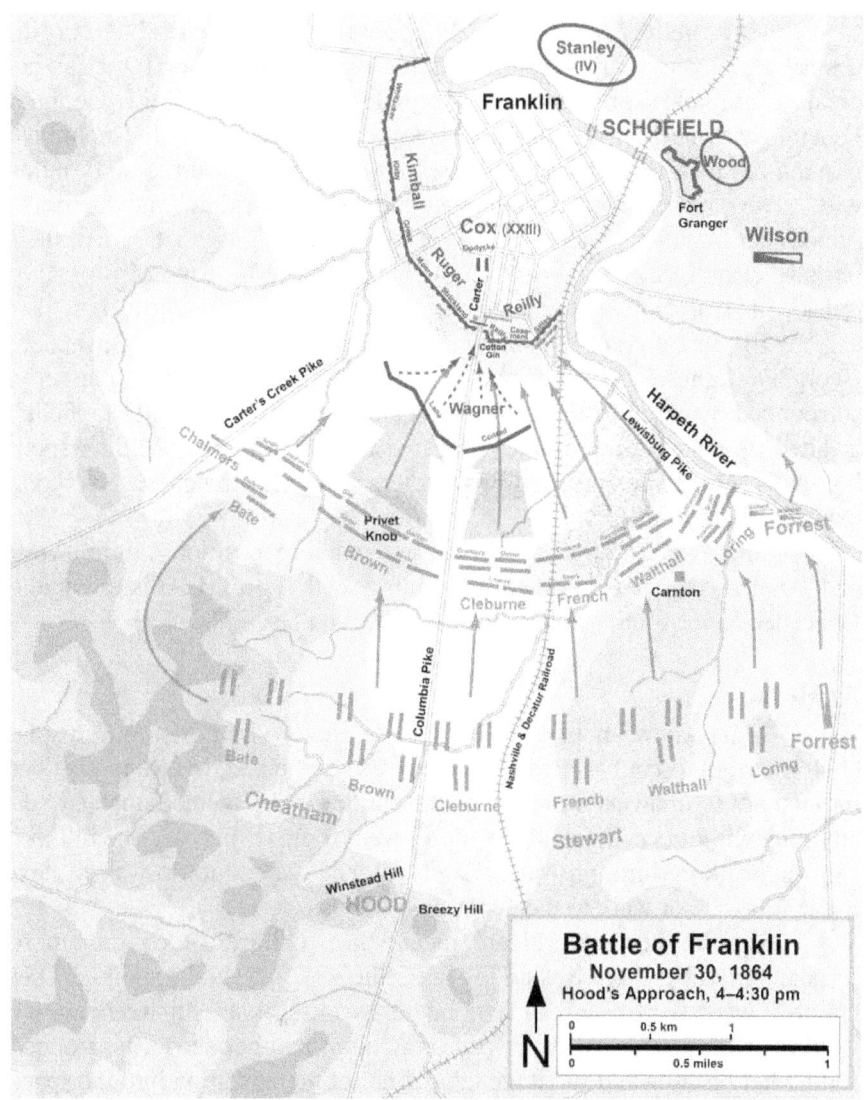

Battle of Franklin, Wikipedia. Map by Hal Jesperson, 2010

Undeterred, weeks later, Hood attacked Nashville, where the Union General Thomas virtually destroyed the rest of Hood's army, effectively ending his invasion of Tennessee. The two battles caused multiple days of worry for the Walker family, who made many trips to the depots in both Monticello and Aucilla. On the 19th of December, the 7th Florida Infantry lost its battle flag. The 1st/3rd lost theirs too but quickly recovered it.

Unimpeded, Sherman disappeared into central Georgia, destroying any military resources in his way, foraging for food for his great army, and shredding the Confederate "heartland" of Georgia. Federals marched on Georgia's red clay roads in four parallel columns, moving ten to fifteen miles daily, picking clean an area up to sixty miles wide. They ripped up her railroads, burned her bridges and factories, ruined her machine shops, and confiscated anything that aided their military efforts. Sherman's trail through Georgia left a band of ruin sixty miles wide from Atlanta to Savannah.

By the end of November, panic and fear gripped Savannah, Georgia's largest city and one of the South's last ports. The city, surrounded by formidable fortifications and swamps, river, and rice fields, awaited its fate. Hardee further prepared its defenses, and William spent his days alongside his fellow soldiers digging trenches. Everyone expected a long siege.

Sherman's 62,000-man army moved into positions north, west, and south of Savannah. Then, beginning with Fort McAllister on the Ogeechee River south of the city, he attacked on December 13th.

At Home

Mary knew about William and the siege. The next morning, she couldn't seem to get her breakfast made. Florrie helped, but Mary sent her into the house to awaken the rest of the children. She seemed unable to do anything without crying, and she didn't want to upset Florrie. She felt like she was walking through water. Lately, all she wanted to do was sit next to the fireplace or walk to the depot.

Her reduced workload meant her children took on more responsibility, but there was no joy in it. She saw their looks and knew her children were worried about her; but the waiting was gut wrenching— waiting to hear if one of their sons or William had perished. She stopped rolling her biscuits and sat at the table. She sat there, staring into the space in front of her with her hands clasped and resting on its surface. With a sigh, she turned her palms down and dropped her head upon them to sob.

Western Theater

Sherman began a series of skirmishes around Savannah. Hardee, outmanned six to one, held as long as he could with his 10,000 men. He called for reserves, but none came. Because the North was attacking everywhere from Nashville to Richmond, the South couldn't spare any troops. On December 19th, Sherman demanded surrender, but Hardee said no, though his engineers built a multiple pontoon bridge to evacuate the city.

The next morning, William watched as the entire civilian population of Savannah, including families, carriages, and wagons as well as men, women, and children on foot streamed from Savannah. To provide cover for this action and his troops' retreat, Hardee bombarded the Union.

The infantry withdrew on schedule, including forty-nine pieces of artillery. Hardee's men set fire to several steamers and the wharf before his navy left. With Savannah's waterfront on fire behind him and the noise of the bombardment in the distance, William marched north with his unit in a single slender line across South Carolina's rice dikes in plain sight of the enemy but too far away for them to do anything about it. Even though it wasn't his home, he still grieved for the beautiful city left behind.

Sherman took Savannah, and he presented it to Lincoln as a Christmas present. The losses at Nashville and Savannah happened within days of each other. Meanwhile, Sherman had been sending his prisoners of war north. Authorities imprisoned Mary's brother William Berry Walker, twenty-four, in Nashville on December 16th. He was then sent to Louisville and Camp Douglas, Illinois.

At Home

On Christmas Eve, Mary mixed cornbread with the last of their mealed corn from the previous harvest. She was thankful for what she had. She was a Walker, and there were lots of Walkers. They all still had their land, land used to subsist on. They saved enough seed from every harvest and grew more corn in each cycle. She darned, cleaned, sewed, and did what she could as barter for the corn. Her children did, too. Standing there in front of the stove in her faded brown dress and butternut apron, she pushed an escaping tendril of hair into the chignon she wore at her nape. She poured the batter into the hot, greased frying pan.

Later, handsome Zech with his father's light brown hair and gray eyes came into the parlor by the fire, and they both sat down to discuss the day's activities. He reminded her of their other two older sons. At night, she worried if they were warm and fed. On other nights, she wondered if they were even alive. Daytime, though, relieved her of more pressing worries. Today, she thought about what they looked like, because she hadn't seen them in years.

They were both far away—James in Alabama with lots of her Walker kin. She didn't worry about him as much, but her Valentine she

227

did. He was still in Petersburg. His letters talked about trenches and the crucial importance of the city and its railroad line. He had been there since early summer. Her prayers were mostly about him lately.

She said to Zech, "Get some paper and let's write to your dad." He went to William's stark bookcase. Zech was so grown now, even though he was only fourteen. Where he used to bound from the kitchen, now he moved like a grown man, the man of their house, doing a man's job. Yesterday he had worked at his Uncle James's place, helping repair downed fences. In return, he came back with dried venison.

"Mama, we are down to only two sheets of paper. I don't know where we can get some more." They wrote on anything they could find, using the backs of documents, the leftover end of former letters, anything that worked. Lately, they tore sheets from William's old journal, using the unused portions.

Mary replied, "I'll finish going through your dad's books. I'm sure there are a few more empty pages there."

Zech sat and dipped his quill as she dictated.

> *December 24, 1864*
> *Monticello, Florida*

Dearest William,

Merry Christmas, my dear. The children and I miss you every day; and like myself, they await your missives.

I have big news from Elizabeth. Uncle Joel's Jane got married to William Shepherd. We knew they were sweet on each other, but we were surprised when it happened so suddenly. They didn't have a big church wedding but did it privately. When they let the rest of us in on their secret, everyone threw a big dinner for them.

The girls and I agree the household is often too quiet with James and Valentine gone and the void felt by your absence. Of course, Zech works too hard to keep us all in line. He has grown a lot since you last saw him…

Zech looked up from the page, and the two of them locked eyes. Mary smiled. Zech smiled and said, "Mama, I really don't mind."

"I know," she replied, and he continued writing.

As 1864 drew to an end, people looked back at its conflicts—The Wilderness, Cold Harbor, Atlanta, and Petersburg. The winter set in severe and long. Life in Virginia's trenches was harder than anyone could recall. While the Rebels froze, the North sent more men to replace those lost.

While the starved and wan South failed in manpower, the North didn't. Rations and equipment dwindled for the South, too.

Searches for firewood to keep warm were constant, and it is said patrols sometimes ran into enemy patrols doing likewise. Sometimes they chatted, pitched in to help each other, divided the cuts, and went their separate ways. The Yankees described these Confederate details as stooped and ragged. On their shoulders were blankets and tents flapping in the bitter winds.

Southern deserters poured in to the other side.

While the eastern theater fought at Petersburg, deep in the western theater, the Federal Navy closed Mobile Bay. This ended all Gulf Coast trade east of the Mississippi River and satisfied the third part of Grant's plan. Mary's brother William, with the 3rd Battery Cavalry, was still in the area.

Finley's Florida Brigade retreated through Alabama and Georgia and entered South Carolina with the remnants of Hood's shattered Army of Tennessee. In South Carolina, they joined Beauregard's army, where William was still with Hardee's men. Meanwhile, Sherman began his Carolina Campaign, marching north from Savannah to link with Union forces in Virginia. Between the two points were South and North Carolina.

All during 1864, Floridians had moved 20,000 head of cattle by the end of the season, 10,000 less than the year before. Florida's cattle supply was dwindling. With winter, the supply stopped.

The remaining Florida herds became emaciated because of lack of forage during the winter. These isolated and unprotected herds were also vulnerable targets, and the Confederate armies up north with their backs against the wall could not spare regular troops to protect these vital herds, their food for the coming spring.

Meanwhile, all throughout the South, large numbers of families moved, especially from cities to safer rural areas. Like Mary, people were restless and began moving to their roots or away to simpler surroundings. These Southern refugees set in motion throughout the South an added element of despondency which only intensified everyone's fears.

Eastern Theater

By the new year of 1865, Valentine's battalion was still near Petersburg somewhere between the Appomattox River and a place called Dinwiddie Court House. His duties included provost work; he served as a military police officer, enforcing discipline and possibly guarding prisoners of war. Most likely, though, he probably had to deal with deserters.

At the beginning of the war, people respected and trusted the provosts. By the end of the war, however, people were assigned to this position for many various reasons. To protect them, the army may have assigned younger men, such as seventeen-year-old Valentine, to remove them from the front lines. They also assigned expert riders, such as Valentine—experienced in working cattle at his grandfather's ranch—to catch deserters before they escaped their units.

Desertion was even more of a problem than previously. By the end of the next month, Valentine's regiment would lose twenty-nine men because of desertion, about ten percent of the men present for duty. The prospects for 1865 probably appeared as bleak to Valentine as it did to his mother in Monticello, to his father in the Carolinas, and to the rest of the South.

Western Theater

From December 1864 until April 1865, the army assigned William's unit to Harrison's Brigade, McLaws's Division, in the Department of South Carolina, Georgia, and Florida. On February 2nd, superiors stationed William at a crossing on the Salkehatchie River near Carter's Ford. The 5th Georgia Infantry was in Bamberg County, South Carolina, along with 1,200 Confederates. Meanwhile, 5,000 of Sherman's men waded through the Salkehatchie swamps and outflanked McLaws. The best McLaws could do was delay the Federal crossing at the Salkehatchie River in the Battle of River's Bridge, where William's unit met the 17th Army Corps.

Outflanked, McLaws had to withdraw toward Branchville, but Sherman did not pursue and instead marched on toward the state capital in Columbia. One can visit the battlefield near the river bridge over the Salkehatchie at the Rivers Bridge State Historic Site near Ehrhardt, a small town in Bamberg County, South Carolina. McLaws's men built and used the earthworks still present at the site.

It is ironic this battle took place near Ehrhardt, approximately five miles away from Carter's Ford but over twenty-five miles away from Colleton County's courthouse in Walterboro. The irony is that in order to preserve Colleton's courthouse records, its officials sent them to the capitol in Columbia for safekeeping when they realized Sherman had landed at Port Royal, north of Parris Island and south of Beaufort. His scorched earth policies resulted in the burning of Colleton crops and homes and in the taking of livestock and supplies. However, Sherman bypassed Walterboro and took Columbia by February 18th. He burned much of the city, along with all of Colleton County's courthouse records.

The devastation was complete in Columbia. Of its 125 squares, the Yankees destroyed eighty-four. The looming facade of the capitol was untouched and conspicuous amongst the sad remains of the city. Several other counties in Sherman's path sent their records to Columbia for safekeeping, too, but it was for naught. Sherman set fire to the building in Columbia that housed all the records.

At Home

Meanwhile, Mary received word her brother Archibald was again in the hospital in Meridian, Mississippi. He was in the Way Hospital, wounded, probably wounded during the Battle of Nashville, which occurred in mid-December the month before. All the news now received was bad.

Later that afternoon, a courier brought her a letter. Thankfully, this one was from William, a relief. Lately, any letter not from him or her sons brought fear, a fear that tugged in the back of her mind. It might be a letter with bad news, news that another family member had lost his life.

She knew she had to open it but always hesitated. Even from William, sometimes it was better not to know. Sometimes, waiting is better; loved ones are still alive until the message says they aren't.

She and Jesse sat in the kitchen to read it.

January 30, 1864
Somewhere on the Salkehatchie River

Dearest Mary,

I am in your homeland. After all these years and stories about Carter's Ford, the Little Salkehatchie River, and Colleton District, I finally got to see them. Unfortunately, Mary, Sherman is here, too. Both our armies are still engaged in a hostile waltz. Our posteriors are against the wall again as we back our way through this land your family calls the Low Country.

In mid-January, one day before daybreak, we crossed the railroad bridge over the Salkehatchie River, and sadly we had to burn it, taking our position in the swamp on the other side above the bridge. Joining us there were Colonel Fiser's Georgia Brigade, Colonel Hardy's North Carolina Brigade, some Texas Rangers, and General Conner's South Carolina Brigade, a sum of three to 4,000 Georgians, Carolinians, Texans, and a few Floridians, including me. It has been miserable, raining all the time, with cold weather thrown in. Your swamps are not a good place to live. Also notice, we are not making a winter camp. Sherman never stops to break now. ...

She told Jesse to bring her the blank pages she found from William's books, because she wished to write back immediately. She had better news about a place called Hatcher's Run where Vollie and J.J. both fought. Mary welcomed any good news and wanted to share it with William. There was so little she could do to help him otherwise. She thought he could use the better news.

Eastern Theater

Vollie and J.J. were still in Dinwiddie County, and though weakened, their units quickly moved forward to engage in battle at a mill six miles southwest of Petersburg, Virginia. The evening before it had rained all night long, and it continued after dawn. All the country around the courthouse was low and swampy. The rain soaked their meager rations and blankets. Mules and horses standing still would sink in the mud and have to be moved again and again.

At one point, Vollie told his cousins, "I expect to see the Ark go by any minute." All of this happened between March 29-31.

When the Union army tried to intercept Confederate supply wagons headed to Petersburg, two Confederate brigades made their third and final assault just as Finegan's Brigade arrived as backup. Thankfully, the situation didn't require Finegan's men.

This was another battle in the siege of Petersburg, which was fought on the Boydton Plank Road, two miles south of Ream's Station. It was a draw, because the Confederates kept the road open while the Union extended their siege works.

Besides its systemic loss of men, the Confederacy suffered heavy costs to its infrastructure. In order to slow the encroachment of the North, the South systematically burned its own bridges, destroyed its own railway tracks, and mined its roads and ports. The Confederacy even had to scour its own land for horses and crops to keep its armies moving. Hunger often pushed people to do what they normally wouldn't.

In February, on all fronts, misfortune plagued the South. Sherman swept from the heart of Georgia into the Carolinas, and Union soldiers occupied Charleston by mid-month. Meanwhile, Sheridan occupied the breadbasket of Virginia, also known as the great valley, and on the South's coasts a Union blockade captured Fort Fisher in North Carolina.

Petersburg, though, was in its eighth month of siege with no end in sight. Grant's plan to force Lee to stretch his lines was working. Lee had fewer men, and this weakened his chances even further. By this time at Hatcher's Run, Vollie was one of less than 14,000 Confederate soldiers fighting against almost 35,000 Union men.

What the Florida Brigade didn't know was later the same month at the Hampton Roads conference, senior Confederate officials rejected President Lincoln's invitation to restore the union with compensation for its emancipated slaves.

At Home

Late in February, the worst news arrived. Mary was in the kitchen about midday when Zech came in and plopped down at her table. He was lower than low and muttered something about not getting a chance to fight and the Yankees suffocating us.

"Zech," she said, "This is a good thing, because we're about to lose this war. You're one of the lucky ones."

But the look on his face was one of anguish. "Mama," he said, "Wilmington fell. We lost Wilmington."

The Confederacy lost its last remaining blockaded port. A major Atlantic Ocean port and located thirty miles upstream from the mouth of the Cape Fear River, it was the South's one remaining lifeline for trade and supplies, including munitions, clothing, and food. The North had completed its blockade of the South. By now, the blockade runners were mostly British smugglers.

Zech was right. The noose was tightening, and in some places flour cost $1,250 a barrel, if you could find a barrel. Stores recently sold flour in five-pound bags. In cities, pigeons, mice, and most rats disappeared. Seventy dollars of Confederate money only brought one dollar in gold.

Meanwhile, forty-five miles southwest of Monticello, the Yankees landed near the St. Marks Lighthouse. Their aim was Tallahassee and the surrounding area which controlled so much of Florida's wealth.

#

Chapter II

A Surmission of the Quietus to Come
March to May 1865

At Home

On a chilly Saturday morning, March 4th, the citizens of St. Marks, Florida heard thundering far to the south. Outside, though, it was a clear day, and they realized it was not a thunderstorm. The Yankees who had been patrolling offshore throughout the war were bombarding the lighthouse. Sixteen ships shelled the vicinity of the lighthouse to prepare the area for their landing force. Before departing, armed Confederate soldiers tried to demolish the lighthouse but failed, leaving behind a single eight-foot hole. They fled north to turn and fight again at a better defended position.

The St. Marks lighthouse is about ten miles south of Newport, the closest village to the advancing Union infantry and the narrowest place to cross the St. Marks River. To get to Newport, the Yankees had to slog through a swampy terrain west of the river. They hoped to attack the river port of St. Marks from the rear, which is about three miles south of Newport on the other side of the river, but the local militia were ready for them at Newport, the narrowest place to cross. The next day in Newport, the local militia with the 5th Florida Cavalry, the retreating Confederates, and cadets from the West Florida Seminary congregated at the East River bridge.

Earlier, at 9 pm the evening before, authorities sounded the alarm in Tallahassee through the use of an unannounced train on the St. Marks Railroad. It brought word that a Union force had landed at the lighthouse. Subsequently, a general call for help swept through the city.

By noon the following day, a West Florida Seminary cadet corps assembled at the school and marched to the state capitol, where they were quickly sworn into Confederate service. The twenty-six boys, ages eleven to eighteen, marched to the train station. Included in the cadets were boys from Jefferson County, including students of Samuel Pasco from the Waukeenah Academy.

They held the youngest cadets behind in Tallahassee, though, while the older cadets boarded and disembarked at Wakulla Station to begin their six-mile march to Newport. There in the late afternoon, the

234

boys marched through town and entered a line of breastworks two at a time while Union sharpshooters fired upon them from the other side of the river. The breastworks ran parallel to the river on its west bank. The 5th Cavalry had partially burned the bridge before the Union arrived. The Confederates fought over the bridge's remains. After the sun went down, in the trenches, the tired, cold, and frightened Baby Corps waited for dawn on their first night of the war.

The West Florida Seminary opened its doors in 1857 after the Florida legislature created it for higher education in 1851. It included classes for military education. Some of the older cadets fought in Olustee.

Meanwhile, on the east side of the river, the advancing Union troops, the US 2nd and 99th Colored Infantry, knew of another crossing upriver at a place called Natural Bridge, where the St. Marks runs underground for a short distance. Former deserters probably gave them the information. The enemy slipped away and started north, along with Martin and Delilah Walker Bishop's son Wesley.

With orders to delay the crossing at Natural Bridge until more help could arrive, the Confederate 5th Cavalry rushed north on the west side to meet the invader. There, help arrived—the 1st Florida Militia under Captain William O. Girardeau of Monticello, the Gadsden City Home Guard, Milton's Dismounted Cavalry, and a company of the 2nd Florida Cavalry.

The cadets and the rest of the force at Newport marched north along an old plank road to join in the fight. They could hear cannon and musket fire in the distance. That Monday, the Confederates formed a great crescent on the west side of the natural bridge. The bridge itself had a dense hammock that covered it. The cadets were under continual fire, but their teachers on the battlefield watched them constantly and made them keep behind cover. They each dug themselves a trench, a hole with a little mound of dirt in front.

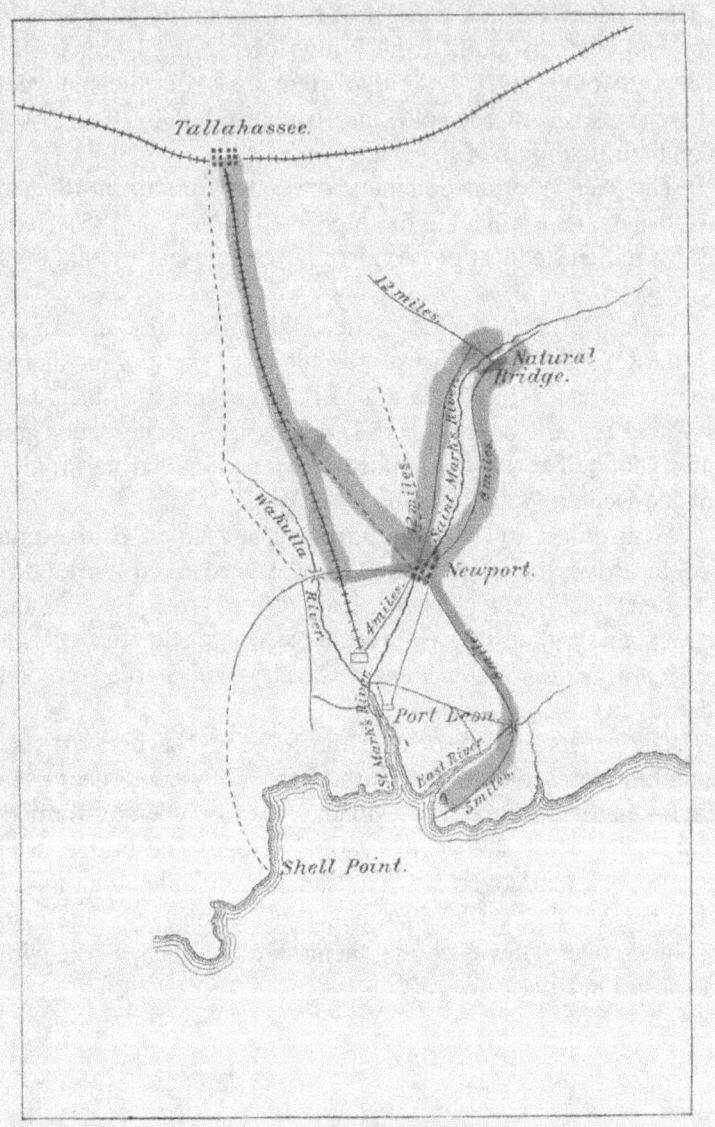

Sketch of operations near St. Mark's, March 1865 as reported by Brig. Gen. John Newton (*War of the Rebellion Official Records of the Union and Confederate Armies* Series I Vol. XLIX, Government Printing Office, 1897, Florida Historical Society Archives)

Blue = Federal Forces, Red = Confederate Forces

Confederate troops repeatedly stopped the Yankees' attempts to cross, inflicting heavy losses each time. With good backup and one last charge, the Confederate troops counterattacked, crossing the bridge and driving the invading force south. Part of this force marched south on the west side of the river to make sure the attackers did not try again to cross at Newport.

With about 1,000 soldiers engaged on both sides, Confederate casualties totaled twenty-six, three killed and three mortally wounded. The cadets suffered no casualties. Most returned to Tallahassee, but some stayed to guard two Confederate deserters. A court tried and executed them. Later, the cadets escorted a group of twenty-five Union prisoners of war back to Tallahassee. Union casualties were 148.

Everyone who took part in the battle had nothing but excellent reports about the cadets. Later, the boys had to guard the prisoners from the battle as there were no adult soldiers in Tallahassee to do the job. Their part in the battle guaranteed that Tallahassee did not fall to Union occupation. It was the only Southern state capitol east of the Mississippi which didn't.

The young cadets returned to a hero's welcome at the train station in Tallahassee, complete with wild olive wreaths and serenading young women. West Florida Seminary is the lineal predecessor to Florida State University, and FSU's ROTC Corps is one of only three colleges in the nation who has a battle flag—a streamer which says *Natural Bridge 1865*.

Rail transported the Natural Bridge casualties to Lloyd and Monticello, where the Jefferson Academy again served as a hospital.

During the three days that the Yankees were trying to invade Middle Florida, Mary watched the fear in her children's eyes. The older boys were raring to go fight. Henry was determined that he could protect his family if they did, but Joseph and the girls looked thunderstruck when the older boys weren't looking.

Laura asked, "How far are we from Newport, Mama?"

She had always tried to answer her children honestly. "About forty miles," she replied. The bedroom was still and dark as there was no moon. It was a comfortable evening with no fire in the fireplace needed.

"How long would it take them to march to Monticello?"

"Hon," said Mary, "Those troops won't come here first. They'll want to take Tallahassee before coming to us."

Laura grew quiet and pulled her knees under the covers. Mary could almost hear her thinking. At night Laura asked a thousand questions and sometimes cried in Mary's bed. Thankfully, little one-year-old Virginia—now sleeping with Florrie—seemed blissfully unaware of it all.

Mary lay on her pillow, staring into the darkness as Laura inched over to fold herself under Mary's arm. She hugged her close and let her child snuggle against her. Mary thought about Laura's last question, though. That army, if they wanted to do so, could be in Monticello by lunch the next day.

Every day, Mary walked to the depot for the latest news, but she walked alone. No use in scaring the children more than they already were. If troops came to Monticello, she considered fleeing back to Elizabeth to be near her kin, most of whom did not have slaves. She thought the family would be safer there but realized she was running out of safe options.

Mary was also worried about William and her older boys. Lately, their letters were few—and those that arrived carried a tone of quiet resignation. The one received yesterday from William shared that the men subsisted lately without pay or rations. Men became independent of these necessities, and mysteriously they found sustenance in the surrounding streams, forests, and fields. "We're all growing quite capable of surviving on nothing much," he wrote.

Several days later, Mary rolled out the dough for her biscuits. "Good news indeed," she said. She was in her kitchen with Zech, who brought in a letter. They paroled James Slicer and exchanged him at Camp Lee near Richmond. Everyone thought this meant he was coming home to Blackshear, his wife, and family.

When John Slicer got home months later, he told his family that on the day they left to be exchanged, he did not know what he was doing or where he was going. They simply marched the men out the gates and to a railroad crossing. They sent them first to Point Lookout in Maryland, but they shipped them out again and sent them to the Boulware & Cox's Wharf on the James River along with over 3,000 other paroled Confederate prisoners of war. Their speculations ran wild, mostly hoping the war was over.

But he didn't go home. Instead, he returned to his unit and learned that Lincoln had begun a second term. In some ways, the family was less worried when he was in prison. The fighting grew fiercer every day.

On March 10th they received more good news. Jesse Allen, Mary Ann and Littleberry's son and Mary Jane Hamrick's husband, received a parole from Elmira Prison in New York. Good news indeed, thought Mary, something so needed during these bleak times. Sadly, though, they also received news that General William Bailey's son of the same name died as a prisoner of war at Hilton Head.

Western Theater

General J. E. Johnston's forces marched north from Columbia, South Carolina while General Bragg's forces retreated from Wilmington, North Carolina. As a part of Johnston's army, William and his unit moved through Cheraw into North Carolina but stopped on March 16th twenty miles southwest of Goldsboro.

They stopped because Sherman's armies moved north in two columns, the right being the Army of the Tennessee, headed for Goldsboro, and the left the Army of Georgia, marching to Raleigh. Earlier Sherman had split his army—the Army of the Cumberland, the Army of the Tennessee, and the Army of the Ohio—into two wings. He designated the other wing the "Army of Georgia."

Goldsboro was important as a railroad hub and a medical center. It was the junction of the North Carolina Railroad and the Wilmington & Weldon Railroad, both vital for the Confederate's supply lines. Several Goldsboro churches, warehouses, and schools became temporary hospitals.

William's unit quickly built breastworks of logs and light wood knots, covering them over with dirt. They used spades and bayonets to dig with. William was as careful in carrying along his spade as he was his gun. Many had lost theirs, though, and had to use their bayonets.

Then they waited. That night around a fire, a crooner sang, "No more from that cottage again I will roam. Be it ever so humble, there's no place like home." William wasn't one for crying, but he wiped his eyes.

Elsewhere at the Battle of Averasborough, thirty miles northwest, McLaws led a division under Lieutenant General Hardee on March 16. Hardee's corps attacked Sherman's left wing, but the Confederate attack only slowed them for a day. In the end, Hardee retreated to join Johnston.

Later, William was glad to see Hardee and Finley's Florida Brigade, especially his son. That evening around a campfire, it was like a family reunion, a Walker reunion, as several of Mary's kin were part of Finley's Brigade.

239

Meanwhile, Hardee joined Johnston in his line of battle across the Goldsboro Road. In a last desperate attempt, the weakened Confederate Army of Tennessee fought here in the Battle of Bentonville on March 19th, two miles south of the town. They attacked Sherman's right column for three days. It would be the last major battle to occur between Sherman and Johnston and did little in the end to arrest Sherman's movement.

This western theater army of 21,000 Rebels was all there was between Sherman's 60,000 Union soldiers and Lee's flank.

At Bentonville, McLaws's Division was hardly engaged because of its vague orders. William worried about his division because there were problems with discipline. Lately, he stood through multiple roll calls daily to prevent desertion and looting. Eventually, because of this, McLaws lost his command.

Amongst the rattling musketry and artillery roar, William waited with his unit away from the front line, but he knew the Confederacy was on its last leg. Still, all around him, men fought as desperate as ever. All that stood between Sherman and Virginia was Johnston's army, of which the 5th Georgia and Finley's Floridians played a role, albeit a small one.

At Bentonville on the other end of the front in the second line was Finley's Floridians, who fortunately also missed the most active part of their last battle. When the battle was over, the Rebel Army at Bentonville lost 239 more men in the fight with over 1,600 wounded and another 673 missing or captured.

One of those wounded was Vollie's young friend and fellow student, William W. Blackburn, who entered a Greensboro, North Carolina hospital and died soon after. William hated to write Vollie and give him the sad news. They buried William Blackburn at Oakwood Cemetery in High Point, North Carolina.

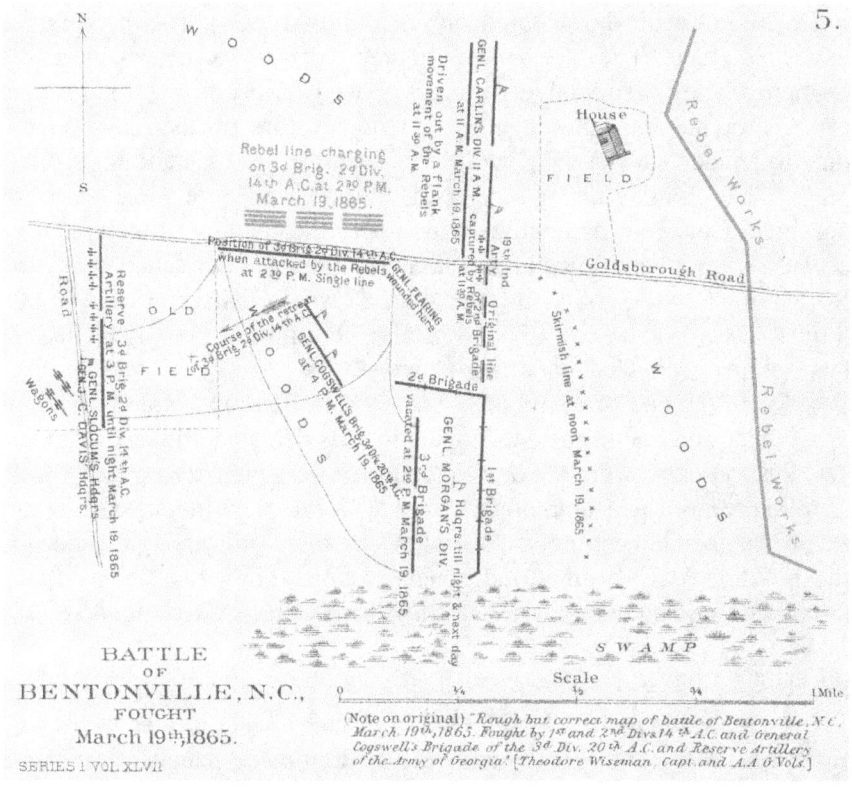

Battle of Bentonville, US War Department, 1895, Wikipedia

The 5th Georgia, though, did not give up. Several days after the overwhelming defeat at Bentonville, a Union unit, in a quick skirmish, reached the edge of the rifle pits where the 5th Georgia held its position. Some of the 5th jumped over their breastworks, collared the Yankees, and brought them back into the works with them. The rest of the Yankees retreated. Thus, the next weeks were so many skirmishes throughout North Carolina as the two armies waltzed.

On the 22nd, General Johnston withdrew across the Black Water River by sunrise and marched ten miles toward Smithfield, leaving General Sherman to continue his march unmolested to Goldsboro, North Carolina.

Far north negotiations proceeded in a peace conference at Hampton Roads, Virginia. Men throughout the ranks on both sides heard rumors that the Confederacy had sent a peace commission.

By April, the Confederacy controlled no ports, harbors, or navigable rivers. The North had captured their railroads, which ceased operating. They destroyed key bridges as well as locomotives and freight cars. Throughout the South, the Confederacy tore up their own feeder lines to replace the lost rails, but heavy use left them weak and worn out.

The South's major food-producing regions were war-ravaged or occupied. Only Florida continued to supply the South with beef, mainly because the Yankees failed at the Battle of Olustee. They failed at Natural Bridge, too. By the end of the war, Florida would deliver at least 75,000 head to the Confederacy, approximately 39.4 million pounds of beef to feed soldiers from Chattanooga to Charleston.

By the end of March, the South controlled only three pockets of its territory and one third of its population. Its defeated armies disbanded. The three pockets were the area of southern Virginia and northern North Carolina, central Alabama down through Florida, and the state of Texas. Really, neither Florida nor Texas interested the North enough to occupy them. While Davis wanted independence or nothing, Lee's army failed through disease and desertion. Lee could barely protect Richmond.

At Home

Meanwhile, in Middle Florida, Tallahassee received word that both Petersburg and Richmond were in imminent danger of capture. Florida's fifty-seven-year-old governor left the city, retired to his home near Marianna, and shot himself in the head.

On April 2nd, the Union broke through Lee's lines at Petersburg. His lines south of the city crumbled. When Mary heard this, she knew enough to know it wouldn't be long before they took Richmond. Richmond was only twenty-four miles from Petersburg, a shorter distance than Monticello to Tallahassee.

Because of the failing mail system, she did not know where Vollie, James, or even William were. The last she'd heard, Confederate soldiers were fighting around Bentonville, North Carolina, and Vollie had spent three months in the trenches at Petersburg, only leaving for brief battles.

Killed at Petersburg was 2nd Lieutenant Alexander Gill of Jefferson County. Also severely wounded was Captain William K. Partridge. They sent Captain Partridge home disabled. Another wound injured Hilary Bishop, but he survived the war. Later, Mary told Ann Lightsey, "He truly must have nine lives." A. J. Watts also suffered a wound.

Eastern Theater

Mary was right. When Petersburg fell, the government fled Richmond. And, like Atlanta earlier, the retreating army torched the city. Now gone was a vital metropolis to the Confederacy, a city that supplied its iron, tents, uniforms, swords, bayonets, artillery, and other munitions. It was an important transportation hub, the terminus of five railroads; as a fall line city, it sat on the James River with hydro-powered plants that fed its factories, foundries, and mills. Now the North controlled access to the Chesapeake Bay and the Atlantic Ocean through its James River and Kanawha Canal.

Fleeing south, President Davis and his Confederate government reestablished themselves in Danville, Virginia. Danville sat near the North Carolina state line, almost 150 miles to the southwest of Richmond, deep in a heart of one pocket of territory still held by the South.

Meanwhile, the same day, Valentine's unit learned that General Ambrose Powell Hill's death at Petersburg meant the Third Corps survivors, including Florida's 11th, 5th, and 8th, would now report to General Longstreet.

"What's the point?" asked Private William Grubbs as they sat around their campfire. Resigned, they were relieved to be out of the trenches of Petersburg after ten long months. Vollie wrote home.

April 4, 1865
South of Richmond, Virginia

Dearest Mother,

Oh, how I would love some of your sweet apple pie! It has been on my mind of late. Rations are nonexistent and reduced to a minimum if at all, both quantity and quality. I'm tired of worm-eaten peas and rancid meat; but I shouldn't complain because we do still get a little coffee and half rations of flour. Last night, we even got some apple brandy.

Mostly, though, you would be proud of me, because I have a flair for foraging, probably the practice I got from sneaking biscuits from your kitchen.

Sadly, we're in rags, barefoot, and many are even bareheaded, but there is scarcely a man in my group who complains. We try to take it as our lot and move on. It is not the same for others in our regiment. Desertion is a common problem here.

We are an army in retreat. Our men are dull and listless as we continue to move ahead of Grant's army. Still, there is always the monotonous call of guard duty. Last night, as the sun went down and as

243

the twinkling stars appeared, we heard the rumbling movement of artillery ahead of us. We huddled around a little fire in our hut, a hut left behind by earlier troops. There is a sand here that pervades all our flour and meal, our pans, and even our hair as we sleep. It filters down through the roof and walls which were built here into the sides of a ravine.

Lying in my bunk tonight, I can hear hymns sung and prayers murmured. Sometimes around our campfire, several of us share about times past and home. In it all is a sad loneliness.

About three hours after we got settled several nights ago, we got word we were on the move again. We destroyed what we could without noise, fell in, and marched slowly away, many without their arms. They believed we were heading to battle and would receive our weapons later. We marched until broad daylight on Monday, the 3rd of April.

That night, as we continued to move, the sky lit with a red glare toward Richmond, and we could hear growls of explosions. Our road, filled with other troops, headed in the same direction as us, all moving quietly and seriously. There was no talking or singing, as usual.

What little sleep we got, mine was against the base of a tree, stretched out on damp ground, my gun by my side. I even said a little prayer but never finished it. This happens a lot lately. I hope God understands.

An owl's hooting overhead quickly broke my quiet slumber. Then I drifted back to sleep. I don't think I've ever been this weary in all my life. My consolation is my memories of all of you and the warm, gentle home you and Dad provided for all of us.

Morning came, and we joined the main road from Richmond, which was filled with a line of refugees. We learned Richmond was burning, and we realized the entire Confederacy was in full retreat.

I will post this letter, Mother, but I do not know if you will get it. We are ready to fight our way back and retake Richmond, and we worry that for every step we take in the opposite direction, Richmond will be harder to recover.

Give my love to all the children, and please keep writing. You don't know how I long to hear and see anything that comes from home.

Love,
Vollie

From their position all the way to Appomattox, Vollie, J.J., and their Walker kin, all in Finegan's Brigade, marched fairly continuously, fleeing for their lives, moving day and night with no stated time to sleep, eat, or rest. Retreating was difficult on country roads strewn with debris and crowded with endless streams of refugee women and children from Petersburg and Richmond. Mealtimes devolved into merely "something to eat." Hot on their heels was Grant's army.

As Lee's army weakened, there was little hope of replenishment, whereas Grant refilled his ranks as needed. This disturbed the men of Finegan's Brigade. Honor and duty had become empty words to them. All they wanted now was to go home, but Vollie, J.J., and the other kin stayed to finish the job.

On the night of Monday, April 3rd, a halt was called, and Vollie lay down in some piney woods to rest. He ate his meager rations, and early the next morning, the 4th, orders came to move again. With only one suit of clothes, his clothes were now black. Soap was rare. He constantly scratched at his scabbed scalp. He wondered if he might burn the lice off his scalp like he did with his clothes by holding them over a fire until very hot. This time, the Florida Brigade and Lee's army moved all day and arrived at Moore's church in Amelia County.

Again, they fell out and Vollie shared what little food he had left before they slept, this time in a nice grove. The Florida Brigade, now under the command of Brigadier Theodore W. Brevard, became part of the Confederates' rearguard. Their job was to delay Grant's army.

Vollie noticed that spring had come. All around him, trees and the understory were turning green with new leaves and white blossoms. There were no more trenches with their cramping misery, though there was the fear of defeat.

They were scarcely comfortable when a detail of four men was called. The rest drifted off, only to be awakened again in the dark early morning to march.

Frequently, "halt" sounded; each time, seventeen-year-old Vollie dropped in his tracks and didn't mean to but slept heavily on the ground. From far away he heard "Forward" ordered again, and before he could regain his own, feet stumbled on him. All the rest of the night he heard, "close up men, close up!" as they marched forward. His mind sank into apathy, as did the morale of his colleagues.

Later that day, on Wednesday, exhausted and starving, Finegan's Brigade got to Amelia Courthouse, almost forty miles southwest of

Richmond. Vollie learned they were now a part of Walker's Division. Someone issued them muskets, though there were not enough for all the men, plus cartridges and caps. Since there were no cartridge boxes, belts, or other conveniences for storage, Vollie put the ammo in his pockets along with his meager supply of corn and salt. Foraging was all they ordered him for his rations, except for the corn on the cob held for their horses. He received two corncobs, and chewing them was hard work for his jaws and teeth.

Still, they waited near the town, and then there was a deafening explosion that caused the ranks to turn and flee. Vollie, like the others, thought he was under attack, but it was the firing of ammunition by their own. Nervous laughter and hilarity prevailed amongst them as they returned to their companies.

They immediately left for another Virginia town called Farmville, marching all night. Vollie and the Florida Brigade were now part of Longstreet's combined First and Third Corps. Two divisions followed them, Lee's main wagon train and John Gordon's Second Corps. Because of so much rain earlier, the roads were muddy, and the creeks and rivers were swollen. Bridges were out, and they had to take circuitous routes. At one point, Vollie thought, "Sometimes I believe it would be better to be shot than to be marched to death."

Earlier, Lee had tried and failed to concentrate his army at Amelia Court House; they were an army on the run, retreating toward the safety of Southern-held territory with the North hot on their heels. He thought that getting to Farmville and its Southside Railroad would allow provisions to be brought up from Lynchville.

Longstreet's combined corps got to Rice's Station about sunrise, and later that morning General Lee joined them there. Lee again ordered them to march through wretched conditions, on what seemed to Vollie to be plantation roads instead of the usual main roads. Other troops and wagon trains crowded these dark roads.

They arrived near Deatonville on the morning of Thursday the 6th. Vollie and his Florida kin didn't know it, but they were now only six or seven miles from their starting point the night before. Food at Deatonville was no better than before. They quickly built a fire and began cooking, but before some of their slower comrades could even get started, the sharp, high-pitched command rang out: "Fall in! Fall in!"

Vollie grabbed his belongings and watched his Uncle J.J. quickly wipe out the hot frying pan, wrap it in his blanket, and drop it into his haversack. "Forward march, double quick," yelled the officers all up and down the line, and they moved at almost a run before the back of the column had to turn quickly and fight. Vollie heard the action behind him as it vanished in the distance.

Drunk with fatigue, everybody was dog tired. Days on the march, they had moved through wood smoke that hung in the still air while dust rose and clouded their ankles. The only noise was the endless shuffle of their feet and the clank of bayonets rattling against their canteens.

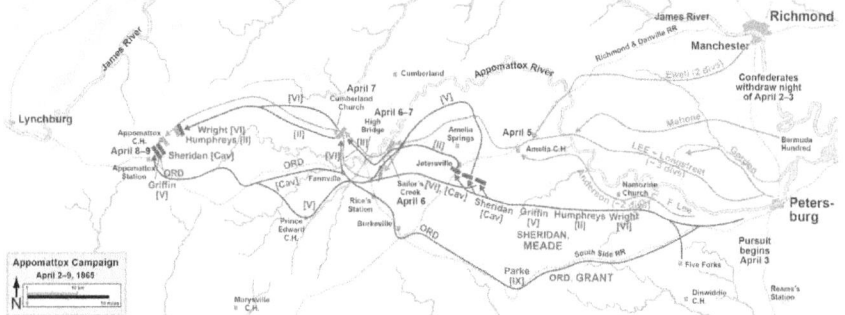

Lee's Retreat and Grant's Pursuit, Appomattox Campaign, April 2-8, 1865,
Wikipedia. May by Hal Jesperson

Longstreet and Lee arrived at Sayler's Creek near Farmville later that day. All around Vollie and the rest of the Walkers, the area was woody, with dense undergrowth and swamps. With Petersburg four days behind them, they had been averaging thirty-five miles a day. On each side of every road they traveled were big guns with broken wheels, broken wagons, emaciated horses and mules dead where they fell, discarded muskets, blanket rolls, tents, and canteens. In the woods, they saw stragglers slipping through the trees.

They came to an area where the creek flowed into the Appomattox River. Two small bridges over the creek and a tributary caused a bottleneck, but the Florida Brigade made it over. However, the bottleneck kept the rest of Lee's army and his wagon train from escaping.

It was chaos back there, and Longstreet's men were too far away to help. Four brigades of Yankee cavalry descended upon the remaining men, fatigued from scarce supplies, exhaustion, sleeplessness, and hunger. Hand-to-hand fighting broke out as the rest of Lee's army turned and tried to fight. Longstreet's men heard bugles sound from the end of the line.

Lee, receiving reports of what was happening at Sayler's Creek, climbed a bluff overlooking the battlefield to get a better look. Vollie, along with the rest of the Florida Brigade, were on the nearby hilltop, too, and watched helplessly as Colonel George Custer's cavalry captured their Southern colleagues, two Confederate army corps. He took thousands prisoner.

With incredulous eyes, Lee watched the chaos, turned to one of his generals, and said, *"My God, has the army dissolved?"* What transpired took another quarter of the South's soldiers, including several of its generals—approximately 7,700 killed, wounded, or captured at the Battle of Sayler's Creek.

Later, on the other side of Sayler's Creek, Lee and Longstreet's columns stopped again to rest near a place with an Indian name called Appomattox Courthouse. The men scattered in search of rations. Many did not return.

Still, Lee thought this was their last chance—to cross to the northern side of the Appomattox River. If they burned the bridges behind them, they might flee to reach the mountains to rest or to join Johnston farther south. They were down to one final Confederate corps, and it was the third and greatest of the three.

With the plan in play, they crossed and burned all but one bridge before a Yankee unit stopped them. Vollie realized they had to flee again because an entire Yankee corps had crossed behind them. Evening fell.

Meanwhile, Grant occupied Farmville. That evening, they lit bonfires on its main street, and Grant went inside a little hotel there to write a formal letter to Lee, which a messenger delivered under a flag of truce. The letter asked Lee to surrender.

Lee's corps found foraging easier on the north side of the river since the war had not come there yet. Dusk came early because the woods were deep. They collected wood for fires to cook the expected rations set to arrive on the railroad.

But General Phil Sheridan had his cavalry in front of Lee's army to its west. To Lee's east was Meade, and to his rear was the VI Corps. Sheridan, Meade, and the VI Corps effectively surrounded Lee on three sides. The noose was tightening when Vollie heard the cavalry bugles sound, clear notes piercing through the atmosphere. Facing them were lines of horses and tense men with sabers raised high. He thought, "This is it."

Out of the Rebel lines a lonesome gray uniformed rider moved wildly across no-man's-land with a staff in his hand and a white flag atop it. He disappeared into the line of Yankees on the other side.

Men on both sides saw there was a truce in the making. Almost immediately, rumors circulated until Vollie heard that Lee and Grant were going to meet in the little village that lay between the two armies. If the whispers were true, Lee's surrender felt near. Then came a quieter hope for Vollie—perhaps he would live to see Easter. Today was Palm Sunday.

Across the way, the Yankees simply sat down and waited, although one here or there would cross the line to talk to their beaten foes. What didn't happen, though, was rejoicing and celebration.

In a greening swell of Virginia farmland, on Palm Sunday, April 9th, what remained of Finegan's Brigade silently watched their leader ride among them in his finest dress uniform, sword at his side. Lee made his way down the lane to the place of surrender. Earlier, they had seen his nemesis ride up in mud-splattered working clothes, a cigar clamped in his mouth. Vollie told his Uncle J.J., "Did you see? He even had mud on his boots."

The grayed Lee dismounted and climbed the stairs of the town's brick house with his shoulders squared and his head held high, the stature of a lifelong military man. Not a sound could be heard except a rustle of leaves in the wind and his knee high-black polished boot steps on the bricks. All around him, his beaten companies' tenderly furled flags snapped in the wind.

Lee surrendered, along with his entire Army of Northern Virginia. As ordered, the remaining impoverished and starving Rebel regiments stayed in the area awaiting their fate. Vollie in Finegan's Brigade noticed that many Union soldiers rode past them up and down the roads as if the Rebel boys were a spectacle to see. Frequently, the Yankees would call, "How are ya, Johnny?" They hung around the camp as if they wanted to be familiar with their surrendered enemy.

Later that same day, the Yankees came from the direction of the village bearing boxes of "hard tack" and crackers for the emaciated Rebels. Another group drove in a steer, a soldierly act of empathy. Vollie realized that nobody spoke ill of General Lee.

On Tuesday the 11th, the Confederate soldiers massed together in a field where Confederate General John B. Gordon spoke to them as a whole. Afterward, generals addressed their divisions, bidding them farewell. General Walker denounced those who threw down their arms and praised those who carried on as heroes. Then they were relieved, and all went into their camps for the night.

That evening, Vollie stood outside in the firelight of their campfire. As far as he could see, campfires dotted the landscape all around them. Later, he lay in his tent encircled by his enemy; and for the first time in weeks, he slept soundly. While he slept, Confederate officers received papers about the size of an ordinary blank check.

The next day on April 12th, a Wednesday, J.J. and Vollie paraded up from a creek bottom where they had camped, with the rest of the Florida Brigade at the top of a hill. They entered what was called the surrender triangle and surrendered their muskets, sidearms, bayonets, and regimental flags. There they received their parole passes. It read:

Appomattox Courthouse, Virginia,
April 10th, 1865
The bearer, Private Valentine Andrews, of Company K, 10th Florida Infantry, a paroled prisoner of the Army of Northern Virginia, has permission to go to his home and there remain undisturbed.

His own commander signed it. His Uncle J.J. got one like it. Both doubted its use but learned in time that all picket officers and patrols of the Federal army would respect it as if it bore the signature of Ulysses S. Grant himself. The remaining Florida Brigade marched from Appomattox toward home, six hundred miles southwest, leaving the surrender triangle behind.

General Lee, during the surrender negotiations, made sure his men received paroles. In return, they handed over their arms, artillery, and any other public property they had on hand. The men kept their horses and mules because families through the next winter needed them for planting crops. With this done, the North allowed everyone to go home undisturbed as long as they observed their paroles and the laws where they lived. No treason trials festered old wounds because all rested on Grant's written word. At home, they would attempt to comprehend their chaotic new world and take on the uncertain task of rebuilding their lives in the war-torn economy.

At the peaceful county seat of Appomattox, the 2nd Florida Infantry Regiment surrendered only sixty-eight men. At Richmond, they paroled Dr. Palmer on April 17th.

They had combined the decimated 1st, 3rd, and 4th Florida Infantry Battalions into other regiments. The Aucilla Guard's 5th Florida surrendered six officers and forty-seven men. The 5th had over 1,000 men when it was first ordered to Virginia. With a loss of thirty-five percent of their force in Pennsylvania, they had left many behind at Gettysburg. They were the only unit in the brigade to not lose their regimental banner in battle.

Out of 1,292 men enrolled, the 9th Florida Regiment surrendered 109 at Appomattox. The unit had only existed fifteen months, though some of their men had fought since 1862.

5th Florida Infantry Battle Flag, Wikipedia

His Uncle J.J.'s 11th Infantry Regiment, an earlier consolidation of the 2nd and 4th Florida Infantry Battalions, surrendered four officers and nineteen men. Hendry, Jackson, and Bradford counties provided most of the regiment's men; the army's retreat left many of them stranded, and they had surrendered earlier.

Lee surrendered 50,000 of his remaining soldiers of the Army of Northern Virginia, but it was still not the end of the war, not for the Army of Tennessee in the Carolinas nor for Mary's brother William who was still fighting in Alabama, where a few hours after the surrender, in Blakeley, Alabama, a battle blazed to control the eastern approach to Mobile. Sixteen thousand Federals charged a 2 1/2-mile front through bursting lands mines, felled trees, and telegraph-wire obstacles.

Western Theater

A mere 140 miles southwest of Appomattox, the distance between Monticello and Jacksonville, Sherman and Johnston prepared for battle as Johnston hoped to link up with Lee. Neither had received word of the surrender.

After midnight the next day, the first word of Lee's surrender reached General Johnston by courier in a dispatch. Johnston's original goal was to unite his army with Lee's somewhere near the North Carolina and Virginia border. It was the South's last shred of hope, but the dispatch dashed it all.

Still, President Davis felt optimistic that Johnston could continue the war effort by recalling deserters and draft dodgers despite overwhelming evidence to the contrary. All this while Johnston's men deserted en masse. Johnston knew his foe outnumbered his men 18 to 1. He thought "It would be the greatest of human crimes to continue the war."

Nevertheless, Davis went farther west to Greensboro to talk to Johnston, and the two men argued their points. Then Johnston opened communications with General Sherman in Raleigh. Sherman worried because unlike Lee's Army of Northern Virginia, Johnston's army was neither surrounded nor in as poor a condition as had been Lee's.

On Easter Sunday morning, Johnston received word from Sherman and rode to Greensboro to see Davis, but Davis was gone, having left Greensboro without notifying Johnston. Annoyed, Johnston continued negotiations with Sherman with no authorization from Davis, and the two generals agreed to meet on April 17th at Durham Station, which is present-day Durham, North Carolina.

In mid-April, William's unit learned of the earlier surrender in Virginia. A few men from Jefferson County—former members of Lee's army—passed through on their way home. They stopped long enough to give them the news. Morale plummeted. William's brigade, along with the rest of the Confederate army, became a howling mob.

On April 16, William's 5th Georgia marched within five miles of Greensboro and formed another camp. William may not have been with his unit, though. In recent days, doctors had hospitalized him again. Only one document, a state of service record dated August 20, 1915, shows him as appearing on a list of medical officers, hospital stewards, nurses, and patients remaining in the General Hospital No. 12 in Goldsboro, North Carolina dated April 28, 1865. We do not know why or the exact date they hospitalized him, but Johnston's army was 150 miles away.

Union records of prisoners of war contain this information, and this hospital paroled him on or shortly after April 28th. The document shows that a military convention signed April 26th, 1865 between General Joseph E. Johnston of the Confederate army and Major General W. T. Sherman of the United States Army in North Carolina authorized his parole.

One must question whether someone gleaned the information in 1915 for a pension application, though modern researchers did not find any such document.

In the hospital, William probably heard rumors that General Johnston, with only 30,000 men, planned to fight his way through the enemy lines of 230,000-plus men. Another person said the general would surrender, sending everyone to Northern prisons. He also heard about angry hordes of men who insisted on being told what was really happening. Another rumor said that the officers ordered the men to stand firm and meet their fate like men.

That night near Greensboro, many men simply walked south along the railroad tracks, leaving the army to go home. This decision was not devoid of danger. The country due south was barren, picked clean of anything to eat. Plus, there was the risk of being captured by the enemy, so men stayed, too.

Meanwhile, order broke down in the camps. Mary's brother Berry heard the talk around the campfires. Rumors abounded. Said one private, "You saw Sherman's men. They look like a race of giants and are well-clad, too. We're nothing more than broken down skeletons compared to them. It is useless."

Said another, "Well, only because there's no food."

Replied the first, "Well, they're getting fed."

Soldiers in every unit refused to go on guard duty that night. William may have worried about his sons and wondered where they were in all this anarchy. He probably worried about Mary and the kids, too. Was it equally bad at home?

In the last weeks, the Army of Tennessee merged all the Florida regiments into a First Florida Regiment, a remnant of 351 men. The Florida Brigade no longer existed. They combined the six regiments into a merged regiment barely the size of a battalion. Union soldiers had captured most of their battle flags earlier in December 1864 on the outskirts of Nashville. The only battle standards saved were Florida's 1st, 3rd, and 7th.

Meantime, in Raleigh, eighty miles east-southeast of Greensboro, Sherman thought about President Lincoln's generous terms which were earlier offered to General Lee for the surrender at Appomattox. He worried that Johnston's 30,000-plus men who were in the area might disband to fight a protracted guerrilla war. He thought that using the terms provided by President Lincoln could be a template for terms offered to Johnston.

On the morning of the 17th, as Sherman prepared to ride to Durham Station, twenty-five miles northwest toward Greensboro, a coded telegram brought him news of President Lincoln's assassination the previous evening. Despite the startling news, Sherman continued to Durham Station, where he met with General Johnston. The two men had never met before, even though both had served in the Old Army. They hastened their negotiations to the Bennett farmstead nearby.

Once at the Bennett place and in complete privacy, Sherman handed Johnston the telegram he had received earlier. Johnston, upon reading it, stared hard at the paper and without looking up told Sherman, *"This event is the greatest possible calamity to the South."* Negotiations began in earnest, and both men left after the first day agreeable to continued negotiations. There was no deal, though.

Upon Sherman's return to Raleigh, word had spread about Lincoln's assassination. He found mayhem and roaming hordes of soldiers who wanted him to refuse any Confederate surrender. The town of Raleigh almost burned to the ground the evening before, and he could barely control his army.

In Alabama

Meanwhile, in Alabama, Mary's brother William A. Walker, who had been riding with the 15th Cavalry Regiment guarding the port of Mobile, fled north with his regiment when the Federals took the last major Southern port. They captured him in Demopolis, Alabama on April 17, 1865, and he had probably lost his horse long ago. Army horses had a life expectancy of only seven months, used up by disease, undernourishment, and wounds. Plus, the South was running out of horses along with many of its resources needed to fight a war.

The Final Surrender

Surrenders do not happen overnight, and the delay for both armies in the western theater was not good. While Sherman's army turned into a revengeful mob, Johnston's army crumbled away with desertions.

On the following day, April 18th, at noon, the two men met again at the Bennett House near Durham Station. Overnight Davis allowed Johnston to surrender the remaining Confederate armies. Johnston offered his armies in exchange for Sherman's assurance of protecting his men's constitutional rights. Sherman assured Johnston that Lincoln's 1863 Amnesty Proclamation and the existing terms of the Appomattox surrender allowed for a full pardon of all Confederate soldiers, from the privates to the commanding generals. They agreed, and the South's Confederacy lapsed into history as a lost cause.

The South was to deposit its arms in their respective state arsenals, usable only within those states. All officers and their men were to sign an oath to cease all hostilities of war.

The president would recognize again all states when their officers and legislators took the oath of allegiance. The president would guarantee all personal, political, and property rights of the Southern people and grant them legal amnesty.

Sherman felt Lincoln had never wanted to punish the South—that the former president instead wanted to fully reestablish the United States in order to ease any further resistance.

With the armistice between Sherman's and Johnston's armies, both sides agreed to a ceasefire. The agreement, though, had its detractors. Many felt Sherman fought a hard war but followed it with terms too solicitous. They felt he delved into political matters that were beyond his authority, and these feelings caused problems for both sides.

Rumors increased while order disintegrated in the Southern army as the two armies waited to see if Washington would approve the agreement. Breaking orders, more Southern men left, marching home on foot following the railroad tracks. Though still hospitalized and unable to leave, William witnessed the surrounding area descend into chaos as soldiers destroyed ammunition, confiscated supplies, and spread rampant rumors, particularly about the intergovernmental agreement.

Unfortunately for Sherman, the assassination of President Lincoln hardened the hearts of Northerners everywhere. Congress condemned Sherman, and one senator even sent President Andrew Johnson a letter asking for Sherman's immediate removal from command. President Johnson and his new cabinet rejected the terms of the surrender. Then they sent Grant to Raleigh to oversee the resumption of combat.

Grant, though, was a friend of Sherman's and understood what Lincoln had wanted before he died. All three men felt that if hatred and bitterness reigned, revenge and reprisal would seize the day. The latter would make any re-union of the states forever impossible.

Lincoln had tried to warn everyone who would listen that win or lose, both sides would have to get along with each other when it ended. Revenge was not the answer.

Though all three men were merciless in their endeavors during the war, by the end, each of them wished to end any vindictiveness or hatred. Lincoln's assassination made the job harder.

Grant quickly turned to negotiate with the establishment in Washington using a letter he had received earlier from Lincoln. The letter reflected the former president's feelings regarding the surrender of the Confederates and, most important of all, the healing of America. It was the same letter he used when negotiating a surrender with Lee. The terms expressed simple human decency and a desire for reconciliation.

Meantime discipline collapsed further in Johnston's army, and general looting and pillaging broke out. As the officers lost control, looting broke out even within Johnston's own camp.

Sherman formally informed Johnston by the next Monday, April 24th, that the agreement's terms were unacceptable and that hostilities would resume at noon on the 26th. Under the circumstances, Johnston quickly replied and asked for another meeting at the Bennett farmstead on the morning of the 26th.

On the 25th, Confederate forces marched six miles beyond Greensboro into new camps. As they marched, thousands dropped their guns by the roadside. There was no order as ranks scattered from one side of the road to the other. Most of the Walker kin marched together and kept theirs, though their guns were cumbersome and grew more so the farther they marched away from Greensboro. Their morale plummeted. When they finally stopped, that same night of April 25th, every man without a gun received no rations. Thousands returned to retrieve their guns, and more deserted.

Negotiations between the two generals began again the next morning and continued throughout the day. The armistice between Johnston and Sherman ended at 11 am, but later that day on Wednesday, the 26th of April, Johnston surrendered his army.

According to the American Battlefield Trust article entitled Bennett Place Surrender, *"Under these final terms, Johnston's army and his naval force would cease all hostilities, each brigade could keep 1/7 of its small arms and soldiers would deposit their arms at their respective state capitols, all officers and men were to be paroled and take an oath to not take up arms against the United States, their paroles would be signed by their immediate commanders, soldiers could retain their horses and other private property, and the Union army would provide field, rail and water transportation home to paroled men."*

Separate from this agreement, Sherman also promised 250,000 rations to the newly paroled troops. These favorable surrender terms allowed former Confederates to return home with relative ease. Lincoln intended the agreement and subsequent surrender to bring the former Confederate states back into the Union and prevent future hostilities.

On that same day, seventeen days after Appomattox, William's former 4th Florida under the newly merged regiment and his current 5th Georgia Infantry surrendered their battle standards at Greensboro along with the remnant of the once great Army of Tennessee. The 4th was part of the newly formed First Florida Regiment (Consolidated).

The 4th Florida Regiment surrendered only twenty-three of its original men. This was all who had survived from the time it organized in the summer of 1861 in Jacksonville, Florida to the end of the war. The First Florida Regiment (Consolidated) mustered Jesse W. Walker, son of Mary's Uncle James, and Mary's brother Arch (Archibald) Walker out of service in Orange County, North Carolina. The two twenty-seven-year-old first cousins began the long journey home. They were probably not alone, as all the Walker kin most likely traveled together when they could. We know from records that all the family members who survived the war were now making their way back home whether by foot, train, wagons, buckboards, or a mixture of all four, probably with their respective companies.

When General Joseph E. Johnston surrendered his army to General William T. Sherman, this ended the war in the Carolinas, Georgia, and Florida. There were approximately 90,000 Confederate soldiers stationed in these states, but it would be weeks before some of the rest of the South received word that the war was over.

One Confederate soldier out of every three died during the Civil War. One in four men of military age in the South died. Only one in ten died in the North.

Later the same day of the surrender in Greensboro, in Hospital No. 12, William may have been sleeping when an orderly downstairs ran inside and yelled to the rafters that Johnston had surrendered to Sherman. At the time of surrender, William's unit was with Harrison's Brigade in Walthall's Division, 3rd Corps, Army of Tennessee.

We should also ask when William wrote his last letter home and what it said. Many of the returning soldiers remembered later that they first wrote home at the end of the war, though they did not know if the letter would get there.

I only imagine this, but it may contain the gist of what he wanted to say before coming home.

April 26, 1865
Greensboro, North Carolina

My Dearest Mary,
Hopefully I will be home before you receive this letter, but I write to let you know I am now in this place and have been in the hospital here in Greensboro, North Carolina. As I'm sure you are aware, the war is

over, my darling. I am on my way soon, but I am told I will need to stop in Atlanta first for my parole since I serve with a Georgia regiment.

My dear Mary, I long to see your face again. It was so good to get your last letter to learn how all of you are surviving and to think that John, James, and Valentine all survive, too. God has truly blessed us.

I have seen so many young men mangled and dying. It saddens me that all over the South, the southland's young men and boys lie asleep in shallow graves.

If one of us had to be mangled, it was better for me than our sons. They have their whole lives ahead of them, and I lived a good life until this heinous war. Saddest of all, though, are not only the lost boys but also the lost crops of bounty, the burned houses and buildings. Sherman did what he had to do, and I'm afraid Georgia and South Carolina are all laid to waste.

Of course, I am one of the lucky ones. Petersburg was freezing, and we hear that so many died of the chills. But it is spring here in North Carolina, and the hospital here at Greensboro is more comfortable than many. I hear that parts of North Carolina escaped this war, and much of it is still pretty. Thankfully, our county escaped it, too. I long for Monticello and Elizabeth and old friends to reminisce with, but of course my dearest old friend has passed.

Mary, I know you miss your father, but I miss Jesse, too. I miss his counsel, and home will not be the same without him. I look back with wonder and thankfulness that he took me, a city boy, under his wing and showed me how to survive in a state which breaks the weak. And also I would not have met you—you being your father's greatest gift to me.

I heard him say many times how blessed he was to have had your mother, and I have felt the same way about you, dear Mary. I too am blessed, and I pray God will allow me to see you again.

I thought about asking for you and one of your brothers to come to me here in Greensboro, for I'm worried about the journey home, but it will be too hard and take too long. Hospital administrators will soon release all patients, and damage has destroyed many sections of the railroads. Plus, there will be waves and waves of soldiers desperately trying to travel the opposite way. Waves of hungry men desperate to survive and return home. It may be dangerous for you, so I am leaving with my unit as they make their way to Atlanta. I will try to travel with them as far as Albany and make my way home from there.

Hug and kiss all our children. Tell our Zech and Jesse that the war did not need them and that it is over. Thankfully, they were only sixteen and fourteen and could not join without your permission. Tell our daughters Sarah and Florrie that I cannot wait to see the young women they have become. Thank them for stepping up and sharing in the responsibilities of our household.

Tell Hattie not to grow up too fast. Your description of her newfound height scares me. She's obviously taking after the Carters. Before long, you won't be able to sweep out the house without dusting one of her beaus. Tell Henry that I'm thankful he is there to help take care of all the womenfolk. He's having to do an awful lot of grown-up work for a boy of only nine. As for beautiful little Laura and the irrepressible Joseph, please tell them more about me so they'll remember their daddy. And Little Virginia, whom I've never laid eyes upon, kiss her for me.

I'm coming south and will be there as soon as humanly possible.

All my love,
William

At Home

Mary probably had Jesse write another letter in case they detained William before his release. Though they weren't sure where to send it, they would post it to the last place where William had been.

Both were in the parlor, she standing near the fireplace, as a front moved through and the day had been windy and downright cold, a late cold snap for Middle Florida. He, with a pen in hand, sat over by the window at William's writing table. The fire crackled and popped behind Mary, who stood with her back to it. Mary said:

May 1, 1865
Monticello, Florida

Dearest William,

It has been chaos here in Middle Florida. Our own Governor Milton committed suicide, and Senate President Allison of Quincy is now acting governor. He plans to call a special assembly into a session to deal with the situation. There is much confusion, and we are in wait for our menfolk to return from the war.

You were right all along. Why did the agricultural South think it could win a war with the industrial North when all the North really had to do was bottle up our ports and squeeze the life out of us?

William, we watch every day for your return. We send this brief letter, having no idea if you are still at your last address, but we still have much hope. Come home to us, darling. We pray daily for grace on your travels south.

All my love,
Mary

When she finished the letter, she told her son goodnight and walked to her room. She felt weary and numb, as if she could not stomach another single disappointment.

Two days later, on Friday, the command ordered William's unit to surrender their guns to their ordnance officers, who then passed them on to Sherman's officers. Confederate records say that Sherman paroled them and allowed them to go home. The official surrender began, but another record said that the men could go home on May 1.

The hospital may have released William on the same date, and they likely prepared him for the long, five-hundred-mile-plus trip home. He was probably living on adrenaline. He was going home to Mary and the children—but he would have to wait five more days before beginning the journey. Thirty thousand men moving at once may have been too much for the area's transportation corridors, and those were only the Confederates.

At the surrender, their clothing was in tatters, and most were barefooted. Haggard and thin, their posture was that of a beaten foe.

On May 1, authorities released the entire army, ordering each regiment to march to their respective state capitols for disbandment. For William, because he was part of a Georgia regiment (even though he was a Floridian), he would first have to go to Milledgeville, Georgia's capital, but a diary says the units went to Atlanta. Sherman had invaded Milledgeville, too.

William Hill Andrews (no relation), a member of the First Georgia Regulars from Cuthbert, Georgia recorded the trip to Atlanta in a diary. He survived the war and later lived in Atlanta. According to this diary, the US authorities permitted the men to return home and "*not be disturbed so long as he observes this obligation and obeys the laws in force where he may reside.*" The diary said that the regiments started on their homeward march south on May 3rd.

When the Georgia soldiers began their travel on that Wednesday, May 3rd, 1865, there was no certainty William was with them. They marched eighteen miles hard with hardly a rest toward Salisbury, North Carolina. Was William in a wagon, or did he have to march with the rest of them?

The next morning they began marching down the broken rail line to Columbia, South Carolina, which took days to reach. Then they marched days more south of Columbia to Georgia, where they boarded an overly packed train probably in Augusta. The men rode in boxcars with flat tops, cars that were so crowded that many of them rode on top where sparks flew in their faces.

Sometime on the night of Tuesday, May 16th, the train reached Atlanta. The men were all paroled in Atlanta and awaited another train going south to Macon. Probably all the regiments headed to Middle Florida and South Georgia traveled this route, even if the Florida units did not have to be paroled through Atlanta. They probably stopped in Albany for the march south.

If William was on this train, his condition may have declined significantly. Whether he was on it or another one or riding the 500 miles in a wagon, he probably suffered. Part of his 5th Georgia probably stopped in Albany, which was closer to Bainbridge, the home of William's Company H. Some of the 5th may have proceeded on to Cuthbert, Georgia. Both Cuthbert and Albany had stations, and both had Confederate hospitals, though Cuthbert's Hood Hospital was larger and stayed open longer.

The reason for speculation with Cuthbert, Georgia is because in its Greenwood Cemetery there is a grave which reads W. H. Andrews. This grave is with several other Confederate soldiers who died at Hood Hospital, one of three Confederate hospitals in the town. Near W. H. Andrews, many more unmarked Confederate soldiers' graves fill an open area in the graveyard.

Grave of W. H. Andrews, Greenwood Cemetery, Cuthbert, Georgia, personal photos

It is truly speculative whether William was on this train when it arrived in Cuthbert, but if he was, he may not have marched the seventy-two additional miles south to Bainbridge, much less the additional forty-two miles to Tallahassee, where several of his fellow Florida comrades were paroled again. Did the trip make him sicker? Did he end up in Cuthbert, too sick to go farther south? Was he unable to go any farther on foot?

Oral history recounts that Hood Hospital, known as one of the best Confederate hospitals in the South, admitted the most severely wounded or sick soldiers. Also, we know that G. L. Musgrove of William's regiment had convalesced there. His company would have known about the hospital's reputation. Even if his company stopped in Albany, did they send him on to the hospital in Cuthbert? Many soldiers died during the train journey to the hospital. Was he the one who made it only to succumb later?

There is also other evidence regarding the grave site of W. H. Andrews. In a newspaper article written a year after the war ended, it says it is the grave of a W. J. Andrews from a Tennessee Regiment. The ladies of Cuthbert identified the men buried in these graves, according to the newspaper article. Our William's enlisted name on records for the 5th Georgia was W. H. Anders, a misspelling probably made by a clerk. This difference in his name may have led the women to decide that the man in the grave was W. J. Andrews from Tennessee. Maybe they thought the middle initial was a transcription error in the man's name. Or maybe someone from the family in Tennessee came looking for their loved one, and the ladies assumed it must be him.

Service records for W. J. Andrews show this Andrews fought in Georgia and that he spent time in this hospital. The records, though, do not reflect his death. No records show he died during the war, nor do they show he returned to his home in Tennessee. Was he missing in action? Did his family come to the hospital looking for him? So many unanswered questions.

That grave holds either W. H. Andrews or W. J. Andrews, but we cannot determine which. For our William, this grave only shares his name. Short of exhuming the body, we may never know which is buried there. Records show W. J. Andrews was definitely in the area. There is no record showing that W. H. Andrews came through the area, but record keeping was scant immediately after the war. There was simply no paper. Paper was at a premium. Even as early as November 30, 1864, Dr. Nichol at Hood Hospital wrote to his superior that he could no longer make his monthly reports without forms. He was out of paper.

And whoever is in that grave may or may not have gotten a casket. We know the Confederacy purchased caskets for these soldiers for $4, though ordinary citizens paid $5. If this is our William, who paid for the casket after the war was over? His burial would have been after the Confederacy fell, and if this were him, did he have any personal effects? No records exist, and no family stories tell of his death.

A book entitled *Confederate Hospitals: Cuthbert, Georgia* by Karan B. Pittman and Dr. Lela B. Phillips searched for any records of the three Cuthbert hospitals. The book mentions W. H. Andrews only in the context of his grave. There was no mention of a W. J. Andrews except for the list in the newspapers dated a year later, where someone tried to give more information as to the men in the marked graves.

We know from all his compiled military records that William survived the war, but there are no further records of William beyond his parole in April 1865. Two unanswered questions remain. Did he return to Mary? And if he did, how did he get there?

#

Chapter 12

Scalawags in the Courthouse
May to December 1865

In the last hours before the Yankees entered Florida's capital, Tallahassee's adjutant general hastily removed the retired battle flags from the capitol and slipped them into his sister's care, urging her to hide them at once—before Union hands could seize them. On Wednesday, May 10, the Union Brigadier General Edward McCook and his staff of officers rode into Tallahassee and proceeded to the capitol quietly and slowly. Everywhere, white people stopped and watched. The colored folks celebrated their liberation by taking to the streets. Later, in one of McCook's orders to the public, he informed local clergy that their Sabbath prayers must include the president of the United States, whether they cared to or not.

It was no different in Monticello, and Jefferson County had a plan, too. In March, before the Battle of Natural Bridge, the commission allowed Probate Judge J. B. Collins to pack the contents of his office and remove them to a safe place for whenever the Yankees "invaded" the county, but the Yankees never came.

This time it would be different, though. Before a McCook unit destined for Monticello arrived, George W. Taylor had a wagon waiting for the judge, and the judge removed the records again.

For the enslaved people of the South, they had been free since New Year's Day in 1863, but the slaves of Jefferson County probably did not know it until the Federals marched into their city. Upon their approach, news probably spread among the slaves like dry grass burning up a hillside, and the world the South knew ended. Freedmen came from everywhere and lined the sides of the road, eager to watch their liberators pass.

In a first order of business, the US Army prohibited Florida's government from functioning. Thus began a funereal reality and a new beginning for the state. Gone was the institution of slavery and, subsequently, its plantation culture. In its place was the beginning of Reconstruction. As the Confederate soldiers arrived in Tallahassee, all

Florida's regiments formally surrendered through Confederate Major General Sam Jones.

In Monticello, Mary probably heard the news about the May 10th Tallahassee surrender from the telegraph office or from those Confederates paroled and returning. Her Uncle David's parole happened on May 12th, and he probably came to Monticello and paid her a visit.

Who Got Home First?

The next day, on Saturday, Mary, wearing her mended and faded blue calico dress, heard a knock at the door. She hesitated to answer it. With the crowds of people in town, all her boys were away escorting their sisters, running errands. The town was bursting at its seams with strangers, and she worried it might no longer be safe for her or any of them to be alone anymore. Left home alone with the little ones, she thought maybe all of them should be more careful in the future.

She lifted the curtains in the parlor and practically knocked over the table in her haste to get to the door. There stood David in his faded and patched cavalry jacket, grinning from ear to ear. He grabbed her in a bear hug, swinging her around. She quickly hissed at him to be quiet, and they disappeared on to the porch.

Her handsome, dark hair and complected Uncle David, a private with Florida's Kilcrease Light Artillery who was close to her age and with whom she had played since a child, was home. More like a brother than an uncle, he had only joined the Light Artillery in 1864 at Camp Milton, near Pensacola, less than a year before.

The two sat and talked. She was glad the younger ones were asleep, the older ones away, and she had him all to herself. They shared all the family gossip before moving to events outside of their tight circle. He told her what he knew of the others who hadn't gotten home yet, but it wasn't much since he had been mostly in Florida.

He leaned forward and dropped his voice to a whisper. "There are rumors that the capitol's records were most likely destroyed before the Yankees occupied it." She frowned, and he added, "to prevent any incriminating evidence in case of prosecution for treason." She nodded in understanding. "Mary, you do not know how strange it was to ride to the capitol and see it surrounded by Yankees, and flying above it the Stars and Stripes." He leaned back in his chair and relaxed again. "I fear what will happen to us all."

They paroled Mary's Uncle David again in Madison on Wednesday, May 16th. The authorities likely didn't formally release him until he signed the oath of allegiance to the US government on May 18th. He may have waited to see if others were signing it. It said he was six foot tall with dark hair, dark eyes, and a dark complexion. The oath said he swore to never bear arms against the USA or give any information or do any military duty whatsoever until regularly exchanged as a prisoner of war. A captain and Provost Marshal G. W. Burns signed the oath, certifying that he gave the parole on the date written. It said he allowed the above-named person to return to his home not to be disturbed by the military authorities of the US so long as the person observed his parole and obeyed the laws which were in force previous to January 1, 1861 where he lived.

So David was home, but what about the scores of others? Mary guessed they were somewhere between Monticello and Richmond, trying to get home. Later, in the silence of her bedroom, she dropped to her knees on the rug by her bed and prayed for all of them, but she added a special prayer of travel grace for William, James, and Valentine.

In Monticello, bands of freedmen roamed about, initially with nothing to do but celebrate their new freedom. Of the county's 6,000-plus recently freed slaves, thousands of men, women, and children celebrated and milled about the town.

There arose many unanswered questions. When would Florida be restored to the Union? With slavery dead, what would be the status of the freedmen? With a worthless currency, failing cotton prices, and thousands of liberated slaves, how could the state rebuild its agricultural economy?

Mary wondered when the Georgia regiments would get home. Did word come quickly that William was on his way south—or was the message instead one of his passing? Did any Monticello men get home by the evening of the parole in Tallahassee, or did they wait for the next day?

There are no *Family Friend* newspapers from this time period to give us a clue what happened. As earlier mentioned, old Jefferson County families said that, during those last days, the newspaper printed a single copy, hung for all to see on the courthouse bulletin board. No known single copies survived, but an article from the *Family Friend* appeared in the September 26, 1865 issue of *The Semi-Weekly Floridian,* a Tallahassee paper, proving the *Family Friend* survived the war. The editor Fildes sold it during the month of November.

Though the Confederate government had ceased to exist, the war's last skirmish occurred near Brownsville, Texas on May 13, more than a month after Lee's surrender at Appomattox Courthouse.

Simultaneously, a Union cavalry detachment near Tifton, less than a hundred miles northeast of Monticello, captured Confederate President Davis, his wife, and others. Authorities accused him of treason and imprisoned him at Fort Monroe in Hampton, Virginia.

Late in May, a company of the 82nd US Colored Troops marched into Monticello, probably up Waukeenah Road from Tallahassee. They were part of Union General Edward McCook's orders from the War Department in Washington. He suspended any plans by Florida's acting Governor Abraham K. Allison and declared martial law in Florida. McCook garrisoned Federal troops in principal towns to see that laws and military orders from Tallahassee were enforced.

Monticello buzzed as the black Union soldiers wore their blues with honor and dignity. They marched to the eastern side of the courthouse, and every boy of color immediately wanted to join.

Authorities stationed the soldiers in Jefferson County where they would remain for several months, hoping they could maintain order amongst the thousands of freedmen who swarmed Monticello's streets, a continuous stream of newly liberated people with their newborn freedom to go anywhere they wished.

By the end of May, the South's world had changed. For over thirty-four percent of the people of Jefferson County, their faces probably showed their desperation. For the rest of the population, there was a newfound freedom never before experienced. Slavery ended and freed over 60,000 slaves in Florida alone. In Jefferson County, it freed over 6,300 men, women, and children.

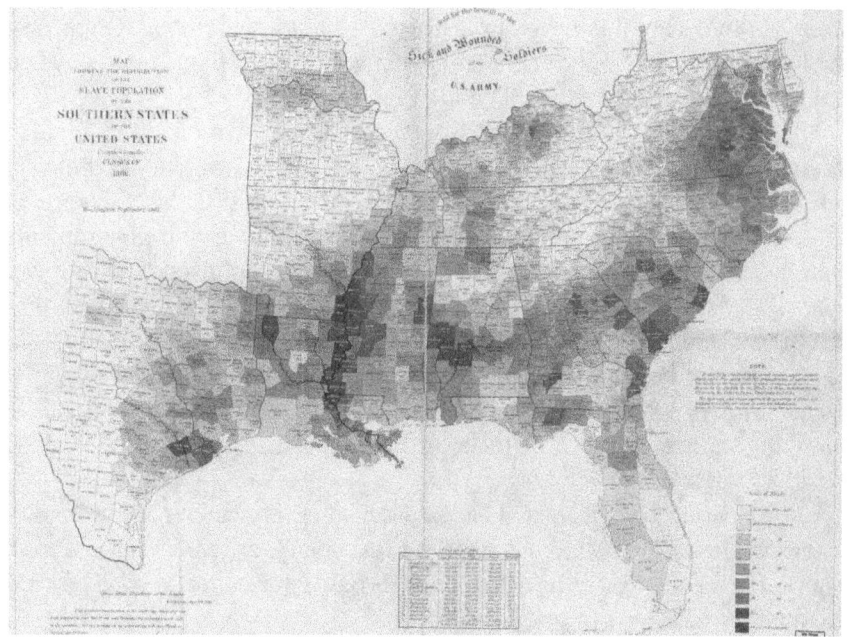

Southern States Slave Population, 1860, Library of Congress

The war destroyed Florida's economy. It caused Florida's villages, towns, and farms to fall farther into disrepair. In human terms, it also took a catastrophic toll. When Florida seceded in January 1861, the voting population was 14,374. Between 16,000 and 17,000 Floridians marched off to war, much more than its voting population. A third of those who left did not return.

By early June, President Johnson announced his plans for Reconstruction, his effort to reintegrate the former Confederate states into the US. It was an unprecedented challenge to reunite the country after four long bloody years of fighting.

Obviously, there were many differing views about when to do it, who should do it, and especially how it should be done. The latter ideas swirled around, and several were particularly onerous for the Southern half of the country.

Our forefathers probably never imagined states would one day secede from the union. Thus, there was nothing in the Constitution or in statute offering any guidelines. What followed was a plan based on President Lincoln's earlier generous and non-punitive plan designed to return the former states speedily into the nation.

Born in North Carolina and a Tennessean, President Andrew Johnson, the military governor of Tennessee after the North occupied his state, put into play this program of Reconstruction which placed power in the hands of white Southerners and eventually forced the former slaves to return to work as dependent plantation laborers.

Johnson's plan gave the Southern whites a free hand to regulate the transition. Except for Confederate leaders and the wealthy planters, he offered a pardon to all white Southerners. He also directed the seceded states to hold conventions and elections to reform their civil governments, and he allowed those pardoned to create them. Johnson also allowed nearly all lands confiscated by the government to be returned to their prewar owners.

In the beginning, most Northerners believed his plan was good. Most simply wanted the country to heal, but others saw the plan as forgiving traitors and turning its back on civil rights for the former slaves.

No one in Jefferson County had done any universal springtime planting. How now would a farmer, whether black or white, make a crop? Many Floridians felt Middle Florida would never reclaim its former prosperity.

The Jefferson County Commission met again a few weeks later to issue rations to indigent families, but they would not again convene until later, in December, before Christmas. Governments all over the South collapsed, waiting for the next elections.

Confederate forces in the trans-Mississippi surrendered on June 2nd. Across the nation, the South was devastated, though the devastation did not reach the same degree in every state. Virginia and Tennessee saw most of the war's fighting, while Florida and Texas saw the least. Military action extensively damaged parts of the South's infrastructure, while it left other parts virtually unscathed.

The war years left behind physical devastation throughout the region. Losing manpower prevented planting crops. Heavy use ruined over forty percent of farm assets. Roads through neglect were in a horrible condition, many impassable.

To fund the war, people bought Confederate currency and bonds, but these were now worthless. The South's investment in the war and in their slaves vanished—its equity vanished overnight. Southern banks and insurance companies went bankrupt.

Most debts became noncollectable. The men who made them simply disappeared—one third of them never returned from the war. Their farms were intact, but their horses, mules, and cattle were lost, much to conscription. Fences and barns needed repair, and this was true whether or not fighting had taken place nearby.

The news about the whereabouts of their menfolk came to the families piecemeal, a little here, someone arriving there. One day Sarah came from downtown with news. "Mama," she said, "Remember the flag Daddy described in such great detail that hung above the speaker's desk at the capitol?"

"Yes," said Mary as she poured vinegar over some cucumbers she had recently sliced. "What of it?" She wiped the jug spout with a rag.

"Well, I heard a Union army officer took it," replied Sarah.

"Well, I'm not surprised. We're under occupation. We could expect nothing less." The flag would not find its way back to the State of Florida until forty-six years later, having gone west before being sent to a Florida member of the United Daughters of the Confederacy in the early 1900s.

Mary thought about James and Vollie, who had left Jefferson County as mere boys seeking travel, to prove their bravery, and to experience battle. When they left, they were high in spirit but lacking the good, sound judgment God strives to give a person of age. Later, she would realize that those who came back were different people altogether, firmly ensconced in their manhood. Mothers, sweethearts, sisters, and wives found each divergent from the boy that left.

She also noticed a divide between those who fought and those who stayed home. What happened to her men and boys who fought would affect their feelings about the enemy when they got home. Mostly, they looked ahead to peace, even peace for the Confederate deserters who ran away. For her men who fought, it appeared they wanted to move forward and leave the veil of hatred behind them.

It was different, though, for those who stayed at home, especially the young but also some of the old. These quiet civilians felt differently. They spoke of hangings, especially for those who infested the swamps and woods of Florida.

Later, as years passed, the sustained war would have an intense effect on every one of the men and boys who left Jefferson County. Their feelings about the effort and each other would grow in magnitude, and because of the wounds and strains of war, many would die earlier in life than was normal. John Slicer would be an example of this, dying of consumption at fifty-nine in 1896. Yet he was one of the lucky ones. So many would die the first five years after the war, maybe even William.

These men, their lingering emotions, were from the heart—overwhelming, entrenched, and catching. Their womenfolk and children experienced passionate feelings regarding the war well into their old age. Several more generations inherited these feelings, reaching even to the author's generation, four generations later. The author's North Georgia-born Dalton grandmother retold her own grandmother's stories as if she had experienced them herself, thus giving the author the powerful impression that Sherman was the devil.

Unlike other parts of the South, those in Sherman's path often saw their land seized, appropriated, or laid waste by Union forces. In some areas, Confederate deserters followed behind like vultures, plundering what remained. Instances of violence—including rape—were not unheard of. This may explain why Mary did not return to Elizabeth until after the war had ended, where it's possible she moved there during the summer.

In their thoughts, the returning veterans probably dwelt on events far to the north, a philosophical place they would soon leave behind. The surrender of Lee, Lincoln's assassination by John Wilkes Booth, and the subsequent presidency of Andrew Johnson left the nation, and especially the South, in a state of estrangement.

For those soldiers who left without the company of their unit, the walk home was hard. There was no money, and even if there had been, there were no horses or mules for sale. Because the North destroyed them, and the South had already used them up, there were no animals left for the soldiers to ride home. By the end of the war, the south lost half of its 2.5 million horses and mules. Many farmers had none, and those who did needed theirs to survive.

Mary woke every morning wondering where her menfolk were. Young Vollie with his sandy blond hair bleached by the sun was probably the first one to show up—thin, ragged, dirty, and crawling with lice.

Mary placed her hand on his slack cheek. She cried, something she seldom did publicly, but these were tears of joy. She had earlier hung blankets in the backyard for privacy, and her wash kettle was ready to go, as it had been for weeks. They saved big hugs for later. Vollie went around back right away while Zech started the fire under the kettle. Vollie would get a good bath—a cold one first, though—until the water boiled.

Later, after his hot bath and maybe even a short haircut, they all ate supper in the backyard while Vollie told them story after story about the trip home, his soldier friends he left behind, and more until his eyelids grew heavy.

Mary noticed and said, "Vollie, your bed is upstairs if you're ready for it." He pushed his chair back from the table and looked at all the surrounding eyes, all watchful of his every move and word. Misty-eyed, he climbed the back porch stairs and disappeared into the hall.

The people of Jefferson County were all poor as church mice. White people had property and status but no money. Black people lacked all three but were happy to be free. About all they had were the clothes they wore and their liberty. With the shock of the defeat, all civic functions ceased. There was little money for anything, anyway. Swarms of freedmen, hundreds, came into the town and Tallahassee, milling around, until smallpox forced the matter of the situation.

Mary barked orders to clean the house and grounds. Henry sprinkled lime freely in the backyard, especially the corner which always stayed damp. Though William, Vollie, and James had been vaccinated, she and the rest of the family had not. With no money for anything, they would have to be extra vigilant about the pox, and this might have been when she moved back into the countryside in Elizabeth.

Both Yankee and Southern leaders noticed right away that there were so many idle men. People looked for work, and the leaders looked for ways to get people employed. Walking through town, Mary noticed the disoriented freedmen. They were grateful for their liberty, but they were unsure what freedom now demanded of them. Many kept waiting on the Yankees to lead them, but all they gave them were instructions to go to their masters and seek jobs.

Yankees and unemployed freedmen quickly overran the county. Many were happy about it, and some were not. Major General John Newton was the military commander in charge of the occupation of Florida, and he quickly met with the major planters of the area, planters such as Burton Bellamy.

On his way from town, Bellamy stopped to chat with Vollie, who was coming in from Elizabeth. Bellamy sat high on his horse and tipped his hat. "Welcome home, Vollie."

Vollie replied, "Thank you, Mr. Bellamy; and I hope it has been a fine day for you? How is the family?"

"The misses is doing better now. She got into something and had a nasty rash on her wrists, but she is almost well. Thank you for asking. Vollie, we all miss your grandfather. Jesse was a fine man."

Vollie listened as Mr. Bellamy talked about his grandparents. He was sad he never got a chance to say goodbye to the only grandfather he ever knew.

Bellamy added, "I just got back from town. Some Yankee officers met with us. They asked us to gather our former slaves and inform them they are free. Of course, most of mine knew it anyway—many are hanging around town. The grapevine, especially among the slaves, works better than our own press." Both chuckled.

"Anyway," he continued, "I'm to ask my former slaves to come to work for me but for wages. Of course, all of us told them we don't have money. All we ever had was property as land and slaves, and now we don't have any slaves.

"So they explained we could pay them for a share of our harvest. We told them that no one will make any money this way, not us and not them, but I agreed to do it because I have no other alternative. All the others in the county agreed for the same reason."

Said Vollie, "I bet they're worried about all the freedmen hanging around town. There are hundreds of them, and half of them are drunk on their new freedom. They're a noisy lot."

Before Lincoln's assassination, in March, Congress created the Bureau of Refugees, Freedmen, and Abandoned Lands, also known as the Freedmen's Bureau. After the occupation in Tallahassee, the bureau was immediately on-site and responsible for both black and white people who needed aid. It came right away to Monticello and provided food, clothing, and medical aid. They even arranged for the legalization of marriages amongst the county's former slaves. The bureau provided for general legal representation and helped secure employment opportunities. It would even settle freed people on confiscated lands and was popular with the freedmen, but not so much with the whites.

Mostly, though, it was quickly apparent to everyone, returning Confederates, the women who stayed behind, the freedmen, the Bureau, and even the occupying army that crops needed to be planted in Florida if starvation was to be avoided in the fall.

Days later, Mary couldn't help feeling like she had lived through this before. Not the waiting for her menfolk, no, but the hard living. It was like everyone was starting over. Everything needed repairing, and some even had to rebuild their homes. Overgrown fields needed clearing.

That night at supper, she reminisced about those early days when her parents started over in Florida. She said, "This is so much like when Mama and Daddy first got here. They both worked hard to eke out a living. Daddy spent his days clearing field after field, bringing each one closer to full planting. I remember him and the uncles girdling trees and waiting years for them to fall. In the meantime, they planted in between them. We hunted wild animals to eat and sometimes would have starved without them.

"Mama was often there right beside him with her dress pulled through and tucked in one of Daddy's belts wrapped around her waist. It made her look like she was wearing pants that ballooned at her legs. She could hoe as well as any of Bellamy's slaves. Her hands, unlike those of the planter's wives, were always calloused."

Mary's children loved to hear about those times. Instead of the little faces from Mary's young womanhood, now staring back were her grown progeny, except for the three youngest. Years later, in retrospect, many felt the war marked the end of Florida's frontier existence, and families like the Walkers and Andrews who had lived through those times felt like they were living them again.

Vollie was most worried about acts of vengeance, especially by the federal government. With so many Yankees in town, the fear was prevalent, staring them in the face daily. People became more despondent and kept to themselves. Any free and forward, back-and-forth exchange of ideas was no longer prevalent. No one trusted the Yankees or those who followed them.

For all the Southern soldiers and officers, there remained in these months and even years after the war the overall question of amnesty and treason. The North discussed holding treason trials, especially against Jefferson Davis. But considering the terms of the surrender, the cabinet was not consensual. They never held treason trials against anyone.

A main issue no one wanted to address was whether the states had the legal right to secede. The Union feared an acquittal for Davis on these grounds, which would have humiliated them. The Federals wanted no court precedent that said it was possible for a state to secede.

Florida's helm, though, was still unoccupied. The state waited for the November elections after the authorities removed Florida's governor. The South began its new normal. Courthouses which were closed during the war reopened. Jefferson County's probably never closed, but courthouses in previously occupied cities like Jacksonville and Fernandina did.

They would not parole John Slicer until June 10th, when he signed the US Oath of Allegiance at Fort Delaware Prison. It said he had a sallow complexion, probably because of his consumption, dark hair, gray eyes, and was 5' 7". He began his journey home to Pierce County, Georgia to his wife Emily and family. His family needed him, and the only way he could leave was to sign the oath. He put his family ahead of the cause. Pierce County may not have warmly received him when he returned.

By mid-summer, the Freedman's Bureau supervised the contracts between the freedmen and their former owners. Bellamy complained to anyone who would listen that his former slaves were undependable. The freedmen were not all that interested in returning to the fields, especially the same fields they had escaped. The promised share of the crop often felt insufficient, though the occupying army made efforts to see that the agreements were upheld.

On June 19th, Juneteenth, the Union army, when it liberated the remnants of the South's slaves, controlled even Texas. All remaining Confederate land forces surrendered by this date. General Edmund Kirby Smith of Florida yielded the last Confederate troops at New Orleans.

Meanwhile, most of the talk around town centered on President Johnson's order that the paroled Confederates could run for local offices, salient positions that subsequently allowed them to form a new state government and local governments. With the coming elections, this renewed hope helped raise spirits that things would soon be back to normal. It did nothing for the freedmen, though, who were questioning liberty and what it really meant to be free.

Mary wiped her face to keep the sweat from stinging her eyes. It was early morning, but the heat pressed in, thick with the promise of a front. Humidity hung in the air. She leaned her face against Flossie's warm, damp side and felt the cow exhale gently as her milk let down. The stream of milk splashed inside the wooden bucket. Today, Mary planned to churn butter and make biscuits. She hadn't felt this much like cooking in a long time. It all came back when Vollie returned.

Vollie walked into the barn, his slender frame silhouetted against the bright sunlight at the door. Motes swirled through the sharp slats of light slashing the floor. "Mama, I can do that for you." He pulled her up and quickly sat down and proceeded. Without protest, she let him do it.

"I thought you might want to sleep a little longer," she said. How good it was to have him back. With his sandy brown hair, so much like his father's, Val leaned his face against Flossie. Mary watched for a moment and thought to herself that Valentine was a good-looking scamp. It would be no time before he found someone and settled down again. Ellen had remarried.

Val added, "I'm here now, and Zech, Jessie, and I can all do what needs to be done. You and the little ones have had to do so much by yourselves. We can take over now."

They discussed the corn crop and the potato patch. Earlier, Zech had mentioned trying to fish cattle from the swamps the way they used to in better times. Those swamps, especially below Lick Skillet, were deep, vast, and dark. The Indians had escaped and hid in them for years. There might be cattle there still. The brothers also wanted to hunt for fresh hog meat. (Lick Skillet is today Lamont.)

The laughter returned, but there was still a note of sadness in the air. William and James still weren't home, and no one knew where William was after Goldsboro. They probably knew his Georgia unit had to come via Atlanta, but they may have been still waiting for news. They also worried he was not well.

By late afternoon, the house and the surrounding rolling pastures were a place of industry. Everyone had a job and was busy at it. Even eleven-year-old Joseph helped Henry split and stack firewood from a water oak blown down during the last storm.

Mary and the girls had supper ready and rang the dinner bell. The sun was dropping low. It was quitting time, and everyone came in for the evening.

Mary loved this. All her family trying to talk at once, chattering nonstop. It was "pass the potatoes" and "have you seen Elizabeth Grubbs?" and "when are we going to town again?" If only William and James were here.

Suddenly, the door flew open and there he stood, or rather leaned against the frame, grinning at his family. William was home. The entire room reached a new level of pandemonium as chairs overturned and children ran to their father. Mary's Uncle James stood behind him.

First, Mary froze. She noticed Joseph, Laura, and Henry stood still, unable to move. William looked at her and grinned from ear to ear, his same old boyish grin. She bolted from her seat.

He was extremely thin and dirty. Ragged would be a better word. She knew right away he wouldn't be able to sleep in the house tonight. Everyone of her menfolk came home crawling in vermin. And the smell!

But she couldn't stand it any longer. They met halfway, and he was at last in her arms again. She would deal with the lice later. Holding her, he reached for the three youngest, and Mary said, "Children, come here and see your father, but keep your distance. You can hold his hand." And she looked up again into his eyes and through her smile said, "He is home."

Though the two youngest were born before he left, they were toddlers and had little memory of him. Virginia, though, was another situation all together. He had never seen his youngest sandy-haired, blue-eyed daughter, nor had two-year-old Virginia ever laid eyes on her father. While he was gone, Mary made sure they knew all about him. She described him and what kind of man he was, but thankfully, God sent him home so they could get to know him for themselves.

William remembered his manners and turned to James, "Join us for supper, James." Uncle James looked to Mary, and she nodded her head because there was plenty enough. He joined them for a quick bite while William explained how he had gotten home.

"Did you get to kill Yankees, Daddy?" asked Joseph.

"Not enough," said William. "The entire state of North Carolina's crawling with Yankees." They all laughed but got somber when Val said, "Well, we're crawling with Yankees here too, Daddy, even in Monticello."

"I heard all about them from Uncle James," said William. And the family talked far into the night. Mary couldn't get enough of the heart-quickening sound of his voice. Now and then his gaze lingered on hers, and in those moments, her heart forgot to beat.

Zech and their son James left to make their father a good, warm, and comfortable bed in the barn. In the back of her mind she thought, "James is home, but when…?" but she noticed William flagged as his adrenaline waned. They could see he looked tired and weak, so everyone decided it was time to get some sleep.

He and Mary stepped outside on the porch as she alone walked him to the barn. She helped tuck him into his bedroll and with the kerosene lamp made her way to the barn door to see herself out. As she stepped into the night, she looked back at him curled in his bedroll. She wondered if he was asleep.

When the barn door snapped shut, she woke up. It was all a dream. Neither James nor William was home. Lying in the dim first light of morning, she cried quietly to herself and was glad she got to hold him, even if only in her dream. Little Laura slept soundly beside her.

What happened to William by the end of the war is a mystery, and there are no papers or documents showing he survived the trip home. All we know for certain is that, if not earlier in 1865, Mary was a widow, possibly a war widow, by 1871. What we have is family lore that says he came home from the war, though the story came from William's grandson, who had heard the story from William's son Henry, who lived until the 1930s. Henry told the story to one of his sons, who lived to be over ninety, and it was he who told the author. But William returned twice from the war, and at which time did Henry remember his father's return?

William may have died immediately after April 28, 1865 of complications from the war and the more than six-hundred-mile journey home. If he got home, he may have been an extremely sick man.

Land records did not contain information that led to a record of his death. The only property sold after the war was a tract which was bought under Mary's name during the war. It may not have required his signature.

Tax rolls for 1863 and 1866 name Mary, probably because the land the family owned was in her name. The 1863 tax roll inventoried nothing other than the land. However, the 1866 tax roll inventories not only the land but also a horse valued at $130, nineteen head of cattle or hogs, a carriage, and various household items. This 1866 tax roll may suggest that William had already passed, since most likely these had once belonged to the entire family, him included.

And then there is the grave in Cuthbert, Georgia—silent, enduring, and still holding its mystery.

William, though, isn't the only person in Mary's life who disappeared after the war. Her Uncle David, who probably came to see her immediately after his pardon in Tallahassee, disappeared as well, with no records beyond May 16, 1865 when he signed the oath of allegiance in Madison.

For a good twenty years after the war, this was often the way of things—Southerners disappeared without a trace while the record keeping of earlier years became a tool for occupiers to stir trouble for those who remained. People stopped recording things in the courthouse. The less the courthouse knew about your business, the better.

Our best guess is William either died at the end of the war before reaching home or he died by June 1870, the date of the 1870 census. There is no birth or death date for the man, so such a statement is completely speculative. With a lack of good records, each must make his or her own assumptions. We can only prove William died after April 28th, 1865 but before the June 22nd, 1870 census. This is the true end of "our" story for Mary's William.

Steel magnolia is a southern symbol of a woman who embodies traditional femininity and uncommon fortitude. Mary, who was southern to her core, became the backbone of her family. Women like her were the foundation on which the new South was built. While William provided for his family and fought wars, Mary taught her children well, had to make do with less, and carried on. She didn't teach her children to read and write, but she taught them a work ethic and good common sense. She was there through their laughter and tears, and she would be there to make sure they survived. It was the women of the South who waited on their men to come home, and the same women who kept the body and soul of their families together when their husbands could not.

By mid-June, almost all their menfolk were home. No one had heard from her brother David, whom they felt was still a prisoner of war at Rock Island, Illinois. His late arrival home can be attributed to his not signing the oath of allegiance until June 22nd at Rock Island. He was 5' 10" with gray eyes and light hair.

On June 30th, authorities paroled Mary and William's son James. He, too, may have been one of the last to arrive home, probably in early July.

In early evening on the day James came home and after he bedded down in the barn, Mary and her children changed clothes, lit a fire in one fireplace, and fried some lice. Tomorrow they would rise early, start a fire outside, boil a big pot of water, and begin the delousing of James. They would throw away and burn his clothes and bedroll.

We know James Jefferson, Valentine, and John Slicer returned, as well as Mary's brothers J.J., William, Arch, Berry, and David. Her Uncle Littleberry survived the war, as did his sons, her first cousins, Jess, Joel, and William. Mary's Uncle James had several sons who served, and they all survived, including Joel P., Isham, Jesse, and Wesley. Mary's Aunt Mary Jane Walker Lightsey sacrificed a son, but her other sons Joel, Archibald, Stephen, and William H. came home. We're unsure what happened to her son Jacob, but according to records, he was still alive in 1862 when John Adams died. Mary's Uncle David's son Stephen J. Walker returned, too.

Those lost before, during, or soon after the war were Mary's brothers Henry, George, and Joseph; her father; her Uncle David; her first cousin John Adams Lightsey, who was the son of her Aunt Mary Jane Walker Lightsey mentioned earlier; and possibly his brother Jacob, too. The Walker family paid a heavy price.

Mary's brother Joseph disappeared during the war, possibly before early 1862, when the state units joined the overall Confederacy. Confederate records do not list him, though his name appears on an earlier state militia roll. There are no more records on him after this. He may have died as young as twenty-five. Several of his siblings named their children Joseph.

Of William's family, some of which fought for the North, his brother-in-law Alexander Newton, who married his sister Elizabeth and who owned and ran his mother's tavern after she passed away, fought for the Confederacy for the 56th Virginia Infantry and survived the war to return and help his wife run the tavern in Leesburg, Virginia. William's sister Julia Ann Andrews Pic passed away in the 1840s, but her son John F. Pic fought for the Union in the US Navy. He survived the war, though he was still in the hospital by July 1865. When he left the Navy, he lived in Washington, DC until his death in the 1880s.

William's older brother Jesse was too old to serve in the war, but four of his sons served and survived. He lived in Smith County, Tennessee, which sent twelve companies to fight for the Confederacy. His son Samuel D. Andrews fought for the South and enlisted in the Tennessee 7th Cavalry Battalion in 1861. He survived and stayed in Smith County.

By the middle of the war, when almost all of Tennessee was Union occupied, two of Jesse's younger sons, Napoleon B. Andrews and William H. Andrews (the latter of which was possibly our William's namesake), enlisted in August 1863 in the North's 5th Tennessee Cavalry, Company B. Both survived the war. Was their enlistment a choice—or a consequence of coercion under military occupation? William H. moved on to Fredericktown, Missouri, where he died in June 1914. Napoleon remained within the Smith County area.

Another son, Jerome Dekator Andrews, fought for the First Mounted Infantry of the Union army but did not enlist until early 1864, when he was twenty-two years old. We're unsure about the other sons, James Byron or Junius Marcellus, the latter of which was in only one census in 1850. James Byron may have joined the Union, too, but in Ohio. William's brother Jesse, who had sons fighting for both sides, died shortly after the war in 1868. Family lore says Jesse came to Monticello to visit the family at least one time when they were young, though we're unsure if it was before, during, or after the war.

Florida played its role in the war and gave a higher percentage of her citizens than any other state in the Confederacy. Half of her soldiers served in the east with the Army of Northern Virginia and the other half in the western campaign in the Army of Tennessee. Her men took part in every major battle east of the Mississippi River.

President Davis was not an efficient administrator. He attended to too many details, displayed a certain weakness for dismissing those who worked for him, and failed to attend to civic responsibilities. His Southern constituency was quick-tempered, daring, and impulsive if not tireless; but the North was tenacious, too. They came down on the South *"with the steady momentum and perseverance of a mighty avalanche,"* as prophesied by Texas Governor Sam Houston before the war. Florida's own former Governor Call warned Floridians in the same way with his earlier fiery secession comment, *"You have opened the gates of Hell, from which shall flow curses of the damned to sink you to perdition."* Both men were widely traveled and, like William, Houston knew what was north of the Mason-Dixon Line.

At the end of the war, the US Army took control of all Confederate territories without post-surrender insurgency or guerrilla warfare against them. However, the coming year in Florida saw local violence, feuding, and revenge killings, though Jefferson County reported nothing significant.

After the war, authorities immediately suspended the hugely unpopular Northern draft; it would not return for over half a century until World War I. Union soldiers sent South after the war could not see why they were there. They did not want the duty and had little sympathy for Reconstruction. They simply wanted to go home.

The knowledge of how many Jefferson County men and boys died brought home the war's reality more than any other event. When the war began, Florida's total population of whites numbered about 77,000. Of that number, approximately 15,000 served in the Confederacy. One third of those that served never came home, and many more died quickly after the war because of their wounds and related illnesses.

It was the same for the rest of the Confederacy. Over half a million Southern men died or never returned. By the end of the war, thirty percent of all white males between the ages of eighteen and forty were missing. People did not consider various soldiers missing until they failed to return from the war, especially by the summer's end.

No one recorded civilian deaths in the South, but over 800,000 people lived in eleven Confederate states before the war. By the war's end, about 681,000 Southerners were alive. The Union army seized control of 162 of the South's 239 cities, with eleven suffering destruction or severe damage, among them Atlanta, Charleston, Columbia, and Richmond. Remarkably, forces destroyed only forty-five of the South's more than 800 courthouses.

Though most of Florida was spared occupation, the devastation throughout the rest of the South brought immense suffering to those left behind—women, children, the elderly, and the enslaved—who bore the weight of the war's aftermath. Many widows abandoned their farms and merged into the households of others. Women who never married were many, but it was less of an embarrassment than it would have been before the war. Now it was more common to remain unmarried.

It was true for the war widows, too. Many didn't want to remarry, as the choices were mostly men in poor health. Mary may have faced this choice. Other customs changed, such as divorce, which became more common, and the independence of women, who were now the mainstays of their fragmented families.

Local widows and even those women whose broken husbands returned faced the absence of able-bodied men, depleted stock, deteriorating roads, filled ditches, disintegrating or washed out bridges, decaying wharves, steamboats in disrepair, railroad tracks grown up in weeds and bushes, and cross-ties and trestles rotted—all of which created an overall crumbling of local infrastructure. Reports surfaced of people stealing wood from the trestle near Olustee to repair their fences. Adding to their problems, the price of cotton never recovered, and no one had any money to spend. A barter system sufficed.

What Mary noticed most, though, was the sight of so many mutilated men and boys. It recalled sad and bitter memories for everyone.

When they thought no one was listening, usually late at night, her sons recalled endless marching, bivouacs, scanty rations, shivering limbs, and half-shod feet. There were wasting sicknesses, horrible wounds, battlefields awash in blood, and the faces of death. They talked about Lee, Jackson, the Johnstons, Bragg, and Beauregard.

She knew, though, that what they didn't witness was what happened on the home front, when their women wept, prayed, toiled, suffered, substituted, made do with what they had, and sacrificed. And now everyone, especially the women, talked about how they could bind themselves to the loved and lost, the ones who would never return. How cruel the awakening.

Mary's life, though, continued, and there are records to prove it. Mary's children will have many memories of when the men came home from the Civil War, which they will call the War of Northern Aggression for the rest of their lives. The South may have fired the first shot, but the North kept trying to resupply its forts on what the South considered Southern soil. For months after the war, several said most men were emaciated, barefooted, and carried their rifles even to church.

By the end of the war, Mary's parents' generation had mostly passed, but among their children and grandchildren there arose an identity with Florida that her parents may have never felt. Probably to Jesse and Elizabeth and the other older uncles, they were South Carolinians, but to Mary and William's children, they were Floridians. Those caught in the awful vortex of the Civil War and the passing of generations helped create this identity, when many soldiers from all over the state fought to uphold their state's name.

Mary came into the house from the kitchen, her hair pulled back severely from her face, which was flushed. It was hot, humid; and she and Sarah finished preparing dinner for the boys, who would come in from the fields soon. She had asked Jesse to stay home today to help around the house. Wood needed cutting, and she needed him to pull the wash urn for the following morning.

Inside, Jesse was waiting with quill and paper. Mary wanted him to write a letter for her. It had been awhile since anyone had written the relatives in Colleton County, and she felt it was certainly time. With her father gone and she the oldest, she felt it was her place.

She sat next to the desk in the parlor with a cup of water and began dictating to Jesse, who sat at his father's desk by the window. He dipped his quill into the ink and kept writing. She added:

"Thankfully, this war is over, and now our mail resumes. I hope this letter finds you and yours well. Our little Monticello is an occupied city with a captain from the Union army as our taskmaster. The poor man has his hands full, I'm afraid. The South does not surrender so easily, and passive resistance is the call to arms here, as I'm sure it is in South Carolina.

"The entire state is still reeling from the searing lashes of loss and death. Men everywhere are maimed—several without an arm, without a leg or both. Our sons and husbands came home, several without boots and a few with, though not their own. Into the toes of his boots, James stuffed whatever he could find. Those boots remain his good boots, his only boots. The girls and I made them all pairs of moccasins. They all exclaimed how good they felt. It's a blessing the womenfolk here have enough spirit for all of us.

"It is sad to see what has happened to our little town, our poor state, and our glorious southland. William wrote about how Colleton County missed Sherman's wrath. Jefferson County did, too, but we hear, though, Sherman pillaged and forced the people of middle Georgia to survive on black-eyed peas and turnips. The Yankees thought the peas were simply forage for their animals, so they left them behind. The turnips were in the ground, so they didn't know their roots were edible. Now these foods, too, are gone.

Everywhere, decrepitude has set in and there is no money to be had for anything, let alone a coat of paint. There are no new boards to mend the decayed, as our boys and menfolk spend every waking hour trying to keep food on our tables."

Jesse wrote quickly as the words spilled forth, and Mary asked about their cousins who remained behind in her home county. Later she took the time to rest and refresh herself before moving on to the next task of the day.

The black-eyed peas and turnips story came from the old-timers who survived in that area. Many later said, "Today we eat black-eyed peas and turnip greens for luck in the South."

One summer afternoon, Vollie came from Monticello with news. During the planning for the registration of the freedmen, surnames were necessary. Vollie said, "Most chose the names of their masters, but several didn't want it."

She listened and thought to herself, "Some of those masters are as mean as a moccasin. I wouldn't want their name either."

She said, "Those who took other names probably are the ones who will move on the quickest. They probably want to put everything behind them as soon as possible and will probably be the ones who will be the most successful."

If not before, by midsummer, Mary and the family moved to Elizabeth. The Walker brothers, uncles, and cousins were all back, and the countryside was safer with all its menfolk home to watch over it.

By the end of summer, all the men were home from the war who were coming back. Most got to work right away with no time for much of anything but survival. The loss and the new world order at home still depressed most, but to add insult to injury, President Andrew Johnson appointed a new provisional governor for Florida, the New York-born William Marvin. Thus began a new phase of many changes in Florida, changes to spark dynamic growth in the state.

Mary remembered when her father and William had grown thoroughly weary of the appointees sent from Washington. It is one reason they worked so hard for statehood. Yet here Florida was again on the receiving end of the same practice. She was glad neither was here to witness it.

A few weeks later, all hell broke loose. If people resented the 82nd Colored Troops, they seethed over the 2nd Florida Union Cavalry. This unit housed Confederate deserters, several of whom had ravaged the Florida countryside during the war, some of whom had once been Confederate citizens, and several of whom drank too much. There were personal animosities still ripe. This was the same unit that had fought against the Confederates in several skirmishes in Florida during the past couple of years.

All kinds of problems arose, culminating in their commander arresting and imprisoning several of them in Monticello's jail. Other soldiers of the 2nd helped them escape twice. The local commander tried to enforce discipline, but this was an unruly company. In the end, they ordered the entire 2nd to Tallahassee by mid-October and mustered them from service by November.

There are stories about a Union unit who used the First Baptist Church as a target from the second-story windows of the courthouse. People in Monticello as late as the 1960s said they remembered the bullet holes that remained in the church's foundation. This may be the atrocity which resulted in the imprisonment of these men. Monticello's citizens probably lost their minds over the desecration, and the authorities removed the cavalry unit to Tallahassee.

Meanwhile, as the crisis between the freedmen and whites escalated, congregations in the county asked their freedmen to seek other places to worship, to organize their own churches. One gentleman didn't take kindly to the order and torched Monticello's Presbyterian Church. It burned to the ground within its brick walls. By 1867, the Presbyterians rebuilt their church on the same foundation, using many of its original bricks.

In August, they hospitalized Joel E. Walker in Georgia; by October 10th, he remained hospitalized. We're unsure if his injuries were so bad that he remained hospitalized all this time.

October brought campaigning for offices, but Mary and her family and most of the Walkers who were at work harvesting their fields hardly noticed, though those who could would all take time to vote.

By fall, Mary's entire family shared in the labor to harvest their crops. The most backbreaking was the cotton, and Mary thought back to those days when she and her brothers and sisters worked in their father's cotton fields. Much time had passed, and she had forgotten how much backbreaking effort it required. The pads of her fingers felt like pin cushions, pierced by hundreds of needles.

Their hopes were high for the cotton, but a flood of cotton on the world market meant depressed prices. They hardly broke even. Even sadder was the condition of the freedmen. With their freedom came responsibilities that most were unprepared for, such as providing shelter, clothing, food, and medical attention for their families. The cotton harvest destroyed their hopes.

Most problems occurred at the end of this growing season in 1865 because of the area's meager corn and cotton crops. Planters tried to collect on their contracts from the fall harvest. Equally problematic was the freedman's practice of buying on credit. Because of the fall in the price of cotton, many freedmen owed more than the value of their crops. This caused them to feel that working was useless. The Bureau tried its best to explain the situation, and they recommended to the freedmen that in the future they buy nothing on credit.

The biggest problem, though, was the freedman's inability to read and write. Landowners frequently wrote the oral agreements, and for obvious reasons, the freedmen didn't trust them. The following year, all agreements would be required to be approved by the Bureau before they became effective.

Another problem was loitering. At the end of their contracts, freedmen returned to the streets, and Monticello and Tallahassee reacted negatively. Florida's general assembly met and debated legislation to cut down on loitering. Vagrancy laws emerged throughout the Southern states.

Late one afternoon, Vollie came in from a quick trip to town with news about the *Family Friend*. He said, "Mr. Fildes sold the paper to two gentlemen, one by the name of Cocke and our own Judge Collins. Mr. Cocke is a Virginian by birth. Mr. Fildes is moving to Memphis." Mary listened and thought, "The only sameness is change—relentless change."

At the general election in early November, a vast majority of the men elected were former Confederates as the freedmen still did not have the right to vote. With the November general elections behind them, Florida was back in business as far as the whites were concerned. Florida's Union-appointment governor, who was a conditional secessionist but not a Unionist, called for a constitutional convention to elect a new delegation from Florida to Congress.

Dominated by ex-Confederates, they held the constitutional convention in Tallahassee later in November. Their task was to repeal the ordinances of secession and ratify the Thirteenth Amendment, the amendment which freed the slaves. They followed their orders and did both, but what also came forth from the convention would eventually send the former slaves back to conditions that resembled slavery. It allowed the provisional governor to issue writs of election for Florida's counties for various offices, including sheriffs. From Jefferson County were delegates William Capers Bird, William B. Cooper, and Asa May.

In the election, they ratified the new Constitution and formed a new state government. They elected Governor David S. Walker, no relation, to take control in January 1866.

The news from Tallahassee was troublesome for both the freedman and the whites. Article 1 said *"no freeman shall be taken, imprisoned, or dis-seized of his freedom, liberties, or privileges, or outlawed or exiled, or in any manner destroyed or deprived of his life, liberty or property, but by the law of the land."* Article XVI outlawed slavery in Florida and permitted blacks to testify in cases involving other blacks but not whites.

That winter with a new state constitution Florida's new legislature produced a set of laws called the "Black Codes," which while recognizing the slaves' freedom, kept them distinctly unequal to whites in criminal procedures, labor contracts, and nearly every facet of daily life. The legislation relegated them to second-class citizenship, restricting them to a status of legal inferiority.

The governor reinstated local civil officials who had held office before the war and directed these reelected officers to carry on as they had done before. Samuel Pasco became Jefferson County's circuit clerk.

For the Unionists in Florida, this caused much consternation. There was vitriol when they saw secessionists simply come home from the war, even from Union prisons, and step back into their elected offices as if nothing had taken place in between. A huge cry erupted.

The Radical Republicans in Congress watched with rage as similar events took place throughout the South.

In reply, Congress refused to seat the new Florida representatives or those from other states and demanded investigations and more protection for the freedmen.

Mary heard her sons and daughters read about the new laws as the family still met in the evenings to read together before the hearth or on the porch. She listened with interest to the articles about the additional duties of sheriffs in the state. The new laws designed to control the former slaves gave sheriffs broad powers to bring in vagrants and vagabonds, to hire them to anyone who would take them for the shortest time and pay the fine. It was really a new form of slavery—a new way to restrict their freedom.

In time, though, when the local sheriffs tried to enforce the new laws, they faced hostile Federal officials, the military who occupied towns like Monticello and who were ready to intercede on the behalf of the freedmen. No way around it. The North won the war, and Federal authority was here to stay.

James said, "Mama, it says here our US marshals will assume their roles as census takers. Mr. Blackburn will continue in his position." E. E. Blackburn of Monticello was the marshal of the northern district of Florida. James skipped a portion and read the following: "It says the Radicals are calling for the impeachment of President Johnson. They say he should be ashamed of himself for betraying those who put him there, and especially the Negroes."

Mary listened and then took her leave. She was sick to death of hearing about all the trouble everywhere in the nation. There were problems in their own county, in Tallahassee, and in Washington. It gave her a headache, so she retired for the evening. As she walked down the hall toward the back of the house, she rubbed her temples and pulled at the pins in her hair. Lately, everything cast a cloud on her every joy.

Later, after everyone had gone to bed, she found herself sleepless. She wandered throughout the house and on the porch heard the older boys talking quietly in the cool evening air. Said James, "Brigham Young has proclaimed polygamy as their right."

Added Vollie, "Well, that should add fuel to their fire." They laughed.

James continued, "He says they will sustain their right even if it requires a force of arms."

There was a pause, and Zech said, "I never remember Daddy reading anything like this when we were younger." He hesitated and added, "Do you think he skipped such lunacy?"

Chilled, Mary tiptoed to her bed before they discovered her eavesdropping. Zech was right. William didn't read about such things to his children, but he had shared it with her. That is how she knew what polygamy was.

Several days later, Mary visited her Aunt Mary Jane Lightsey who was hosting her sister-in-law Ann Lightsey. The ladies and several of their daughters sat around a quilt doing handwork for Joel Walker Lightsey, whose wife was expecting their first child.

Ann said, "I heard something, Mary Jane, that I don't want you to hear from outside of the family." Mary Jane looked at her, stunned, and Ann added, "The Union has taken steps to move their dead from the many Southern battlefields to have them reinterred elsewhere."

Mary looked over at her Aunt Mary Jane, whose son John Adams had died and lay buried at Sharpsburg. Mary Jane replied, "Only 'their' dead?"

"It appears so," said Ann.

Mary Jane teared up, and Mary reached over to hold her hand. Her aunt asked, "What do they plan to do with the bodies?"

Ann replied, "They will place them in the new National Cemetery at Lee's Arlington, but I'm hearing there are efforts for each state in the South to do likewise for our own."

"Surely not send them to Arlington, I gather?" added Mary Jane.

Ann replied, "No, I think not."

No one recorded the whereabouts of her son Jacob Lightsey after 1862, but many were missing in action. Sometimes there was nothing left —no proof of loss.

Meanwhile, a bitter struggle ensued between the president and the "radical" Republicans in Congress, and a story spread throughout the South that southern lands would be confiscated and all blacks given "forty acres and a mule" on January 1, 1866. Mary's brother Arch told her he overheard one freedman say to another, "Who's gonna eat crow now? Them masters will have to farm with little acreage, just like us.

#

Chapter 13

Crawling with Carpetbaggers
1865-1866

With all the children at home, the 1865 holidays were special, though there was no money to be had for anything. Still, the children, several of whom were now grown, made gifts and proved again how resourceful they were. The little ones, several of whom had only known these lean times, were more than excited by the decorations and gifts— eight-year-old Laura most of all.

A few days after Christmas Mary was making hoecakes in the kitchen when Laura with her cascading dark hair and faded emerald green dress that reached to her knees said, "I wish every day was Christmas." Mary stopped and looked at her daughter whose dark, wavy hair reminded her so much of her mother's. Mary wiped her hands on a rag and sat next to Laura.

"I know, Hon. It is a special time." She smiled and added, "But Jesus could only have one birthday."

"I know."

Mary placed her hand on Laura's cheek, "Wasn't this Christmas extra special because of who was here?"

Laura smiled. "But they are here for good now." Mary thought about it for a minute and smiled.

Vollie was smitten, though, and not by only one girl. It was by women. There were several who had their eyes on him, and his on theirs. He wasn't shirking his responsibilities at home, but he spent more and more time in the evenings elsewhere. She knew someone would take him away eventually.

Several days later, they got a letter from John Slicer and Emily, who still lived in Blackshear, Georgia. John's consumption was chronic, but he was doing well for the moment, probably because Emily had given him another son, Charles Walton, their fourth son. "Poor Emily," said Mary to Florrie who read the letter to her on the back porch in the cool afternoon. "I don't know what I would have done without you and Sarah. Women need their daughters."

Elsewhere in the county, the Freedmen's Bureau had an ongoing thankless job. While there were planters who tried to cheat their freedmen employees, there were also cases of freedmen who tried to renege on their agreements. In between were the many misunderstandings which required ongoing negotiations between the sides. And planting time was only a month away.

1866

Mary and the family observed New Year's Day by calling on friends and family. It was a door-to-door typical celebration, but in downtown Monticello, it was different this year. The freedmen who had so recently gained their freedom celebrated downtown with a parade, speeches, and music to commemorate the day President Lincoln signed the Emancipation Proclamation. Most likely it culminated with a program held at the new Bethel Church—a benediction followed by the reading of the proclamation itself. Subsequently, the Florida legislature formed a Freedmen's School Superintendent.

One night in front of the hearth as Mary darned Vollie's socks, James read from a week-old Tallahassee newspaper. "Many '*returning soldiers escaped the dangers of the battlefield only to find a more invulnerable foe in the malaria of a southern climate.*' Mama, this is true here, too. So many of the older soldiers have succumbed. I guess they're weakened and fall easier." The family mentioned several other families affected, as the flames from the fire cast their shadows on the walls of their parlor.

James went back to the paper. "The railroad announced a new stagecoach service between the Pensacola and Georgia Railroad and Thomasville."

In February 1866, word on the street was General Nathan Bedford Forrest had fled the country, either to Mexico or Cuba, according to the source. Federal officials placed a warrant for his arrest. Meanwhile, four days of cold and cloudy weather struck, the kind that goes through one's clothes. It rained for four days, but by the second week, sunshine broke through and temperatures moderated to the 70s, typical for Florida's winters.

On the Gulf Coast, commercial traffic still languished. For nine months, lighthouses remained unlit from Egmont Key at the entrance of Tampa Bay to Cape San Blas.

The president declared reconstruction complete, but the result was disbelief and distress among Southern white men when an increasingly hostile Congress still refused to recognize the South's new senators and representatives, including over sixty former Confederates. They denied these elected officials their seats in Washington. However, they did not target Florida. They treated all the seceded states equally.

One night at dinner, James said, "Congress say they exclude our representatives from their seats so they can examine their credentials, but we all know this is a pretense—an impudent, dishonest trick." Without the sixty members from the South, the Republican minority became a two-thirds majority, and they could vote in alterations to the Constitution. James added, "It is usurpation."

Vollie said, "So much turmoil throughout the land. Our governments are butting heads at every turn. Did you hear about Kentucky?"

"No," came the reply from several.

He added, "About a week ago, a court fined a freedman for possessing a pistol, which is a violation of Kentucky state law."

"So what happened?" asked Sarah.

"The governor told the judge that he was correct since he had no power to make, unmake, or attend laws. The judge ruled as if the freedmen's agent didn't even exist. He ignored him completely."

Mary added, "Well, that won't last long. The long arm of our Federal government will reach and smite them like they've done us."

There was a break in the conversation when Hattie said, "Oh, let's stop talking about our political predicaments. It is so depressing. Can we change the subject?"

"Sure," said Vollie with a half-smile, "I hear there is a conflict brewing between our widows and maidens?"

Mary said, "Yes, there is, since there is such a scarcity of marriageable men." Both Sarah and Hattie rolled their eyes.

"But certainly no scarcity in marriageable women!" said Zech. "And the widows look to be the most successful at marrying." Sarah threw down her napkin and left the room.

Hattie replied, "Yes, the widows appear to be well-versed in the grab game."

Added seventeen-year-old Jesse, "Sweet sister, they do have superior wiles and strategies." Mary noticed the looks exchanged between her sons. He added, "You girls are too modest and retiring."

Said Mary, "Also, the widows own land and property. In early colonial times, there was a law that restrained young men from marrying those who had been married before. I wonder if it will be used again?"

One day in mid-March, Mary rose early and worked on breakfast while Sarah got everyone to the table inside. Thirteen-year-old Hattie shuttled food between the kitchen and dining room. Mary could hear the chatter, giggling, and raking of chairs on the wood floors inside. She was waiting for them to settle before joining them.

In her kitchen, though, she had also made one of her strawberry cakes with the last of her garden's strawberries. She was putting on the finishing touches and would add strawberries for garnish later when twenty-two-year-old Sarah walked into the kitchen. She was wearing her lavender "Sunday-Go-To-Meeting" dress with its full skirt and boat neckline. Her skirts were less full than usual. Sarah kept her eyes on the fashions, and now women were wearing fewer petticoats and no hoops. The article in *The Semi-Weekly Floridian* stated that the wide hoops, "*once ubiquitous,*" had completely disappeared (in New York) and remained only among domestic servants.

"Mama, I fixed the rip in its side, but it is so faded," Sarah said.

Mary replied, "Sarah, honey, everyone's clothes have faded. It wouldn't be right if you wore something new to J.J.'s wedding. No one would understand since all of us have had to do with a lot less. It is a badge of honor to look worn and faded." Mary grinned and winked at her daughter.

Sarah looked at her dress and then at her mother's. "I know. It is so boring, though, this pretense that everything is fine. It isn't." And she turned and walked through the dogtrot toward the porch. Mary heard the big back door open and slam.

Poor Sarah, she thought. Everything is so hard. So many boys lost and so many more maimed, if not in body, then most certainly in their minds. It was Sarah's age group of boys that were so decimated.

Later, before noon, the entire family met at the Baptist church south of the courthouse for Mary's brother, J.J., and Hannah's wedding. J.J. was marrying Hannah Raysor Walker, a distant cousin. Hannah's family came with the second wave of Walkers. Like J.J., she too was born in Colleton County, South Carolina, but she was almost fifteen years younger than J.J. Her parents were David M. Walker and Rebecca Raysor. After the service, everyone celebrated with dinner on the grounds. Mary's strawberry cake was one of the first to disappear, but she could not help thinking about her brother Henry all day long. The war and his mill cut his life short; otherwise Julia would have given him many children by now.

Later that evening, as the families dined together, Mary listened to Uncle James talk about the distant battlefields. He said, "Word was that many of those fields lie fallow with the debris of the battle, but I read in the *Semi-Weekly Floridian* that nature is taking over. One correspondent said he saw a rose growing from a busted drum and other flowers growing from ammunition boxes. It is surely a cycle and inspiring—peace may yet bloom where war once ravaged."

A few days later, Mary got a tax notice on the land near the Nash community. Her 160 acres were now worth only $800. Normally the family would be upset the land had decreased in value over $400, but not this time. She was glad they devalued the land because of the taxes owed. They also taxed her other property, including one horse, nineteen head of cattle, and one carriage. It said her household did not include any males between the ages of twenty-one and fifty-five. William would have been fifty-five, and though their oldest son James was twenty-one, they may have said he was younger since he may have had to be counted as a separate tax holder. This is another sign William was dead by 1866, though not proof. Mary and Zech made a trip to the courthouse to pay the taxes.

This photo appears to have been taken east of the courthouse, though the house behind the men could be the Wirick-Simmons House. Still, there look to be no stairs on this side of the courthouse. The stairs to the second floor were on its north side. The picture was taken in 1895 after the "great snowstorm." Locals said the temperature dropped to zero degrees. In the hunting wagon is Britt Bythewood and George Shoemaker. (Information from Rebekah Sheats) Photo at Florida Memory Collection.

Not all could pay their taxes without hardship. On Judge Randall's plantation in Jefferson County, an auctioneer sold his stock of cattle, sheep, hogs, a young horse, sugar, syrup, and chewing tobacco. The selloff was even worse at the plantation of the late George Anderson.

The evening after her trip to the courthouse, Mary sat on Ann Lightsey's porch with Sarah, who had come into town with her. They rocked and listened to the riot of the crickets and frogs along with the sounds of the city. Inside, Ann's grandchildren played a game in the parlor. Their voices wafted into the street where, in the fading evening light, a small band of soldiers walked by. They tipped their hats and moved on. They looked dapper in their brass and blues, and Mary noticed Sarah reached to tidy her hair.

Said Sarah, "It is so strange to see them walking by, when only a short time ago they were shooting at our boys." Ann sighed and agreed.

Last fall, after they withdrew the Second Florida Union, the authorities placed Major General John Foster in command, and a regular army company commanded by Captain Allen Jackson reoccupied Monticello. Ann stated, "It's rumored that they may transfer Captain Jackson to General Foster's staff in Tallahassee." None of them knew it, but the entire company was soon to be sent to Leon County. From then on, the local Freedmen's Bureau would send small groups of soldiers to Jefferson County as needed, but no military companies would remain stationed in the county. Many bureau's agents, though, were ex-Union army officers, and the bureau was an agency within the US Department of War.

Because President Johnson withheld pardons, Confederate officials and owners of large taxable plantations had to personally apply to him to obtain them. Most applied, and Johnson quickly reappointed them to their former political positions. He would pardon over 7,000 by the end of spring.

Adding to the pardons was a battle between him and Congress over control of Reconstruction. Congress overrode Johnson's veto of a civil rights act to shield the freedmen from overt discrimination and to extend the wartime Bureau of Refugees, Freedmen, and Abandoned Lands. Subsequently, Congress pressed into service the army as the chief Reconstruction agency.

Meanwhile, a newly formed vigilante group surfaced in the South —the Ku Klux Klan.

Around the end of March, James came in before supper and quietly made his way to the fireplace. It had been cool all day long. He poured himself a drink and sat in front of the hearth where the fire had nearly burned itself out, though someone had banked one side of it to keep the coals alive. Mary brought him a cup of tea. He had fallen back into his chair with his head back, eyes closed, and his hands hanging down. For the moment, he did not open them when she entered the room. In the county, all male residents from sixteen to forty-five worked five days annually on the roads or paid a tax of $5, so James, Vollie, and Zech had to do their time on the roads because money was scarce. A road tax also applied to black males, but because of their extreme poverty, they were given relief.

"Mama, I try my best to put myself in their shoes and understand their trials, but it isn't fair. The freedmen have so much less to do than we. We never owned slaves, and we can't afford to pay the $5 tax any more than they can." Mary thought about the endless labor of her sons as they tried to survive. Though young, James appeared bent and ravaged by the constant demands war and farming made on his body. Cords of muscle stood out on his forearms. His hands were rough and swollen from work.

He added, "Have you heard the news from town?"

She nodded no.

"President Johnson stays crosswise with his congress. He vetoed their Freedmen's Bureau bill." He looked deep into the amber liquid in his glass.

She said, "So this means the existing bureau will expire soon?" He looked at her and frowned, whereupon she sighed. Tired of the discord, she had hoped the move into the country would bring less of it to her door.

He explained the bill, but she heard little of it until he mentioned the Supreme Court. "...Court proposed to resume consideration of the Southern states' cases."

"What did you say?"

"The courts resumed all the Southern states' laid-aside Supreme Court cases. Some think this is a legal endorsement, and the Southern states can now occupy their former position in the Union."

Even more confused, she sighed. "We can only hope."

Most of the streets of Monticello were in terrible shape after the war. After a heavy rain, one resident said, "*One needs a batteau in places on Washington Street while in other places, you need a 'running jump' to get over the larger puddles of water.*" People often needed planks at the frequently flooded intersection of Washington and Cherry. One wonders if this area was once a bog and the reason for the town spring, which was on lower ground south of Palmer's Mill Road, below where Cherry Street dead-ended into that street.

The roads were a problem, especially for Monticello when its county farmers began traveling north to Thomasville to do their business, because traveling was far easier once they crossed the state line. Thomas County's roads were far superior to the ones in Jefferson County, and their better roads diverted trade. Something needed to be done. People also said the county's bridges were dangerous.

One early evening on a cool spring day, Vollie came into Mary's kitchen, pulled out a chair, and seated himself at her table. He immediately leaned back, balancing himself against the wall. She poured him a glass of sweet milk, and he took a long drink. "What's wrong?" she asked.

He looked over the glass and smiled. "You always know before we do when something's bothering us."

"Oh, I've had practice," she replied as she pounded the fresh beef they brought from Uncle James.

Vollie hesitated but then lit into the conversation. "Mama, there are so many strangers in the county, and you don't know who you're dealing with." It was true. The whole county was crawling with carpetbaggers. They had descended on the area because they saw money to be had. Vollie added, "They hang over us like carrion."

His feelings were legitimate. Every day they heard stories about people who lost their land. And there was always someone, a stranger, who would swoop in and offer a pittance to help the poor soul be on their way. People were leaving as hordes were moving in.

Mary, though, listened with interest as her sons discussed Texas and other regions of the country. Plantation owners on the Brazos in central Texas divided their lands into small lots and rented them to the poor for planting cotton. Said James, "People are moving all over the South, trying to find a better financial toehold."

By April, the South, and Florida in particular, had been living under the new Black Codes which Florida passed in December, codes which suppressed the rights of all Florida's black citizens. A storm of protest from the Northern people intensified until the Black Republicans in Congress retaliated.

The Republican majority in Washington brought their own reconstruction plan to the table in the Civil Rights Acts of 1866 and the Fourteenth Amendment to the Constitution. Both had passed, and the latter, if ratified, would permanently change the nature of American citizenship. Both actions paved the way for the federal government's responsibility for protecting all Americans' civil rights. It also paved the way for a new era in the South. It meant registration for voting would include all adult black males over the age of twenty-one. Any Confederate state that balked would find itself denied full admission to Congress.

They also gave the Bureau of Freedmen, Refugees, and Abandoned Lands added responsibilities by granting it the power to protect blacks. The bureau was in Monticello to oversee contractual arrangements between the white landlords and their black tenants, and because it was under direct military protection, it coordinated its activities with the army. It also created schools, clinics, and legal advice for the freedmen. They also pushed the freedmen again to return to the plantations and sign labor contracts with the owners to raise the state's agricultural economy.

Later in the spring, Mary and James rode out to see their fields. The boys had them planted earlier, including cotton, to give them extra spending money. On the way as they rode through the undulating hills and swamps, she thought to herself there was no more beautiful place on earth than these hills east of Monticello, especially the shaded beauty of their swamps in the springtime with their wild azaleas in the floodplains, lilies, jasmine, and many other brilliant wildflowers all set against a canopy of the feathery spring-green cypress trees.

She mentioned it to James, and he agreed. "Mama, I thought a lot about this while I was up north. Winter here has its beauty, too, when the cypresses turn to copper and the magnolias and silver bays become more noticeable." They rode a little farther in silence when he added, "I heard yesterday that they've removed the obstructions our army placed in the St. Marks River during the war. This means the river is free for commerce again."

Suddenly both heard the crack of a rifle in the distance. It could be a hunter trying to feed his family, but both knew that the owner of the gun could also be on the wrong side of the law. Livestock was being shot or taken so frequently that people sold off their cattle. Every gunshot could mean someone was stealing livestock. There was an unwritten code that someone with a sizable herd expected a certain amount of cattle to be stolen by the hungry, but this went far beyond feeding one's family.

One day, Mary noticed that her favorite laying hen Eudora was missing. She also found no signs of a violent struggle such as one would expect from a fox or wild animal. She heard of others who missed their chickens, but this was her first. Even her garden produce had been vanishing lately.

Later, when she returned home, she walked into her kitchen and pulled a big frying pan off the stove and poured from it the grease left from frying squirrel earlier that morning. Because she had cooked in it several times, it was time to retire this grease to the soap making. She poured it into the bucket by the stove.

Mary created her best soap with oak ashes. She had left the ashes mixed with water to decay. Outside, Jesse placed the large barrels which she would use for tubs. They planned to make soap tomorrow.

By the end of the next year, any attempt to rear a stock of poultry would become ridiculous as the hungry invariably stole every feather. It reminded her of the hungry Indians during the Second Seminole War, only far worse this time. There were thousands of people who were scrounging food for their families. The family began keeping their livestock deep in the river swamp near her father's old home.

Panthers and bears were less worrisome, mainly because people shot and snared all there was moving in the woods. Everything became edible if one was hungry enough. Florida's wildlife population decreased because people would eat anything now, and she couldn't remember the last time she heard a Carolina parakeet.

In mid-April 1866, Mary got a wonderful surprise. Ann Lightsey came for a visit and brought her thirteen-year-old grandson, George Henry, with her. He and Jesse quickly disappeared to explore, but not before twelve-year-old Hattie locked eyes with George Henry. Mary noticed their fleeting glances. It appears George Henry was interested, too.

She and Ann retired to the sitting room, and the two women shared coffee and their news. Said Ann, "Have you heard about Colonel Dilworth and his unchristian-like behavior? His church's elders asked him to appear before them."

Mary didn't like the sound of this one bit. She still liked the colonel and felt he had looked after her James during the early days of the war. Still, she listened intently. "Well," continued Ann, "when the session met again, the colonel didn't bother attending." Mary laughed, but then she realized Ann wasn't and was staring at her, her lips pursed.

Mary, though, was worried about the colonel. War was ugly business, and she had heard it was his drinking that had everyone in a dither, but it might have also been his help for the freedmen. She hoped he could forgive himself for any indiscretions and get on with his life. He didn't, though, because his church, Monticello Presbyterian, found him to be "*walking disorderly*," and by the end of June they excluded him from all church privileges on the charges of immoral conduct when he showed no signs of penitence. Mary added him to her prayers.

Later, she heard Dilworth was taking heat again in town. It appears he arose and spoke vigorously to a jury during court one day. He railed against the frequent attacks upon the freedmen by whites, attacks with impunity. She was told that he said, "this thing has got to be stopped...These people have the same rights before the law as whites, and it is to our interest to give them justice..."

At the end of the month, on April 29th, the ladies of the Elizabeth Community met at the cemetery and placed their floral tributes on the graves of the loved ones they lost in the war, but these were only the ones who died at home. Reverend Mays offered a prayer. Many of the men joined them. The same ceremony took place in Monticello, but only the women were there. Some men, because of their oaths, had to stay away.

On May 1, Captain Alfred B. Grumwell arrived in Monticello— the new Freedmen's Bureau agent, a slender, dark-haired, thirty-two-year-old veteran of the Union Army's Reserve Corps. An outsider, he embodied Washington's long reach into Middle Florida. His charge was to oversee the county's Black population, though before long every white resident believed he favored the freedmen, while the freedmen themselves felt he did not favor them at all. In time, his greatest challenge would prove to be the negotiation and enforcement of labor contracts between the freedmen and their former masters.

By mid-May, when Washington was at its worst, a glimmer of goodwill came forth. General Grant wrote a letter to the president asking for the release of Senator Yulee from Fort Pulaski. Said James that night on their porch, "They released him, and I guess we have to give General Grant the credit. It was obviously a gesture of goodwill to the South."

Zech added, "Mama, you were right as usual. You tried your best to help all of us realize we are a vanquished foe and needed to worry more about survival than getting involved in the head games people play. Your advice, as always, is spot on."

Val changed the subject, "Did y'all hear about the Indians in Arizona? Over 2,000 Indians took a fort there and killed 120 men, except one man who escaped because he was out hunting."

In late May, Mary heard something that gave her pause. Reports surfaced that the town children had attacked the Freedmen's Bureau Agent Grunwell twice. They pelleted him with clods of dirt once in the back while he was riding through town. Later, at dinner, she made sure her offspring understood they had better never be among the culprits. Said Mary, "We don't act like that, and you don't either. If I ever hear of it, you boys won't be able to sit for a week."

Later, on the porch, Vollie told James, "Damn, I felt like she was even talking to me."

Then Vollie changed the subject. "Sarah, you and Hattie are going to love this new drink they have at the drugstore. They call it soda water. It is going to be a great convenience this summer." All gave their attention as Vollie explained what it was.

Said Hattie. "Do they serve it warm?"

"No. St. Marks has an icehouse, and they bring it up from there. And there is now another icehouse in Jacksonville."

The conversation changed yet again. Said James, "I heard today Congress voted for Colorado to be our newest state."

Val added, "They're still considered an immature territory. They can't even agree on how many people live there. I hear their people are an unsettled horde of roving adventurers. Plus, our own statehood is still uncertain. Our representatives are still excluded."

Mary looked from face to face, especially her sons and their worried countenance.

June came, as did the sweltering heat and rains. The rainy season, which usually begins near the end of June, began early in the first week of the month. It rained for four straight days, with the first day including hail. Mary watched her sons come home each day from the fields with their faces etched with worry. The more it rained, the more weeds and grass covered their fields. The rains nearly destroyed their small cotton plot; however, the corn thrived, as did the surrounding weeds. They couldn't hoe it fast enough. Its prospects became poorer as the rains fell.

Meanwhile, things were no better in Washington for the South. Congress sent the Fourteenth Amendment to the states for ratification, which defined citizenship as including the freedmen and increased the government's power over the states to protect citizens' rights. The whites hated it, and the freedmen were disappointed it stopped short of giving them the right to vote without the Fourteenth Amendment.

Congress repassed its vetoed supplemental Freedmen's Bureau Bill, which added more power to the agency. Later, Tennessee became the first state to be readmitted to the Union. A stipulation of readmittance was ratification of the Fourteenth Amendment.

By now, it was common knowledge that President Johnson had lost his support within the Republican Party for his reconstructionist policies. Congress passed bills, he vetoed them, and they consequently overrode his veto. Neither the Black Republicans, the freedmen, nor the

Southern whites liked the unpopular President Johnson. He was by now a lame duck president.

The news, though, wasn't all from Washington. Jesse read one night from an old copy of the *Semi-Weekly Floridian*, "*All goes smoothly with the Atlantic Cable. It is now coiling at the rate of two miles an hour.*" "Do y'all know what this means? They'll be able to send messages across the Atlantic, like we do here with our telegraph. They sent a message over a distance of 1,506 miles."

During the first week of July, the county got a reprieve from the oppressive heat. Mary noticed it was remarkably cool and dry—well suited to slowing down the weeds, but their crops needed rain. It had been a hard summer for her boys.

Later, they came in from their farm work. Vollie said, "Mama, Colonel Dilworth's law office burned to the ground yesterday. It started at Mr. Stephen's livery stable." Mary had heard about the colonel's problems, and now this.

James, though, had the most memorable news. "Guess what? There is now telegraphic communication across the Atlantic Ocean."

"So the Atlantic cable was a success?" said Mary.

"Yes, Isn't it grand? It runs over 1,600 miles. They say when they send a cable to London, it only takes eight hours to get a reply. What used to take months at sea is now done in less than a day. That's progress!"

Mary, lost in thought, marveled at what she had seen in her lifetime—messages sent over wires, railroads that ran on steam, and hot air balloons that allowed people to float over the treetops. Progress indeed!

The following week would astound James, though. *The Semi-Weekly Floridian* reported "*The President's reply to the Queen was acknowledged by Osborne at 5 P.M., or one hour and eighteen minutes after its reception here. It passed through the cable in eleven minutes.*"

Northern investors, government officials, and general opportunists trickled into the South. One sultry August night, Vollie said, "Several New York capitalists bought the Florida Railroad." Staring at Mary, everyone frowned.

Mary rocked, her chair making a soft squeak against the boards of the porch, the coolest spot there. She said, "Maybe they'll have the money to complete it." She meant from Fernandina to Cedar Key.

Mary sighed and stopped rocking. She felt extra weak and tired lately. The blazing heat for the past week left everyone listless and sluggish. No one replied until James added, "Well, let them have it. It won't mean anything to us over here, anyway."

Vollie filled the void. "These hot, dry days are most grievous for our cotton. There's a little more rust every time I walk that field."

Asked Hattie, "What is rust?"

James replied, "We don't rightly know. No one understands it, and no one knows what to do about it."

"What does it look like?"

"Red and yellow ulcers on the bottom of the leaves."

"Will it affect the crop?"

"Maybe it could reduce the size of the bolls."

Added Vollie, "And I found caterpillars near the stream."

Zech said, "Thank the Lord, it is late in the season, maybe too late for any significant damage from those buggers."

Changing the subject, Mary said, "I heard today Lieutenant Governor Walker passed away. You know he followed the Randolphs here. He had old family connections in Virginia, even though he came from Kentucky. During the Indian wars, he was most eloquent in raising volunteer armies. My mama disliked him, but to Daddy he was a hero."

Hattie added, "Lots of these newcomers think we're kin to him."

Replied Mary, "Well, of course we're not! Back home, Walkers are as thick as hair on a dog's back." She meant South Carolina.

Survival was easier and cheaper in Elizabeth. Mary loved being where every home had roosters crowing and hogs grunting, where her family's voices laughed and crooned in the evening, sounds that made her feel she was truly home. She yearned for the "good old days" when her father and mother took the world on their shoulders and her responsibilities were few. Sometimes, sitting on the porch in the evening, she felt nostalgia sweep over her. It was soothing for her soul.

Sarah, at twenty-two, broke the silence. "Mama, I heard the Paris ladies no longer wear bonnets like ours. They've been getting smaller and now are little more than a ribbon worn around their head with a black veil attached."

"Goodness, obviously the sun doesn't shine there like it does here. I'll keep wearing my bonnets, but it will be pretty on you young girls, especially for the frolics."

In the fall, the family was lucky. Before cotton picking time arrived, according to reports from the *Semi-Weekly Floridian*, *"The reports of the ravages of this cotton-destroyer are truly distressing. Whole fields have been literally devoured in an incredibly short space of time."* It destroyed the crops near Tallahassee. Thankfully, it did not get to their part of Jefferson County.

Cotton picking time came in the fall, and the entire family either picked cotton in the field or picked cotton seeds from the bolls afterwards. They weighed and bound it in bags. At home, while the youngest were picking cotton seeds that evening, Mary spun her own thread. She planned to weave it into fabric for the family. For herself, she wanted to make a cotton skirt tinted with the indigo leaves she had left to rot in water to stain the dye.

The other day she had overheard Sarah and Hattie talking about old times when they could go to the store for whatever they needed. They talked about a new double-springed hoopskirt, the patented Bradley's duplex elliptic. Said Sarah, "It is supposed to have a perfect shape and be the lightest spring made. They say it is perfect for any crowded assemblages, such as theaters or railroad cars." She sighed. "I don't guess either of us will ever own one, let alone go to any of those places again." Mary stepped away without hearing more.

Only last week, Mary had watched Jesse tan and cure a cowhide by placing it for several days in water with oak bark. After letting it dry in the sun, he cut out soles, measuring it with his own shoes. He tacked them on to the bottom of his shoes with small tacks made of maple wood. Others in the family brought him their shoes to repair.

After mid-October, the family made a trip into town for supplies, something done infrequently now. Mostly, though, they wanted to see the damages from the fire earlier in October. Fire destroyed the stores of Messrs. Marvin and J. D. Turner & Co., but other stores, such as Denham & Palmer, Williams, and Bernhard, saved theirs, though they had to remove their contents. Hundreds of people answered the first alarm and added their exertions. They removed much of Messrs. Marvin and Turner's stock before the fire consumed the stores.

What was most noticed, though, was the help of so many freedmen. The papers reported they even helped in finding the perpetrator. Also noticed was the help of Captain Grunwell of the Freedmen's Bureau, who rendered his most active help. All worked hard to protect the roofs of adjoining buildings and houses. They saved a large amount of goods. The town began talking about starting a fire company as this was the second instance of arson, possibly by the same perpetrator.

Another instance of arson was the Presbyterian church. It burned the year before. It would be many years, though, before the church body discovered who set the fire. Years later, a freedman made a deathbed confession. He was mad because the church session required the freedmen, who had always attended there, to find another church body to join.

For the family, the trip to town was exhilarating and the weather clear, beautiful, and bracing. Mary couldn't remember a more pleasant fall season. James and the older kids stayed home, picking out what the worms had left in their cotton fields.

Jesse, who accompanied them, was frustrated because they would accept no mail contracts and establish no post offices unless they found people willing to swear the 'ironclad' oath. The only exception was in locations far from the state's major transportation routes. He added, "The Tallahassee paper suggests using women, who weren't disqualified, to fill the positions."

Mary hated all the dissension. It came from all quarters. While in town, the talk of four hangings to take place in Quincy the next Saturday reached her children. A court had convicted the four men of murdering the town's marshal.

All this led to the midterm elections in the fall. Both Vollie and James wanted to vote, and it would have been Vollie's first time at the polls since he turned eighteen last February. On the same morning, Mary sat at breakfast in the dining room, and both boys dressed for a ride into town. She could not help reminiscing about how special these days were when she was young and her father voted. Extra special was the day he and William rode into town to vote for statehood, but this was different. Disenfranchised, her boys could not cast their votes today.

Wearing a white blouse open at his neck, James passed around a plate of bacon. "Mama," said James, "don't expect us from town until late. In fact, we might spend the night with our buddies there, so don't expect us at all."

A silence fell in the room, and Mary looked at all the faces staring back. She smiled and said, "I expected nothing less," and they all laughed.

Added Vollie, "We can't vote, but we still want to hear the returns from the rest of the country."

Mary said, "Well, I guess the telegraph office will have information. Maybe you boys should hang around there and try to stay out of any trouble. The town will probably be full of people. Keep your heads and stay out of the jug."

Two days later, the boys returned with tales and news. After sharing what they knew, James said, "Vollie, tell them about the four Confederates who recently surrendered in Virginia."

Sitting at the dinner table, he started his tale. "They described them as ragged Rebels from Lee's army who said they stopped during the evacuation of Petersburg to rest, but they said they fell asleep and got cut off from their unit during the confusion. The Yankee officer to which they surrendered last week said they were the raggedest lot he had ever seen. He said they looked like four apparitions."

Added James, "Frankly, all of Lee's army by the end of the war looked like an assembly of apparitions."

The officer reported they had tied, sewn, and stuck their clothes together with string, thread, and thorns, leaving no square inch unbound.

Said Mary. "Where were they all this time?"

"They hid in a cave on the banks of the Appomattox, living on wild game and fish. They said they did not know the war was over until an old Negro man passed through and told them."

The conversation waned when James said, "Mama, ladies in town are forming a memorial association. If you want to be a part of it, I'm sure one of us can take you there when they meet."

"Let me think about it. There is too much happening here, but it would be good to remember those we lost. Maybe I can plan my shopping trips around the meetings and can spend time with Ann and Betsy."

In the November midterm elections, the Republicans won in a landslide even though President Johnson supported Democrats, both War Democrats like himself and Peace Democrats, the latter of which favored a negotiated settlement with the Confederates. The win by the Republicans gave them enough seats in Congress to provide them a veto-proof majority, further diminishing the president's power, something he had tried to prevent by campaigning against the Radicals earlier in the summer.

By the end of the year, El Destino Plantation and its mills between Tallahassee and Waukeenah were for sale.

#

Chapter 14
Eating Our Distractions from All This Misery
1867-1870

In early January 1867, Mary heard they were creating Monticello's first public school, but only for black people of all ages. She didn't like it one bit. Her own children needed an education, but they didn't have the money to send them to school. What she heard was not entirely true, though. The schools required money to pay the teachers, and they had trouble raising the money.

Northern mission groups financed many of these freedmen schools around the state. The school in Monticello was being built east of town on Pearl Street. They named it the Howard School, probably after Major General Oliver Otis Howard, a former Union officer who headed the Freedmen's Bureau. He strongly supported education for blacks. The first county school taxes would not follow until 1869.

At first, white teachers operated Howard School, which was still in the Bethel Church, but teachers of color later replaced them. About the same time as the school opened, churches opened with black ministers in their pulpits; many freedmen congregated in makeshift homes in an area described as "Rooster-Town" by their residents. The community still exists in the southeastern part of Monticello.

Congress and President Johnson continued to spar as the South bristled under their new laws. If Floridians were expecting a return to peace, they were ill-informed. Congress worked on several more reconstruction acts, and the South's struggles were only beginning. These acts would rip apart the social fabric of the state and usher in an even more radical Reconstruction.

About this time, Colonel W. O. Girardeau, who had once been principal of Jefferson Academy, bought the local newspaper *The Family Friend* and renamed it the *Jefferson County Gazette*. He became its publisher.

One night on the porch, Vollie read from a week-old copy of the *Semi-Weekly Floridian* from Tallahassee. He said, "Y'all listen to this. *Crop Prospects in Texas. Our farmers are energetically preparing for a large crop. Industry, energy, and public spirit seem rife in the community. Railroads are being pushed forward in various directions. Schools are flourishing—churches are well sustained. Politics are generally avoided, and progress—physical, mental, and general—seems to be the order of the day."*

Said Sarah, "Sounds like we should all move to Texas, especially if they avoid talking about politics!"

Replied Henry, twelve, "Sounds good to me. Someday I'm gonna get me a girl and move to Texas."

Said Vollie, "Wait a minute. There's other news from there. *'Indian spoliations continue, and it is rumored that twelve families have been massacred.'"*

Replied Mary, "Moving to Texas reminds me of when we moved to Florida. Better stay here and keep your scalps."

At the end of April, women across Jefferson County decorated the graves of their Confederate dead. Mary and her daughters, along with their many female kin, gathered at Elizabeth Churchyard Cemetery to do the same.

She looked around at the worn, carefully mended dresses—their faded skirts billowing in the wind. Overhead, the strong arms of the oak trees stretched wide, draped in floating veils of Spanish moss.

So many lives lost now rested here in this quiet graveyard since she first came to Florida.

In May 1867, for Mary and her family, their primary struggle was for survival in a broken economy. The political scene in Washington was a long way away, and the one in Tallahassee was silent since the family had no one there to witness it firsthand. Like many Floridians, they may have quit reading their papers to avoid knowing what else was happening.

At home, though, especially in Monticello, the family listened to the dialogue between the freedmen, the planters, the Federals like Capt. Grunwell, and everyone else. Said Vollie, "I heard that at the very well-attended meeting of the freedmen in Monticello, they allowed Colonel Bird to speak and respectfully listened to what he had to say."

James replied, "So what did he say?"

"That there is a necessity of obedience to the laws of the land, and that above all, all of us should work to preserve friendly relations between the races. Like I said, it appears they listened to what he had to say. Afterward, Captain Grunwell talked to them about coming into town in such large numbers. He suggested each plantation pick a few trusty men to come in for meetings like this and to report back to the group.

"What did they say about that?"

"Well, from what I heard, not much; but it is to be expected. They believe he hung the moon anyway."

Southern newspapers were indignant about the new Reconstruction acts, but the Northern radicals were equally indignant about the release of Jefferson Davis from prison on bail. A court charged him with treason, but he was never tried. The only person tried, convicted, and executed in the south was Henry Wirz, the commandant of Andersonville, but the charges were conspiracy and cruelty, not treason.

The recent act of Congress was the Military Reconstruction Bill. The bill deemed the governments of Florida and other Southern states illegitimate, stating that their restoration to the Union required constitutional amendments incorporating specific language. The bill declared Florida's current government provisional, to last only until its constitution was revised. In Florida, the US military held the authority to "*abolish, modify, control, or supersede*" the state government. In the meantime, Congress withheld the state's right to congressional representation.

After Zech read this to Mary on the porch one evening, James said, "What is Florida to do now? Especially since we are neither in the Union nor out of it!"

Added Vollie, "Exactly. The US government controls us, and we have no voice in making national laws."

They continued sitting in silence. Mary listened to the wind in the pines and thought about how lonely the sound was. She said, "The only escape will be a fully restored Florida."

James cut in, "Mama, you cannot be that naïve. How can you seriously think that is the answer?"

She replied, "Naivete or not, there is no other option; and the faster you do it, the better. We need to change our constitution to become a fully recognized state again. Then all of you need to bite the bullet and get yourselves the right to vote. It is the only way to take back our state. At least under this law, you can take an oath and vote. They would have disqualified your father since he had held office and taken up arms against the Union, but none of you held office."

Vollie couldn't believe what he heard. "Mama, you know the freedman here will outvote us. They'll vote Republican, and we will have no power at all in this county."

Mary replied, "No, not in this county, but people have been pouring into the areas downstate—Southerners from throughout the

South. They left behind their war-ravaged lands and broken-down farms, and in time they will outvote the carpetbaggers, scalawags, and freedmen. They will eventually carry the state." She meant downstate counties like Marion, which had grown so quickly that by 1867 it was fifth in population in the state.

Zech said nothing and thought about his mama—how strong she was while all the older menfolk were away. He also remembered his father talking about how smart she was. She seldom gave her opinions and never in public, but he remembered she spoke her mind to their father, and he listened.

Changing the subject, Vollie said, "They caught the cow killers in Tallahassee; four soldiers from the 7th Infantry Regiment were involved. They imprisoned them, and an officer stripped one of his rank on the spot."

Before Florida rejoins the Union with its full representation in Congress, it must change its constitution to guarantee the right of suffrage to all males over twenty-one, regardless of race. Despite daily letters to Northern newspaper editors demanding women's suffrage, women still faced exclusion. Also, Florida's constitution had to ratify the proposed amendment to the US Constitution. Third, it required the election of senators and representatives in Congress who qualified under existing laws. Only after these modifications of Florida's constitution could its military provisional government cease to operate and the military give way to regular civil government.

One night on the porch, Mary's brother Arch stopped by for an early evening visit. He had news from town. "I heard the county commissioners were told to revise their list of jurors into a list of registered voters without discrimination."

James said, "So now they're gonna even be on our juries?"

Arch replied, "Well, it is part of the responsibilities of citizenship. If they are full citizens, I guess they'll be serving on juries, too." Quietness overtook them, and the singing of the cicadas sounded in a cycling crescendo.

Henry asked what the younger ones had been wondering, "What all are we expected to do when we come of age to vote?" Mary felt a pang —William wasn't here to guide Henry in his duties as a citizen. Uncle Arch seemed to feel it, too. He paused and began working his way down his mental list.

He added, "I guess they may ask the black people to serve on Sheriff Ellis's jury." The sheriff's repeated drunken incapacitation displeased both the county commission and the Freedmen's Bureau. General Pope eventually replaced him with Daniel Oakley.

By order from General Pope, by midsummer a Jefferson County Board of Registration was at work. Appointed to the board were John W. Powell, Edward Murphy, and Robert Meacham, the black AME minister. The town roared against the two whites, labeling them as scalawags— Floridians described as deserters who fought on the side of the Union.

Under the new laws, "*all adult males, regardless of race, were eligible to take the oath and have their names placed on the registration lists who could swear that they had never taken an oath to uphold the United States Constitution and subsequently never participated in the rebellion.*" The requirement would have kept William from voting because of his position as sheriff, which required him to take an oath to uphold the nation's constitution. Although the new law disenfranchised only a handful of county residents, by this time men were so aggravated and confused they refused to take part. Plus, the oath requirement confused any who wished to do so. Many thought they could not vote. The whites tried to urge the freedmen to do the same.

Meanwhile, by the end of the summer of 1867, of the twenty-seven needed, fifteen states had ratified the Fourteenth Amendment. Nebraska ratified it in June. Mostly, the individual Northern states gave the black man the vote anyway. Also, Congress passed (over the president's veto) an act giving the district military commanders the authority to remove state officials from office.

By the end of summer, President Johnson toured the country to regain his public and political support. He attacked the Radical Republicans in Washington and accused Congress of inciting black violence in the South and poisoning the American public against him. Leading to the fall midterm elections, his tour did not include the South.

In September, Mary was almost home. She had been at Martin Bishop's near Aucilla. Her first cousin Delilah had another boy, which they named John Calvin. This was their eighth boy of eleven children born to the couple. On horseback, she let the mare walk easily toward her home on the clay and sand roadbed with its shoulders blanketed in pines and its understory of green palmettos. The wind blew through her skirts, which draped on each side of her sorrel mare.

Beside her was Vollie, whom she had encountered in Aucilla, back from another visit to the pretty little red-headed Elizabeth Connell. Last week, James told her that Vollie was buzzing around Elizabeth lately like a bee dancing on a honeysuckle blossom. She hoped the insinuation wasn't too literal.

While Vollie talked about Elizabeth, she got lost in her own thoughts and remembered when the family came down from South Carolina. Delilah had just been born, and Aunt Elizabeth made the trip with the baby through two months of sleeping in a wagon, cooking over an open fire, and bouncing eight to ten miles every day of what had to be the worst roads in Georgia. It amazed her she never thought about what that was like for her aunt.

And yet here is the same grown baby girl who has birthed eleven children and may have more on the way later. Mary thought Delilah was of a tougher stock, more so than she was. Thankfully, William had backed off and allowed Mary's body to heal, especially when Dr. Palmer worried Mary couldn't have more children without risking her health. Of course, he was wrong. Virginia was the proof, but little Virginia did her damage, too.

Mary's mind wandered to a conversation she and her mother had had years ago about how her grandmothers rode horses astraddle everywhere they went. Her mother's generation changed that, and it became no longer proper for a woman to sit astride a horse.

Mary learned, though, that women's rolls change out of necessity, and now this had changed again, instigated by the war. Such a short time ago she only traveled in carriages, and now she mounted a horse, having come full circle to her grandmother's time.

Mary realized she had spent years now making do with almost nothing. During the war she wove, sewed, cooked, and cared for her family and livestock. She made shoes and soap, much like her mama did before they had enough money to buy those things from the store. Now they even made coffee from dried peas and tea from the green needles of the longleaf pine. She heard at Delilah's that somebody near Aucilla had made flour from cattails.

From making a flag from her crimson shawl that William had given her for her thirtieth birthday to handling their business at the courthouse, she worked all jobs now. Lately she cut trees, rolled logs, cleared fields, and grew crops like her father and brothers did when they first came to Florida.

Last week she had cut an armload of broom sage and made herself another fresh broom. Still, the work made her feel closer to her parents. Virginia, three, and Laura, ten, helped. She taught them how.

Mary felt the rolling motion of the horse between her legs, and she realized she spent a lot of her time lately in the saddle. It was quicker to get around, and it was impossible to help pen cattle without one. She also needed her horse when trouble came. When needed, its transport made for a much quicker exit with the valuables. For almost two years after the war, the county had crawled with vermin—men who lived on the edge of the law in a land with laws that no one trusted—Yankee laws.

All her girls were getting good at riding, like their brothers. This war had changed all of them, sometimes for the better. Her girls were far more independent than she had been at their age. To her thinking, "fragile Southern womanhood" had sucked all autonomy out of its women before the war. In its place was a new Southern woman, who rode astride horses, worked in the fields alongside her men, and oversaw her properties when her men were unavailable.

Still, she never learned to read or write. She could count money and could put words in their right order. She was a good conversationalist, and she had become a good judge of character. Though she was thankful, she was raised in a sparsely populated county where she knew whom she could trust, but that was changing. The county was filling up with strangers since the war.

Within a couple of weeks, Vollie came home one Sunday afternoon with Elizabeth Connell and her mother. All the family had met her at different functions, but this was the first time Mary had a chance to really talk to the girl. Initially, Elizabeth was a little shy, but as soon as she got used to everyone, she talked a mile a minute. Elizabeth had porcelain skin and looked fragile, though her carrot-top hair probably made her skin even paler. It was plain to see why Vollie was smitten.

Big news came on September 23rd when the locals formed a county Republican party in a mass meeting in Monticello. It was all her boys talked about that night at supper. Said Vollie, "I guess that means we are again a two-party system."

Replied James, "Not in my book. It comprises outsiders, deserters, and illiterates." Then he looked at his mama and realized that she fell into the latter category. He looked at his lap and murmured, "Mama, I'm sorry."

Later, on a Tuesday in early October, Mary sat in her rocking chair near the hearth, listening to her older boys talk. James, Vollie, and Zech were reminiscing, remembering their childhood. She realized it was a type of goodbye, and she wondered if they realized it. Their home life between them would never be the same. Bringing someone else into the equation changes everything, though she wouldn't have had it any other way for Vollie.

The next day Val and Elizabeth Connell were getting married, and this was Valentine's last night at home. She remembered how much she appreciated getting the older boys back after the war. It made life so much easier for all of them, especially Zech, who had managed everything alone.

She mostly listened tonight, though, because they talked about camp life and drilling. They seldom talked about the war, so she sat with them, silently listening, afraid that they might stop. Said Vollie, "I can still feel the muscle memory of loading and priming."

Added James, "That's probably because of the continual drill. I wish I had a cotton boll for every time I had to do it. I'd be a rich planter by now." They discussed the drill of loading and priming, a drill important during combat, when it had to be done without thinking and under immense pressure. The faster they loaded and shot, the more successful they were in battle.

"Yes, they taught us to fight in closely knit formations," said Vollie. "And two rows deep. We walked into battle shoulder to shoulder."

Added James, "Yep, but it wasn't much use by the time of the rifle musket."

Vollie interjected, "That's when the casualties rose so high."

They talked about camp life as Mary's thoughts drifted. Vollie turned to her. "Mama, you should have seen us in our camp kitchens."

"If you could call them that," said James, "a fire, a stand, and a pot. But the coffee pot was the most important item on the field."

Added Vollie, "And our bayonets not only cut meat, but we also used them for candle holders and to grind coffee beans and anything else that needed doing."

Mary waited, thinking they had finally wound down, but Zech added, "It must have been grand."

Both brothers thought about that for a moment, then Vollie said, "Well, except for losing friends...."

He paused, and James added, "and the early morning calls and late-night marching. They used drums to announce everything. We heard them from sunrise to sunset. Reveille was usually about 5 am. We assembled for the roll call, and they called for the sick, usually early after breakfast."

Vollie agreed and added, "We could also hear the cavalry's buglers in the distance. They used bugles instead of drums. Somehow, it helped to know that the cavalry boys were being harassed as much as us."

James turned to Mary and added, "And there was no need for you and Daddy there. Those sergeants and lieutenants were always on us like we were all children. They doled out punishments for everything, from shirking camp duty to keeping our guns clean."

"Yes," added Vollie. "I dug a few latrines myself, and I walked many an extra mile on guard duty, but I never once had to carry a log around camp or stand on a barrel." Mary frowned. He added, "That's what they do if you get caught doing something bad, like stealing from another soldier or for insubordination. It wasn't unusual to see a man standing on a barrel for half a day. It was especially bad if it was raining."

Leaning forward with his elbows on his knees, James looked at his hands. He said, "For really serious offenses like desertion or threatening an officer, a guilty verdict meant imprisonment and sometimes execution by a firing squad."

The next day on October 2nd, Vollie and Elizabeth were married. The girl's family threw a dinner, and people came from all around to wish the couple their best. Then Vollie was gone.

Mary noticed right away a change in Florrie. Florrie, who was now every bit of twenty-seven, was still living at home. She was an attractive girl with dark hair which she wore pulled back in a tight chignon at her nape. One evening on the porch, Mary suggested maybe Florrie would like to go visit her married sister Ellen, who lived near Ocala. Florrie jumped at the idea. She said, "Mama, are you sure you can manage without me?"

Mary leaned forward and took her hands. "Why, of course, though I'll miss you. Florrie, you have been an angel from God for me. No one has been by my side as often as you." Florrie jumped up, gave her a hug, and disappeared into the house. By the next morning, she was ready to post a letter.

As quickly as Vollie transitioned, Florrie did, too. By the end of December, Mary got word that Florrie and Joseph Hogg, the brother of Ellen's husband Thomas, had married three days after Christmas in Romeo, Florida. It was so sad that only her sister was there for the quick wedding. Mary thought a lot that day about Elizabeth, Florrie's mother, and how much time had passed since she died. So much had changed.

Florida Andrews, daughter of William Henry and Elizabeth Andrews

Mary missed Florrie. The young girl was more than a daughter; she had become a friend. Mary hoped that the young Joseph treated her well. Joseph F. Hogg was the son of Joseph Hogg who lived in Marion County according to the 1860 Marion County, Florida federal census. The elder Joseph Hogg was a planter with $4,000 in real estate and $12,000 in personal estate, probably slaves. Both the father and the sons were born in

South Carolina and appear to have come from Richland County, near Columbia.

Joseph, the youngest, served in the 4th Florida Infantry, Company G, with others from Marion and Levy Counties. Perhaps he knew William, who served in Company A of the 4th. Joseph's company remained at Fernandina until its evacuation in March 1862.

It is uncertain how Ellen initially met Thomas. One cannot find an answer other than there were many in Marion County who may have lived earlier in Jefferson County. There were many Carters, Gambles, Aldermans, Driggers, Lovells, Scotts, and Williams, and we know that Col. W. L. Bowen was from a company there. The county was full of South Carolinians and their descendants.

This area of Florida filled with people during the land rush of the mid-1840s, about the time Florida became a state. Its large migration was brought by a widely advertised sale of over 280,000 acres of the Arredondo Grant, which was most of Alachua, Marion, and Levy Counties. This land sold for an average of thirty-nine cents per acre and had been a private land grant from the king of Spain to a man named Arredondo that predated the American Revolution. Also in the treaty with Spain in 1819, the US agreed to honor these prior land grants.

A few days later in October, several of Mary's sons went downtown to a meeting at the courthouse to form a baseball club. They probably made a diamond on the parade ground behind the school. Meanwhile, even though it was only mid-October, the weather had been delightfully clear and cool, cool enough for a fire in the hearth, but all the girls could talk about was the circus coming to Tallahassee, the Messrs. Barnum, Van Amburgh, and Dan Castellos Museum and Menagerie. Pasted high on the walls of several stores in town were enormous pictures of clowns, elephants, lions, hippopotamus, and a ring-tailed monkey. The cotton crop, though, came in even less than the two years before, the result of a cotton worm and too few hands to pick what survived.

Elsewhere throughout the state, though, was a constant chatter about the coming election for the constitutional convention. The election took place over three days, starting on November 14th. They reported the total whites registered in the state as 11,151. The total number of black registered was 15,441. The *Semi-Weekly Floridian* reported 556 white and 1,747 black registered voters in Jefferson County.

Every so often, Mary took the carriage and visited with her Uncle James. At first, she thought she did it simply as part of being a good family member. But later, she noticed that Uncle James had a cadence to his voice that mimicked her dad's. She had never noticed it before, but now, after an afternoon visit, she felt an overwhelming feeling as if she had spent time with her father. Her Uncle James became more important to her as she aged.

One evening in late November, the family had supper and was sitting by the hearth discussing the news and events of the day. Said Sarah, "I hear there have been several robberies in town and in Tallahassee, too."

Zech said, "Yes, people are posting guards over their premises. I heard that someone stole every single bit of Judge Randall's pork and bacon from his basement while the family slept."

Added Mary, "I hear it is happening everywhere. Maybe we need to post a guard, too."

"Well, it has been a hard year," said James. "It has rained nonstop. Hungry people are stealing us blind, and everything looks gloomy. Maybe it is time for 1867 to pass into history. The weather was bad, our crops uncertain, finances scarce, and we're all disenfranchised. Hopeless to do anything to change anything!"

In November, the day of the election came, and despite the emotions on both sides, there was little violence in the campaigning or on voting day. The agent Grunwell reported employers had threatened only a few freedmen.

The election yielded the expected results. Votes for the constitutional convention were unanimous. Powell and Meacham, two men who had served on the county's board of registration, won election as Republican delegate candidates to the convention. The whites unanimously abstained from voting.

Because Congress kept passing several more Reconstruction acts, the political system kept changing for the South. Congress followed the first act with two more Reconstruction acts. Designed to resolve both the political and constitutional issues of the war, their primary objectives were to end Confederate nationalism and slavery. It effectively did this by both ratifying and enforcing the Thirteenth Amendment.

1868

In mid-January 1868, the family gathered after church one Sunday, and Vollie stood and asked if he could make an announcement. His wife Elizabeth turned beet red, and Mary knew before Vollie uttered another word. He said, "Elizabeth and I are going to be parents," and everyone jumped up to hug the happy couple. Mary hugged both and said, "I'm not sure I'm ready to be a granny yet." Then she covered her mouth and giggled.

That night, Mary sat in her bedroom at her dressing table, brushing her long, dark brown hair. In the mirror, she could see the flashes of gray, especially around her face. She wished more than anything that William was here to share this. Setting her brush down, she opened a small drawer to her right and retrieved a cameo breast pin. Her memory drifted to that special day when William, with his captivating eyes, gave it to her. It was after the birth of Laura.

Goodness, she thought, we were in high cotton then. She covered the pin in her hand and placed it back in the drawer. She also thought about her mother and wished she could be here to share this joy. Then she planned a trip to the graveyard for tomorrow.

In Tallahassee, though, the political scene was anything but joyful for the whites of Florida. Due to all the Congressional Reconstruction changes, the Republicans dominated the state's constitutional convention. For the first time in history, black and white lawmakers would have to work together in constitutional conventions all over the South, including Florida. Union troops camped west of the capitol when the convention began on January 20th.

Of its forty-six delegates, forty-three were Republicans, of which eighteen were freedmen. About a dozen were Southern Unionists and another dozen recently arrived Carpetbaggers. The other three delegates were Democrats, also called the Conservative vote. The small number of Democrats led to expectations of a harmonious session, but the session became anything but. Vast differences arose between a radical wing of the party whose priority was civil rights and another group whose primary consideration was the state's economic development. They believed white Floridians, whose support was necessary for Florida's reconstruction, deserved more consideration.

The bitter differences continued until one Monday when the Radicals arrived to begin work. They found themselves alone. The moderates had seceded from the convention and moved their meeting to Monticello. They wrote their own version of the constitution which became known as the "Monticello Constitution." The Radicals in Tallahassee asked the military commander General George Meade, who had recently replaced Pope, to arrest the missing delegates. But Meade was in Atlanta. Subsequently, the Radicals decided not to wait and wrote their own version of the constitution, which called for the disfranchisement of people who had supported the Confederacy, among other elements.

On February 10th, the Moderates slipped into Tallahassee, and in a post-midnight candlelight session, without knowledge of the Radicals, they reorganized the body. The Radicals protested, and freedmen by the thousands gathered at the capitol to regain possession of the convention hall. Colonel F. F. Flint, who commanded the soldiers in Tallahassee and who had placed a guard at the capitol, prevented the masses from storming the building. After a week of disorder, General Meade came to Tallahassee and ordered all the delegates back to work and called for new officers.

The Moderates worked hard to secure additional support for their side. As a result, they controlled the convention following the election of new officers. The convention adopted the Monticello Constitution two days later. It called for an elected governor with the power to appoint nearly every state and local official and a disproportionate representation in the legislature that favored whites. It did not disenfranchise anyone because of prior Confederate support. An uproar ensued, so the colonel sent both documents to Congress for their consideration. Congress approved the Monticello Constitution, whereupon they sent it back to Florida for ratification.

Said James a couple of nights later on the porch, "We are living with a Congressional oligarchy, I tell you," whereupon he disappeared into the house, slamming the front door.

Mary uttered under her breath, "Well, if they keep this up, we'll need a new door." To her, it was simple. They might get their right to vote back, and that was the most important thing.

When its work was done, this constitution conferred upon the Republican governor the power to appoint all local officials except constables, legislators, and municipal officers. The state ratified the new constitution the following May, and the Republicans, mostly Unionist and outsiders, governed Florida in short order. The newly elected Republican Governor Harrison Reed quickly appointed all county officials, including sheriffs.

Meanwhile, several days later, Mary rode her mare through a herd of cattle. That morning she had carefully penned her hair into a tight chignon, but it kept escaping. It had already fallen and hung down her back. With it free, she dug her heels into the mare and started off into a fast lope. It felt good to race through the pasture with her hair streaming down her back and her bonnet held only by its ribbons.

By spring, the tough winter, with its frigid temperatures and heavy rain, delayed planting by several weeks. In addition, the boys reported that the game was getting scarce. One cool evening, Mary was in the kitchen when Henry came in with a mess of songbirds—several robins, a couple of jays, and an oriole. Mary frowned, and he quickly said, "Don't worry, Mama. I didn't mess with the mockingbirds."

She sighed and turned her back on the scene as she rolled the dough. She replied, "Well, go on and clean 'em." As he walked out the door, he heard her add, "It's a sad day when we have to resort to eating our distractions from all this misery."

She referred to a lifetime of the birds' cheerful choruses which arose each morning from the oak trees near their homes. Years later, Henry would tell his children that he never once heard his mama complain, but it wouldn't be entirely true.

By mid-May, Congress impeached President Johnson, but he avoided conviction and kept his office by a slim margin. A week later, the Republican National Convention nominated Ulysses S. Grant for president. Grant ran his platform on the very popular "Let us have peace."

In June, the Southern states began their readmittance into the Union. Their new Republican-led houses met the required conditions. First Arkansas, then Louisiana, followed by Florida. By the end of July, Congress ratified the Fourteenth Amendment, guaranteeing dual US and state citizenship to all native-born residents regardless of race. These changes by Congress and the earlier changes ushered in a period of Republican party rule in Florida where none existed before.

Probably sometime later, around midsummer, Mary's first biological grandchild arrived. They named her Sarah E., most likely after the pretty red-headed Sarah Elizabeth who disappears from the picture by the 1870 census for Jefferson County, when Vollie is again living at home with his two-year-old daughter Sarah. His cute red-headed wife may have died in childbirth, as so many women did.

Late in July, James came home with more news about the nation. "Mama, Wyoming is now a territory. We keep adding more land, especially with the railroads being built in the west." The big news, though, came several weeks later when the Wyoming Territory granted women's suffrage to attract new settlers. Sarah and Hattie were positively ecstatic about the territory, but Mary made sure they understood what was at stake. The last thing she needed was one of her girls traipsing off with a man to parts unknown over an illusion.

By mid-fall, Florida was holding its midterm elections. That is when James noticed that the combination of freedmen, Northerners who had recently moved into the county, and Unionists (Loyalists) gave the new Republican party more power. This combination actively worked to guarantee black voting rights, and they elected Ulysses S. Grant as president. Freedmen voted for the first time, as did Vollie and Zech. Grant took office in 1869. General William Tecumseh Sherman succeeded him as the army's general-in-chief.

The Confederate veterans, though, felt increasingly embittered by the reconstructionist policies and occupying troops. James and Zech described to the rest of the family one evening at supper how Yankees remained camped west of the capitol in Tallahassee. They placed troops in Tallahassee and in towns throughout Middle Florida to enforce the reconstructionist policies regarding voting for the election.

Most of the offices in the state were now Republican in their political affiliation, and most of the people holding these offices found it dangerous if not impossible to perform their duties. Jefferson County's current sheriff had a most difficult problem doing his job because most native white Jefferson Countians were determined not to accept Republican rule.

Reconstruction violence took place throughout the South. A testimony in Congress in 1871 said that substantial numbers of people perished in the Florida counties of Jackson, Madison, Columbia, Alachua, Suwannee, Hamilton, Taylor, and Lafayette Counties. Despite the 1871 testimony omitting Jefferson County, the era was turbulent.

Mary realized that for years now, her hopes rose and fell with the passing of time. Calls for troops in the early days emptied the county of its men, and then the war devastated it socially, politically, and economically. It was hard to keep a straight face, but tradition required it —the ability to remain sane. Where she used to ride in a carriage, now everywhere she went, she rode in a saddle. Like her sons, she penned cattle, picked cotton, and snared hogs. They did better than most at maintaining herds because of the river bottom that skirted their property. This is where they hid what they needed to survive, safe from the foragers.

Reconstruction politicized the office of sheriff more than ever before. Sheriffs still collected taxes, but their job was compounded by the unrest. Many in protest refused to pay their taxes. Many found loopholes in the law. For example, hotels became boardinghouses because hotels paid taxes but boardinghouses did not. Business was bad everywhere in the South, and wages were down. Desperate farmers did what they could. Reigning supreme was political, economic, and social confusion—a total disruption of society. Thus, the Freedmen's Bureau was often used to help maintain control.

1869

In February Congress passed the Fifteenth Amendment, which made it illegal to deny the right to vote to anyone because of race. Mary noticed no one had added anything regarding gender. She didn't complain, though. What was the point? At her age, the men seldom listened, unlike her William. She always felt she had a voice with him. With her sons, it was different. She stopped offering it.

Meanwhile, in Washington and in state capitols all over the nation, men continued to debate whether a state could legally secede from the United States. She thought, *what's the point?* They had already fought a war to answer the question, but she kept her thoughts to herself.

After the war, though, there was a court case about bonds and the state of Texas. The case went all the way to the Supreme Court. Its outcome depended on a state's relationship with the Union. The ruling affected whether a state had a right to secede. On April 12, 1869, the US Supreme Court in Texas v. White ruled the US is "*an indestructible union*" from which no state can secede. They decided that the US Constitution did not permit a state to secede unilaterally, and therefore all the ordinances of secession were null under the Constitution. This ruling found that the Union is perpetual and indestructible under Constitutional law. In effect, it means that no state can leave the Union except through revolution or through consent of the states. She thought, "Well, we revolted, and the North squashed it. Discussion closed."

It repudiated the earlier position of the South that the Union was a voluntary compact between sovereign states. The South's argument about states' rights was negatively settled.

By the next summer, Republican Governor Harrison Reed and the Republican legislature assumed control of all state affairs, but that was in Tallahassee, and the community of Elizabeth was far away and secluded. The Walkers and Andrews may have even stopped their papers by now.

Even though President Johnson issued a general amnesty to all Confederate participants, Congress had trumped him with their Amnesty Acts in May 1866 that restricted the holding of office. Confederate veterans were no longer permitted to hold public office, nor could they until Congress passed another Amnesty Act in May 1872 to lift the prior restrictions.

In Monticello, officials removed Samuel Pasco, an ex-Confederate, from his office, and Republicans installed Robert Meacham as the new circuit clerk of Jefferson County. Robert Meacham was the son of a slave and a white planter and became Florida's first black circuit clerk.

When Meacham became clerk, Samuel Pasco protested, and on the day he left office he wrote in the circuit court order book that Robert Meacham came to his office and claimed the office of clerk of the court by a paper, a commission from *"one Harrison Reed claiming to be governor of the State..."* One can still read Pasco's written protest today in the courthouse. Pasco surrendered all records, seals, and other public property in his custody to Meacham.

After his election to the state senate, Meacham would soon resign his lucrative clerkship. The rules prevented holding both offices simultaneously. He would serve in the senate from 1868 to 1879 as Jefferson County's senator. They appointed John W. Powell sheriff.

Later, Mary made a carriage ride to the home of Dr. William Joseph Carroll to see her sister. It was a beautiful late summer day, and she felt better with all the sunshine and fresh air. Though it was stifling hot, the breeze from the moving buggy gave some relief.

Summer growth made the woods dark green, and shade covered most of the ride. It was truly good to get away from the kitchen. She left Sarah, who was almost twenty-five, in charge. She worried about Sarah, who was still not married. So few eligible men existed, but the Walker women were known for taking their time.

Earlier, Mary's sister Jane took care of Dr. William Joseph Carroll's five small children, ages one to nine. Their mother Mary Rebecca Walker Carroll, a cousin through the second set of Walkers, had passed away earlier in May.

Jane was waiting for her on Dr. Carroll's porch, holding the baby. As Mary climbed from the carriage, Jane said, "Sweet sister, you don't know how much I've been thinking about you lately." They sat on the porch, but not before Mary took the baby.

She said, "This reminds me. We got a letter from John Slicer and Emily. After five sons in a row, Emily got a baby girl. They named her Cora."

Replied Jane, "Didn't one baby fail to thrive?"

"Yes, little Charles didn't live a year. It about tore them apart, especially Emily. We think that's why they moved to Levy County (Florida), somewhere near Barnesville Lake, though I'm not sure where that is."

Jane and Dr. Carroll married before the 1870 census. Both he and Jane had been friends for most of their lives, so it was no surprise when they married. Jane turned to Mary for help since their marriages were so alike. Both became mothers instantly to several young children, and both of their husbands were key citizens in their communities. Jane, though, was much older than Mary had been. She was thirty-six. Mary was nineteen when she married.

Mary said, "I've been thinking a lot lately about Mama and Daddy. Daddy was such a quiet man, much like my William was."

"That probably had to do with how they were raised. Little boys were seen and not heard, and they knew better than to speak when old people talked. That generation was more silent. I think they learned a lot by all that listening. My Dr. Carroll is the same way. It was hard to get him to talk about himself in the beginning."

"I had the same problem with William. Courting was tough with him. You know, all three men were or are very smart. Maybe all that listening means they think a lot. All three seemed to have the wisdom of Solomon."

Jane's husband William served with Company G, the Aucilla Guards, of the 5th Florida Infantry. However, they sent him home in 1863 with paralysis on his right side, unfit for further service.

Meanwhile, Jefferson County's abundance of resources attracted Northern men who showed a decided interest in the freed slaves. Called "carpetbaggers" because of their traveling bags, these men sought to advance their political advantages. Charles Parrish, a former slave and very good carpenter, told James one day, "They're buying our votes to get us to vote for the ones who would be favorable to their politics." James had heard it from others, too, but Charles was the most reliable source.

That night, James told his mom what he heard. On the porch the two rocked, and in the woods among the evening chorus of crickets and frogs, they heard the warbling whistle of a calling whippoorwill. Mary murmured something about "Jack marrying a widow," but she couldn't exactly remember how the story went. James noticed something different about his mother. The older she got, the quieter she got. She had less and less to say lately. It worried him. Still, when she responded, they were often words of wisdom. She often brought to the table a view that no one had thought about before.

The next day Mary stood in the yard stirring a big pot of boiling water as a wagon went by filled with baskets of cotton. Atop the baskets were several of the Parrish children along for the ride. Their harvest looked good. She knew that the Parrish's first year sharecropping was as hard as theirs had been, but things were getting better for most. Those not willing to work, both black and white, were failing and moving on. Most everyone left was learning how to do for themselves. She and the children talked about the black families who were saving to buy their own land.

By November, it was cane grinding time. Uncle James would grind the bit of cane they grew. They looked forward to it, a gala with plenty of juice, its skimmings, and fresh syrup for later. Tomorrow night she planned to fry cornmeal hoecakes and mix the syrup with butter for a treat. Tonight, though, there was dancing and music with a fiddle. With a crisp white blouse, Mary wore her bright blue indigo skirt that she had dyed for the occasion. When her son James walked into her room, she was already pulling on her burgundy shawl for the ride over. James said, "Mama, you look positively radiant. You could turn heads tonight!"

"Aw, hush," she said as she reached to push a comb securely into her hair, raising it up above her right ear. She had worn her hair down tonight since she had just washed it earlier that week. The silver curls that framed her face with the cascading darker hair became her.

When they got to Uncle James, she quickly found her group of women. Ann Lightsey was there with Aunt Mary Jane, but cousin Amanda Sledge Lightsey glowed. She had big news. She and Uncle Littleberry's son Joel E. Walker were obviously spending a lot of time together, and they had an announcement to make. They set the wedding for December 22nd, and they invited everyone.

Mary was happy for both of them. Amanda had struggled so hard to raise her and cousin John's five children, the youngest of whom was born after John was killed at Sharpsburg. It had been hard on all of them, and now she had someone to help her. Joel and Amanda would marry and add four more children to their union.

330

In 1869, the biggest news of the new year was the funeral of General William Bailey, considered the richest man in Florida. Mary thought about the day she and Vollie visited the general to purchase fabric at a discount to make uniforms for Jefferson County boys. During the war, Bailey had moved his wife and children to the Columns in Tallahassee, but they brought him back to be buried close to Elizabeth with the rest of his wife's family at Bellamy's place. Mary realized that almost all her father's generation were gone now, including the old general. Many called the old generation the pioneers of Florida.

1870

In mid-May 1870, James, Vollie, and Zech went to Monticello to celebrate the connection of the rails of the transcontinental railroad at Promontory Point in Utah. The family had been reading for months about the two sets of tracks as they inched east and west toward each other. There were stories about the men who worked on the rails, many veterans from the South and former slaves all looking for employment wherever they could find it. Earlier that day, though, the family talked about the final spikes which were to be sledged at noon, connecting the two tracks. The boys went into town for what they believed would be a celebration.

The next day, around noon, they returned for dinner with all kinds of stories. Zech, eyes aglow and a wide grin on his face, said, "The telegraph announced that the two locomotives steamed until their pilots touched, *"facing on a single track, half a world behind each back."*
"Did you just make that up?" Mary asked Zech.
However, before he could respond, Vollie cracked him on the back of the head, stating, "No, Zech received the information from a reporter who telegraphed it to our railroad office. Mama, I'm glad none of you were in Monticello last night. Everybody and his brother shot their guns into the air. It was pandemonium." She looked at Sarah, and Sarah was hanging on every word, positively green with envy.

Homeless families from Georgia and Alabama came to Florida in hopes of a better life. The sale of several estates to outsiders saddened Mary and her family.

Best news of the year was when the Freedman's Bureau ceased activity in the county. Worst news of the year was when the Freedman's Bureau ceased activity in the county.

331

That fall, Robert E. Lee, sixty-three, passed away because of a stroke he suffered in September. Whites all over the South grieved.

Said Mary, "Sad that all the war veterans keep dying off. War seems to take its toll whether or not they're fighting."

James added, "I heard that Monticello's businesses will close the day of his funeral." The newspaper reported that on the day of his funeral a procession of people formed at the courthouse to pay their respect.

By this time, some Southerners had laid aside their bitter sectional feelings and their rancor, but some never would.

#

Chapter 15
To Come Full Circle
1870-1871

Mary, in a faded long-sleeve green calico dress, sat on her back porch staring at an expanse of shaded woods with little understory. In late afternoon, the sun penetrated the canopy at an angle. She marveled at the sunlight as it filtered through the trees, the soft greens and the bit of color of a changing sweet gum tree. A soft breeze feathered through, and a yellow star-shaped leaf floated down until it rested on the shaded ground. With a few freed tendrils of her dark and gray hair around her face, she sighed and thought about how much she missed all of them, her father, mother, Julia Ann, Henry, David, Joel, and now William, too. Inside, she heard two of her girls talking. With sorrow etched in the lines of her face, she remained acutely aware of how fragile their existence was. If she were the weeping kind, she would have wept.

Inside, Laura told Hattie, "Thank you for your help with this. I don't want it to look too childish." Each valentine contained a hand-written missive with no particular rhyme or meter. The girls worked at their father's desk in the sitting room before a fire in the fireplace. It was and always would forever be Daddy's desk. They called it nothing else.

Some girls got four valentines, and a few only one. Most were anonymous. This year, Laura planned to give three valentines: two to her best friends and one to George Lightsey, now a school graduate.

As they finished, Laura added, "I'll give this to his sister Mary tomorrow. She's agreed to place it in a book George has been reading. When he isn't looking, of course." Because Laura was only thirteen, someone had to hand deliver the valentine. She and Hattie, who had another beau, decided on an anonymous delivery. The thought of their plan made Laura giddy with excitement. Laura's soft brown hair shone in the firelight. Her unusually small mouth bowed as she contemplated whether George could guess who sent it.

Laura was still too young, especially to her mother, but several of her siblings had married. John, Ellen, and Florida were gone. Sarah was smitten by the handsome Jacob Hartsfield, and Valentine had moved back because he needed help with little Sarah after his wife passed. Of the older siblings, only James and Zech were still unmarried, though James spent more time with Florida Grubbs. For Zech, Lizzie Hammonds had her eye on him, though he hardly noticed. He was all work. The other day her mama told him, "Zech, all work and no play makes Jack a dull boy." He wrinkled his nose and paid her no mind.

Laura's mother and George's father, Henry Lightsey, had known each other since South Carolina. The Lightseys lived next door to them in Florida, and Laura spent many days playing with George as a child in Ann Lightsey's yard. George was almost four years older, and for a while she was just a kid. It had all changed, though, within the past year. Suddenly she noticed he noticed the changes. She had her mother's height and was growing into the shape of a young woman.

Even with the ravages of war, Jefferson County grew another thirty-six percent between 1860 and 1870. Now, with a population of over 13,000 residents in Jefferson County, a new Florida emerged with a different social, political, and economic order. The 1870 map of Monticello reflects little growth, with much fewer new businesses open than during the decade between 1850 and 1860. Documents reflect only three new buildings built. (See Appendix 2)

Most of the county's population growth was freedmen, as there were more black people living in the county in 1870 than there were in 1860. Since Jefferson County offered less trouble for black men than nearby counties, more may have moved there in the five years following the Civil War when the freed could live where they pleased. Also, one wonders if this was because of families separated earlier by slavery. There was a pipeline of slaves brought to Florida from Virginia and the Carolinas before the war, and those left behind may have been seeking their relatives in a milder climate.

Or they may have needed to leave their place of liberation. A statistic showed there was a great migration of blacks to Florida from the Carolinas in the 1860s. Tallahassee's *Semi-Weekly Floridian* reported on September 28, 1866, *"in consequence of the persistence of the land holders in South Carolina in refusing to lease or sale lands to the Negroes, thousands of them are preparing to immigrate to Florida."*

Also in the same paper was the following, *"Information Wanted: A colored woman named Amanda Linn who formerly belonged to Mr. Leroy Jones and who then lived about 15 miles from Raleigh, North Carolina, is very anxious to hear from her child Robert Linn and from her mother Jane Thompson who belonged to Mr. George Brogdon living in the same neighborhood. She has written to both Mr. Jones and Mr. Brogdon for information but has been unable to get any answer. Any person who knows anything of these parties will confer a great favor by communicating with her at Tallahassee, Florida, in the care of SW Myers."* This notice was also sent to the Raleigh paper.

By June 1, 1870 (the date of the 1870 US Federal Census), Mary lived east near Elizabeth, near her cousin Joel P. Walker and her Uncle James and Aunt Elizabeth Walker. The census lists Mary at age forty-seven but omits William. Living with her is Sarah (twenty-five), James (twenty-four), Valentine (twenty-three), Zech (twenty-one), Jesse (nineteen), Henrietta (seventeen), Henry (sixteen), Laura (thirteen), Joseph (eleven), and Virginia (seven). Valentine's Sarah E. (two years old) lived there, also.

Following the war, Florida was still a largely unsettled frontier. The only people downstate were the later waves of pioneers straightforward in their thinking, doggedly determined, and self-reliant, much like the early settlers of Jefferson County in the 1830s. Many in Florida did not want to accept Republican rule, and the areas in the peninsula provided for escape.

By the 1870 census, John Slicer and Emily lived near Sanderson in Bradford County with their five children, and Ellen Andrews was married and living with Thomas Hogg in Marion County, Florida. He is the brother of the Joseph Hogg whom Florrie married after the war. Interestingly, though, living with Thomas and Ellen is Florrie. It appears her husband, Joseph, may have passed away. Florrie is twenty-nine, probably widowed, and has no occupation listed.

Monticello and the entire nation went through major changes, the biggest of which occurred in farming. Unlike most families before the war, Mary's family had income from other sources besides farming.

The entire nation between 1860 and 1870 changed economically to become more like Mary's family had been before the war. Before 1870, American farmers were in the majority, but the 1870 census showed a change. By 1870, farmers were no longer in the majority, though deep in the South in places like Florida, most people farmed for survival. Without their patriarch and his special skills, the Andrews farmed for survival, too.

Mary's eldest, James, did what he could to support the family. Rev. H. S. Linton passed, so James approached the Linton family and negotiated an agreement with William Marvin, who administered the estate. James agreed to pay the estate two bales of cotton, weighing 900 pounds, in order to use sixty acres of their land. It was New Year's Day in 1870. James was now officially a sharecropper.

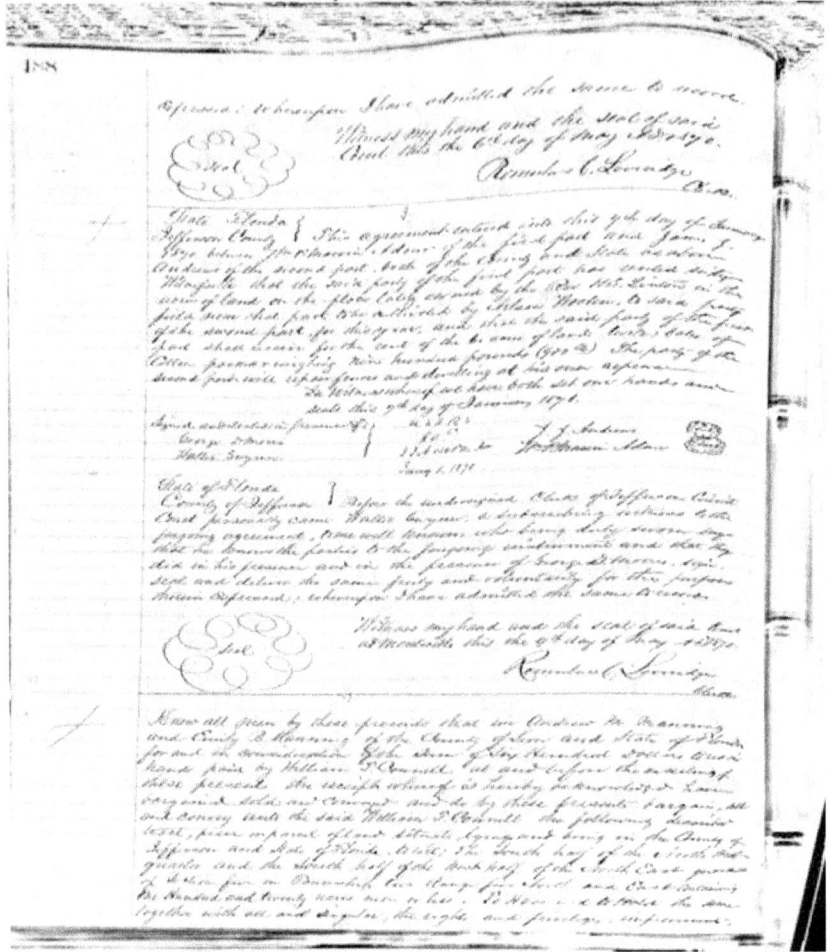

Land leased by J. J. Andrews and recorded in the Jefferson County courthouse, Monticello, Florida, personal photo

He knew his yield was about a half-bale per acre, so he felt certain he could meet the lease. By the end of the week, every one of them was in the field, yanking and whacking down the stalks, getting the ground ready for the next crop. Before they knew it, they would be digging and manuring the new furrows. They planted in April and continued the cycle by thinning in May.

One day, deep into the field and out of sight of James, the kids had hoed their way to the far reaches of the rows which stopped short of a little stream. A beaver had dammed it, and there was a pool of clear water perfect for a dip. Henry and Joseph stripped and jumped in while their sisters giggled behind their hands. Unbeknown to them, James caught them frolicking instead of completing the work needed before the sun went down. He yelled, "What the blazes are y'all doing? Get back to work!"

The girls scattered into the rows, but the boys had to wait because they needed their clothes. James lost his temper and flogged both of them as they scampered for their clothes and rushed into the cotton.

Later, Joseph's temper got the better of him. He had been grumbling to himself for some time, and then he started yanking on the tender cotton plants and tossing them aside.

"Stop! Stop! What are you doing?" screamed Hattie as she rushed to him. Crying, he wiped his eyes on his shirtsleeve, smearing the mud on his face. She looked at the massacred row, about ten plants in all. "Oh, dear Lord." Then Hattie hugged him and said, "It's okay; let's replant them."

Weeks grew into months, and it was time to harvest the cotton. June and July were when the plants blossomed. By fall, they picked the open bolls, placing them in long, cloth sacks which hung down their backs behind them. It was backbreaking work, but it paid money—something hard to find in those days. Plus, it could make homespun clothes.

People carded the raw cotton using two wooden cards with teeth to pull the fibers and align them. Then Mary spun the fibers into threads on her spinning wheel. Next she used her loom to make the fabric. It was the same color as the cotton bolls.

It took the longest to make their dresses, and all her grown daughters required floor length skirts. Their homespun, coarse and heavy skirts were trimmed with rows of buttons. The buttons were pieces of gourds cut round about the size of an inch and covered in scraps from the dress.

Mary, after feeding her crew, walked onto the front porch and reached for her hat woven from palmetto buds. It always hung on a nail by the front door. She herself had split and braided it. It had a wide brim to protect her from the sun's rays, though she wasn't sure why she even bothered anymore. Her mother said the sun caused the age spots on her hands. Her life was far too hard for her to wear gloves all the time. Although her face was clear, her hands caused her embarrassment.

She joined the family, who were in the field picking cotton. Later, as Mary was working a row, suddenly she stopped, straightened her spine, and bent it backwards, trying to relieve the kinks. She said, "Look at this, James." He was only a couple of rows away. He stopped and pulled his bag off his shoulder before coming to her. She continued, "What do you think happened to these plants?"

He stared and looked around at all the other plants nearby. Running his grimy hand through his hair, he said, "I don't know what happened here. It looks like none of these made it."

Mary replied, "There's about eight or ten plants missing." The rest of the family stopped and said nothing.

They knew how to subsist on the land, but still some items needed to be bought, such as coffee and tobacco. Prices, though, were still ridiculous. At J. T. Budd's store, rope cost sixty cents a foot, and a barrel of kerosene cost a whole dollar and a half. A coat could cost almost five dollars. Most families didn't have the cash to spend even after their crops came in. If they had a crop to sell, there was little market for it. Mary couldn't remember the last time she went to town for anything. She had even taught her boys how to make rope from the tails of cattle. Everyone spent so much time working to survive. Going to town was no longer practical.

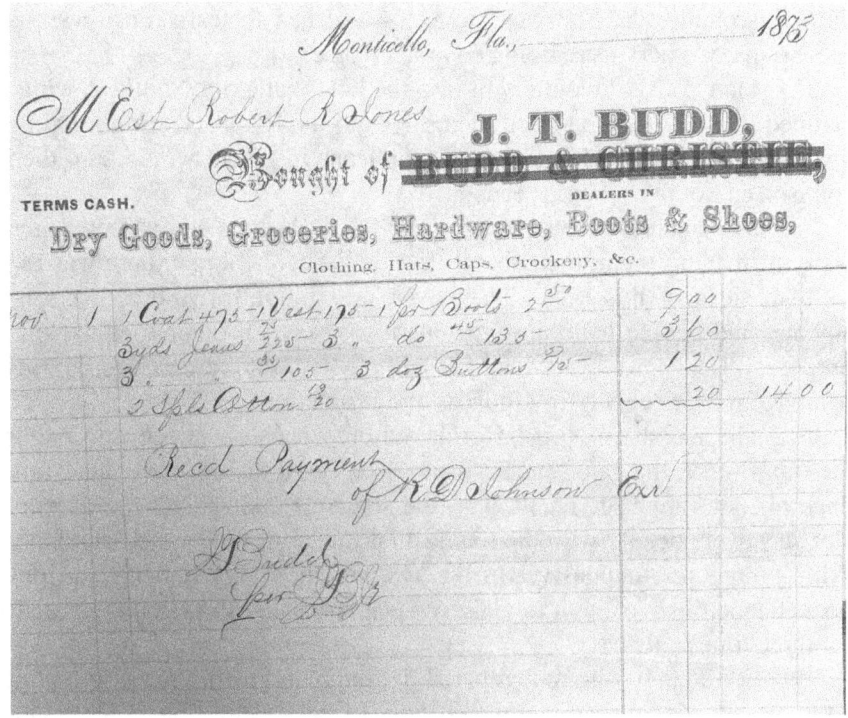

1873 receipt from J. T. Budd's store, Keystone Genealogical Library, personal photo

These were hard times, as hard as toward the end of the war. Mary noticed the swelling, calluses, and coarseness of her daughters' small, delicate hands. Before the war, theirs was a life of carriage rides and tranquil times. Now each of them could chop wood, drive a two-horse wagon, and do all the housework. She had to do it when her family was new to Florida and living came hard, but she never thought it would happen to her children. The war swept into their lives and changed everything. Nothing was the same. Life had been so much easier before the war.

Now it was hard labor, dirt, and poverty—every hour of every day spent trying to survive. The boys plowed, trapped, snared, and fished while she and the girls planted, hoed, and gathered. Light for their lamps came from alligator oil, and they made candle wax from the pale green wax boiled from wax myrtle berries. Sometimes they feasted when the boys brought in a gopher tortoise. Mary thought they were lucky because the boys had learned from William and her father Jesse how to survive in the wilds of Florida. She was lucky she had had to learn those lessons, too. So many others were doing so much worse.

Many of the freedmen fit into the latter category. Southern whites claimed the freedmen had tied themselves to the Radicals, clinging to the mistaken belief that helping keep Republicans in power would earn them confiscated Southern homesteads.

Mary hated the entire debate. If the scalawags and carpetbaggers were misleading them, then shame on them; but she knew there was evil on both sides of this issue. There were no straightforward answers for anyone, and people have always sought to use each other for their own purposes. Her sons described her simple answers as naïve, but she believed in the necessity of kindness and justice.

The woods in North Florida suffered because of the poverty. In the war's wake, the game such as bear, deer, coon, turkey, dove, quail, and duck all but vanished. Thankfully, the squirrels and rabbits fared better. Her sons were deadly with their slingshots and slings, a learned childhood skill. Ammo was expensive. In the swamps they gigged frogs and pin-hooked small fish, enough to make a meal. It was hard work, this trying to eat three times a day.

Fortunately, she remembered her mother showing her how to find wild tubers. She even remembered how to bake using the flour ground from the coontie plant. The Indians taught her parents the safe preparation of the plant's taproot for flour, though the plant was highly poisonous.

Beginning early in November, she made homespun fabric for her and the children. The little ones had picked the cotton seeds from the bolls, and one afternoon she began carding. She broke it into manageable steps, carding an hour one afternoon, then an hour spinning it into thread or yarn.

Sometimes she left it the same color of cottony white, but for the children and girls, she died the thread or yarn using indigo for blue, sumac berries for red, or bark for a golden-brown color. Subsequently she wove the thread or yarn using a loom. For skirts she needed six yards, and it took her two weeks to make the thread and another week to weave the fabric. Then she still had to make the skirt or dress, which took another week. Thankfully, many hands make easier work.

For the latter, she invited a few of her other family members to a sewing circle. She missed the socializing she had had while they lived in Monticello. Several came one afternoon, and each did their own needlework and discussed each other's happenings. There was her uncle's wife Elizabeth Padgett Walker, Mary's cousin's wife Mary Jane Hamrick

Walker, another cousin's wife Amanda Sledge Walker, and Mary's daughters Ellen, Hattie, and Laura.

Her Aunt Elizabeth said, "I heard Queen Victoria is still in mourning clothes for Prince Albert. Didn't he die around the beginning of the war?" She meant the Civil War.

Amanda replied, "Yes, he did. She must really be distraught."

Mary added, "Well, obviously she doesn't have to make her own mourning clothes and share with each other, like we did. So many of our men folks died, and it happened so often we hardly had time to grieve and wear our widow weeds before someone else needed them."

Mary Jane added, "Yes, we had a dress in our family that went from house to house. It was so sad. Thankfully, the deaths don't come as often as they did."

While Mary Jane was talking, Mary looked around the room and realized another difference. Their gowns didn't overlap between their chairs like they did before. Everyone was using less fabric in their skirts, and no one had the crinolines to make them fuller, either.

Mary noticed everyone wore the same dress for everyday while reserving a better one for special occasions. Even with help from her girls, it took them too long to make clothing for more than a couple of outfits each at any time.

She remembered how before she married William, she and her dad noticed William had more clothes than most. She realized she got to live that life, but now it was all gone. They returned to living like they did when Florida was still a territory.

Late in 1870, Laura listened to the preacher at Elizabeth Baptist. George Lightsey sat three pews back in the corner with two other older boys, and the rumors that morning were that the boys had been in town the night before, arriving in Elizabeth just before church. She heard they imbibed. She knew George was probably in for it when the service was done. His father and stepmother kept looking back at the boys. They had probably heard the rumors, too.

The sermon was how one sinner can cause so many to go astray. The preacher looked directly at George's group, and George's dad turned to look, too. Then, as if he were addressing the boys, the reverend said, "If anyone is determined to be wicked, you need to remove yourselves from society and be a hermit." People turned in their seats, and George and the boys got really still with folded hands, looking like cherubs. Laura almost giggled but saw her mom staring at her. Laura's grin folded, and she dropped her head.

The next Saturday, the youth met at the reverend's house for a sing. The reverend's wife played the piano. Favorites were "Home Sweet Home" and "Carry Me Back to Old Virginny."

During a break, Laura told George, "My father's people lived in Virginia."

"I thought your dad was from Washington, DC?"

"Yes, he was born there in Georgetown, across the river from Virginia. His part of Washington, DC was once a part of Virginia."

"I didn't know that. All my people were from South Carolina." Laura knew this because it was the same for all her mother's relatives.

George continued, "Before South Carolina, my people came from southern Germany in Baden-Wurttemberg. They say it is beautiful there, with dark green forests and cliffs. It sits at the foot of the Swabian Alps near Stuttgart." Laura listened to George, who added, "They came here a little more than a hundred years ago."

Laura replied, "I've never seen mountains before."

"Neither have I, but my dad and cousins got to see them during the war."

It was fall and a cool breeze wafted through the open windows. The reverend's wife's muslin curtains carried on the breeze, folding this way and that. Young people sat throughout the room on chairs, the sofa, and chairs brought in from the dining room and kitchen. They started another song as their voices filled the evening air.

Several weeks later, Laura was helping her mother in the kitchen pack a basket of food. She looked at her mother, who was now forty-seven. Her hair was gray, and she looked tired. Eleven babies, the three motherless children, plus several wars had taken their toll. Mary wore a faded green satin dress whose bodice dipped low to drape over her narrow hips. The neckline was modest, as always, hugging her neck. Puffed sleeves gathered below the shoulders and again below the elbows. Her gloves matched perfectly, and she wore a small boxy hat to match. Her mother was always so elegant, even now when she looked so tired and money was so tight.

They traveled to Monticello for a Christmas reception at the courthouse. It was sad her dad wouldn't be there to escort her mother; only her children escorted her now.

Several days later, Laura went with the other children to the school in Elizabeth. They read a Bible verse and sang a hymn. Whereupon their teacher dismissed them and divided them into smaller groups for the respective recitations. Today, she and her first cousin Lizzie Pillans talked while they waited to begin.

Said Lizzie, "I hear some students call it the 'Jefferson Jail.'" She was talking about the Jefferson Academy in Monticello. She added, "Burt Bellamy says that no one can call on them on Sunday, and it is hard to be received on any other day unless one's parents approve."

Replied Laura, "My older siblings went there, but I don't think it was the same before the war. I got to go for a year, but then we moved out here. I liked it, though."

In the 1870 census, all Mary's boys were farm laborers. Of all the children, it says only Joseph and Laura attended school. There was a school in Elizabeth at least in the early 1900s, and records show there was a school in Aucilla, though it may have been too far away. The younger children in the house were Virginia, age seven, and Sarah E. age two, Valentine's child. School usually began for eight-year-olds.

This census signals how well William and Mary did as parents. Of the fifteen children, they lost only one. Julia Ann died of a sickness, probably malaria, judging from the newspaper account.

The family still had a personal estate of $300. The records show Mary was forty-seven years old, but they do not list William. We believe William died after his parole in Greensboro, NC at war's end but before the census death schedule date.

There is an old family Bible in the possession of a great-great-granddaughter at Citra in Marion County, Florida. It records the birth of William Henry and says "W. H. Andrews resigned as sheriff of Jefferson County to go to the Confederate War." The date recorded is April 22, 1860.

The book *Soldiers of Florida in the Seminole Indian, Civil and Spanish-American Wars* shows that state officials mustered him into the 4th Florida Infantry in July 1861. The earlier date may have been the local militia. Also, there were sheriffs elected after W. H. Andrews served from 1855 to 1857, so we know he did not resign to go to war in 1860. Someone may have recorded this at a later date when memories were less clear. Instead, William resigned as Monticello's railroad agent to go to war. Newspapers reflect this, as does the 1860 census.

That Christmas, Mary sat as the children opened their presents from her. Each of the girls got a new skirt, made from the homespun fabric they all lovingly made and dyed. Sarah, though, was the happiest. She loved the rich, burgundy-colored skirt. The boys got new blouses, except for Joseph, who needed trousers more.

They decorated the hearth with palmettos, pine boughs, and sour oranges for color. Hattie even added moss to it and dried orange circles.

1871

On New Year's Day, James and Vollie dressed and used ashes to draw mustaches and ferocious eyebrows. The rest of the boys got into the act, and the entire gang rushed out and into the kitchen. Surprised, Mary and the girls were in there cooking black-eyed peas with ham for seasoning and a big pot of turnip greens. With squealing and shuffling of feet, the brothers chased the girls around the big table. Mary laughed and laughed. William might be gone, but he left her with all this joy.

Later, Mary about rubbed Joseph's face raw trying to get the ashes from his hairline. He had smudged the soot all over his face. When finished, she pushed her left hand's fingers into the pad of flesh at her thumb's base. It was sore, and she rubbed pine oil there for her rheumatism, which had flared up again. She rubbed it into both hands and wrists and thought about her Grandmother Walker, who suffered the same pains. She even thought about adding a bit of the oil to her next bath.

By the following year, she and the children noticed changes. Both whites and blacks were leaving their homes and pursuing other opportunities. Many of the whites moved farther south while the freedmen migrated to the cities. In South Florida were jobs in logging, cattle, and citrus. Tourists came to the St. Johns River valley to their east. The boys read about steamboats which took passengers as far south as Mellonville, now called Sanford. By the 1870s, Florida's population had grown to over 187,000 people. A demographic shift was clear. (See Appendix 2.)

On January 1, 1870, Mary sold the 160 acres near Nash, south of Monticello. The family's assets were dwindling, and Mary liquidated her last available property. She sold it to a known Republican and Southern Unionist, the Sheriff John W. Powell.

William's railroad was still in miserable condition and in the hands of receivers. The road still ended in Chattahoochee. Woodburning locomotives pulled small wooden coaches with open platforms. The trip between Jacksonville and Lake City alone took six hours.

Lately, Mary spent a lot of time remembering how they had found this area when her family arrived forty years ago and how it prospered before the war. She remembered the earlier planters who were the children and grandchildren of several of the well-known aristocratic forefathers of the country, but today everything was shabby and broken down. Florida's economy was in shambles.

She thought about the flowers and birds she saw when she got to Florida. Several had disappeared, because during the war and after the war, people had to eat. Thankfully, songbirds were still flying, especially the loquacious fuswahaya, the name given the mockingbird by the Indians. The other night one sang all night long on a full moon.

She told Laura the other day that the swamp lilies bloom with no one to see them anymore. The Indians are gone, as are men like her father Jesse who worked in those river swamps to find the stray cattle. She said, "Now, those lilies bloom entirely for their own enjoyment."

*The swamp lily is a type of amaryllis native to Florida and is also known in
Florida as a spider lily, personal photo*

Mary lived to witness Jefferson County's transformation from a
quiet frontier into a bustling county—weathering deep economic
depressions, flourishing during the boom of the 1840s and 1850s,
enduring war and Reconstruction, and entering a period of economic
stagnation. She was glad William wasn't here to see his beloved county
decay.

But it wasn't just her county—it was all of Florida, all of the
South. Her thoughts drifted to the days of prosperity when Monticello
thrived, William's easy smile brightened her world, and their children
grew strong and kind under their care. None of them could have imagined
the hardships secession would bring to their world, stripped of its men and
boys, and daily life reduced to bitter want—no salt, no tea, no coffee, no
sugar, no cloth except what their own hands could weave, until at last
there was nothing at all.

One night, Mary awoke after going to bed early. She could hear her sons' voices murmuring in the sitting room. Silently she slipped from her bed and tiptoed barefooted into the hall to listen. They were sitting around the fireplace, passing a jug and talking about South Florida and Texas and the possibilities elsewhere for a better life.

Said Val, "They say it will be the Cuba of America. It is mild, soft, and balmy in climate and rich in production, especially its tropical fruits. Its forests abound in game like our forests used to here."

Added James, "It rarely gets too cold there—hardly any frost. And they have perpetual sea breezes. But I also hear it is easy to live and support a family and that action and energetic labor are unneeded. I think someone is overstating its advantages."

Mary leaned against the wall and thought about her own parents and uncles whose South Carolinian progeny once sought a better life in Middle Florida. She remembered that night when she overheard her own father and uncles discuss the frightening Florida frontier. Now she had lived long enough to witness her own children as they discussed new frontiers farther south and west. She marveled at these places, places she would probably never see, but which her own descendants might one day inhabit.

Finis

Epilogue

Mary Adeline Walker Andrews

We do not know when or how Mary died. Her last records are the 1870 census and when she sold her land to Sheriff Powell in 1870. We believe Mary lived her remaining life in Jefferson County and likely rests near her parents in the Old Elizabeth Baptist Churchyard Cemetery. Her death is believed to have happened in 1871 or 1872 since several of the children married and left home in 1872. The 1880 US Federal Census and the 1885 Florida State Census (the only surviving state census for Jefferson County before 1900) do not list her. The June 22, 1870 census, her last record, shows she died sometime after this date.

Researchers studied tax lists, and Mary appeared on an 1863 tax list with her 160 acres of land. The pertinent pages of the 1864 tax books are missing, as are the 1865 tax books in their entirety. County authorities list her again in 1866, this time as Mrs. M. Andrews, with the 160 acres of land. This tax listing says her household did not include any men between the ages of twenty-one and fifty-five.

Tax rolls did not list Mary again after 1866, though her property did not sell until January 1, 1870. On this document, Mary placed her mark rather than writing her name. A. Lacy, Asa Anderson, and W. L. Granger witnessed the transaction.

An examination of marriage records for Jefferson and surrounding counties did not find a marriage for Mary after the war, though there was a Mary A. Andrews who married G. A. Burton in 1877 in Jefferson County, Florida. This Mary, though, proved to be a maiden of only twenty-three years old and could not be our Mary. Andrews was this woman's maiden name.

Mary probably didn't have an occasion to marry again after William passed. There were so many widowed women after the war. While looking at the families who lived near her children in the 1880s, there were several ancient men married to young women. There was a dearth of marriageable men, and there were many more young maiden women who were of marriage age. Mary, forty-seven, was an older woman by 1870, and the Civil War years had been hard on everyone. She may have looked even older.

Reliable sources show the Old Walker Cemetery (also known as the Elizabeth Baptist Churchyard Cemetery) on Walker Cemetery Road, off Old Salt Road, is the burial place of Mary's deceased parents, Jesse and Elizabeth Wilson Walker, and grandparents, Joel Sr. and Elizabeth Carter Walker.

There are three Walker cemeteries in Jefferson County. We sincerely believe Walker Cemetery #1, near her parents, is Mary's burial place. Walker Cemetery #1 is the original Elizabeth Churchyard Cemetery which predates the current Elizabeth Cemetery, which is not a church cemetery but rather a graveyard for the community at the corner of Bassett's Dairy Road and Old Salt Road.

William H. Andrews

Following William's 1862 deed, all subsequent Andrews land records after Mary's 1870 deed concerned his daughters-in-law: Florida, married to James Jefferson, and Julia, married to Valentine. We found no other deeds.

The 1866 tax rolls for the county do not list William, though they do list Mary. If her household did not include any men between the ages of twenty-one and fifty-five, where was William? He would have been fifty-five years of age in 1866. The lack of William's name in tax assessments, even after the war, suggests he may have died or become incapacitated, no longer considered the head of household responsible for taxes.

There was an inordinate toll of veteran deaths within the early years after the close of the conflict, and this shows the resultant effects of the war's damages on men's bodies. These men did not receive listings as war casualties, nor did they receive disability benefits like their Union counterparts.

William's last record, dated April 28, 1865, shows he survived the war. He is not in the 1870 US Federal Census or its Mortality Schedule. If he returned home from the war but died in the year before May 31, 1870, census takers would have recorded his death in the 1870 Mortality Schedule, which recorded deaths between June 1, 1869 and May 31, 1870. He was not in this mortality schedule, so a correct death date for William is between April 28, 1865, and June 1, 1869.

William fathered sixteen children between his two marriages, and he was a grandfather to seven by 1870 through John Slicer and Valentine. The following records show five children from his first wife and eleven more with his wife Mary. His family must have revered him, because almost every child of his eventually named one of their children after him. There are several William Henry Andrews.

If he returned from the war, they may have buried him in Walker Cemetery #1 (the Old Elizabeth Churchyard Cemetery) beside Mary.

William and Mary were both deemed Florida Pioneers through the Florida State Genealogical Society's Florida Pioneer Descendant Certificate Program, which honors descendants of Florida pioneers who settled in Florida prior to statehood on March 3rd, 1845.

The Children of William H. Andrews and His Wives Elizabeth and Mary

All of William's children settled in Jefferson, Madison, Bradford, Marion, and DeSoto Counties in Florida except for William Henry Jr., who settled in Corsicana, Navarro County, Texas in the 1870s. The 1870 census record shows that none of Mary's household residents could read or write, but it lists two of her younger children as attending school. Later censuses list all of those surviving as being able to read and write. Records show all the boys, including the youngest, Joseph (age eleven), worked on a farm during Reconstruction.

Researchers found no burial records for **Jesse, Henrietta (Hattie), Joseph,** or **Virginia**. Their trails, except possibly for Jesse and Joseph, run cold in 1870.

John Slicer Andrews

After the war, John Slicer returned to Pierce County to his wife Emily and family. Because their local economy was in shambles, the family moved to Marion County, near Ocala, and then to Levy County. They lived there for some time before moving on to Bradford County by 1888, where they permanently settled. They had eleven children. **John** stayed in this area for the rest of his life. None of the rest of the Andrews family settled nearby other than Walkers of unknown origin.

The area they settled is now in Union County. Their first home in Union, according to their family, was two miles south of the Baker County Line near Dowling Lake. One wonders if the lake carries his wife Emeline Dowling's maiden name. Later they moved to Ellerbee, which is now part of where the old state farm dairy was located.

A local doctor described John's condition as chronic bronchitis, a wartime malady, and Emily fought hard to take care of him and her family in the hard years following the war. Thankfully, during the war, she learned on her own how to grow cotton and gin it with a hand gin. Like Mary, she spun it into thread with an old-fashioned wheel, then wove it into cloth on an old hand loom. This is how she fed and clothed her family while John was away.

Their daughters married men by the names of Bryan, Hendricks, and Carroll.

John and Emeline made their final home near the Scout Hole Road, Lake Butler, Florida. John Slicer died of consumption on March 7th, 1896. Emily would live another twenty-four years. They both lie buried at Elzie's Chapel Cemetery in Union County.

Graves of John Slicer and Emeline Andrews

Ellen Lou Andrews

Ellen Andrews Hogg appears to be a widow by 1880 and lives with her sister Florida Mae Andrews Guilfoyle in Precinct 5, Marion County, Florida. They lived in Romeo, which is on US 41 about mid-way between Williston and Dunnellon, west of Ocala in Marion County. Again, there appears to be none of the Andrews family living nearby except for the two sisters.

Ellen's second husband, Thomas Hogg, passed away, too. Ellen died between 1885 and 1900, possibly in Romeo, Florida, where she last lived with her sister Florrie according to the 1885 census. Researchers found no further marriage records.

Florida Mae (Florrie) Andrews

Also living in Romeo was Florida Andrews Hogg, who later married William Timothy Guilfoyle on December 28th, 1867 in Romeo. He was eighteen years her senior. Florrie changed her name to Mary Elizabeth, possibly after her stepmother Mary, who was the only mother she ever really knew.

Several of her daughters never married or died young, but one daughter married into the Loos family.

Florrie died in Romeo, Florida on November 1st, 1926. The death certificate listed her birthday as September 22, 1840. It listed her father as W. A. Andrews and mother as May E. Goff.

Mary Catherine (Florida) Andrews Guilfoyle

Sarah Andrews

Sarah married by July 4, 1872 to Jacob Franklin Hartsfield, and they lived in Precinct 2 of Jefferson County in the Elizabeth area. They had three daughters, named Julia, Sarah, and Adeline, the last possibly named after her mother, Mary Adeline. Researchers believe Sarah died sometime between 1880 and 1882, but they found no death certificate. She may have died giving birth to Adeline. Researchers were unable to find marriages for the daughters or death records. By the time of the 1900 census, Jacob had remarried to a lady named Harriett.

James Jefferson Andrews

Tax lists from Jefferson County show James Jefferson Andrews in 1872, 1878, and 1879. He was still in the county in the 1885 census in District M Eight. He was missing in the 1880 census. Also missing in the 1880 census were **Jesse W., Henrietta, Joseph, and Virginia,** all of Mary's younger children.

James had married Florida Grubbs by February 14, 1872. Earlier, her Grubbs family settled north of US 90 and east of Big Joe Road as early as the 1840s. This may have been what the *Family Friend* newspaper called the Grubbs and Walker community. Her father was John Grubbs and her mother a Kinsey. Their daughters married into the McLeod and Clayton families.

James was a farmer and died November 16, 1908 near Harmony, Florida in Madison County. The Andrews Family Cemetery in Madison County is the burial place of him and many of his descendants. This family has reunions annually.

James and Florida Grubbs Andrews

Valentine E. Andrews

Vollie married again by September 12, 1872 to his second wife Julia "Judy" Kersey. He had moved to Hernando County, Florida to the 5th enumeration district by June 22nd, 1880. Research showed no other family living near them. By 1900, he and the family lived in Pine Level, DeSoto County, Florida. His daughters married into the Easter, Johnson, and Kelly families.

He was a farmer who died on February 18, 1902 and lies buried in the Joshua Creek Cemetery in Arcadia, Florida.

Valentine Andrews

Zechariah (Zachariah, Zachery) Taylor Andrews

Zech was still in Jefferson County in Districts 15, 16, and 17 in June 1880, but he married by October 1, 1874 Elizabeth Telulah "Lizzie" Hammonds. Jefferson County tax lists for 1877 and 1879 include him. He was a farmer and one of the last children to marry.

In 1880, living in his home was a three-month-old daughter named Mary Virginia. One has to ask if he named this child after his mother and baby sister, who were both missing in the 1880 census. His daughters married into the Morris, Henderson, and Worley families.

Zech was one of Mary and William's longest living children. He died on April 24, 1924 in Tuten, Madison County, Florida. His death certificate says his father's name was William and his mother was a Walker.

They buried him in Walker Cemetery #3 on the north side of US 27 between the Aucilla River and Eridu, not too far from one of my tree farms, and on the Old Bellamy Road (Federal Highway #1 also known as the Old St. Augustine Road) between Harmony, Florida in Madison County and US 19 east of Lamont.

Zech and his wife Elizabeth Hammonds Andrews

Jesse W. Andrews

Researchers did not find Jesse W. Andrews in the 1880 census, but a Jesse W. Andrews served as postmaster in Harmony, Madison

County, Florida in 1905. Harmony is near where his brothers, James and Zech, later lived. The search yielded no other records.

Henrietta (possibly Hattie or Hennie) Andrews

Hattie, seventeen in the June 22nd, 1870 census, simply vanishes from history after this. No other later records state her whereabouts. It appears she did not marry in Jefferson County or nearby. Perhaps she lived with older siblings, but researchers found no records or marriage certificates in those locations. The names Hattie and Hennie are nicknames for anyone named Henrietta, and Henrietta's little sister Laura named her first daughter Hattie.

William Henry "Henry" Andrews Jr.

Henry went to Texas when he was twenty-four years of age, where he was working as a laborer in Navarro County in Sub Division E #131 by June 1880. He lived with the William McCarter family. The mother in this family was a Woolf from Jefferson County.

Also moved to Texas and living in the same county was Sarah Walker Pillans, Mary's sister. She lived with one of her daughters and her son-in-law. There are several McCarters, Pillans, and Woolfs in Navarro County in 1880. These families may have moved to Texas together, maybe leaving from Texas Hill in Monticello, named for the many Jefferson County residents who so often gathered there to begin their journey westward. It is here families came to say their goodbyes to those moving west.

Henry would marry three times in Navarro County, outliving his first two wives. The first wife, Cinda Sheppard, died in childbirth in 1884 while Henry was on a cattle drive with the McCarters. She died in the Pillans home.

Henry and Cinda Sheppard Andrews

With his second wife, Martha Beard Floyd, Henry had one son. She died, and his third wife, Annie Bell Boyd, gave Henry nine more children. He may have named his oldest son after his baby brother Joseph and his first daughter after his little sister Laura, who had recently passed away. He may also have named his second son after his father, William. His daughters married into the Jones, Hart, and Burris families.

Henry and Annie Boyd Andrews

Henry lived the longest and died at seventy-six on May 15th, 1932 in nearby Melrose, New Mexico, where he lived with one of his sons. This is near Hereford, Texas, where most of his family settled.

His death certificate appears to have several errors. The death certificate names Fred Andrews as his father, but the family says Fred was the name of his last father-in-law. Henry's second son received the name Fred. Henry's death record also showed the initials "DK" for his mother, signifying "don't know." Nineteen thirty-two was seventy years after

1872, which was believed to be his mother's death. They buried Henry in Melrose Memorial Cemetery.

Henry's oldest son, Joseph Edward Andrews, remained in Hereford, Texas and lived a long life. Apparently, during the Depression, he needed help and approached his banker. The two devised a plan for Joe to recover financially. He borrowed money to drill an irrigation well and bought lots of sheep. According to his descendants, every day Joe took the sheep to a new pasture to graze, where he sat in his car with a jug of water and a sack lunch to wait.

Each evening, he drove his old Ford car back to the barn, followed by a goat named old Pat. The sheep followed the goat, and Joe's sheepdog followed in the rear as the convoy made its way to the home place. Whereupon Joe placed the sheep in his barn for the evening because of coyotes.

The artist, Joe's great granddaughter Lynette Andrews Butler, took some liberties and painted her grandparents' home as she remembered it. She painted the buildings and property, as described by an older generation. Of the home place, on a hill above the Frio Draw south of Hereford, only the foundations of the well house, large hay barn, and a few fence posts remain. Hardly any still living remembered Joe raised sheep during the depression.

Joe passed in 1962.

"Go Pat Go" by Lynette Andrews Butler

Laura R. Andrews

Laura married George Henry Lightsey, grandson of George and Ann Lightsey and son of Henry William Lightsey and Mary Martha Howell in October 1875 at eighteen. He is mentioned several times in the story as the grandson of Ann Lightsey.

Laura gave him one son and three daughters before she died on March 9, 1896 in Monticello at thirty-nine. We're uncertain what the R. stands for in her middle name, but they named one of their daughters Roberta.

Laura probably attended school in Monticello and in the Elizabeth community. She and George could both read and write. According to the 1870 census, it appears the family had enough money to pay for her education even though there was still no public education system during Reconstruction or most of her school years.

Laura Andrews and George Lightsey

By 1880, Laura and George Henry lived in the Elizabeth area of Jefferson County near her sister Sarah and several of her Walker cousins, including Uncle James. They lived in Precinct 2 of Jefferson County, and Laura's and George's descendants still own land in this area today.

As the author, I am a descendant of Laura and George, and I, too, come from Jefferson County. Their daughters married into the Hamrick and Kinsey families.

They buried Laura at Elizabeth Cemetery, the Elizabeth community one at the corner of Old Salt Road and Bassett's Dairy Road, alongside her husband George, who never remarried.

Laura and George both qualified for the Florida State Genealogical Society's Florida Pioneer Descendant Certificate Program as Settlers & Builders of Florida. This is for those who settled or were born in Florida between March 3, 1845 (statehood) and December 31, 1900. Both were born in Florida after 1845 but settled as adults in Florida before 1900. Laura and George are my second great grandparents.

Joseph Andrews

The 1880 census did not list **Joseph Andrews**, but there is a Joseph of the correct age in the 1910 census living near his oldest half-brother, John Slicer, in Bradford County. There is also a Joseph M.

Andrews of the same age married to Esta with one son Gene living in Cedar Key, Levy County, Florida in the 1900 census of that county. He lists himself as a fisherman. This Joseph is also in the 1910 census, but we can find no definitive evidence that this is Joseph Andrews from Jefferson County. This Joseph has relatives who believe he was born in St. Johns County, Florida.

Virginia Andrews

Virginia was nowhere to be found after the 1870 census, when she was seven years old. Like her sister Henrietta and mother Mary, she vanished.

Mary's Siblings and Their Families after 1870

Henry L. Walker appears to have had no children when he died in the mill accident in 1860. When the railroad came through, it is his and J.J.'s mills at Walker Mills, which today are called Drifton. Their father's brother, Uncle Henry, had established one or both mills earlier. The 1860 census showed Henry L. at thirty-five, with personal assets of $12,000, living with several of his brothers and next door to his sister Sarah Jane "Susan" Pillans.

It is uncertain what happened to his wife Julia after he died, nor has anyone found his grave, but we speculate it is in the Old Elizabeth Churchyard Cemetery. Though the later Smiths of Drifton were kin by marriage to a Mary Virginia Walker, nee Hinton, whose husband was John Isham Walker, the youngest son of David and Rebecca Walker, there is no evidence that John Isham ever owned the mills. He was a distant cousin, though, of Mary's.

Sarah Jane "Susan" Walker, who married Isaac Pillans, appears to have died in 1881. Along with several of her Pillans offspring, they moved west to Texas with William and Mary's son Henry Andrews, the McCarters, and the Woolfs. The family in Texas said Susan was a Walker from Jefferson County.

In the 1870 census, she lived in Jefferson County with four children named William H., Jesse B., Walker, and Elizabeth. Except for William H., possibly named after his Uncle William H. Andrews, the other names are common Walker family names. Her daughter married into the Jeffries family.

They buried Susan in Winkler, Texas in Freestone County. Her son William Henry married Edna Surles in Monticello on November 11, 1870 before they moved to Texas. She was the daughter of Major (Mager) Surles and Rebecca Moore.

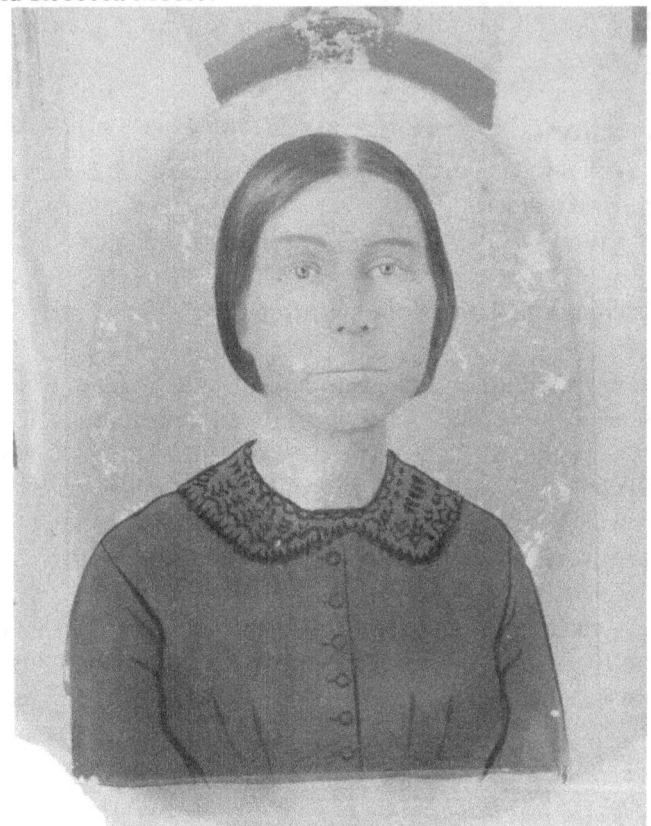

Sarah "Susan" Walker Pillans

James J. "J.J." Walker and Hannah had three children. By the 1870 census he, his wife, and children lived in Madison County. The census listed him as a farm laborer with $4,000 in real estate and $1,035 in personal property. His brother Archibald (Arch) lived with him. His son Joseph H. was only one year old. His daughter married a Henderson.

J.J. passed away in the summer of 1889. His place of burial is unknown, but he may also have been buried in the Old Elizabeth Churchyard Cemetery.

William Allen Walker married Amanda Porter, and they had nine children. He lived until 1901 and died in Tallahassee, where he lived with his daughter at seventy-one. He named one of his sons George Leonard Walker, possibly after his brother George who died in Kentucky during the war. His only surviving daughter married a Wilson.

William's burial place is Roseland Cemetery in Monticello. He lies buried next to his brother-in-law, 2nd Lieutenant Alvin Brainard Munger, a Union soldier. Finley's Brigade, Sons of Confederate Veterans Camp 1614, and the 2nd Infantry Regiment United States Colored Troops Living History Association honored both men with headstones in 2018.

Jane E. Walker is listed in the 1860 census as still living with her father. By May 5th, 1869, it appears she married Dr. William J. Carroll in Madison County, Florida, whose first wife was a distant cousin of Jane's from the second set of Walkers to move into the county.

He and Jane had four children, the oldest boy named Jesse possibly named after her father and the youngest son named David Walker Carroll, possibly after her brother or her Uncle David. Their daughters married into the Brinson and Bonnell families.

She passed away on August 31, 1894 in Suwannee County, Florida, where it appears she lived with her son Charles.

Joseph Walker is an enigma. He is living at home with his parents in the 1850 census in Jefferson County at sixteen, but he disappears before the 1860 census, when he would have been twenty-six. He may have already left home. There are no further records. However, several of his siblings have children whom they named Joseph, including Mary and J.J.

George Walker's last record is his death during the war in Kentucky. He likely rests near Bardstown. His last census record shows him at twenty-five as a carpenter and living with his brothers, but his father also shows him as living at home in the same census. He probably worked both on his father's farm and in his brothers' Walker Mills.

Archibald Jesse "Archie" or "Arch" Walker came home from the war and married Anna Martiel in 1872. They had five children, one of whom was named Agnes Elizabeth, possibly named after his mother.

He lived with his brothers in the 1860 census and probably worked with them in his brothers' mills, but by 1870 he lived with his brother J.J., wife, and children in Madison County. His daughters married into the Prescott, Wimberly, and Cross families.

The 1880 census listed him, Anna, and three of their children as living in Precinct 1 of Suwannee County, Florida, where he died in 1923 at eighty-five. They buried him in the Antioch Cemetery in Live Oak, Florida. The Florida State Genealogical Society, too, deemed him a Florida Pioneer through his descendants.

Arch Walker

William Berry Walker still lived with his father in the 1860 Jefferson County census. He married on January 25, 1871 and died October 4th, 1889.

By the 1870 census, there was a William Walker of the right age who lived with Jane Lightsey, possibly his aunt. His occupation is listed as "farmer." He lived with a twenty-year-old Mary Walker who worked as a cook.

By an 1880 Jefferson County census, W. B. Walker was forty and lived with his wife, Caroline Lightsey Walker, with three children. Joseph was his oldest son and Mary E. his oldest daughter. He also had sons named William Henry Walker and George. His daughters married into the Hamrick and Oglesby families.

William Berry Walker

His wife was the granddaughter of Ann Lightsey, sister-in-law of the Jane Lightsey mentioned earlier. This means his wife Caroline was the sister of George Henry Lightsey, who married Laura. So after the marriage, Laura's Uncle Berry was also her brother-in-law. Oh, the tangled web! The offspring of both William Berry's marriage and Laura's marriage are double kin.

Berry and Caroline had eight children, and he died October 4th, 1889 in Aucilla. They buried him and his wife in the Old Elizabeth Churchyard Cemetery.

David L. Walker as a young man lived with his father before the war, though records also show him living with his brothers at Walkers Mills, where he attended the Davis Academy. He survived the war, and his prisoner-of-war release took place at Rock Island, Illinois. Records showed him at 5' 10 1/2" tall, fair with light hair and gray eyes. They captured David at Missionary Ridge; however, like William, he disappeared at the war's end after they paroled him in Madison. This proves, though, that unlike William, he returned home from the war.

Mary's Walker Uncles and Aunt

Mary's Uncle **James W. Walker**, who was closest in age to her father, lived a long life and never left Jefferson County. He and Elizabeth Padgett Walker had ten children in twenty-two years. Their daughters married into the Bishop, Bell, Howell, and Smythe families.

His daughter Clifford, who married a Bishop, had thirteen children. Her daughters married into the Clark, Sledge, and Scruggs families.

Her father James died on February 13, 1886 at eighty-three. He and Elizabeth are buried in the Old Elizabeth Churchyard Cemetery, and their graves are marked.

James Walker

Mary's Aunt **Mary Jane Walker** married Stephen Lightsey, brother of George, husband of Ann Lightsey. Stephen and Mary Jane had eight children in eighteen years, seven boys and one girl. They lost one son to the Civil War and possibly another. Two sons moved to Texas. Their daughter Mary A. Lightsey died at the age of three. Stephen died in 1860 and Mary Jane in 1890. Mary Jane lived to be eighty-two years old.

Mary's Uncle **Littleberry Walker** lived a long life. He died after 1885 but before 1892. He and Mary Ann Kinsey had ten children, most of whom remained in Jefferson County, except two daughters whose husbands moved them to Manatee County. One married a Clair and the other a Hampton. Littleberry and Mary Ann's oldest daughter married a McClelland, and their youngest married a Harp.

Mary's Uncle **David Walker,** who was like a brother to her, was forty-two when the war began. He married his second wife, Caroline Goodman. The census listed him as a farmer. They had eight children. He had another daughter by an earlier marriage, Sarah Elizabeth Walker, who married William Samuel May. His other daughters married into the Farquhar and Moore families.

Mary's Uncle David fought with the Kilcrease Light Artillery as a private, as did his brother J.J. Records show he survived the war and also received parole in Madison County, Florida. The 1870 census lacked a record for him, but it listed his wife and children still living in Jefferson County.

He may have died before this date and possibly lies buried in the Old Elizabeth Baptist Churchyard Cemetery. By 1880, his wife is in Navasota, Grimes County, Texas. She lived with her fifteen-year-old daughter Rosa and her son Stephen Jesse Walker. Their daughters Frances and Harriet died in childhood. Emma married and moved to Navasota, Texas, too.

Senter. *Navasota, Texas.*

Rosa Walker, wife of Robert Moore Jr.

Mary's **Uncle Joel Walker** died young at the age of thirty-six in 1859. A former Jefferson County sheriff, he left behind his wife Betsy Howell and five children. Their daughters married into the Shepherd, Kinsey, Divine, and Thomas families.

Jefferson County, home to both the Andrews and Walker families, began as a thriving planter economy—its leading figures often descended from the nation's forefathers. Today it is a rural, quiet county without a single stop light—the last county of its kind in the great state of Florida. According to the last census in 2020, its population was 14,510, with 5,816 households and 3,762 families living in the county, many of whom are descendants of its earlier settlers.

Current Jefferson County courthouse, built in 1904 on the site of the last courthouse in the story

#

Appendix I
Which David?

There were several David Walkers. Mary's Uncle David S. Walker was also her childhood playmate. There is also Mary's baby brother David L. Walker and Mary's distant cousin David M. Walker, who moved to Jefferson County in the 1850s.

Still, there are other problems. There are three service muster roll cards for David S. Walker, the first of which at the bottom says, "*See also 3 Florida Inf. as David L. Walker.*" It appears the Confederate authorities confused David S. and David L. with each other.

Three cards show David S., Mary's uncle, enlisted on December 11, 1862 in Monticello under Captain Stockton for the war. Another card says December 11, 1861 in Monticello by Captain Stockton for the war. It says they transferred him to the 3rd Regiment in February 1862, about the same time they recorded him absent without leave on the 5th.

On the third card, David L., Mary's baby brother, enlisted on December 11, 1862 in Monticello under Captain Bailey for the war (this would be the 5th Florida). It says they transferred him to the 3rd Regiment Florida Volunteers on the 1st day of May 1862. The cards need to be clarified, and therefore we think they confused these two David Walkers frequently in record keeping. Also, did they transfer him seven months before he enlisted?

When studied, records show Uncle David S. Walker was in the Kilcrease Light Artillery and later transferred to the Florida 1st Battalion. Brother David L. Walker was in the 5th Florida, Company A.

It is unclear to which company Mary's cousin David M. Walker belonged.

#

Appendix 2
1870 Census: Growth of the Town and County

Even with the ravages of War, Jefferson County grew another thirty-six percent between 1860 and 1870 to a population 13,968 residents while a new Florida emerged with a very different social, political, and economic order. In the 1860 census, Jefferson County had a population of 9,876 people.

By 1870, there were thirty-nine counties in the state, with Alachua County leading in population, followed by Leon, Jefferson, Duval, Madison, and Marion. Alachua and Marion Counties grew quickly because of the Armed Occupation Act passed before 1860 and the sale of the massive Arredondo Spanish Land Grant which had covered almost 300,000 acres in Alachua County.

By 1870, there were 187,748 people living in the state—96,057 whites and 91,689 coloreds. The state's population in 1860 was 140,424 people—77,747 whites and 62,677 coloreds.

In Jefferson County, by 1860, the county had fifty-five plantations with thirty or more slaves each. It was second only to Leon County in numbers of plantations or slaves. After emancipation, the number of former slaves was large and growing. Where before in 1860, 64% of Jefferson County was black, by 1870, its black population had increased to 72%. So many plantations in Georgia and South Carolina were destroyed, unlike those in Florida, which is one reason Florida's and Jefferson County's Freedmen population may have grown.

The 1870 map of Monticello reflects very little of that growth, as it appears much fewer businesses opened than did during the decade between 1850 and 1860. Documents reflect only three buildings built between 1860 and 1870.

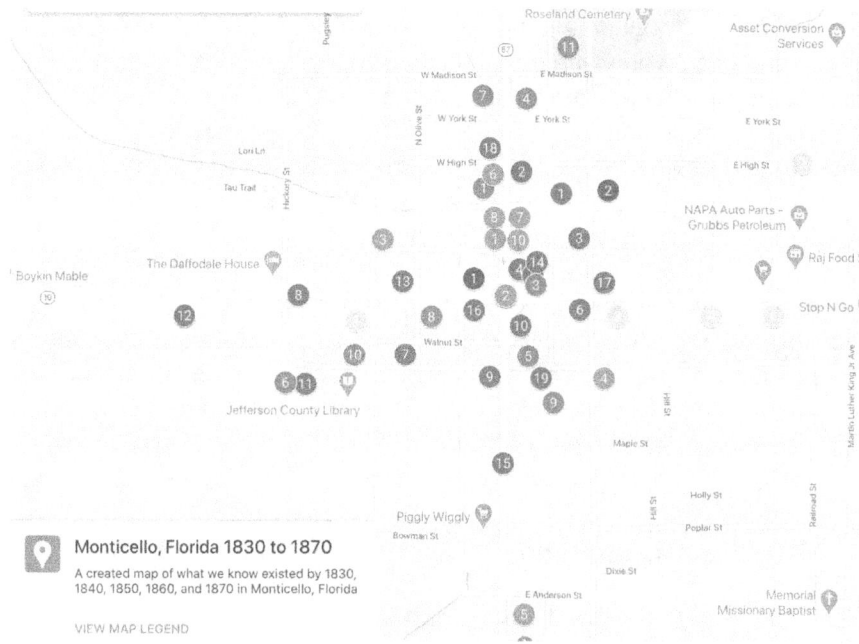

Monticello, Florida 1830 to 1870
A created map of what we know existed by 1830,
1840, 1850, 1860, and 1870 in Monticello, Florida

VIEW MAP LEGEND

Green Disks - Buildings Built Between 1820 and 1830
Blue Disks - Buildings Built Between 1830 and 1840
Maroon Disks - Buildings Built Between 1840 and 1850
Yellow Disks - Buildings Built Between 1850 and 1860
Purple Disks - Buildings Built Between 1860 and 1870

1870: Population 13,968—Jefferson County grew by 3,522 people, for a thirty-six percent overall growth

Businesses and Buildings Added Between 1860 and 1870 - Purple Disks

1. Simon and Simon sold their building and moved to the brick building and warehouse erected by Edward B. Bailey and later occupied by Carroll. This sat on the courthouse square where the *Monticello News* currently sits facing W. Washington St. This may have been an existing building.

2. Howard School–The Freedmen's Bureau built this school with their money in 1868 on Pearl Street between Pinhook (now Waukeenah) and Howard Street (now Magnolia). It was constructed of wood, and the nearby Bethel AME church congregation spurred its creation. The church

held school in its building until the construction of Howard School. Many Bethel members volunteered their labor. It opened in October of that year and charged one dollar per student. Jefferson Academy received Peabody Funding support and only charged fifty cents per student. Grunwell thought the Bureau or the state should do more, so he went to the community's white leaders and raised enough money to support two more teachers. The school soon had 100 students.

 3. Bethel AME Church—Built after 1865, Robert Meacham, a freedman from Quincy, served as its pastor and later served as a state senator for Jefferson County from 1868 to 1878. Bethel's members created the original church on its current site. It was the site of the first freedmen's school in Monticello. After the original church burned, they built the present building in 1975.

Businesses and Buildings Added (Unknown Locations)

 4. Darius Williams Mercantile moved to a new unknown location.

 5. Denham and Palmer continued in business until William Denham's death in 1874. Location Unknown.

 6. John Tatum opened a store after the war. Location Unknown.

 7. Reid & Turnbull. Location Unknown.

#

Appendix 3
The Four George Walkers

This is a list of the George Walkers from Jefferson County that we know of. It was difficult to tease them apart, but their Confederate enlistment dates and places helped.

Mary's brother George of the 3rd Florida Infantry, Company H, died in Kentucky near Bardstown.

A second George Walker in the same regiment but in a different company also died near Bardstown just after they left the city. He was from Jacksonville.

George R. (Raysor) Walker died at Gettysburg and was the son of David M. Walker of Jefferson County.

Another George Walker died of his wounds at Chickamauga and was the son of James Sims Walker from Jefferson County. He also served in the same regiment as the others, but in Company H, the same company as Mary's brother, the earlier deceased George. This George Walker had a sister, Anna Martiel Walker, who married Mary's brother Archibald (Arch) Jesse Walker.

His father identified this George in a later plea for monetary help. We are unsure how this George is related to Mary's family except through marriage.

It was unlucky to be a George Walker from Jefferson County.

#

Appendix 4
Family Trees

Mary and Her Husband's Family Tree
William Henry Andrews Family (all the children Mary raised)

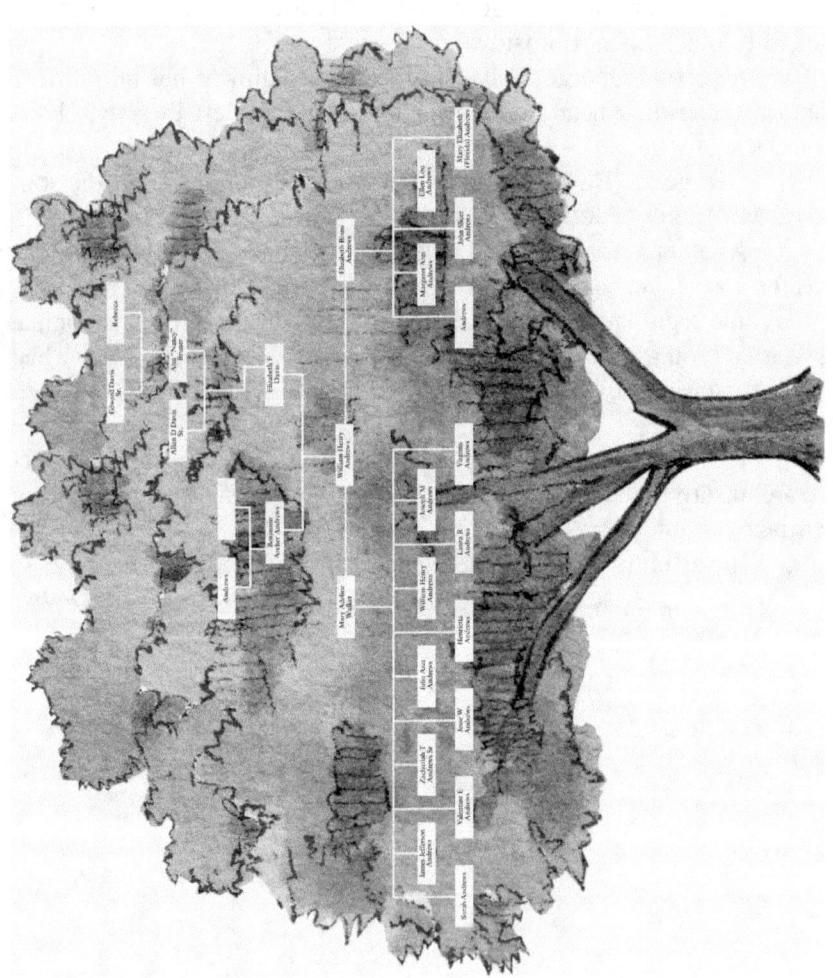

Mary's Parents and Siblings
Jesse and Elizabeth Walker Family Tree

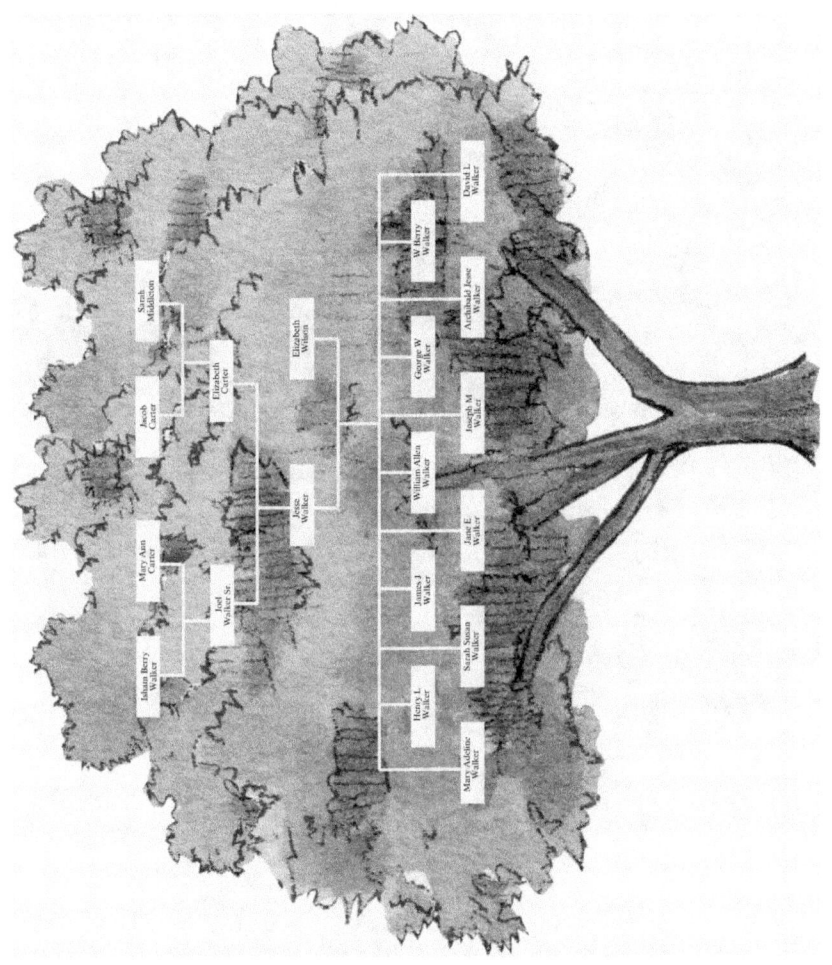

Mary's Walker Grandparents
Joel Senior* and Elizabeth Walker Family Tree

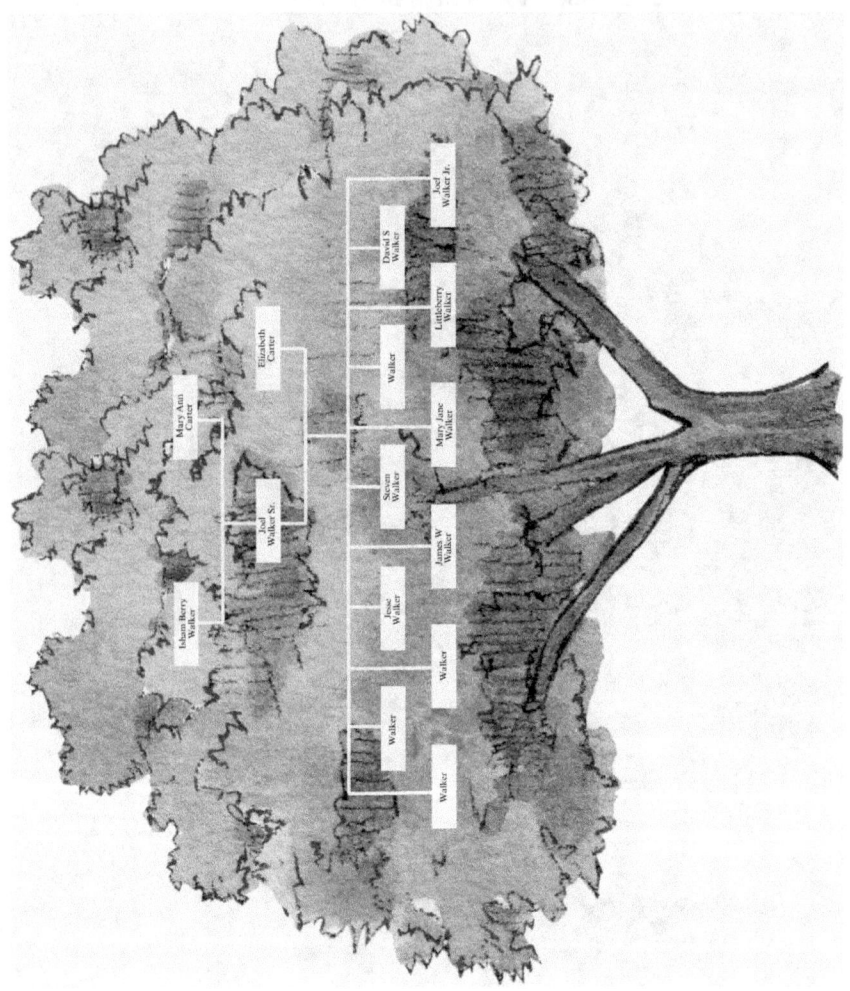

*There is no evidence that Mary's grandfather Joel Walker ever used the title "Senior" or that his son was known as "Junior." These designations appear to have been added later by genealogists simply as a way to distinguish between the two men.

Afterword

Thank you for reading *Yankees in the Courthouse*. I hope you enjoyed this book as much as I enjoyed writing it.

Keep an eye out for my next series, *Florida's Builders & Movers*, stories about later generations of Lightseys and introducing a new family called the Hamricks. It covers the time between the 1880s and the 1920s, when one of Mary and William's grandchildren leave North Florida to move to South Florida to another unsettled area of the state. Also, I plan to write a middle-grade children's book about Mary's life before she married. My goal is to publish it in 2026.

If you have a moment, please leave a rating for the *Palmetto Pioneers* books at any online store that carries them. A rating requires nothing more than rating it by stars, no written review is necessary. A review means leaving several sentences letting everyone know what you liked about the book. I am asking for a rating only, but I would value a written review if you have time. Help other nonfiction historical readers by telling them why you enjoyed the book.

Please remember to visit the *Palmetto Pioneers* website at https://www.palmettopioneers.com, where you can find more information about the series, its characters, and its places.

Want to stay updated with news about this series?

- ❖ Join my mailing list at: https://www.palmettopioneers.com/
- ❖ Like me on Facebook at: https://www.facebook.com/CindyRoeLittlejohn.Author
- ❖ Follow me on Instagram at: https://www.instagram.com/PalmettoPioneers
- ❖ Follow me on Tiktok at https://www.tiktok.com/@palmetto.pioneers?lang=en

Thank you again, dear reader, and I hope we meet again between the pages of another book.

About the Author

Cindy Roe Littlejohn was born in Thomasville, Georgia, at the nearest hospital to Monticello, Florida. Her parents brought her home to Monticello two days after her birth.

With residences in Tallahassee and Wakulla County, Florida, she has mostly lived in Monticello, where she is married to Chuck Littlejohn. They raised a son and two daughters. They now have seven grandchildren.

Acknowledgments

My research stands on the shoulders of so many others. I was fortunate to have worked with all the following relatives and researchers:

Thank you to the late Andy Andrews, whose ancestor was John Slicer Andrews, who has descendants who spread across central Florida; to the late Julius "Sonny" Williams, whose ancestor was James Jefferson Andrews of Madison County, Florida; to the late Clint Andrews and Lynette Andrews, whose ancestor was William "Henry" Andrews Jr., our Texas cousins; to Vicki Cureton and her brother Ray Diehl of Tallahassee, whose ancestor was Zachery "Zech" Taylor Andrews.

Thank you to the late Anita Griffin Collins and Donna Wiehaus for their Walker family research; to the late Mrs. Theo Delp who cataloged all the known cemeteries in Jefferson County, Florida; to the Jefferson County research of the late Jerrell H. Shofner commissioned by the Jefferson County Historical Society; and to the men and women of the wonderful Works Progress Agency from the Great Depression who wrote a book about Jefferson County during that era.

Much thanks to Wesley Pippenger and his expertise in Washington, DC research; and to Ancestry's ProGenealogists, who reviewed my research and identified no further records on William but found three records overlooked for Mary. They also identified other records, but we found no further information.

Thank you to Ronald Wirick, a native Jefferson Countian whose family reaches back as far as mine and who was always on the lookout for my family and its allied surnames. To the late Derylene "Dee" Counts, who knew more about Jefferson County than I can ever learn and who edited the first two books for local historical content. To my high school classmate and friend David Ward, who came to my rescue and read this third book for local historical accuracy. His knowledge of the county's history trumps mine. To Tallahasseean John Clark, who edited the first book for territorial Florida historical content. And to all the volunteer staff in the Genealogy Room of the Jefferson County Library, who come together to open the room every Wednesday from 10 to 3. To the late Joan Linn, its director, whom I just loved and whose ancestors were the Grays massacred in the first book.

My sincere thanks to my friend, author, and Civil War historian Clint Johnson, who has written eight nonfiction books on the war. Johnson, born in Fish Branch, Florida in Hardee County, now lives in the

North Carolina mountains, but he and I worked in the 1970s for a lobbyist and association manager named Bill Owens in Tallahassee. Clint edited the last two books in the series for Civil War accuracy.

My greatest gratitude to the late Dr. James Sledge, who spent hours with me and provided photos and research I had never seen before he passed earlier this year at 100. I believe that his ancestor James Walker was Jesse's closest brother because they were older and closer in age than the rest. James Sledge is a descendant of James Walker, as I am a descendant of Jesse, Mary's father; but Dr. Sledge, who was also my childhood dentist, was the only person allowed to read the full manuscript of all three books in their very first draft. He was very elderly at well over ninety years of age, and the book took over six years to research and write. Toward the end of writing, one day he said, "Cindy, if you don't finish this book soon, I'll die and never get to read it." He got to read all three books of the series first.

I am extra thankful for my Walker cousin Linda Gramling Demott, who spent hours with me going over family documents and Elizabeth Baptist Church documents. Her help was invaluable.

Thank you to my friend John Finlayson, who spent an afternoon with me talking and looking over old documents that his family has. His family lived across the Aucilla River from the Walkers. We speculated why the two families never seemed to cross in documentation or otherwise. We talked about how the road across the Aucilla then was Sandy Ford and that both families lived far north of that road. I think, though, that John's family was in a different class. Jesse Walker was a cattleman while the Finlaysons married the Shehees, who were in plantation society. Jesse and his brothers were yeomen farm families, the middle-class of that era. The Walkers worked their land with their families and hired hands.

Many thanks to the late Mary Elizabeth Brown and her late mother Mary Jane Hartsfield Brown Lightsey, both of whom passed before the book was even in its first draft. They showed me a picture of William and Mary Andrews's daughter Laura and her husband George Lightsey. Since daughters often look like their mothers, this is the picture I used to describe Mary. The first time I saw this picture, I saw the resemblance between her and my mother, Laura's great granddaughter.

Years later, Mary Jane Hartsfield Lightsey's stepdaughter, my cousin, the late Doris Jean Lightsey Wright, provided a copy of the photo. The two earlier mentioned women gave me rich material about the Lightseys and the Hamricks. Both families lived down the road from the

Walkers during this antebellum period, during the War, and after the War. Mary's granddaughter married a Hamrick, and I am an offspring of that union. When interviewed, both women lived on Lightsey land bought from our nation's government in the 1830s, land still owned by a Lightsey.

Thank you to my Hamrick cousin, Bubba Greene, and his wife Maria of Madison, Florida, who were always on the lookout for photos and documents from that era.

A special thank you to Frankie Smith Rosie, who is a distant Walker cousin. She read the first book and offered valuable information I did not know. For example, in the first book, I questioned whether the Walker families might have built a fort for protection during the Second Seminole Indian War. Frankie shared her memories of their evening walks on her grandparents' farm with her Grandmother Elizabeth "Lizzie" Walker Stanley. Aunt Lizzie described a family fort near the Fort Pond. When Frankie was a young girl, one could still see scattered logs and tree trunks where the fort once stood by the pond. The family named the pond Fort Pond. The land initially belonged to Mary's Uncle James Walker.

Also, a special thank you to Bruce Warren, another Walker cousin, who allowed me and Linda Demott an opportunity to walk around the pond one winter day. It was a wonderful experience. As far as we know, the Walkers faced no attacks during the war.

The Fort Pond, Personal Photo

Thank you to the late Auley Rowell from Perry, Taylor County, Florida, next door to Jefferson County, who read the first book and shared information he discovered many years ago. His Jefferson County ancestor is William Rowell, who is in the book and who married Peniopy McSwain Hamrick, my third great grandmother from another lineage who moved to the county after statehood.

While working on the Rowell genealogy for his family, he and his son made a trip to visit the late Mrs. Ethel Hartsfield Lewis, who was born in Jefferson County in 1898 and attended Elizabeth Baptist Church since she was a child.

Mrs. Lewis told Auley the first Elizabeth Baptist Church building burned. Before this information, none of us in Jefferson County remembered what happened to the first church. We only knew that the site of the current church is not where the first church was located. She also told him that all its records burned, too. Many thanks to Auley for sharing this information. It was important to the second book, especially since he also shared the approximate date it burned.

Again, a sincere thank you to my dear friend and watercolor artist Susan Starbuck Rissman, who painted the artwork for the cover, and to my sweet niece, Hannah McDonald Dryka, who created the cover's graphic design. Thank you both so much!

My profound thanks to Lynn Palermo with The Family History Writing Studio who taught me this new genre of writing called "creative nonfiction." She has helped hundreds of family historians turn their research into entertaining and shareable stories.

This book is in a style of writing called "creative nonfiction." Also known as narrative nonfiction, it uses literary styles and techniques to create accurate narratives. Although I remained faithful to the research, passing over a century and a half erased many memories forever. These stories are like heirlooms, passed from generation to generation. Where necessary, I used the research and my imagination to fill in the gaps. The essence, though, related here is true, as related by biographies, diaries, journals, and other research.

I got rich material from the 2016 Great Florida Cattle Drive, a reenactment of an 1850s drive. It offered an opportunity to go on a fifty-mile cattle drive and provided wonderful information to recreate the Walkers who pushed their foundation herd from South Carolina to Florida. Many thanks to Doyle Conner Jr., for his untiring work to preserve the heritage of Florida's cattle industry.

My sweet husband Chuck never failed me and listened to hours ad nauseam about this family. One day we were walking on a battlefield northwest of Atlanta when he took a phone call from his boat motor mechanic who worked with us for decades. Chuck told him, "Pete, we're walking a Civil War battlefield." Then, when Chuck thought I was out of earshot, I heard him say, "No, Pete, it is not that interesting." Thank you, Chuck, for always persevering!

This author believes this subject is exhausted—at least until someone finds something buried in an attic, an unopened box, or releases information someone has withheld.

Bibliography

Media

Appomattox Campaign. Wikipedia, June 1, 2025. https://en.wikipedia.org/w/index.php?title=Appomattox_campaign&oldid=1293455797.

Appomattox Campaign of the American Civil War, *Drawn in Adobe Illustrator CS5 by Hal Jespersen. Graphic Source File Is Available at Http://Www.Posix.com/CWmaps/.* March 31, 2011. Own work. https://commons.wikimedia.org/wiki/File:Appomattox_Campaign_Overview.png

Atlanta Campaign - Kennesaw Mountain National Battlefield Park (U.S. National Park Service). Accessed July 1, 2025. https://www.nps.gov/kemo/learn/historyculture/the-atlanta-campaign.htm.

Barnard, George N. *City of Atlanta, Ga., No. 2.* 1863. Graphic. PH - Barnard (G.), no. 46 (B size) [P&P]. Library of Congress Prints and Photographs Division Washington, D.C. 20540 USA http://hdl.loc.gov/loc.pnp/pp.print. https://www.loc.gov/resource/ppmsca.33069/.

Barry Lawrence Ruderman Map Collection - Spotlight Exhibits. "Florida Map by J. Lee Williams, 1837." Accessed July 1, 2025. https://exhibits.stanford.edu/ruderman/catalog/yc980cc9111.

"Battle of Antietam." Wikipedia, June 28, 2025. https://en.wikipedia.org/w/index.php?title=Battle_of_Antietam&oldid=1297713471.

"Battle of Atlanta." Wikipedia, June 1, 2025. https://en.wikipedia.org/w/index.php?title=Battle_of_Atlanta&oldid=1293333604.

"Battle of Bentonville." Wikipedia, January 22, 2025. https://en.wikipedia.org/w/index.php?title=Battle_of_Bentonville&oldid=1271053078.

"Battle of Chickamauga." Wikipedia, June 3, 2025. https://en.wikipedia.org/w/index.php?title=Battle_of_Chickamauga&oldid=1293689687.

"Battle of Davis's Cross Roads." Wikipedia, June 1, 2025. https://en.wikipedia.org/w/index.php?

title=Battle_of_Davis%27s_Cross_Roads&oldid=129345642
1.

"Battle of Franklin." Wikipedia, July 1, 2025. https://
en.wikipedia.org/w/index.php?
title=Battle_of_Franklin&oldid=1298339283.

"Battle of Kennesaw Mountain." Wikipedia, June 3, 2025. https://
en.wikipedia.org/w/index.php?
title=Battle_of_Kennesaw_Mountain&oldid=1293825466.

"Battle of Nashville and the City's Historic Bass Neighborhood (U.S.
National Park Service)." Accessed July 1, 2025. https://
www.nps.gov/articles/000/protecting-legacy-battle-of-
nashville-and-bass-neighborhood.htm.

"Battle of Spotsylvania Court House." Wikipedia, May 21, 2025.
https://en.wikipedia.org/w/index.php?
title=Battle_of_Spotsylvania_Court_House&oldid=12914961
09.

"Battle of Stones River." Wikipedia, June 3, 2025. https://
en.wikipedia.org/w/index.php?
title=Battle_of_Stones_River&oldid=1293825590.

"Battle of the Wilderness." Wikipedia, June 3, 2025. https://
en.wikipedia.org/w/index.php?
title=Battle_of_the_Wilderness&oldid=1293689599.

"BATTLE_OF_PEACHTREE_CREEK.jpg (1318×1760)." Accessed
July 1, 2025. https://upload.wikimedia.org/wikipedia/
commons/d/d9/BATTLE_OF_PEACHTREE_CREEK.jpg.

Boetticher, Otto. *Union Prisoners at Salisbury, N.C.* Graphic. New
York: Published by Goupil [...], January 1, 1863. PGA -
Sarony, Major & Knapp—Union prisoners [...] (D size)
[P&P]. Library of Congress Prints and Photographs Division
Washington, D.C. 20540 USA http://hdl.loc.gov/loc.pnp/
pp.print. https://www.loc.gov/resource/pga.02608/.

"Chattanooga Campaign Battles November 24-25.pdf - Wikipedia,"
December 24, 2022. https://commons.wikimedia.org/wiki/
File:Chattanooga_Campaign_Battles_November_24-25.pdf.

City of Atlanta, 1864, Peachtree Road, *photo by George Barnard,
official Army photographer during the war, Library of
Congress*

Franklin-Nashville Campaign of the American Civil.
*War,*en.wikipedia, User:Andrein at. *October-December 1864.*
November 22, 2008. Own work. https://

commons.wikimedia.org/wiki/File:Franklin-
Nashville_campaign.svg.

Florida, State Library and Archives of. "Battle of Olustee Florida
Memory • Kurz and Allison Lithographic Print of the Battle at
Olustee - Olustee Battlefield, Florida." Florida Memory.
Accessed July 1, 2025. https://www.floridamemory.com/
items/show/154548.

"Forrest's West Tennessee Raid Historical Marker." Accessed July 1,
2025. https://www.hmdb.org/m.asp?m=72213.

Frank Leslie's Illustrated Newspaper. *Camp Chase, Columbus, Ohio
—Prison of the Rebels Captured by U. S. Forces*. February 6,
1862. Library of Congress Catalog: https://lccn.loc.gov/
2007675765 Image download. Original url: https://
tile.loc.gov/storage-services/service/pnp/ppmscd/
00000/00001v.jpg

"Franklin–Nashville Campaign."Wikipedia, June14, 2025. https://
en.wikipedia.org/w/index.php?
title=Franklin%E2%80%93Nashville_campaign&oldid=1295
508866.

Gibson, James F. ; Civil War Glass. *Field Hospital after the Battle of
Savage Station, Va. June 27*. 1862. https://
commons.wikimedia.org/wiki/
File:Savage_Station,_Va._Field_hospital_after_the_battle_of
_June_27_LOC_cwpb.01063.jpg.

Siege of Petersburg of the American Civil War, Capture of the Weldon
Railroad. *August 18-19, 1864*. Drawn in Adobe Illustrator
CS5 by Hal Jespersen Graphic. March 26, 2011. Hal
Jespersen's Wikipedia Civil War Maps https://
commons.wikimedia.org/wiki/File:Petersburg_Aug18-19.png.

Jaxson, The. "Jacksonville - Civil War Photography of Jacksonville,"
February 18, 2022. https://www.thejaxsonmag.com/article/
the-civil-war-photography-of-jacksonville/.

"Kentucky-Tennessee, 1861 Confederate Withdrawal from Kentucky
to Stones River." Accessed July 1, 2025. https://
s3.amazonaws.com/usma-media/inline-images/academics/
academic_departments/history/AmCivWar/
ACW17Combined.jpg.

Library of Congress, Washington, D.C. 20540 USA. "Atlanta and
Vicinity." Image. Accessed July 1, 2025. https://www.loc.gov/
resource/g3924a.cw0144200/.

Library of Congress, Washington, D.C. 20540 USA. "Atlanta, Ga. Civilians Crowded on Tops of Boxcars at Railroad Depot as Soldiers Gather around an S.D. Goodale & Sons Stereoscopic Viewer next to Office of the Daily Intelligencer Newspaper]." Image. Accessed July 1, 2025. https://www.loc.gov/item/2018666984/.

Library of Congress, Washington, D.C. 20540 USA. "Distribution of the Slave Population of the Southern States of the United States. Compiled from the Census of 1860." Image. Accessed July 1, 2025. https://www.loc.gov/resource/g3861e.cw0013200/.

Library of Congress, Washington, D.C. 20540 USA. "Olustee [Ocean Pond] and Raids on Jacksonville)." Image. Accessed July 1, 2025. https://www.loc.gov/resource/g3701sm.gcw0094500/?sp=22.

Library of Congress, Washington, D.C. 20540 USA. "The Snowball Battle near Dalton, Georgia." Image. Accessed July 1, 2025. https://www.loc.gov/item/2004660878/.

"Richmond 1862.jpg." Wikipedia, October 26, 2017 https://en.wikipedia.org/w/index.php?title=File:Richmond_1862.jpg&oldid=807150529.

"Salt Works - Division of Historical Resources - Florida Department of State." Accessed June 21, 2023. https://dos.myflorida.com/historical/museums/historical-museums/united-connections/foodways/food-in-wartime/civil-war-salt-works/.

"Siege of Petersburg." Wikipedia, June 27, 2025. https://en.wikipedia.org/w/index.php?title=Siege_of_Petersburg&oldid=1297643482.

"Southern Bread Riots." Wikipedia, April 2, 2025. https://en.wikipedia.org/w/index.php?title=Southern_bread_riots&oldid=1283518224.

Team, 50FISH Dev. "Winter Is Coming." Civil War Monitor, December 15, 2017. https://www.civilwarmonitor.com/winter-is-coming/.

"The Fall of Chattanooga - Braggs Counterattack, 1863." Accessed July 1, 2025. https://s3.amazonaws.com/usma-media/inline-images/academics/academic_departments/history/AmCivWar/ACW41

Waud, William. "Prisoners of War Exchanging Their Rags for New Clothing on Board Flag of Truce Boat New York." Image.

Library of Congress, January 1, 1864. https://
loc.getarchive.net/media/returned-prisoners-of-war-
exchanging-their-rags-for-new-clothing-on-board-flag-2.

Research—The War Between the States 1862-1865

"2nd Battalion, Florida Infantry (Confederate) Genealogy -
FamilySearch Wiki." Accessed July 9, 2019. https://
www.familysearch.org/wiki/en/
2nd_Battalion,_Florida_Infantry_(Confederate)

"4th Regiment Florida Infantry1." Accessed September 25, 2017.
http://www.rootsweb.ancestry.com/~gatroup2/
fl4threginfantry1.html.

"11th Florida Infantry." Wikipedia, August 22, 2018. https://
en.wikipedia.org/w/index.php?
title=11th_Florida_Infantry&oldid=856031549.

"11th Regiment, Florida Infantry (Confederate) Genealogy -
FamilySearch Wiki." Accessed October 24, 2019. https://
www.familysearch.org/wiki/en/
11th_Regiment,_Florida_Infantry_(Confederate).

"Amazon.com: Historical Findings Photo: Pocotaligo, Railroad
Station, South Carolina, American Civil War, Theodore
Davis: Home & Kitchen." Accessed October 21, 2019. https://
www.amazon.com/HistoricalFindings-Photo-Pocotaligo-
Railroad-Carolina/dp/B00UGDSVFC.

American Battlefield Trust. "Battle of Natural Bridge Facts &
Summary," December 19, 2008. https://www.battlefields.org/
learn/civil-war/battles/natural-bridge.

American Battlefield Trust. "Battle of Rocky Face Ridge Facts &
Summary," June 14, 2012. https://www.battlefields.org/learn/
civil-war/battles/rocky-face-ridge.

American Battlefield Trust. "Bennett Place Surrender," October 23,
2018. https://www.battlefields.org/learn/articles/bennett-
place-surrender.

American Battlefield Trust. "Wilderness - May 6, 1864," October 20,
2009. https://www.battlefields.org/learn/maps/wilderness-
may-6-1864.

American Battlefield Trust. "Winter Encampments." Accessed April 24, 2025. https://www.battlefields.org/learn/articles/winter-encampments.

"American Civil War Soldiers - Ancestry.com."Accessed April 5, 2021 https://www.ancestry.com/search/collections/3737/records/2933182?ssrc=pt&tid=23894133&pid=1441728990

"Ancestry.com - U.S., Civil War Prisoner of War Records, 1861-1865." Accessed April 5, 2021. https://www.ancestry.com/imageviewer/collections/1124/images/M598_46-0227?pId=356557.

"Ancestry.com - U.S., Confederate Army Casualty Lists and Reports, 1861-1865." Accessed April 5, 2021. https://www.ancestry.com/imageviewer/collections/2401/images/33124_b042407-00631?pId=55455.

Anderson, James Patton. "Southern Historical Society Papers, Volume 24, Autobiography of James Patton Anderson, C. S. A.," 1896. zotero://attachment/199/.

Andrews, W. H. *Footprints of a Regiment: A Recollection of the 1st Georgia Regulars, 1861-1865*. Taylor Trade Publishing, 1992.

"Battle of Appomattox Court House." Wikipedia, October 15, 2019. https://en.wikipedia.org/w/index.php?title=Battle_of_Appomattox_Court_House&oldid=921437587.

"Battle of Jonesborough." Wikipedia, February 15, 2022. https://en.wikipedia.org/w/index.php?title=Battle_of_Jonesborough&oldid=1072035305.

Battle of Nashville. Accessed October 24,2025. Wikipedia. https://en.wikipedia.org/wiki/Battle_of_Nashville.

"Battle of Natural Bridge Florida. Accessed October 24, 2019. American Battlefield Trust. https://www.battlefields.org/learn/civil-war/battles/natural-bridge.

"Battle of Olustee." Wikipedia, October 22, 2019. https://en.wikipedia.org/w/index.php?title=Battle_of_Olustee&oldid=922508095.

"Battle of Olustee Festival: Revisionist History Where Black Lives Didn't & Still Don't Matter." Accessed October 24, 2019. http://www.columbiacountyobserver.com/master_files/Florida_News_2015/19_0128_battle-of-olustee.html.

"Battle of Stones River - Wikipedia, the Free Encyclopedia."
    Accessed March 3, 2015. http://en.wikipedia.org/wiki/
    Battle_of_Stones_River.

"Campaign of the Carolinas." Wikipedia, October 9, 2019 https://
    en.wikipedia.org/w/index.php?
    title=Campaign_of_the_Carolinas&oldid=920438749.

Cash, W. T. "Taylor County History and Civil War Deserters." *Florida
    Historical Quarterly*, n.d. "Widow's Pension Claim Valentine
    Andrews." Accessed April 5, 2021.

Charles, Harry K. "American Civil War Postage Due: North and
    South," February 15, 2016. http://stamps.org/userfiles/file/
    symposium/presentations/CharlesPaper.pdf. *Confederate
    Veteran*. 4th ed. Vol. 20, 1912.

Counts, Derylene Delp. "How Did Grandma Make Do?" Jefferson
    County Historical Association, Winter 2025.

"Cuthbert Cemetery, Randolph County, GA - Confederate Dead."
    Accessed January 12, 2018. http://files.usgwarchives.net/ga/
    military/civilwar/other/cuthbert.txt.

Daily Dispatch, accessed 7/22/2025, https://dispatch.richmond.edu/
    1862/1/29/1/5?utm_source=chatgpt.com.

Department of Military Affairs. "Florida's Soldiers Beyond the
    Borders 1861-1865," June 15, 2012. http://
    dma.myflorida.com/floridas-soldiers-beyond-the-
    borders-1861-1865/.

Woodward, Eddie. "West Florida Seminary Cadets at the Battle of
    Natural Bridge." *Illuminations* (blog), March 6, 2013. https://
    fsuspecialcollections.wordpress.com/2013/03/06/west-florida-
    seminary-cadets-at-the-battle-of-natural-bridge/.

Family Search Wiki. "2nd Regiment, Florida Infantry (Confederate)."
    Accessed July 14, 2020. https://www.familysearch.org/wiki/
    en/2nd_Regiment,_Florida_Infantry_(Confederate).

FamilySearch Wiki.. "3rd Regiment, Florida Infantry (Confederate)."
    Accessed June 30, 2020. https://www.familysearch.org/wiki/
    en/3rd_Regiment,_Florida_Infantry_(Confederate).

FamilySearch Wiki.. "Florida Civil War Confederate Infantry Units."
    Accessed July 14, 2020. https://www.familysearch.org/wiki/
    en/Florida_Civil_War_Confederate_Infantry_Units.

FamilySearch Wiki. "11th Regiment, Florida Infantry (Confederate)."
    Accessed June 30, 2020. https://www.familysearch.org/wiki/
    en/11th_Regiment,_Florida_Infantry_(Confederate).

"FL 4th Inf Co. H." Accessed June 12, 2020. http://myweb.fsu.edu/ rthompson2//cw/4-fl-inf/4-fl-inf-h.html.

"FL 11th Inf Co. A." Accessed October 24, 2019. http:// myweb.fsu.edu/rthompson2//cw/11-fl-inf/11-fl-inf-a.html.

Florida. Board of State Institutions, and Fred L. Robertson. *Soldiers of Florida in the Seminole Indian, Civil and Spanish- American Wars*. Live Oak, Fla., Democrat print, 1903. http:// archive.org/details/soldiersofflorid00flor.

Florida Genealogy Trails. "Civil War Florida Infantry Rosters." Accessed July 14, 2020. http://genealogytrails.com/fla/ military/civilwar_infantry3.html.

Florida, State Library and Archives of. "William T. Stockton." Florida Memory. Accessed September 21, 2017. https:// www.floridamemory.com/exhibits/floridahighlights/stockton/ page4.php.

Fold3. "Civil War Service Records (CMSR) - Confederate - Florida." Accessed December 29, 2021. https://www.fold3.com/ publication/30/us-civil-war-service-records-cmsr-confederate- florida-1861-1865

Fold3. "Civil War Service Records Compiled (CMSR) - Confederate - Florida." Accessed April 5, 2021. http:// www.fold3.com:9292/image/110748004/?xid=1022.

Fold3. "Page 1 Civil War Service Records (CMSR) - Confederate - Florida." Accessed April 5, 2021. http:// www.fold3.com:9292/image/110766705/?xid=1022.

Fold3. "Page 1 Civil War Service Records (CMSR) - Confederate - Florida." Accessed April 5, 2021. http:// www.fold3.com:9292/image/109144270/?xid=1022.

Fold3. "Page 1 Civil War Service Records (CMSR) - Confederate - Florida." Accessed December 31, 2021. http:// www.fold3.com:9292/image/264682304? terms=walker,war,civil,george,united,confederate,america,ar my,states.

Fold3. "Page 1 Civil War Service Records (CMSR) - Confederate - Georgia." Accessed April 5, 2021. http:// www.fold3.com:9292/image/52401716/?xid=1022.

Fold3. "Page 1 Civil War Soldiers - Confederate - FL." Accessed January 24, 2020. http://www.fold3.com:9292/image/ 109140148?terms=war,us,palmer,civil,thomas,confederate.

Futch, Ovid. "Florida during the Civil War. By John E. Johns.
(Gainesville: University of Florida Press, 1963. x + 265 Pp.
Maps, Illustrations, Notes, Bibliography, and Index. $6.00.)."
Journal of American History 51, no. 1 (June 1, 1964): 107–8.
https://doi.org/10.2307/1917949.

Gates, Paul Wallace. *Agriculture and the Civil War*. New York, NY:
Knopf, Inc., 1965.

Georgia Historical Society. "Confederate Dead and Hospitals
(Randolph County)." Accessed January 12, 2018. http://
georgiahistory.com/ghmi_marker_updated/confederate-dead-
and-hospitals-randolph/.'Hardee's Flank March,' Bonds,
Russell S. War Like the Thunderbolt: The Battle and Burning
of Atlanta, Yardley, Pennsylvania, Westholm Publishing 2010,
Wikimedia Commons

"Hood Hospital - U.S. Civil War - Cuthbert, Georgia - Field Hospitals
on Waymarking.com." Accessed January 12, 2018. http://
www.waymarking.com/waymarks/
WMAB9G_Hood_Hospital_US_Civil_War_Cuthbert_Georgi
a.

Ives, Washington, and Jim R Cabaniss. *Civil War Journals and Letters
of Sergeant Washington Ives, 4th Florida C.S.A*. Tallahassee,
Fla.? J.R. Cabaniss, 2008.

Johnston's Surrender | eHISTORY. Accessed October 22, 2019.
https://ehistory.osu.edu/articles/johnston%E2%80%99s-
surrender.

Jonathan C. Sheppard. *Everyday Soldiers: The Florida Brigade of the
West, 1861-1862*. Florida State University Libraries, 2004.
http://diginole.lib.fsu.edu/islandora/object/fsu:176255/
datastream/PDF/view.

"Jonesborough Confederate Order of Battle." Wikipedia, December
27, 2021. https://en.wikipedia.org/w/index.php?
title=Jonesborough_Confederate_order_of_battle&oldid=106
2233031.

Loderhose, Gary. *Far, Far from Home: The Ninth Florida Regiment in
the Confederate Army*. 1st edition. Carmel, Ind.: Clerisy Pr,
1999.

Mike Wright. *What They Didn't Teach You about the Civil War*.
Novato, Calif.: Presidio Press: Presidio Press, 1998.

Mitchell, Reid. *Civil War Soldiers*. Viking Penguin, Inc., 1988. "78th
Pa. - Tells of Capturing the 4th Florida Battle Flag at the

Battle of Stones River!" Accessed November 9, 2017. http://
www.mqamericana.com/
78th_PA_Capturd_4th_FL_Flag.html.

Nulty, William H. *Confederate Florida: The Road to Olustee*. First
Paperback edition. Tuscaloosa: University Alabama Press,
1994.

"Confederate Florida - University of Alabama Press." Accessed June
8, 2020. http://www.uapress.ua.edu/product/Confederate-
Florida,690.aspx.

Pasco, Samuel. "Jefferson County, Florida, 1827-1910." *The Florida
Historical Society Quarterly* 7, no. 2 (1928): 139–54.

Pasco, Samuel. *Private Pasco: A Civil War Diary*, 1990.

"Pensacola & Georgia Railroad, Confederacy," n.d.

"Photo Album: Nurses - US Civil War Era." Accessed March 29,
2023. https://www.wikitree.com/wiki/
Space:Photo_Album:_Nurses_-_US_Civil_War_Era.

"Pocotaligo River - Pocotaligo, South Carolina." Accessed October
21, 2019. https://www.scpictureproject.org/jasper-county/
pocotaligo-river.html.

"Resaca Battle - American Battlefield Trust." Accessed October 24,
2019. https://www.battlefields.org/learn/civil-war/battles/
resaca

Riley, Darrell G. "Marion County History, The Civil War Years." *Star-
Banner*, 1997.

Sheppard, Jonathan C. *By the Noble Daring of Her Sons: The Florida
Brigade of the Army of Tennessee*. University of Alabama
Press, 2012.

Smith, Steven D., Christopher Ohm Clement, and Stephen R. Wise.
"GPS, GIS and the Civil War Battlefield Landscape: A South
Carolina Low Country Example." *Historical Archaeology* 37,
no. 3 (2003): 14–30.

Stallings, James E. *Georgia's Confederate Soldiers Who Died as
Prisoners of War 1861-1865*. Macon, Ga.: J.E. Stallings, Sr.,
2008.

Strickland, Michael. *The Red Cotton Fields - Newly Edited Edition*.
Edited by Elaine Blackburn. Mayport Publishing Company,
2014.

Taylor, Robert A. "Rebel Beef: Florida Cattle and the Confederate
Army, 1862-1864" 67, no. 1 (1988).

The Civil War in the East. "10th Florida Infantry Regiment."
    Accessed July 8, 2019. http://civilwarintheeast.com/
    confederate-regiments/florida/10th-florida-infantry-regiment/.
The Semi-Weekly Floridian. Accessed April 30, 2023. https://original-
    ufdc.uflib.ufl.edu/UF00086645/00081/2x?search=semi-
    weekly+%3dfloridian.
"Uniforms of the Confederate States Armed Forces." Wikipedia, June
    10, 2021. https://en.wikipedia.org/wiki/
    Uniforms_of_the_Confederate_States_Armed_Forces
"United_States_Civil_War_Nurses.jpg (3600×2679)." Accessed
    March 29, 2023. https://www.wikitree.com/photo.php/5/5d/
    United_States_Civil_War_Nurses.jpg.
"U.S., Civil War Soldier Records and Profiles, 1861-1865 -
    Ancestry.com." Accessed March 4, 2015. https://
    www.ancestry.com/search/collections/1555/records/4104990
"U.S., Civil War Soldier Records and Profiles, 1861-1865 -
    Ancestry.com." Accessed December 29, 2021. https://
    www.ancestry.com/discoveryui-content/view/159407:1555?
    ssrc=pt&tid=23894133&pid=312126167172.
US National Park Service. "3rd Florida Regiment - Battle Unit Details
    - The Civil War (U.S. National Park Service)." Accessed July
    14, 2020. https://www.nps.gov/subjects/civilwar/search-
    battle-units-detail.htm.
"Valentine E Andrews, Widow Pension Application of Julia Kersey
    Andrews." Accessed April 5, 2021. https://
    www.ancestry.com/mediaui-viewer/collection/1030/tree/
    23894133/person/1441729069/media/
    751906ce-717c-479d-9c77-4f0eff1f5b22?
    _phsrc=Eul7590&usePUBJs=true.
Venet, Wendy Hamand. "A Changing Wind." *Georgia Press* (blog).
    Accessed January 28, 2022. https://ugapress.org/book/
    9780820351360/a-changing-wind.
https://www.ancestry.com/mediaui-viewer/collection/1030/tree/
    23894133/person/1441729069/media/19f65458-9c46-4c07-
    bb96-3e35a3a62c87?_phsrc=Eul7589&usePUBJs=true.
"2nd Florida Infantry." Wikipedia, January 1, 2018. https://
    en.wikipedia.org/w/index.php?
    title=2nd_Florida_Infantry&oldid=818150009.

"3rd Florida Infantry." Wikipedia, October 16, 2019. https://
en.wikipedia.org/w/index.php?
title=3rd_Florida_Infantry&oldid=921630509.
"Lafayette McLaws." Wikipedia, July 28, 2020. https://
en.wikipedia.org/w/index.php?
title=Lafayette_McLaws&oldid=969967025.
"Woodard on Taylor, 'Rebel Storehouse: Florida in the Confederate
Economy' | H-CivWar | H-Net." Accessed May 27, 2020.
https://networks.h-net.org/node/4113/reviews/4416/woodard-
taylor-rebel-storehouse-florida-confederate-economy.

Research—Life after the War

"1880 US Census, Florida, Bradford County.," n.d.
"Ancestry.com - 1860 United States Federal Census." Accessed April
5, 2021. https://www.ancestry.com/imageviewer/collections/
7667/images/4211366_00387?pId=10615443.
"Ancestry.com - 1860 United States Federal Census." Accessed April
5, 2021. https://www.ancestry.com/imageviewer/collections/
7667/images/4211366_00386?pId=10615426.
"Ancestry.com - 1860 United States Federal Census." Accessed April
5, 2021. https://www.ancestry.com/imageviewer/collections/
7667/images/4211366_00386?pId=10615420.
"Ancestry.com - 1870 United States Federal Census." Accessed
December 11, 2017. https://www.ancestry.com/interactive/
7163/4263357_00143/13864792?backurl=https://
www.ancestry.com/family-tree/person/tree/23894133/person/
1441730272/facts/citation/130183358416/edit/record
"Ancestry.com - 1880 United States Federal Census." Accessed
September 28, 2017. https://www.ancestry.com/imageviewer/
collections/6742/images/4240121-00063
"Ancestry.com - 1880 United States Federal Census." Accessed April
5, 2021. https://www.ancestry.com/imageviewer/collections/
6742/images/4240122-00735?pId=2620413.
"Ancestry.com - 1880 United States Federal Census." Accessed April
5, 2021. https://www.ancestry.com/imageviewer/collections/
6742/images/4240121-00225?pId=5047289.
"Ancestry.com - 1880 United States Federal Census." Accessed April
5, 2021. https://www.ancestry.com/imageviewer/collections/
6742/images/4240118-00095?pId=3828871.

"Ancestry.com - 1880 United States Federal Census." Accessed April 5, 2021. https://www.ancestry.com/imageviewer/collections/6742/images/4240121-00300?pId=5929449.

"Ancestry.com - 1900 United States Federal Census." Accessed April 5, 2021. https://www.ancestry.com/imageviewer/collections/7602/images/4120049_00080?pId=34132975.

"Ancestry.com - 1900 United States Federal Census." Accessed April 5, 2021. https://www.ancestry.com/imageviewer/collections/7602/images/4118535_00074?pId=43960136.

"Ancestry.com - 1900 United States Federal Census." Accessed April 5, 2021. https://www.ancestry.com/imageviewer/collections/7602/images/4120038_00419?pId=430341.

"Ancestry.com - 1910 United States Federal Census." Accessed April 5, 2021. https://www.ancestry.com/imageviewer/collections/7884/images/31111_4327451-00283?pId=3045773.

"Ancestry.com - 1910 United States Federal Census." Accessed April 5, 2021. https://www.ancestry.com/imageviewer/collections/7884/images/4454393_00307?pId=28425307.

"Ancestry.com - 1920 United States Federal Census." Accessed April 5, 2021. https://www.ancestry.com/imageviewer/collections/6061/images/4295794-00835?pId=7184693.

"Ancestry.com - 1930 United States Federal Census." Accessed April 5, 2021. https://www.ancestry.com/imageviewer/collections/6224/images/4548195_00728?pId=65050989.

"Ancestry.com - Florida, State Census, 1885." Accessed September 28, 2017. https://www.ancestry.com/interactive/7605/FLM845_6-0190?pid=204105&backurl=https://www.ancestry.com/family-tree/person/tree/23894133/person/1441728990/gallery&usePUB=true&_phsrc=xKK43&usePUBJs=true.

"Ancestry.com - Florida, U.S., State Census, 1867-1945." Accessed April 5, 2021. https://www.ancestry.com/imageviewer/collections/1506/images/FLM845_9-0176?pId=269044.

"Ancestry.com - Florida, U.S., State Census, 1867-1945." Accessed April 5, 2021. https://www.ancestry.com/imageviewer/collections/1506/images/FLM845_9-0176?pId=269037.

"Ancestry.com - Florida, U.S., State Census, 1867-1945." Accessed April 5, 2021. https://www.ancestry.com/imageviewer/collections/1506/images/FLM845_8-0258?pId=252738.

"Ancestry.com - Florida, U.S., State Census, 1885." Accessed April 5, 2021. https://www.ancestry.com/imageviewer/collections/7605/images/FLM845_9-0176?pId=269037.

"Ancestry.com - Florida, U.S., State Census, 1885." Accessed April 5, 2021. https://www.ancestry.com/imageviewer/collections/7605/images/FLM845_6-0201?pId=204669.

"Ancestry.com - Texas, U.S., Death Certificates, 1903-1982." Accessed April 5, 2021. https://www.ancestry.com/imageviewer/collections/2272/images/40394_b062620-02914?pId=83050909.

"Andrew Johnson: Campaigns and Elections | Miller Center," October 4, 2016. https://millercenter.org/president/johnson/campaigns-and-elections.

"Cinda Sheppard Andrews (Unknown-1884) - Find A Grave." Accessed September 20, 2020. https://www.findagrave.com/memorial/175955466/cinda-andrews

"Deed From Mary Andrews to Powell, 1870." Accessed July 16, 2015. http://mv.ancestry.com/viewer/2d83ca1a-0c1c-4e51-96c9-eba2b78b202b/23894133/1441730272?_phsrc=eOt3&usePUBJs=true.

Find a Grave. "Laura R. Andrews - View Media - Ancestry.com." Accessed March 3, 2015. http://trees.ancestry.com/tree/23894133/person/1441729020/media/1?pgnum=1&pg=0&pgpl=pid%7cpgNum.

"Florida, U.S., County Marriage Records, 1823-1982 - Ancestry.com." Accessed April 5, 2021. https://www.ancestry.com/search/collections/61369/records/901369369

"Florida, U.S., County Marriage Records, 1823-1982 - Ancestry.com." Accessed April 5, 2021. https://www.ancestry.com/search/collections/61369/records/977671

"Florida, U.S., County Marriage Records, 1823-1982 - Ancestry.com." Accessed April 5, 2021. https://search.ancestry.com/cgi-bin/sse.dll?indiv=1&dbid=61369&h=1051678490

"Florida, U.S., County Marriage Records, 1823-1982 - Ancestry.com." Accessed April 5, 2021. https://www.ancestry.com/search/collections/61369/records/900978123

"Florida, U.S., County Marriage Records, 1823-1982 -
  Ancestry.com." Accessed April 5, 2021. https://
  search.ancestry.com/cgi-bin/sse.dll?
  indiv=1&dbid=61369&h=900977685
"Florida, U.S., County Marriage Records, 1823-1982 -
  Ancestry.com." Accessed April 5, 2021. https://
  search.ancestry.com/cgi-bin/sse.dll?
  indiv=1&dbid=61369&h=977695
"Florida, U.S., County Marriage Records, 1823-1982 -
  Ancestry.com." Accessed April 5, 2021. https://
  search.ancestry.com/cgi-bin/sse.dll?
  indiv=1&dbid=61369&h=977993
"Florida, U.S., Marriage Indexes, 1822-1875 and 1927-2001 -
  Ancestry.com." Accessed April 5, 2021. https://
  www.ancestry.com/search/collections/8784/records/10531
"Jefferson County Deed Book, pg 188," Courthouse archives. January
  7, 1871.
"Laura R. Lightsey (1857-1896) - Find A Grave." Accessed April 5,
  2021. https://www.findagrave.com/memorial/39726719/laura-
  r.-lightsey
Leslie, Frank, ed. *Frank Leslie's Illustrated Newspaper*. New York:
  Frank Leslie, 1855.
"Marriage Certificate." Accessed April 5, 2021. https://
  www.ancestry.com/mediaui-viewer/collection/1030/tree/
  23894133/person/1441729069/media/66f5c8e9-
  ca36-441d-95cd-fe725d3e2b1c?
  _phsrc=Eul7591&usePUBJs=true.
"Mary Elizabeth 'Florida Mae' Andrews Guilfoyle...Unknown Burial
  but Died in Romeo, Florida." Accessed April 5, 2021. https://
  www.findagrave.com/memorial/143732829/mary-elizabeth-
  guilfoyle.
"Occupied Troops Camped at Capitol." *Frank Leslie's Illustrated
  Newspaper* 1855–1891, no. October 31, 1868 (n.d.).
"Reconstruction Timeline | American Experience | PBS." Accessed
  September 9, 2020. https://www.pbs.org/wgbh/
  americanexperience/features/reconstruction-timeline/.
Rogers, William Warren. *Thomas County, 1865-1900*. First edition.
  Tallahassee: Florida State University Press, 1973.
"The Colonial Williamsburg Official History & Citizenship Site."
  Accessed November 5, 2024. https://

research.colonialwilliamsburg.org/Foundation/journal/ Winter04-05/smoke.cfm.

The Semi-Weekly Floridian, January 16, 1866 (UF Digital Collections), "Turnbull & Reid, Freedmen Loitering." Accessed November 29, 2021. https://ufdc.ufl.edu/ UF00086645/00020/zoom/3.

The Semi-Weekly Floridian, February 23, 1866. https:// newspapers.uflib.ufl.edu/UF00086645/00029/images

The Semi-Weekly Floridian, March 2, 1866. https:// newspapers.uflib.ufl.edu/UF00086645/00031/images

The Semi-Weekly Floridian, March 13, 1866. https:// newspapers.uflib.ufl.edu/UF00086645/00033

The Semi-Weekly Floridian, July 30, 1866. https:// newspapers.uflib.ufl.edu/UF00086645/00068

The Semi-Weekly Floridian, August 6, 1866. https:// newspapers.uflib.ufl.edu/UF00086645/00070

The Semi-Weekly Floridian. November 10, 1865. Accessed February 7, 2022. https://newspapers.uflib.ufl.edu/UF00086645/00006

The Semi-Weekly Floridian. May 4, 1866. Accessed May 8, 2022. https://newspapers.uflib.ufl.edu/UF00086645/00044

The Semi-Weekly Floridian. May 8, 1866. Accessed May 21, 2022. https://newspapers.uflib.ufl.edu/UF00086645/00045

The Semi-Weekly Floridian. May 11, 1866. Accessed May 22, 2022. https://newspapers.uflib.ufl.edu/UF00086645/00046

The Semi-Weekly Floridian. June 1, 1866. Accessed June 25, 2022. https://newspapers.uflib.ufl.edu/UF00086645/00052

The Semi-Weekly Floridian. July 26, 1866. Accessed January 22, 2023. https://newspapers.uflib.ufl.edu/UF00086645/00067

The Semi-Weekly Floridian. August 27, 1866. Accessed February 26, 2023. https://newspapers.uflib.ufl.edu/UF00086645/00074

The Semi-Weekly Floridian. September 4, 1866. Accessed March 19, 2023. https://newspapers.uflib.ufl.edu/UF00086645/00076

The Semi-Weekly Floridian. December 7, 1866. Accessed January 14, 2024. https://newspapers.uflib.ufl.edu/UF00086645/00098

The Semi-Weekly Floridian. January 11, 1867. Accessed June 16, 2024. https://newspapers.uflib.ufl.edu/UF00086645/00106

The Semi-Weekly Floridian. February 5, 1867. Accessed November 17, 2024. https://newspapers.uflib.ufl.edu/UF00086645/00113

The Semi-Weekly Floridian. February 12, 1867. Accessed November 30, 2024. https://newspapers.uflib.ufl.edu/ UF00086645/00115.

The Semi-Weekly Floridian. April 26, 1867. Accessed August 3, 2025. https://original-ufdcuflib.ufl.edu/UF00086645/00139/zoom/2

Unknown. "State Archives and Historical Records Survey," Unknown, possibly 1830s. Bailey Family Folder. Keystone Genealogical Library, Monticello, Florida.

"U.S., Find a Grave Index, 1600s-Current - Ancestry.com." Accessed April 5, 2021. https://www.ancestry.com/discoveryui-content/ view/77370006:60525? ssrc=pt&tid=23894133&pid=1441729077.

"U.S., Find a Grave Index, 1600s-Current - Ancestry.com." Accessed April 5, 2021. https://www.ancestry.com/discoveryui-content/ view/26651398:60525? ssrc=pt&tid=23894133&pid=1441728990.

"U.S., Find a Grave Index, 1600s-Current - Ancestry.com." Accessed April 5, 2021. https://www.ancestry.com/discoveryui-content/ view/17241515:60525? ssrc=pt&tid=23894133&pid=1441729083.

"U.S., Newspapers.com Obituary Index, 1800s-Current - Ancestry.com." Accessed April 5, 2021. https:// www.ancestry.com/discoveryui-content/view/ 734096449:61843?ssrc=pt&tid=23894133&pid=1441728978.

"U.S., Social Security Applications and Claims Index, 1936-2007 - Ancestry.com." Accessed April 5, 2021. https:// www.ancestry.com/discoveryui-content/view/ 629535913:60901?ssrc=pt&tid=23894133&pid=1441729077.

"U.S., Social Security Applications and Claims Index, 1936-2007 - Ancestry.com." Accessed April 5, 2021. https:// www.ancestry.com/discoveryui-content/view/ 611135229:60901?ssrc=pt&tid=23894133&pid=1441729069.

"U.S., Social Security Applications and Claims Index, 1936-2007 - Ancestry.com." Accessed April 5, 2021. https:// www.ancestry.com/discoveryui-content/view/ 611127468:60901?ssrc=pt&tid=23894133&pid=1441729083.

"Valentine E 'Vollie' Andrews (1848-1902) - Find A Grave." Accessed April 5, 2021. https://www.findagrave.com/ memorial/32032890/valentine-e-andrews.

"Web: Florida, Find A Grave Index, 1800-2012 - Ancestry.com."
    Accessed April 5, 2021. https://search.ancestry.com/cgi-bin/
    sse.dll?indiv=1&dbid=70504&h=208399

WPA. "Elizabeth Baptist Church." Florida Memory. Accessed
    September 20, 2020. https://www.floridamemory.com/items/
    show/249016.

Zornow, William Frank. "State Aid for Indigent Soldiers and Their
    Families in Florida, 1861-65." *The Florida Historical
    Quarterly* 34, no. 3 (1956): 259–65.

Research—Life in Florida during Reconstruction

"1880 United States Federal Census - Ancestry.com." Accessed
    March 2, 2015. https://www.ancestry.com/search/collections/
    6742/records/5042694"1880

United States Federal Census - Ancestry.com." Accessed June 26,
    2015. https://www.ancestry.com/search/collections/6742/
    records/5042612

"American Election Campaigns in the 19th Century." Wikipedia,
    March 10, 2019 https://en.wikipedia.org/w/index.php?
    title=American_election_campaigns_in_the_19th_century

"Ancestry.com - 1870 United States Federal Census." Accessed
    December 11, 2017 https://www.ancestry.com/interactive/
    7163/4263357_00143/13864792?backurl=https://
    www.ancestry.com/family-tree/person/tree/23894133/person/
    1441730272/facts/citation/130183358416/edit/record

"Andrew Johnson." Wikipedia, October 29, 2019. https://
    en.wikipedia.org/w/index.php?
    title=Andrew_Johnson&oldid=923538895.

Van Dam, Andrew. "What Southern Dynasties' Post-Civil War
    Resurgence Tell Us about How Wealth Is Really Handed
    Down." *Washington Post*, April 4, 2019. Accessed October
    31, 2019. https://www.washingtonpost.com/us-policy/
    2019/04/04/how-souths-slave-owning-dynasties-regained-
    their-wealth-after-civil-war/.

Ellen Lou Andrews Hogg Residence in 1880 US Census for Florida,
    Marion County. n.d https://www.ancestry.com/search/
    collections/6742/records/5083095.

Fildes, F. R., editor. *Family Friend*. Accessed February 18, 2021
    https://ufdc.ufl.edu/UF00079911/00046/3j?search=jefferson+
    %3dcounty+%3dflorida.
Find a Grave. "Laura R. Andrews - View Media - Ancestry.com."
    Accessed March 3, 2015. http://trees.ancestry.com/tree/
    23894133/person/1441729020/media/1?
    pgnum=1&pg=0&pgpl=pid%7cpgNum.
"George H. Lightsey (1853 - 1918) - Find A Grave Memorial."
    Accessed June 25, 2015. http://www.findagrave.com/cgi-bin/
    fg.cgi?page=gr&GRid=39726760.
"Monticello, Jefferson County, Florida, 1884 Sanborn Map."
    Accessed June 28, 2015. http://ufdc.ufl.edu/
    UF00074203/00003/2x?search=monticello+
    %3dflorida&vo=12&vp=0,368.
Obituary dated Sept. 1, 1955. "Jesse Walker Hamrick - Facts and
    Sources - Ancestry.com." Accessed March 6, 2015. http://
    trees.ancestry.com/tree/23889890/person/1441242834/fact/
    13932290927?msg=me&et=burial.
Shofner, Jerrell H. *History of Jefferson County*. First edition. Sentry
    Press, 1976.
Stone, Alva T. "Diary of a Freedmen's Bureau Agent: Alfred B.
    Grunwell in Jefferson County, Florida." *Florida Historical
    Quarterly* 96, no. 1 (2017). chrome-extension://
    kdpelmjpfafjppnhbloffcjpeomlnpah/https://
    stars.library.ucf.edu/cgi/viewcontent.cgi?params=/context/
    fhq/article/4795/&path_info=Vol96Iss1_DiaryFreedman.pdf.
The Semi-Weekly Floridian. April 27, 1866.Accessed April 24, 2022.
    https://newspapers.uflib.ufl.edu/UF00086645/00042/images
The Semi-Weekly Floridian. *October 16, 1866*. Accessed September
    7, 2024. https://newspapers.uflib.ufl.edu/UF00086645/00087
The Semi-Weekly Floridian. January 25, 1867. Accessed September
    21, 2024. https://newspapers.uflib.ufl.edu/UF00086645/00110
The Semi-Weekly Floridian. January 29, 1867. Accessed October 19,
    2024. https://newspapers.uflib.ufl.edu/UF00086645/00111
The Semi-Weekly Floridian. March 1,1967. Accessed January 26,
    2025. https://newspapers.uflib.ufl.edu/UF00086645/00120
The Semi-Weekly Floridian.. March 15. 1967. Accessed March 9,
    2025. https://newspapers.uflib.ufl.edu/UF00086645/00124
The Semi-Weekly Floridian. March 26, 1867. Accessed March 29,
    2025. https://newspapers.uflib.ufl.edu/UF00086645/00127.

The Semi-Weekly Floridian. April 2, 1867. Accessed April 12, 2025. https://newspapers.uflib.ufl.edu/UF00086645/00129

The Semi-Weekly Floridian. April 5, 1867. Accessed April 27, 2025. https://newspapers.uflib.ufl.edu/UF00086645/00130

The Semi-Weekly Floridian. April 9, 1867Accessed May 11, 2025. https://newspapers.uflib.ufl.edu/UF00086645/00131

"UFDC Search Results - Florida Digital Newspaper Library." Accessed September 29, 2015. http://ufdc.ufl.edu/fdnl1/results/brief/?t=jefferson+county&f=ZZ&o=10.

Works Progress Agency. "Image 382 of Federal Writers' Project: Slave Narrative Project, Vol. 3, Florida, Anderson-Wilson (with Combined Interviews of Others)." Image. Library of Congress, Washington, D.C. 20540 USA. Accessed September 6, 2020. https://www.loc.gov/resource/mesn.030/?sp=382.

#

www.ingramcontent.com/pod-product-compliance
Lightning Source LLC
Chambersburg PA
CBHW060403130626
46555CB00005B/1978